THE
NINE NATIONS
OF
NORTH AMERICA

THE
NINE NATIONS
OF
NORTH AMERICA

Joel Garreau

Boston
HOUGHTON MIFFLIN COMPANY
1981

Library of Congress Cataloging in Publication Data

Garreau, Joel.
 The nine nations of North America.

 Bibliography: p.
 Includes index.
  1. North America. 2. Caribbean area. 3. Garreau,
Joel. I. Title.
E38.G37   970.053   80-28556
ISBN 0-395-29124-0   AACR 2

Printed in the United States of America

A 10 9 8 7 6 5 4 3 2

The author is grateful for permission to reprint material from the
following sources: "Margaritaville," words and music by Jimmy Buffett; © 1977 Coral Reefer Music. "Life at Ground Zero"; reprint
permission *Seattle Post-Intelligencer*, copyright © 1980; all rights
reserved. *The Serial*, by Cyra McFadden; copyright © 1976, 1977 by
Cyra McFadden; reprinted by permission of Alfred A. Knopf, Inc.
Talking Columbia, words and music by Woody Guthrie; TRO —
Copyright © 1961 and 1963 Ludlow Music, Inc., New York, N.Y.; used
by permission.

To Adrienne

WHO NEVER KNEW WHICH TO
ANTICIPATE WITH MORE RELIEF:
MY COMING HOME OR
MY HITTING THE ROAD AGAIN.

Home, in the twentieth century,
is less where your heart is,
than where you understand the sons-of-bitches.
— Dave Hickey, *The Texas Observer*

CONTENTS

Maps follow page 204

PREFACE

THIS ALL STARTED as a kind of private craziness.

A small band of newspaper people who spent their time on the road across America, reporting on it for the *Washington Post*, started getting used to a certain question from me, their desk-bound editor. What, I wanted to know, was it *like* wherever they found themselves?

They knew that I'd get a big kick out of hearing that if you got a Big Mac attack in Langdon, North Dakota, you'd have to race 114 miles to the nearest McDonald's. Or that the view from Ken Castner's outhouse in Homer, Alaska, is the finest vista of its kind in North America. But, apart from the trivia, they knew that I was asking the question in order to help me — and them — see patterns in the news.

After a while, a sort of shorthand began to evolve. Three of the reporters, for example, started trying to explain the American Southwest to me as "MexAmerica." A "nation within a nation," they called it.

It's a place, they said, that appears on no map. It's where the gumbo of Dixie gives way to the refried beans of Mexico. The land looks like northern Mexico. And the sound of Spanish in the supermarkets and on the airwaves is impossible to ignore. The news stories it produces point up the trouble Anglo institutions have in dealing with enormous cultural strain. It's a place where cops sometimes shoot third-generation Americans of Mexican descent for very controversial reasons, a region faced with the question of whether the American Dream applies to innocent kids born of people who have crossed the border illegally. It's hot and dry. It has more big dreams per capita than any other place you'll ever know. Its capital is Los Angeles, but it stretches all the way to Houston. The politicians have difficulties comprehending it, because it ignores political boundaries. But it's there, it's there.

Then other reporters began to offer alternative visions that made their own regions easier to understand.

Ecotopia, about which you'll find a chapter in this book, was one reporter's way of grasping the Pacific Northwest. A third view saw the Intermountain West as a land called the Empty Quarter. Somebody else observed that Miami is on the way to becoming the capital of an offshore Latin American realm. And so on.

Sometimes we saw this business of viewing areas of the continent as semiautonomous nations as a serious and useful way of describing the source of events. At others, it was no more than our own strange private joke. Then *Outlook,* the Sunday "think" section of the *Post,* started casting around for controversial, iconoclastic views of the world and on March 4, 1979, it carried an article that I wrote, expanding on over two years' worth of these musings.

"Whatever the political maps may say," the headline led off, "our continent is not divided into 50 states and three countries. What we really are is: *The Nine Nations of North America.*"

I had written this article as provocatively as I could, with the idea that if this new vision was going to raise a few hackles, it might as well raise a lot of them.

And in a few days, the letters to the editor did begin to arrive. In torrents. But, lo, to my surprise, they were letters from people who *agreed* with me. Not only were they agreeing, but they were offering refinements and improvements on the strange theory. "You should have put more of Saskatchewan in the Breadbasket," wrote one fellow. "The nation of the Islands," suggested another, "extends to Daytona."

Then came the reprints. The *Minneapolis Star* and the *St. Petersburg Times* ran it on their front pages. In England, the *Guardian* serialized it. At least one major newspaper in every "nation" of the nine — including Québec — published the piece.

It began to dawn on me that I had hit some kind of nerve with this idea. The subsequent flow of letters from politicians, businessmen, and ordinary readers began to suggest that I might be on to something important. "I read your article," an Oregon woman wrote, "and something snapped. I could only nod my head and agree and feel excited and read it to my friends and watch them nod and agree." One thing led to another. Soon I'd been talked into writing this book. And I found myself abandoning desk and telephone and suddenly out on the road, wondering what I'd done.

I relate this tale in order to try to explain how — now that the book has seemed to acquire a life of its own — everything began. I hereby testify that this book is nonfiction. After almost one hundred thousand miles of travel and hundreds of interviews, I'm more confident than ever that these Nine Nations are really in being. But that doesn't mean that I haven't spent some dark days wondering exactly where their borders came from, these lines first traced on the backs of cocktail napkins.

Especially in the early days of the formal research for this book, it was unnerving to discover how few primary data existed to "prove" many of my points. For example, MexAmerica is obvious to the eye and the ear. But wherever you look, there is no good answer to basic questions like "How many Hispanics are there?" The Census Bureau admits that in 1970 it blew its count of United States *citizens* of Hispanic origin. Estimates of the number of illegals vary by a thousand percent, like a replay of those absurdist Vietnam War briefings. Academic studies that simply ask the number of those apprehended by the U.S. Border Patrol, and where in Mexico they come from, are considered pioneering work.

Similarly, the United States Geological Survey National Atlas map called "Total Interstate Energy Movement," from which, in 1979, I wanted to draw conclusions about the Empty Quarter, showed nothing coming out of Alaska's North Slope. It was drawn in 1976 and had 1974 numbers. Statistical cartographers faced with a complaint about this look pained. That's good, fresh material by the standards of their profession.

Nor does this address the problem of collecting data in a way that ignores state and national boundaries. Never mind that East Texas is a different place from West Texas, or north Alaska different from south Alaska. Never mind that these are regional distinctions recognized by everyone who's ever lived there. You want numbers? You get them mixed together for all of Texas or all of Alaska. If you want a more serious analysis, you are directed to county-by-county computer tapes. For which, of course, you need a computer. And even that, while hideously expensive, is possible. Matching up most transnational numbers is beyond the scope of nations, much less a single author. No matter how much Montana looks and acts like Alberta, or New Mexico like Chihuahua — no matter how their problems, opportunities, and people intertwine — the twain of their bureaucracies will only, with extreme difficulty, meet.

It was similarly unhelpful to dwell on what might be termed "hard theory." Thinkers with impressive credentials in regionalism have produced monographs that are endlessly fascinating but don't produce much in the way of coherent patterns.

Cultural geographers have mapped, for example, the physical location of vodka drinkers, Muslims, Notre Dame football fans, long-distance-telephone users, bluegrass-music enthusiasts, stock-car racers, high-rolling gamblers . . . anything you can imagine. And the scholars who have done this mapping have come up with many thoughtful ways of explaining why people are distributed the way they are.

But if you took these maps and their attendant explanations, imagined them as transparent plastic overlays, and tried to sort through them to find out what combination would yield my Nine Nations, you would fail. Or at least I failed. These overlays, those spider webs, are so complex and ambiguous that they yield little save microregions. In fact, the lesson offered is that, John Donne notwithstanding, every man *is* an island. Given enough time with these maps, I guarantee you can find the only vodka-drinking, Muslim, Notre Dame football–loving, long-distance-phone-using, bluegrass-music-playing, stock-car-racing, high-rolling gambler in the world. You might even find an enclave of them. But I don't know what that would prove.

And these fastidious concerns reflect only the problems of describing the then and there. My researcher, Nancy Balz, soon discovered that getting around statistical time lags even by going to the most specialized and exotic sources didn't always help. My map, she was startled to find, sometimes seemed to be of the near future.

Of course, on mature reflection, that figures. The Nine Nations process began among people who were trying to "get on top of" events. It was designed, by newsmen, for their private use, to help them judge, region by region, what was going to happen next and how important that event would be. "We've got to stop chasing fires" was their phrase. That meant a desire to stop reacting constantly to events, and start understanding them and anticipating them.

Take Houston, for example. Houston as a town that's building is not news to anyone. Houston as a town that's mortgaged may well be.

Civic boosters still like to recall that the first word spoken from the surface of the moon was not the business about the Eagle having landed. The very first word was "Houston?"

But Houston in the eighties, like everything else, will be defined by far more down-to-earth considerations. During the good years in Houston, no one wanted to brake growth by taxation — not for highways, schools, police departments, welfare structures, sewers, or water. No one in the capital of oil and gas wanted to face the implications of building a city even more air conditioner- and automobile-dependent than Los Angeles. Houston's greatest pride was in its dedication to a complete lack of zoning — a robust wad spit in the eye of pointy-headed urban planners. The advocates of press-on-regardless growth pointed to the vast wealth accruing to Houston as proof that cities like New York were overserviced, overtaxed, and overrated.

Well, the news in the 1980s coming from Houston is going to be about whether these theories are valid. Houston has run up what residents of other — especially eastern — cities view as huge social debts. The lack of new freeways is slowly beginning to result in all-day rush hours. The lack of new water mains is producing breaks in overtaxed lines on an almost daily basis. The police force is spread so thin that some businesses and some of the wealthy are now relying on private police forces ("site-specific enforcement") to protect valuable property.

The significance of this is in the time sense with which you look at a city like Houston. Houston is no longer "a city of the future," as it has been referred to. Houston, instead, is a city of *now* that is getting jerked around hard by the choices of the past, the results of which are clearly catching up.

This time sense, of course, clearly could affect the map, and it did. When I asked Nancy to collect the murder statistics for Houston, I did so with the clear image that the figures would be astronomical, as would befit a town that has undergone so much rapid social change.

She came back slightly bewildered. The actual slaughter was only beginning to occur as we spoke. The best she could do was to cite fresh news stories talking about the 40 percent murder-rate increase so far that summer. The numbers from the FBI, confirming the jump in murder rate, for example, won't be available until after this book goes to press.

Similarly, the Empty Quarter's identity is inexorably bound up in energy resources, and that's how I think of it. But that vision is largely anticipatory. The tall buildings in Denver and Calgary belonging to the likes of Amerada Hess and Amoco are going up. The exploration rigs are drilling in Wyoming's Overthrust Belt. The 100-car unit trains to haul coal are being built.

But statistically, the Empty Quarter is still far more a land of reserves, as I write this, than a land of production. The first quarts of crude are only beginning to be cracked commercially from tar sands. Technically, oil shale is still viewed as experimental. The continent's increase in coal burning is insignificant. Of course, all this will change, just as sure as there's an Exxon, but again, that's, strictly speaking, a future reality.

New England's turn toward the burning of wood for heat, for that matter, may speak volumes about that region's drive for self-sufficiency, but its implications lie in the future. You would never guess from the current U.S. Commerce Department map entitled "Primary Home Heating Fuel by Counties of the United States" that tens of thousands of wood-burning stoves have been installed in New England in the last few winters. The data simply have not had enough time to catch up with reality. But more important, the answers about what all this wood burning will do to the air, the forests, and people's attitudes toward electric companies are to come.

If news, as has been observed elsewhere, is the first rough draft of history, and this book, at least partially, anticipates the news, then perhaps I'm in the disconcerting position of writing a book that will be more true when you read it than when I wrote it.

• • •

What, then, is to be made of this Nine Nations business?

Ultimately, I think a good way to judge it is on a sheerly utilitarian basis. Does it work for you? Do things begin to click into place? Has some nagging fact or observation about this continent — something that had been there, like a piece of corn stuck in your teeth — finally work itself loose, as it did for me, a handful of reporters, and some newspaper readers?

But another way of viewing this volume is to discover whether the process that went into it is useful. I found the United States impossible to understand when it was presented to me as one great place, three thousand miles long, fifteen hundred miles deep, 3,615,122 square miles in area, ending mysteriously at some lines on the other side of which were voids called Canada and

Mexico. It didn't help me much to turn to subdivisions I had been taught, like the "Midwest." To this day I can't figure out why people would want to lump Ohio and Nebraska in the same region. I do not find Cleveland much like Omaha. Neither do I find the tomato fields of western Ohio much like the multithousand-acre grain operations along the 100th meridian.

But if you don't like my map, draw your own. I don't feel particularly protective about the boundaries I've drawn (he lied, in order to make a point).

I do find that dividing the continent into more comprehensible chunks helps put imponderables like energy, inflation, unemployment, and water policy into perspective. This is a time when issues seem so overwhelmingly complex that ordinary people have come to try to ignore them. An open-minded person trying to peer into the future to decide for whom to vote or what to think can easily find himself or herself frustrated by a maze of considerations seemingly *designed* to provoke paralysis and prevent good, hard decisions. These problems can seem more manageable when confronted in a geographical size a person can feel comfortable with.

The object is to find a useful way of looking at the world, to define entities that are much more than parishes and provinces and are therefore large enough to be meaningful. But these entities must be limited to a understandable concept for each one — a concept that relies on a certain intuitive, subjective sense of the loyalties that unify it. It is very important that your region, as bounded and defined, *feels* right to you.

For there's a certain subconscious, subliminal level to the line-drawing process that responds to truths that you sometimes can't name. As you get into this book, for example, you'll find I've drawn a boundary through Colorado, Wyoming, and Montana that divides the Empty Quarter from the Breadbasket. When I originally drew it, I felt sure that there must be some factual ridge there. In important ways, events occurred differently west of this line from the way they did east of it, and the difference was something I could describe. It's the explanation for the behavior that took a while to catch up. It wasn't until seven months later that I noted that my boundary happened to describe the very place where federal control of western land in the form of national parks, forests, wildlife refuges, public land, and Indian reservations becomes overwhelming, and private ownership peters out.

The region "feeling" right can work on a personal level, too. In a continent with a population as mobile as ours, it is no surprise that the second most commonly asked question in casual conversation after "What's your name?" is "Where are you from?"

For better or worse, in North America, the answer to the question "Where are you from?" transmits a great deal of information, not all of it accurate. "Where you're from" is taken as a good indicator of "where you're coming from." You can hear that in the way folk modify their answers. A person not proud of coming from Oklahoma, for instance, might add, hurriedly, "But from right down near the Texas border." A Texan might add, "But I went to school back east." An administrative assistant in Washington, D.C., might hasten to stress his ties to California. But in California you'll find people who make a point of looking you right in the eye and stressing that their people came from Oklahoma. In the *Depression*. ("Want to make something of it?")

Even if you don't completely understand the subtle webs of pride and shame in each of these exchanges, undoubtedly you've heard ones like them that apply to your home. Your identity is shaped by your origins. Thus, to come away with a new understanding of regionalism is to come away with a better understanding of yourself.

The final point to be made about thinking in regional terms is that, more often than not, it offers a reassuring view of the future.

I do not think that North America is flying apart, or that it should.

But I've spent some time talking to a University of Texas professor, a folklorist and regionalist, who does. For what it's worth, I'll pass on what he likes about Nine Nations.

He thinks it shows that if Washington, D.C., were to slide into the Potomac tomorrow under the weight of its many burdens and crises, the result would be okay. The future would not be chaos; it would be a shift. North America would not suddenly look around to discover a strange and alien world. It would see a collection of healthy, powerful constituent parts that we've known all our lives — like Dixie. He sees Nine Nations as a resilient response of a tough people reaffirming their self-reliance. It's not that social contracts are dissolving; it's just that the new ones are being born.

What he's saying, essentially, is that our values are separable from our regimes. We can preserve what is important to us, no matter what violence is done to the federal system, and the sooner we recognize that, the more confident of our future we'll be. This confidence, he adds, ironically may serve to bolster that very federal system.

I don't know. In some ways I think he's crazy. But this whole thing started as a kind of private craziness.

THE
NINE NATIONS
OF
NORTH AMERICA

A nation is the desire of many individuals
to do great things together.
— Marcel Rioux

THE NINE NATIONS

FORGET the pious wisdom you've been handed about North America.

Forget about the borders dividing the United States, Canada, and Mexico, those pale barriers so thoroughly porous to money, immigrants, and ideas.

Forget the bilge you were taught in sixth-grade geography about East and West, North and South, faint echoes of glorious pasts that never really existed save in sanitized textbooks.

Forget the maze of state and provincial boundaries, those historical accidents and surveyors' mistakes. The reason no one except the trivia expert can name all fifty of the United States is that they hardly matter.

Forget the political almanacs full of useless data on local elections rendered meaningless by strangely carved districts and precincts.

Consider, instead, the way North America really works. It is Nine Nations. Each has its capital and its distinctive web of power and influence. A few are allies, but many are adversaries. Several have readily acknowledged national poets, and many have characteristic dialects and mannerisms. Some are close to being raw frontiers; others have four centuries of history. Each has a peculiar economy; each commands a certain emotional allegiance from its citizens. These nations look different, feel different, and sound different from each other, and few of their boundaries match the political lines drawn on current maps. Some are clearly divided topographically by mountains, deserts, and rivers. Others are separated by architecture, music, language, and ways of making a living. Each nation has its own list of desires. Each nation knows how it plans to get what it needs from whoever's got it.

Most important, each nation has a distinct prism through which it views the world.

The Foundry, the declining industrial nation of the Northeast, for example, still tends to see the other eight nations as subservient, as the tribute-paying colonies they once were. It views itself as the "real" center of power in the continent, shrugging off the inexorable slide of population and ambitions to other places as temporary aberrations susceptible to some quick fix, to some new "program."

Viewed from the emerging nation of Dixie, however, the Foundry is a different place. Dixie, which has traded populations and histories with the Northeast for over a century, sees the Foundry as a collection of mistakes to be avoided as wealth flows south. To Dixie, the Foundry is the smell of the New Jersey Turnpike through Elizabeth; the question of the moment is whether that odor must soon permeate North Carolina and Louisiana, too.

Yet the northern Pacific Rim nation of Ecotopia views the Foundry in yet another way — as irrelevant. Even quaint. Foundry-like unemployment and recession are simply not overwhelming concerns in the Pacific Northwest, which is developing the industries of the twenty-first century: lightweight alloys, computer chips, and ways to use them that are still in the future. Its natural markets and its lessons about living are in Asia. The Foundry, on the other hand, is tied to Europe and thinks that the rest of the continent should be. The mistakes Ecotopia fears it may repeat are not those of the Foundry, but those of the boom towns of dry, sunny MexAmerica. If Ecotopia feels kin to any of the Nine Nations, it is to New England, from which so many of the Pacific Northwest's original settlers came, and with which so many of its successful social patterns are traded.

Each of these Nine Nations has a different future. Some are energy self-sufficient or exporting; most are desperate for oil. Some are chronically damp; to others, water is the primary concern, without which no future is thinkable. These nations attract different kinds of inhabitants — the assembly line or farm around which one person can build a life, another person may find supremely maddening.

It's valuable to recognize these divergent realities. The layers of unifying flavor and substances that define these nations help explain the major storms and excursions through which our public affairs pass.

Studying them is certainly far more constructive than examining misleading ideas, such as "Colorado."

Colorado is clearly two different places: the eastern half, which is flat, fertile agricultural land, and the western half, which rises dramatically in the suburbs of Denver to become the Rocky Mountains. Back when there were few people to speak of in the territory and it didn't make much difference, "Colorado" was boxed off into a neat, perfect rectangle, and now the idea it represents has been around long enough to become self-perpetuating. People speak and think of Colorado as one identifiable place, despite abundant evidence to the contrary and for little better reason than that their fathers did it that way. That does not, however, make the idea useful.

Take the farm protest movement that in the late seventies resulted in thousands of tractors blocking the traffic of downtown Washington, D.C. It was born of a frustration that spoke of parity and adverse farm prices, but it went far deeper. Actually, it was a cry declaring that no one cared about the farmers' problems; no one acknowledged the importance of the farmers' existence; no one was listening. That frustration did not first manifest itself in the heartland of Iowa or Nebraska. The American Agriculture Movement was born in the wheat fields of eastern Colorado. That's not much of a surprise. If any farmer was likely to be mad as hell, it would be he who sent his taxes to Denver, despite that capital's obvious interest in loosening its agrarian ties. Denver's great pride today is its shedding of the label "cowtown." As Denver flourishes (it's been called the nesting place of the forty-story crane), it clearly cares less and less about wheat. Denver sees its future in the oil, coal, gas, uranium, copper, molybdenum, and snow to its mountainous, winter-scoured west. Denver is the capital of, and the staging area for the assault on, the Empty Quarter — the most mineral-rich of the Nine Nations. The irrigated farm country to its east is rightfully part of a completely different nation — the Breadbasket.

"California" is an even worse idea than Colorado.

The Empty Quarter's attitude toward the Breadbasket is cordial inattention. The two Pacific nations that divide California, by contrast, are openly antagonistic. They're as antithetical as sunshine and rain.

The problem is simply stated: the thin strip of the Pacific shore along the Coast and Cascade Mountain ranges from Northern California to southern Alaska is the only place in the West with enough water. Everything else for a thousand miles in any direction is basically desert. It's no wonder that essentially different civilizations have grown up on the Pacific coast as a result.

The metropolises of MexAmerica, for example — adored for their dry, sunny climes — are designed like fragile moon bases. All the essentials to support life — water, power, and even breathable air — are imported from someplace else a long way away.

Power for the air conditioners of Los Angeles is sucked in from as far as Utah and Arizona. By buying electricity generated at such great distance, Los Angeles also effectively exports its pollution to these distant outposts, which is a way of importing clean air. For that matter, the smog of the Southern California coast is occasionally scoured by a "gift" of the desert to the east. The hot, violent Santa Ana winds surge over the mountains to make the cities sparkle, at the same time as they shrivel the chaparral to the explosive brush-fire stage.

But most important is water. "You can make gasoline out of cow manure if you have to," points out the western grower. "But you can't make water." Every developmental decision here — be it the growth of homes, industry, or agriculture — is based on the availability of water. Tucson is depending on water pumped over the Rocky Mountains and through manmade concrete riverbeds in the sand. San Diego depends on the Colorado River, also pumped over mountains. The unmatchable vegetable harvests of central California's San Joaquin Valley are absolutely dependent on water imported from the north. The whole civilization is based on engineering ingenuity of the first order.

There are several ways of looking at this.

In MexAmerica, such ingenuity is both father and child to a sense of the miraculous. A discussion of "limits" doesn't ring true here. After all, seven million people demonstrably can live in a Los Angeles Basin, which God saw fit to endow with the resources to support only two hundred thousand. If the difference is a manmade miracle, why stop at this point? The only real limits, it would appear, are those imposed by an inability to dream. Look at the wealth here. Look at the abundance and quality of the food. Look at the property values! This is obviously where people want to be and where people will continue to want to be. We've never let nature stand in the way of building canyon bungalows and sowing plains of rutabagas before. Why start now? In fact, there are serious men in these deserts who even propose diverting the waters of the Yukon River to further their sun-ripened visions of a rich tomorrow.

On the other side, of course, are those who think this is all patently insane, if not blasphemous. Chief among them are Northern Californians and other residents of Ecotopia who like their part of the world just fine the way it is. They worship different gods from those of their neighbors. They certainly have no reverence for the dams, channels, and diversions that would seize their assets and dump them into the unquenchable maw to the south. The forests of the Pacific Northwest are sufficiently blessed with resources to inspire thoughts of husbanding what exists, where it exists, in order to make it last forever. The implication is that others should consider doing the same.

Thus, in MexAmerica, the idea of a freshwater supply flowing unchecked into the sea is considered a crime against nature — a sin. In Ecotopia, leaving a river wild and free is viewed as a blow struck for God's original plan for the land.

Along such faiths are divergent social arrangements made.

San Francisco and Los Angeles are not just two cities. They represent two value structures. Indeed, they are the capitals of two different nations — Los Angeles the capital of MexAmerica, and San Francisco that of Ecotopia. So viewed, Sacramento becomes less the capital of anything terribly important than it is merely a border town between hostile forces.

So it goes, across the map. State legislators in Virginia correctly perceive any idea conceived north of the Rappahannock River, in the wealthy suburbs of Washington, D.C., as foreign and suspect. Most of Virginia is part of Dixie, where tax money, characteristically, is spent strictly on roads and schools, and sometimes not all that much on schools. Northern Virginians, with their ideas about social services and mass transit, obviously are not part of this tradition. They're Yankees. Northern Virginia is part, not of Dixie, but of the Foundry.

Chicago is not a capital city, because there is no such thing as the "Midwest." Chicago is properly an important border metropolis directing the trade in values and enterprise between the Foundry and the Breadbasket. Its hybrid status explains why it gets along so poorly in a political way with the rest of Illinois.

Canada, which is little save moose, Aleuts, and energy wealth north of the allegedly temperate strip along its border with the

United States, has migraines about losing its "identity." It shouldn't. Apart from French-speaking Québec, which is properly a nation unto itself, Canada shares five perfectly respectable and different identities with the northern United States.

Of course, the oil-rich "sheikdom" of Alberta defies Ottawa. Economically and philosophically, Calgary is far more kin to Fairbanks, Salt Lake City, or Denver than it is to Ottawa. It's part of the Empty Quarter. By the same token, the grain belt of the north, centered on Winnipeg, is visibly and temperamentally part of the Breadbasket. The industries of Windsor, Toronto, and Ottawa are part of the Foundry. Vancouver shares far more with Seattle than it does with Halifax, Nova Scotia. And the poor but proud Maritimes are in the same boat as New England.

These realities should come as no more of a shock than that South Florida is not part of any Confederate dream. Miami, after all, is now less a tourist mecca for the pasty-fleshed than it is the trade and intrigue capital of that Caribbean nation, the Islands.

Yet the existence of interstate highways, dense air connections, cheap long-distance rates, ubiquitous television, and the celebrated franchised hamburger has lulled many, incorrectly, into some sense that North America has become utterly homogenized, if not bland.

Granted, some cherished old regional idiosyncrasies have disappeared since World War II — widespread starvation in the South, for example. But focusing on certain absorbed folkways is to ignore what has been dispersed: power. Power, money, thought, talent, information, resources, and population. What's been happening for the past few decades is that North America has been maturing. Houston, Kansas City, and Atlanta, for example, only twenty years ago were crossroads not even their Chambers of Commerce could love. Now they're world-class cities.

Malarial East Texas became a technologically plausible alternative to New York City, for example, only in the 1960s. Shell Oil didn't dream of leaving Manhattan for Houston until it became thinkable to air-condition an employee's entire life — home, office, automobile, parking garage, shopping center, redneck bar, bedomed baseball stadium. Now, not only is Houston the world headquarters of oil, but the number of foreign banks there rose from six to forty-five in the last six years of the 1970s, with as many as twenty more expected in the very near term.

In 1972, the Soviet Union demonstrated that the North American Breadbasket could have as much strategic world importance as the Middle East by secretly contracting for massive, bargain-priced grain imports. When this happened, Kansas City proved to have better global sources of information and communication than did Washington, D.C. Washington got the first detailed reports on the "great grain robbery" — which rocked the U.S. economy, driving up food prices — by reading *Milling and Baking News*, the Kansas City weekly that had the scoop.

And Atlanta, in 1976, demonstrated conclusively that it had acquired a critical mass of financial, political, and media expertise. That's the year it propelled a former state governor, more unknown than which few were, into the presidency of the United States.

The significance of the evolution of these cities is that their regions and peoples are gaining sophistication, too.

Twenty years ago, if you were young, smart, ambitious, and from Des Moines, you fled to the bright lights of Chicago, if not New York, at your earliest opportunity. Getting *out* was of prime importance. The action was elsewhere; the opportunities to test your mettle were in some more glamorous site.

Today, abandoning Iowa at a tender age is not an indefensible action, but it's no longer an inevitable one. As one farmer put it, "In the old days, if you weren't smart enough to get a job in the city, you could always farm. Today, if you're not smart enough to farm, you can always get a job in the city."

In Sioux City, which is proud of the fact that it recently got the stockyards to move the block-long hill of manure that used to dominate the view of the city from the south, I chatted with two young men who had seen the light. Both had left Iowa in their teens, vowing never to return. But each came to the conclusion that the action was back home. The twenty-six-year-old was a commodities futures speculator who'd plowed some of his gains into a full-sized luxury sedan with a tiltable steering wheel in which he looked a little odd — as if both the car and the job would fit him better if he had either thirty pounds more paunch or thirty more years of age. A similar sense of the incongruous was offered by his friend, the corporate officer in a grain-trading outfit. He was twenty-five.

This new maturity is more obvious to regions flexing their newfound muscle than it is to older power centers reluctant to think of the rest of the continent as anything but a collection of branch offices.

"The [rest of the United States] is lagging so far behind us," says Walter Hoadley, chief economist of the Bank of America, the

major financial institution of the West. "We're backing into a tremendous period of growth in the nineteen eighties out here. The
West has a lot of potential resources and a dynamism which simply doesn't exist back east."

Similarly, the 1980s will be the decade in which majority control of the U.S. House of Representatives will pass out of the
hands of New England, the Foundry, and the Breadbasket. Massive losses of population in old Foundry cities such as the Bronx
will see New York state alone lose five seats, while Dixie, Mex-
America, Ecotopia, the Empty Quarter, and the Islands gain seventeen.

When the site of what is now Washington, D.C., was selected
for the capital of the fledgling Republic in 1790, it was virtually
on top of the United States population center, then just east of
Baltimore. In the 1980s, the population center of the United
States will move west of the Mississippi River for the first time.

There are three major results of these changes.

• The more self-assured each of these Nine Nations becomes,
the less willing it is to be dictated to by outsiders who show no
interest in sharing — or even understanding — local values. This
hinders a search for continentwide answers to political questions.

• As resources and opportunities are dispersed, each nation, at
least theoretically, becomes increasingly capable of solving its
own problems at its own level, although habit and institutions
often do not cooperate.

• Increased sophistication may lead to the decline of marginal
continental differences. (The classic southern drawl is on the
wane, for example.) But it emphasizes the real, enduring, and
basic economic and social differences of each region, manifested
in attitudes toward everything from nuclear power to unions to
abortion.

Recent public policy is replete with propositions that were par-
alyzed by their initiators' ignorance of these new implications
about power.

Jimmy Carter's political weakness in the West, for an obvious
example, was made permanent in the first hundred days of his
administration, when he promulgated his "hit list" of waterproj-
ects that he did not feel to be cost-effective. As chief of staff Hamilton Jordan was later to admit candidly, in Dixie, "Water is just
another word." It's something that floods your basement every
spring, not the linchpin of your agricultural, industrial, or urban
survival.

Foreign policy is affected, too. An ill-fated flap over an alleged Soviet combat brigade in Cuba was stirred up in 1979 by a scholarly Idaho senator, chairman of the Senate Foreign Relations Committee Frank Church. He was desperately and unsuccessfully trying to counter a vigorous conservative re-election challenge that centered on one charge: that he had succumbed to the pressures of the eastern seaboard and had become "soft" and "liberal."

The new diversity affects financial thinking. Recently the "multi-tier" theory of industrial performance has gained popularity. It demonstrates, for example, that recessions hurt the creators of expensive durable goods, like automobiles or steel, worse than they do the purveyors of energy, electronics, services, food, and ideas. This was a much-needed explanation of how the Foundry can be failing at the same time that the Breadbasket can expect continued stability, and MexAmerica, strong growth.

The more pressing the continental concern, the more abundant the regional complications. Energy is the classic example. Long have the pundits deplored the seeming inability of North America to come up with an energy program. Unstinting was the derision heaped on Jimmy Carter's declaration of the "moral equivalent of war." Brief was the reign of Canadian prime minister Joe Clark, who called for austerity and a tax on gasoline of eighteen cents a gallon.

Yet the problem has not been a lack of energy plans. The problem has been their abundance. North America has nine energy programs up and functioning right now, each tailored to the demands of a particular nation.

New England, for example, is dedicated to austerity and conservation, which is appropriate for a nation marked by compact geography, good public transportation, and extremely limited resources.

By contrast, Québec's hydroelectric potential is so vast as to be inexhaustible. Québec is actively seeking out heavy energy demands, such as the manufacturing of aluminum products.

Dixie is more reliant on nuclear power plants than any other nation, which is a logical outgrowth of few choices coupled with an unquestioning commitment to growth.

Ecotopia, on the other hand, with abundant renewable-energy options and a jaundiced view of development, sees atomic energy as the poisoned fruit of a technology gone berserk.

The Empty Quarter, which is in the catbird's seat in terms of energy reserves, and is marked by enormous distances between everything, views conservation in the form of a fifty-five-mile-per-hour speed limit in the same light as Ecotopia views nukes — as self-evidently crazy.

MexAmerica, like the Empty Quarter in having significant energy deposits, is like the Foundry in having intractable pollution problems. Unlike any of the others, its growth is fueled by refugees who flee from the cost of heating a home through a northern winter.

The nation of the Islands is similarly filled with "snowbirds" escaping the chill, but unlike people in MexAmerica, few are asking, yet, where the energy to drive the air conditioners will come from.

Meanwhile, the Breadbasket carries on a lonely love affair with gasohol — a fuel partly distilled from grain — a course that every other nation is convinced will drive up food prices.

In this light, it's far less mysterious why, for example, there's a continental inability to agree on a plan so basic as standby gasoline rationing. It is difficult to imagine how, in the face of such diverse interests, coupons could be distributed in a fashion that would fairly distribute hardship.

More critically, unlike during World War II, it's impossible to imagine how a plan aimed at benefiting the industrial Northeast could be rammed down the throat of the rest of the continent.

"Partly, I think, our problems are insoluble unless we change the way we do things," says Jeff Faux, a Maine economist who has studied the plight of New England closely, but who, as codirector of the National Center for Economic Alternatives, a Washington, D.C., think tank, sees broader implications to the current federal system.

"Take Dickey-Lincoln, for example."

(Dickey-Lincoln is the name of a proposal by the U.S. Army Corps of Engineers to dam a river in northern Maine to generate hydroelectricity. Opponents claim it would ruin a pristine wilderness in order to produce an insignificant amount of energy at an astronomical cost.)

There've been analyses — and assume for a moment that they're right — that the environmentalists have put forward, that say if you take the eight hundred million or billion dollars they propose to put into Dickey-Lincoln, and used that in a series of alternative energy projects — low-head hydro, small things, solar, wood burning, insulation, the whole gamut of what we know — you would produce more energy than with Dickey-Lincoln, more of it would be baseload rather than peak power, you'd have less environmental damage, and you'd create more jobs.

Just assume for a moment — assume — that that is right. The problem is that we don't have that choice. The way the system comes down to the state of Maine, and to New England, is that you've got a program that the Corps of Engineers has, and it's willing to put a billion dollars into this. Yes or no. A billion dollars this way, or nothing.

Now there's an obvious problem there. The region cannot make a rational decision on that basis. My point is that we're going to have public spending, no matter what happens in the future. We ought to be thinking about this public investment. Probably not just in energy alone, but in roads and in transportation and all the other major decisions, in a way that provides a region with the flexibility to make the choices between Dickey-Lincoln and nuclear power and an alternative. We need a framework of, okay, what are the region's needs for the next twenty years, how are we going to supply those needs?

I mean, I am a person who feels that, yes, there *is* a position that says we ought to have nuclear power in New England. I don't think Central Maine Power has made the case for it, but clearly, given New England's situation, it is not an unreasonable position. The case for Dickey-Lincoln, I think, is a reasonable case. And the case that the environmentalists make, to say now wait a minute, if you did it this way you could have more jobs and all that, is a reasonable position.

The problem is that there is no forum for the region in which we say, all right, add up all the social costs and the social benefits, and recognize that the public sector is going to put money into whatever it is — nuclear power doesn't stand on its own any more than Dickey-Lincoln or some of these other things. Okay, what is the best decision we can make?

But what we have is the corps saying, hey, you want this program? Yes or no. I mean, a *billion* dollars. Well hell, in a poor state . . .

This sense of regional frustration is hardly limited to old New England. Utah, with its immense coal reserves, is not a poor state. And Kent Briggs, the administrative assistant to the governor of Utah, and the son of an Idaho reclamation farmer, is by no means either a bleeding-heart environmentalist or an opponent of industrialization. Yet he, too, feels chafed by shortsighted federal policies devised far away that block local control over the majority of Utah's land.

"We see the Yankees putting restrictions on our development and continuing colonial shackles," he says. "My vision is that we might need a new western nation from the Mackenzie River to the Rio Grande."

Whether or not Briggs is correct about what his part of the continent should, in the future, do, the fact is that the various portions of the continent are, right now, bringing a new sense of sovereignty to the way they view the world. The ultimate demonstration is that most North Americans, at some level of consciousness, feel a dual citizenship. While their passports may say "United States" or "Mexico" or "Canada," they are also bound to another nation — the heartland of the Breadbasket or the row houses of the Foundry.

The power of these ties to the Nine Nations is confirmed by what would appear to be a contradiction: the extraordinary mobility of citizens who move from one nation to another. These migrants retain some of their old trappings, but they push to embrace the styles and attitudes of their new nation.

The standard amusement among MexAmerican Anglos is watching newcomers turn "mellow" — beguiled by the relentless sun despite their vows never to succumb.

Carolina developers become almost a little apologetic about the deep partisanship for Dixie displayed by European industrialists transferred there. It's hardly uncommon to hear stories of their later reluctance to accept a posting to other parts of North America, or even back to the home office.

With never-ceasing amazement do natives of Idaho or Wyoming watch how quickly a newcomer picks up the habit of referring, with suspicion, to all nonresidents of the region as "them."

To New Englanders, it's tiresomely obvious that one of the region's employment problems stems from the many outlanders who first come to the region just to get four years of college, but then stay — even accepting starvation wages — because they can no longer conceive of living somewhere less "civilized."

The Rand McNally Road Atlas is not a perennial paperback best seller because North Americans think they are all the same. Travel is the great North American pastime because of our enduring diversity. We look forward to picking up our belongings and taking a new job in a different region out of a sense of adventure. It allows us to try on different values, different senses of the pace at which life should be lived, different attitudes about art, food, and ethnic origin, different relationships to nature. It allows us to discover, with some perspective, what empty place there is that only Georgia, say, can fill.

A newspaper reporter told me of the time he gave up the prestige of being a Washington correspondent in order to return to the quieter life of the medium-sized western paper from which he had originally come.

The drive across the continent for him was a long and silent one. As he drove through Pennsylvania, Illinois, Nebraska, he hardly noticed his surroundings, wondering whether the choice he had made was right.

He told me he remembered with great clarity finally losing his indecision on Interstate 80, not far from Cheyenne, Wyoming, as the flatlands gave way to the mountains and their small towns.

It was there, he said, that suddenly a knot disappeared from his stomach, a knot he hadn't known was there. It was there that he discovered a feeling of familiarity with the colors, the horizon, the names of the towns.

Every North American knows a place like that, a place where, on your way back from your wanderings, surroundings stop feeling threatening, confusing, or strange.

Ultimately, that's the reason we are Nine Nations. When you're from one, and you're in it, you know you're home.

NEW ENGLAND

EAST OF THE GREEN MOUNTAINS, under a bridge that carries the main street of the town of Randolph, Vermont, over the Third Branch of the White River, lies a small mill.

With the words SARGENT ROUNDY CORPORATION fading on its smokestack, the place might seem to be abandoned. There are many deserted factories in this beautiful land, much of whose industry has seen hard times for a century. But even from a distance, walking down the steep, hairpin turn that leads from the bridge to the river's edge, one can see hints that the place, though ramshackle, is not empty.

In the yard are great stacks of twelve- and fifteen-foot-long logs, piles of three-foot-wide tree-trunk rounds, heaps of irregularly shaped slabs, and cords of tarp-covered firewood. They suggest that the place has been made into a sawmill, and, indeed, the distant whine of ripsaws can be heard. But those sounds turn out to have nothing to do directly with the felled trees. The tools are actually being used to expand the old mill — to increase the size of a showroom.

Inside the decaying, shingle-covered building, the windows are covered with plastic; pink fiber-glass insulation pokes through an occasional hole in the wall; the mood is of bustle barely under control.

It's the kind of purposeful chaos that can be invigorating if one is young enough not to find it maddening. And the crowd swirling through the cramped quarters is definitely young. A girl with a jeweled pin in her nostril, wearing a floor-length skirt, sweeps around one corner just as two dogs explode out of an office and, at a dead run, bang through the side door toward the river. The sounds of thump, clang, and grind fill the air with a resonance that seems to belong to the past.

Baskets of gray metal parts are heaped on shelves, where workers quickly select what they need, and have at them with grinding wheels throwing off orange streams of sparkles. Down the line, a young man with a pony tail sprays black paint at a finished assembly, after which nickel-plated controls are attached. In a side room, artists are making wooden models of proposed new products, which will be converted to aluminum master molds that will then be translated into iron.

Away from the noise of metal on metal, in a space no larger than a good-sized living room, a bank of perhaps a dozen telephone cubicles has been set up, the partitions between them fashioned of two-by-fours that are still exposed, no attempt having been made to cosmeticize them. A box of apples and a large bag of doughnuts sit near a beat-up wood-burning stove at the center of the room. It is throwing out strong heat. The conversations of the folk on the long-distance lines are of chimneys, drafts, thermostats, combustion efficiency, and dampers.

But the conversation always comes back to wood. For this is the headquarters of one of the biggest employers in central Vermont, and certainly the fastest-growing. It's Vermont Castings, makers of arguably the finest air-tight cast-iron wood stoves in North America. In less than five years, Vermont Castings has gone from nothing but one impoverished yet curious tinkerer freezing his butt off, trying to figure out how to stay warm, to an operation employing hundreds, selling more than fifty thousand stoves a year at prices that can approach $600 apiece. The White House, in order to demonstrate its commitment to energy independence, bought six.

In its display of such Yankee virtues as ingenuity and shrewd trading, and in its ability to take the liability of Vermont's cold winters and dependence on imported heating oil and turn it into a sparkling asset, Vermont Castings is a fascinating display of the contradictions that make New England so distinctly one of North America's Nine Nations.

At first glance, New England's future is bleak. That becomes clear in a study done by the National Center for Economic Alternatives. The results, based on per capita income figures, adjusted state by state for differences in cost of living, are startling. The poorest of the United States is not Mississippi; it's Maine. Vermont is third poorest. Rhode Island, eighth. Except for Connecticut, with its New York bedroom communities that are not part of this land, no state in New England comes anywhere near being in the top two-thirds in wealth.

Yet this, the poorest of the nations, prides itself on being the only really civilized place in North America, a kind of Athens of the continent. It is hardly a contradiction that thousands of highly educated New Englanders each year abandon their central heating in order to go into the woods to hack at the oaks with ax or chain saw. They are feeding this expensive, hot lump of cast iron they've just ordered from Vermont Castings. They're not only happy about this development; they have acquired a sense of smug superiority about it, matched only by the pride they take in coaxing peas out of the frozen ground in April. The various models of Vermont Castings' wood stoves have names like Defiant, Vigilant, and Resolute. It may sound as if this shop is trying to refloat the Royal Navy, but that's not so. What it's doing is redefining what New Englanders like to think of as their independent national character.

Geographically, New England is unusual on this continent in having political boundaries that are meaningful. Practically since the American Revolution, New England has been described in terms of states: Maine, New Hampshire, Vermont, Massachusetts, Rhode Island, and Connecticut — and that's still basically true.

But there are exceptions. The southwestern third of Connecticut, for example, is not part of New England. That area, like western Long Island, is firmly in the orbit of New York City and belongs to the nation of the Foundry. These familiar scenes of John Updike–studied commuter affluence, like Darien, Stamford, and New Canaan, are identical with Shaker Heights outside Cleveland or Grosse Pointe outside Detroit. These big-city suburbs have matured to the point that even the expensive tract homes on the curving streets that were such a novelty thirty years ago are beginning to look a little tacky. They're being bought up by people who realize that they may have to drop as much as another hundred thousand dollars or so on renovations and extensions to return them to their proper status position. This is consistent with the now decades-old theme of places like Great Neck, Oyster Bay, and Larchmont, which is to try to prove that money doesn't have to go hand in hand with vulgarity, despite nagging local evidence to the contrary. That is hardly New England.

Perhaps the most telling perimeter clue: most of those people in southwestern Connecticut or on Long Island are Yankee fans. The New England line is firmly drawn at the point where fanatic Boston Red Sox rooters become the minority.

New Englanders consider it a triumph if the Sox wind up the season forty-one games out of first — as long as the Yankees are forty-two out. Their faith, however, is seldom rewarded because of the Sox's crazed habit of staying in contention until September, when they suddenly get tired of the game and blow a twelve-game road trip. Year after year, the Boston club teaches New Englanders a lesson they have thoroughly internalized: you just can't win.

Farther up the map, northern Maine — like those Connecticut counties — is only marginally New England. If Québec were not so politically defined, it could be part of that nation. The international boundary in Aroostook County has always been a bit vague and arbitrary. It didn't settle into its present position until 1842, decades after southern Maine had been admitted to the Union. The boundary clues up here include a dominant French culture and — an accompanying social phenomenon — the way English-speakers have of being nasty to their French-speaking cousins.

This is also true in northern New Brunswick, which, with its lively French-speaking Acadian movement, could easily be called part of Québec. The only reason not to include it is that Québec, as one of the most distinct of the Nine Nations, deserves to be considered within the confines of its current political borders. Most of New Brunswick, however, is akin to the other Maritime Provinces of Canada (Nova Scotia and Prince Edward Island) and the other Atlantic province, Newfoundland. And, in turn, all of them are really an extension of "the Boston states," as the Atlantic provinces call their United States comrades.

The major difference between the Maritimes and New England is what the schoolchildren are taught about George III. If you grow up in Boston, you are told that the American Revolution was a good idea. If you grow up in St. John, you're told it was a controversial and messy one.

Apart from that, the differences between the two regions are quantitative, not qualitative. The Maritimes are more cold, more poor, and, remarkably, even more beautiful. In the hills off the North Atlantic coast around Mahone Bay in Nova Scotia, winter comes through your clothes in late September.

From Chatham to Moncton in New Brunswick, you can see people digging for potatoes with their hands. Potatoes are so cheap, and this work so hard, that nobody has even thought to sing the blues about it, as they did about chopping cotton.

Yet the farms and pink beaches of Queens County on Prince Edward Island are such an Eden in the summer that one is tempted not to tell friends about it lest it be "spoiled." Already the lobster catch has been reduced to the point that the shellfish are too valuable to be plowed into the fields as fertilizer. That's how plentiful they once were.

The Maritimes are so much a part of New England that businessmen wishing to travel from Edmundston, New Brunswick, to, say, Montréal, Québec, 390 miles away, find the best way is to fly 800 miles via Boston.

The case of Cecille Bechard, of New Brunswick and Maine, was celebrated recently in the *New York Times*:

Cecille Bechard is a Canadian who visits the United States several dozen times a day — when she goes to the refrigerator or the back door or to make tea, for instance. To read and sleep she stays in Canada, and she eats there too if she sits at the north end of the kitchen table. Mrs. Bechard's home sits on the United States–Canada border. The frontier cuts through the kitchen wall and across the sink, splits the salt and pepper shakers, just misses the stove and passes through the other wall to sever the Nadeau family's clothesline and cut off the candy counter in Alfred Sirois's general store. Almost anywhere else in the world, Mrs. Bechard might need a passport to take a bath.

Maritimers work and vacation in New England. Maine teenagers drink in the Maritimes because the age limit is lower there. The border checkpoints are jammed at quitting time and when the bars close.

And if any more proof were needed that Maritimers and New Englanders belong to one nation, it is provided by the ubiquitous cable TV connections, which allow Nova Scotians to be driven just as crazy by the Red Sox as the Worcester tenement-dweller. When the boys boot another one to the Yankees, you can hear the curses all over Halifax.

The argument has been made that if North America had been settled from west to east, instead of the other way around, New England would still be uninhabited, and there's something to be said for this theory. It's only inertia, for example, that preserves any commercial agriculture in New England. The standard story about the Vermont dairy industry is that it is trying to breed a cow whose left legs are two feet shorter than her right so that she can negotiate the slope of her pasture. You may recall that during the Vietnam War, then-Senator George Aiken, that quintessential Vermont Yankee Republican, suggested that the way to disengage from the conflict was merely to announce that the war was over, declare a glorious victory for the United States, and leave. In Washington, that has long been regarded as a typical New England solution. It's no more eccentric than making a declaration that all those Yankee acres of rock and clay, with their four-month growing season, are actually farmland fit for plowing.

Not only is New England unblessed agriculturally, but it has precious little raw material and, with approximately thirteen million people, a diminished population. Long ago the texile manufacturers moved to Dixie, with its plentiful cotton and cheap labor. The iron-makers moved to the Foundry, where the ore and coal were. And, in general, industry continues to march west — partly because it's easier to distribute goods from a central point on the continent than it is from, say, Manchester, New Hampshire.

The most critical point, though, is that New England lacks the oil of MexAmerica, the thundering cascades of hydro power found in Québec and Ecotopia, and the uranium and synthetic fuel stocks of the Empty Quarter. Except for its proximity to the fishing riches of the Georges Bank, New England has sparse resource assets — apart from the remnants of an industrialism that derived from the historical accident of first settlement.

Paradoxically, the scenery and the surroundings have become New England's primary asset. New England is rapidly transforming itself into North America's first truly twenty-first-century, postindustrial society, and, as such, it is again a land of pioneers.

Says one Boston banker, who thinks that New England's economically stable state is a euphemism for stagnation, "We don't have any theories about what you do when you reach this state of economic maturity. The finest brains have been telling us how to *grow*. Nobody seems to know what to do when you *get* grown."

But New England, intuitively and inexorably, is about to show the world how to find out, for it is producing an amazing consensus, considering its circumstances, about the futures that it will and will not accept.

Take its energy future, for example.

People in other parts of North America might think that a nation this short on cash, this cold, and up to 80 percent dependent on imported fuel oil for home heating, would be racing headlong toward any promise of relief.

But that is not the case.

The Pittstown Company, of New York, has been trying for almost a decade to put an oil refinery in Eastport, Maine, the easternmost point of land in the United States. In 1979, Eastport had an unemployment rate of 20 percent. Four hundred families in this town of two thousand were getting food stamps. The sardine canneries that used to be the major industry had closed down long ago. At 250,000 barrels a day, this proposed refinery could meet 19 percent of New England's gasoline and home heating oil needs.

But will it ever be built? Don't bet on it. Half of the waters in which the tankers would have to travel belong to Canada, which says that an oil spill would endanger its fisheries. (The more cynical think that the Canadians really see it as a threat to their own underutilized refineries.) The summer home of Franklin D. Roosevelt, an international park, is a mile downwind of the refinery site, and that outrages a select constituency. But more important, beyond the blueberry-covered hills, in Cobscook Bay, dance humpback whales. And of crowning significance, through the local spruce glide more bald eagles, making more baby bald eagles, than any other place in the Northeast. Both the whales and the United States national symbol are endangered species, and it has been made abundantly clear that as long as oil refineries issue mercury, sulfur dioxide, and other pollutants, there is no way that one is going to be built anywhere near those eagles.

Does the local population buy these priorities? In a recent Fourth of July parade, the Little League's vastly popular Red Sox float was defeated for first place honors by the Youth Conservation Corps' entry, with the theme "Don't Let Eastport Become a Pits Town."

This, in fact, represents a general New England belief in the equation that energy development in its backyard equals an inevitable decline in the quality of its civilization.

The subliminal part of this is an a priori assumption that New England sets a standard of civilized behavior that is far more rare than kilowatts, and is thus more valuable. That is the reason New Englanders see no contradiction in asking the rest of the continent to subsidize the price of their home heating oil at the same time that they frantically resist efforts to drill for it off their coast.

It's a defensible position. It might, in fact, make sense for Houston to subsidize Boston now so that, when they finally come to their senses, Houstonians will be able to go to Boston for a sight of what a truly civilized city looks like.

The problem is that New Englanders have yet to display the guts necessary to put this argument in a forthright way. When they agitate against drilling for oil in the fertile fishing grounds of Georges Bank, they state the argument in terms of one natural resource versus another. They contend that an oil spill could kill a lot of fish, ruining one of God's great gifts to man. That's certainly true, but if the Georges Bank were to disappear tomorrow, a less than 1 percent increase in beef production in the Breadbasket could make up for any loss in protein, according to the Department of the Interior.

What really bugs New Englanders about energy development is not the threat to fish, as such, but the prospect of having their tidy and carefully ordered portion of the planet screwed up. Take the example of the big idea that the Army Corps of Engineers has for the northern tip of Maine.

That's where, as mentioned in the first chapter, the corps wants to build the twenty-seven-story-high, two-mile-long Dickey-Lincoln dam across the St. John River. The proposal, grander than Egypt's Aswan Dam, would flood 267 miles of river and streams and eighty-eight thousand acres of timber in order to create a reservoir 57 miles long. The power it could produce would replace 2.3 million barrels of oil a year.

For a time, this project was blocked by a three-foot-high plant with unimpressive little yellow flowers, the furbish lousewort. That, too, is an endangered species, and the dam would jeopardize the existence of the skinny weeds. The louseworts' habitat, propagation, and microclimatic requirements are under detailed study to determine if they can be grown elsewhere, and the corps is now looking into buying lousewort sanctuaries. But meanwhile, the dam's cost estimates have quadrupled since it was originally authorized in 1965. A projected cost of $218 million is now pushing a billion, and at that price, some of its drawbacks are becoming glaring — such as the fact that there is so little water in the St. John River during the summer that the dam would operate, on the average, only two and a half hours out of every twenty-four.

But the torrent of economic arguments thrown up by Dickey-Lincoln's increasingly sophisticated opponents is not the real reason this dam probably will never be built. The real reason is that northern Maine has some of the prettiest wilderness in the Northeast. You can dip into a river and safely drink its waters. And in a land as crowded as this continent's Northeast, that's a rare, and thus valuable, commodity. If politics allocate resources, then it would seem that in this case, New England politics are again based on the premise that recreational wilderness is more scarce than Middle Eastern oil, and that, of course, is in fact a defensible position.

Hampton Beach, New Hampshire, is by no means wilderness. The North Atlantic surf curls in the same gray-green, foam-flecked fashion there as it has for millennia, but behind the white sandy beach, the Hampton Beach Casino ("Jewelry, Ice Cream, Food, Snack Bar, Rides, Golf, Gifts, Doughnuts, Fashions, Leather, Boutiques, Jewelry") is jammed. So are the taco parlors, fried dough stands, sweet shops, T-shirt emporiums, discos, and motels that make up the resort.

The competition for a few linear feet of New Hampshire coastline is fierce because there is so little of it — only seventeen miles between Massachusetts and Maine. Hampton Beach State Park marks the spot where the Atlantic breaks through the dunes to form a pleasant harbor, where meandering creeks with grand names such as Browns River, Blackwater River, and Hampton River create salt marshes. The salt marshes, in whose sensitive and fecund ecology the marine food chain begins, boast reeds and cattails that, rippling like wheat in a breeze, are hypnotic. The small harbor guards from the riptides both the wide, high-prowed, low-gunwaled commercial fishing and lobster boats, and the sleek cabin cruisers with names like *Shenanigans* and *Anstrice*. Bright-colored lobster buoys line a wall by a small store where you can buy bait, tackle, and cold drinks.

If you're careful not to let your eyes wander a few hundred yards inland, it's possible to forget that the town just across the inlet from Hampton Beach is Seabrook. The motel operators of Hampton make a point, for example, of quickly correcting guests who think they've come to Seabrook.

But although the map of Seabrook put out by Preston Real Estate does not choose to take note of the town's most famous landmark, it's impossible to ignore forever the concrete forms of the largest construction project ever attempted in New England. They're easily visible over the roofs of the shore cottages. For that matter, looming over the forms are dozens of red and white

striped cranes, so much more massive than the ones on the lobster boats that aircraft warning beacons flash from their sides.
Every residential road, as it comes to a dead end in the marsh,
offers a spectacular view. You can sit at the Dairy King, eating
your dip-topped ice cream cone, and marvel at it. Or you can stop
at Captain Berk's Lobster Pond ("Live Lobster, Live Crabs,
Spawns, Oysters, Smelts, Haddock, Shrimp, Salmon, Swordfish,
Scallops, Halibut, Bass, Eel, Bait, Eel Worms") and catch the act
from there. Of an evening, it's much more brightly and starkly lit
even than the row of honky-tonks on the beach. It is Seabrook
Station. Twin 2300-megawatt nuclear reactors. Strategically located practically on top of the East Coast's main tourist
roads — old U.S. Route 1 and Interstate 95. Seabrook Station. The
birthplace of the American antinuclear movement.

One thousand, four hundred, and fourteen people were arrested
at Seabrook on the afternoon of May 2, 1977, and charged with
criminal trespass.

The chief public relations person at Seabrook is enamored
enough of the right-wing Heritage Foundation account of the proceedings to press it on visiting reporters.

Abridged, it goes like this:

With the issuance of the original Seabrook construction permits in July
of 1976, a new and unexpected turn of events took place. Most of the
planners engaged in the construction at Seabrook assumed that winning
the battle in court and before the regulatory agencies meant an end to
opposition to the facility. In this they were mistaken. A group of individuals unhappy with the results of the legal process felt that the time had
come to go outside the law. Towards this end they formed the Clamshell
Alliance, a group which is by its own declaration "unalterably opposed
to the construction of this (Seabrook) and all other nuclear plants". . .

Certainly, in 1976 no one would have been prepared to believe that
over May Day Weekend, 1977, the Clamshell Alliance would return with
a thoroughly trained, coordinated group of some 2000 persons . . .

The company allowed the demonstrators to enter the site and occupy
an area used for parking, and to set up their tents and camping equipment . . . as long as they were peaceful and agreed to leave [before construction workers arrived Monday morning]. Early Sunday afternoon, it
was decided that the time had come . . .

The [Clamshell] leadership, after conferring with the demonstrators,
indicated that they would not be willing to leave, and that they would
also insist on being arrested . . . and 1414 were.

As they refused to post bail, they were temporarily incarcerated in a
number of National Guard Armories around the state. Their stand

against posting bail was maintained for two full weeks during which time they continued to be housed in the armories.

One result of this incarceration [and these are the Heritage Foundation's words] was that it gave them time to organize. In a real sense, those two weeks amounted to the period of incubation for the birth of the national anti-nuclear movement . . .

The cost of renting the National Guard Armories, along with certain services required from the Guard during the period of incarceration, such as feeding the prisoners and caring for the sanitation facilities, came to $310,863.90. Public health services came to $13,082.26. State police (including those borrowed from other states) cost $51,169.75. Local police, $5,090.84. Finally, the initial cost estimate for the services of the Attorney General's staff as a result of the arraignments associated with the arrests of the demonstrators came to $10,000. This cost, of course, as has been mentioned, will escalate severely with time, as a consequence of the appeals process. Thus, the total for the demonstration which took place over May Day Weekend, 1977, comes to $389,206.85.

Further, those figures do not reflect any increased costs which might have been incurred by Public Service Company of New Hampshire [the utility whose idea Seabrook is] in preparing for the demonstration, and which would be reflected eventually in the customer's electric bill.

Of course, since all this, the Three Mile Island nuclear accident has occurred. Antinuclear demonstrations have brought out hundreds of thousands of people. Meldrim Thomson, then governor of New Hampshire, who backed a surcharge on the electric bills of the state's residents to help pay for Seabrook's construction, has been ignominiously defeated at the polls twice. A plan to build reactors of the Seabrook design on Narragansett Bay in Rhode Island has been rejected. (The 604-acre site considered for that power plant will, in classic New England fashion, instead be made into a wildlife refuge.) Public Service of New Hampshire is in deep trouble with its financiers. By 1979, delays had increased Seabrook's total price tag by an estimated $1,997,492,200. It's perfectly possible that if arguments in Congress over nuclear technology's safety don't get Seabrook, arguments on Wall Street over its affordability will.

So I asked Norman Cullerot, the public relations man at Seabrook, about the problems. I had just taken the tour of this mind-numbing, you've-never-seen-so-much-steel-and-cement, makes-the-Pyramids-look-like-sandcastles construction project. I was sitting among the natural wood surroundings of the $1.7 million "education center," and I said, Look, I know you've already spent

nine hundred and ninety million dollars on this project, and
you're still counting. And I know this must be like questioning
Lyndon Johnson about Vietnam. But, just between you and me.
All questions aside about radioactive waste lasting for a hundred
thousand years. Did nobody in this whole, big company ever walk
the beaches around here, look out over the salt marshes and the
lobster boats and the tourists and say, hey, if we build this thing
here, there's going to be trouble? Did it ever occur to anybody
that a nuclear reactor here is emotionally impossible for New
Englanders?

I guess he responded to my question. He launched into praise
for the plant's cooling system. Remember those tall, curved
water-cooling towers that became the symbol for Three Mile Island? Seabrook Station doesn't have any of those, he explained.
Instead, a little east of the reactors there are two holes, 375 feet
deep and wide enough to swallow a small house. On a platform
275 feet down have been pieced together a couple of 340-ton machines called moles. These moles bore through rock with fifty-two
cutter blades, pressed up against the stuff by hydraulic rams that
produce a thrust of 995 tons. The moles' average speed is about
four feet an hour. The granite here is referred to as "stubborn."
These moles are drilling two tunnels straight out to sea, one 16,-
483 feet long, the other 17,410 feet long. These tunnels pass directly under Hampton Beach State Park and the harbor on their
way a mile or so out into the ocean. When completed, they'll be
more than big enough to drive a trailer truck through, although
that's not what they'll carry. One of the tunnels will carry 850,000
gallons of the North Atlantic every minute into the power plant,
where it will cool and condense the steam generated. The other
pipe will take this water, instantly made 39 degrees hotter, and
dump it back into the ocean. Much to the surprise of the fish.

And that, he explained, is why Seabrook was built here. It's as
close to this big beautiful body of cooling fluid as possible while
being as far away from the city of Portsmouth as it can be without leaving New Hampshire.

And he waited for my next question.

I think that means that the answer to my original question is
no.

It never occurred to the planners at Public Service of New
Hampshire that their ideas would be viewed as controversial,
much less that in the eyes of some New Englanders, observing
what was being done to their ocean, Seabrook Station would be-

come the classic and enduring example of technology gone berserk.

This is not, however, to say that management is unaware that it has a public relations problem. And that's why, outside the nature trail with the carefully labeled plants, just down the way from the redwood picnic tables, across from the entrance to the education center with its diagonal wood siding, has been built Seabrook Unit Three.

One and Two, of course, are the 2300-megawatt reactors. Three is a windmill. Very futuristic-looking, it's shaped something like the head of an eggbeater, with three bowed, fifteen-foot blades revolving around a vertical axis, allowing it to accept wind from every direction. It will supply 12 kilowatts of electricity.

On Block Island, twelve miles off the coast of Rhode Island, looming 160 feet tall, is another windmill. It's rated at 200 kilowatts, but has a completely different story.

The U.S. government in 1979 spent over $60 million on windmill development, and this island, on which 459 people were recorded at a recent Ground Hog's Day census (an annual event that takes place at a local bar) has, quixotically, managed to snare $2.3 million of that in the form of its new monster.

Block Island was thought to be a dandy place for this wind machine, which has a 125-foot wing span and sits on a 100-foot-tall tower. The islanders claim they pay the highest electricity rates in the country — twice as high as the mainland — because their power is generated by inefficient diesels, the fuel for which must come from the mainland on barges. Fortunately, the wind gales up to a hundred miles an hour over the island in the winter. The average breeze is a stiff seventeen miles per hour, which is just a hair under small-craft-warning strength.

Equally important, the island gets hundreds of thousands of tourists in the summer, so the sleek orange and white National Aeronautic and Space Administration–built turbine is good p.r. for the government's energy program.

There are a few hitches, but they're being worked on. One is that the wind turbine is calculated to save only $30,000 worth of diesel oil a year, and so, in order to become independent of OPEC, the island will need a platoon of these things to be self-sufficient. At several million dollars apiece, of course, this is no small thing.

There is the question of what the Department of Energy calls "airborne fauna." Block Island is in the migration path of everything with wings that calls the coast home, and the tips of the windmill's blades travel at 178 miles per hour. But an expensive federal study has come to the tentative decision that birds can see and hear a windmill, and most normally fly higher than the windmill, anyway.

And, of course, there's the TV reception. It's been discovered that big whirring aluminum blades cause television signals to bounce. Henry Hutchinson, the septuagenarian Yankee who heads up the Block Island Power Company, was quoted as saying, "Television means an awful lot — particularly to the people who are out here in the wintertime. The movie theater is closed, and it's the only steady source of entertainment." So the federal government has obliged by spending another $700,000 to push an undersea cable from the mainland to Block Island and to wire the entire island for cable television.

In such a fashion is the twenty-first century built in New England.

One of the more instructive parts of the Block Island saga is that the project was financed by federal money. The way one receives federal money in this world is to be political, and from the first days that the locals started shooting at Redcoats from behind the trees of Bunker Hill, political is something New England has always been. In fact, politics is one of New England's leading industries. Perhaps the most celebrated political novel of this century, *The Last Hurrah*, is very solidly based on the career of James Michael Curley, the Boston mayor who ran for re-election from jail and won. The Kennedy legacy alone marks New England as being overendowed with politicians. There is so much government that New England Telephone has a separate section for its telephone numbers — the Blue Pages.

But this has not been an unmixed blessing for New England, because the flip side of government is taxes, and with those New England also abounds. The property taxes in New England are among the highest in the nation. Until recently, houses evaluated at no more than $40,000 in Boston could be taxed so heavily that the assessed value of the structure was handed over to the government in cash once every four years. In 1980, a statewide tax revolt changed this, but probably at the cost of other taxes. Meanwhile, every single New England state is in the top 30 percent, nationwide, in per capita property taxes. And the burden is more onerous when you remember how low the adjusted per capita income here is. When a stiff sales tax, like Maine's, and a nongraduated income tax, like Massachusetts', are figured in, clearly the bite of local government is one of New England's causes of poverty. And since the money often as not goes to ameliorate the effects of being poor, what you have here is, if not the government causing poverty in order to cure more poverty, at least the government enforcing a great leveling of wealth.

Taxation has other effects. Ironically, an argument can be made that if the state of which Boston is the capital were not in a position to be known locally as Taxachusetts, Seabrook would not have been thought necessary.

New Hampshire is a renegade in New England in that it is the only state with no sales or income tax. The philosophy is to provide as much state income as possible through dog tracks, state lotteries, and bargain-basement state-run liquor stores.

As a result, businesses from all over the rest of New England are flocking to southern New Hampshire in order to be as close to Boston — aptly nicknamed "the Hub" — as possible while escaping heavy taxation. This creates jobs, which create housing starts, which demand power, which results in projected growth, which leads utility companies to build nukes.

When Governor Thomson of New Hampshire was gloating about all the growth, Michael Dukakis, then governor of Massachusetts, sniffed that, though his colleague might be right about New Hampshire being a nice place for talented young workers to live, its services were so shabby that it wasn't a nice place in which to be old or sick or handicapped or uneducated or down and out. It is selfless concern for the less fortunate, he implied, that is the core of old-fashioned Massachusetts liberalism. (Massachusetts was the only state to go for George McGovern for president in 1972. Hence the Watergate-era bumper sticker DON'T BLAME ME, I'M FROM MASSACHUSETTS.)

Well, that may be true, but there's more than a chance that all this humane liberalism has its roots in old-fashioned intellectual snobbery.

There is no getting around the point that one Boston investor makes: "This is a pretty elitist group of people who live in New England." What's tough is to describe how it is that an entire population — even the lower classes of it — can aspire to a little moral arrogance, and by the same token, to describe precisely on whom they are looking down.

When it comes to discussing New England elitism, there is one obvious place to start. It makes no difference that a Boston banker asserts that "you couldn't find anything any dumber than a sixth-generation A.B. from Harvard in general studies. I think twenty-five or thirty years ago they had to create that special program for general studies to take care of these people who have been suffering from inbreeding." Nonetheless, Harvard retains a mystique. It is nurtured by the fact that for every Harvard graduate, there are eight or ten very smart, and sometimes ultimately very powerful, people walking around North America who tried to get into that university but were turned down.

But Harvard is no more New England than Cambridge is like the gritty town of Woonsocket. You have to go beyond that, to the fact that New England, in another example of its faded industrial legacy, has an absolute glut of educational institutions originally endowed by pre–income tax entrepreneurs. In the Boston area alone, there are sixty-five colleges and universities. And, as one observer put it, sixty-four of those are trying to be just like Harvard — some to the point of caricature. Then you begin to grasp how some cultural values are diffused among the educated.

But that still doesn't explain how elsewhere uncommon ideas, such as respect for the furbish lousewort or reading or public television broadcasting, are so widely accepted in New England. It certainly doesn't explain the north star of New England moral certitudes: Houston-based oil companies are always lying.

It's true that polls have shown that the non-college-educated are increasingly taking on a lot of the attitudinal and sociological characteristics of the college-educated. It's also true that New England is overburdened with people who do sport degrees. ("Overqualified is the name of New England's game," said one teacher who has been out of work ever since he fell off a roof in the course of trying to make it as a carpenter.)

But try this idea:

"The roots of the [average] people's disbelief in anything that comes from the private sector goes back to that old heritage of the sweatshop and the textile mill. It really shouldn't be rooted in that area, but it goes back to their worries about being exploited."

The man who said this (he asked to remain anonymous) has invested a lot of money in New England's booming computer business. He went on:

"There's a great antipathy between the owner and the worker that goes back to the Industrial Revolution. The people generally perceive people in business as being those old-line Yankee bastards. Don't believe a goddamn thing they say. Don't believe the facts that they come up with, because they're *their* facts, and they're not the truth!"

This is a singular phenomenon. A postindustrial phenomenon. What you have here is the privileged members of an educated elite — the "best and the brightest" — coughing out warnings about our dire future should we continue to depend on nonrenewable resources and massive corporate solutions to our problems.

At the same time, descendants of Italians, Irish, Québecois, Portuguese, and Jewish mill laborers are listening to these alarums and buying them — or at least giving them careful consideration. So what you have is the progeny of the oppressed identifying with the progeny of the oppressors.

In Detroit, it wouldn't work like this. In Detroit, the ideology of the United Auto Workers is so ingrained — jobs, more jobs, more jobs with more money, more money — that the UAW has literally come around to the old capitalist slogan that what's good for General Motors is good for the U.S.A. Only there's a minor twist. The twist is that it's Chrysler in whose interest the UAW labors in Washington. Bail out Chrysler, whose products have always been associated with fat-cat consumption, the union pleads.

By contrast, in New England a different kind of philosophical union, cutting across traditional class lines, is being formed. And this new sense of everybody being in it together is reinforced by the aforementioned tax structure, which affects the trappings of the class structure. This is to say that a New Englander making $25,000 a year doesn't live in terribly different circumstances from a New Englander making $12,000. Neither is starving; neither frequently dines on steak. Both inhabit modest houses or apartments. In the summer, they swim off the same public beaches.

In Houston, the contrast would be much more marked. The difference is that in New England poverty has become rather chic.

I have a theory that the entire history of twentieth-century New England has something to do with the sad surplus of Harvard architects. Here are these fellows, superbly trained and motivated to modify man's habitat. They find New England so stimulating intellectually that they don't want to leave. Yet New England is so poor that nobody can afford to put up new buildings. So they're broke. But clever. And so they get into mischief.

Take Duncan Syme. He's not a Harvard architect; he's a Yale architect — but close enough. Syme is the man who designed the Vermont Castings wood stoves mentioned in the beginning of this chapter, thus creating from scratch an important manufacturing operation in central Vermont.

I asked him, so, one morning you woke up and said, hey, what this country needs is a good airtight wood stove?

He turned to one of his colleagues and asked him whether a captain of industry of his stature should still be telling the truth about this, or whether maybe it wasn't time for somebody to cook up a new story. But then, in the absence of a tasty lie, he said:

In the winter of 'seventy-four–'seventy-five, I was living in Warren, Vermont, about twenty miles from [Randolph]. Warren at one point had the highest per capita ratio of residents to architects of any community in the world. Warren had something like thirty-two licensed, practicing architects in a population of five hundred.

It was a big ski area — Sugarbush — so there was some building going on. But, while some guys were doing reasonably well, a lot of guys were starving. If a guy is born in a particular country, he hates to leave and go someplace else. I spent most of my life in Essex, Connecticut, which is a little sailing, bedroom town on Long Island Sound a little west of New London.

Anyway, at the time, Dindy [his wife] and I were living in a building I'd designed for a guy as a woodworking shop. The deal was that if I built it, I got to live in it for a year for nothing. So we were living in this wood shop, freezing. Freezing to death. Our only source of heat . . . we had this old wood stove, which was *horrendous*. The thing went out. It was kind of an old stove, and it was real leaky and stuff, and it wouldn't hold a fire overnight. I had to get up at two o'clock every morning to fill this damn thing up, to keep it going so it would make it through the night. One morning in March, I said screw it, I'm not going to get up. And so I reached over and turned on the electric blanket and I went back to sleep. The next morning we woke up, and our inside air temperature was eleven.

So I ended up doodling around on a piece of paper about it — what would a good wood stove be like. My eleven degree experience became a catalyst for becoming interested in stoves per se. Not totally as a marketable entity, but just because I've always been a curious kind of guy in terms of mechanical gizmos and stuff. A couple of us went and talked to a whole bunch of people, did some research, began to get some papers on studies that had been done during the war, state-of-the-art papers from Europe, and stuff like that.

I came up with the stove I wanted. I didn't know whether you would want one, or anybody else, but it seemed like a pretty nice stove. It had all these features that combustion-technology research said was important, and it had all the features I wanted from a kind of user number.

I hadn't even heard of half of the major activities which are required in order to build a wood-burning stove five years ago. I didn't even know what the names meant, or what the jobs were, or anything.

I had this stove all designed. Murray [Syme's partner] and I built one out of steel, welded it all up. And it took two *days*. And we said this is *hopeless*. The thing is so labor-intensive that there's no *way* we're going to make any money out of this. And to put all those goddamn air channels and stuff in them . . . much too much time is involved. So at that point I said to myself, well, lookit. We got twenty-seven parts to this stove, but the old wood cookstoves — beautiful, magnificent things — must have had eighty billion parts, and I'll bet that a guy assembled one of those things in three or four hours, bolting them together. So I said, it must be that, because you have the ability to kind of cast all these little things in place . . . cast iron must be the solution.

So we started calling up foundries. The first foundry we called up, we said, "Listen, do you guys cast iron?" And the guy said, "Yeah, we're a class thirty gray shop, what do you need done?"

And there'd be a long pause from Murray, and he'd say, "I'll get back to you." And he literally went and got a book out of the library to find out what a class thirty gray shop was. That's why we have our own foundry today, because it turns out that making stove plate is such a specialized thing.

And it turns out that the stove I drew up . . . It just turns out that quite a few other guys on the continent have my kind of leanings.

Yeah, I said, but how many of those guys are sitting in New England farmhouses where they've got a couple of two-by-fours propping up the chimney and a pie pan over the flue hole, just waiting for your stove to be installed? Wood burning in New England is now becoming attractive to the middle class. If that's not what it amounted to, you wouldn't have designed your latest model so that it slips comfortably into the opening of a suburban fireplace.

And this is how he got launched on a discussion of poverty chic:

"I would not give up wood heat now, even if I could afford to have a nuclear power plant of my own. I would not do that because I like the type of heat you get out of wood."

What do you mean? I asked. Heat's heat. Either you're warm or you're not. I was greeted by a chorus of dissent from the stovemakers. Syme went on:

A single source of radiant energy that ultimately heats the entire habitable envelope is incredibly different from having this whole envelope amazingly uniform in temperature.

You're busting your butt, trying to get the car out of the ditch, or help the kids go sledding, and they're whining because the snow's inside their mittens, and you're frozen and you come inside.

In nineteen fifty-one, you came into a house that had hot-water radiant heat under the slab and your toes would kind of slowly get warmed up, but it took forever before you were thawed out. If you come into a house with electric baseboard heat, it's the same way. I mean, where the hell do you dry your mittens? Now, maybe that's putting regional emphasis on all of life that exists only here in Vermont, but the point is that when you come into a house that has a single source of radiant heat, the first thing you do is you kind of walk up to it ass first with your hands back there behind you like people used to do to fireplaces. You can take the chill off within seconds because there's this intense radiant energy. The idea of having all of your house within a quarter of a degree diminishes your life. There's an esthetic coefficient to the quality of heat.

It's a survival statement. The guy takes a look at the future and doesn't like it, and is looking around for some alternative.

This is something a guy can relate to one on one. He either bought a little wood, or he went out and he chopped it himself and *he* made that fire. It isn't a fire that came from galaxy L Twelve-Fifteen like at Seabrook. What I'm talking about is a guy getting a hell of a lot closer to the source than the dial on the wall.

I think we must become replugged in to the subtleties of the planet if it's going to sustain us. Wood burning is a relaxing thing, and it allows a guy to get plugged back in, and that's why I see the wood-stove boom as a real hope. It is a basis for people becoming intimately involved with a basic energy source. And energy is everything.

Almost two hundred miles southeast of Randolph, in Lowell, Massachusetts, amid the narrow, twisted streets that were laid out along patterns literally established by the meanderings of long-dead cows, there's a small monument to a single, basic source of radiant energy that has nothing to do with poverty chic. It's a less-than-romantic reminder of what is behind New England's present predicament. This is a faithful re-creation of an old kitchen of a textile-mill worker, and its centerpiece is a big, black coal stove.

The stove was called a Glenwood C, and in this model room, it is carefully dated "circa 1900." Note is taken that "thousands of tenement buildings were erected to accommodate" the immigrants who flocked to the mills of Lowell in the nineteenth century.

Although the neighborhoods were separated by nationalities, the houses were, for the most part, similar in style. The kitchen played an important role in the lives of the tenants, in that it was generally the only room in the apartment with heat. All of the rooms were built off the kitchen as a result. The kitchen thus became a vital part of tenement life, the center of all the family's activities.

Everything in the re-creation of "a typical tenement apartment" during the Depression of the 1930s is brightly labeled and noted:

The furnishings include pressed tin ceilings, and printed linoleum floors. The ice box is roughly dated at 1915. Although electric refrigerators were in use by 1930, we can assume that a tenant of this apartment wouldn't have been able to afford one. Of particular interest is the coal [clothes] iron, circa 1895, which weighs seven pounds without the coal. The soapstone sink has a clothes wringer attached to it. Clothes were normally washed on a washboard and hung on clothes lines across the kitchen in winter . . .

The lunch pail on top of the ice box is dated at 1910. It had three compartments. The bottom of the pail held a drink. The second layer was used for either soup or stew. The top for meat, vegetables, bread or fruit. The pail was generally carried down to the mill by one of the younger children at lunchtime . . .

The cheerful singsong of the plaque ends:

Try asking your parents or grandparents about the kitchens in their homes. It should prove quite interesting.

Yes, indeed, I thought to myself, ask your parents and grandparents about the years of the Depression, when the textile industry was in full flight from New England to places like Calhoun, Georgia. Ask them about the stained oilcloth covering the rickety kitchen table. Ask them about the neighborhoods "separated by nationality." And about how much they loved carrying the lunch pail down to the mills.

Ask them if they remember the *Sunday Advertiser*, the paper that once boasted the largest Sunday circulation in New England. A yellowed promo recalls its glories:

EXPOSED! Starvation wages, unhealthy surroundings, grinding toil, crooked shop owners, revealed in actual stories of work in Massachusetts. SWEAT SHOPS! Stories of shocking abuses, cruel treatment, and deplorable conditions. The truth about sweat shops, that cancerous evil eating out the lives of underpaid workers in Massachusetts. Exclusively in tomorrow's Sunday Advertiser!

And while you're at it, ask them what they think of the federal government spending tax dollars not to bury these memories, but instead to make the whole city of Lowell into a national park to *preserve* them. For that's what's being done. Nearly $50 million is being spent to celebrate "America's first planned industrial city."

The museum in which the tenement kitchen is so lovingly restored is in one of the old mills. Its walls are two feet thick, and its tall windows are made up of small panes, over which are diamond-shaped iron security grilles.

The wooden floor is a rich, varied, honey-brown, made uneven by a century of heavy carts trundling over it, but the looms that stand on it are not pretty. Run by unguarded belts and oversized bicycle chains, they prickle with sharp objects, around which one had best be very careful.

A tour guide explains that this museum is attached to the only functioning and, everyone hopes, profit-making textile mill left in Lowell. "We just rent this space," she explains. "The rest of this whole complex is in operation and they're using these old looms for part of their operation. The man who owns it wears overalls and a rolled-up plaid flannel shirt and he looks like a Teddy bear. How does he compete? He brings in, first it was Puerto Ricans, and then it was Jamaicans. Then it was Colombians. It's tough for the mill to keep afloat, but everybody's reluctant to let it close down because it's the only one left. You should go over there, it's like the Tower of Babel."

As it has always been in the mills of Lowell.

"It's like the whole town is one big museum," she continues. "There's an antique on every corner. Some are not in the best of condition, but they're all there. They may not have been restored to their former splendor yet, but that's what the federal money is going to do, and that's what the tourists, we hope, will come to see.

"What they're hoping for in the long run is a Sturbridge Village kind of thing, or Williamsburg."

Lee Cott, a young restoration architect whose office is halfway between Harvard and MIT in Cambridge, is one of the people who came up with the idea, utterly mad on the face of it, of making one of New England's grittiest cities into a theme park to misery, after the fashion of Colonial re-creations the tour guide mentioned.

One of the reasons the Lowell project was so relevant to us [Cott explained], was that it really brought together a whole lot of things for us in this office. General Motors grew out of the tradition of Lowell.

As an architect or a designer — or a visionary, in your best moments —

you have images of what you want the world to be like. Lowell conforms to the image. It has the kind of thing you push for. The idea of doing a large building, then a couple of buildings together — until you end up doing a whole city. This was the ideal situation for a group of young, creative architects and planners who wanted to get it all out of their system. Here's a city. What do you want to do to it? Redo a city.

Eight years ago, when we first started — we were among the first to do this kind of large-scale adaptive reuse of older buildings — people had real trepidations.

"I'm going to live in a factory?" they'd say. "S***, I grew up there. I worked in that building. I don't want to live . . . who wants to live there?" They don't see it as part of their life that is worthy of recall. We did have a lot of that attitude about Lowell, among the local people.

The people's attitudes about themselves had deteriorated. The city had gone to hell. In fact, the city was so far behind the times, they never even got their act together to apply for federal urban renewal money in the fifties and sixties. Which is exactly what saved the city. None of the old buildings was torn down. The old buildings, too big, too monstrous to tear down, are now the city's great hope for the future.

Cott says that he's lost interest in the project on a day-to-day basis, now that it's off the ground, "mainly because I never saw the Lowellians having confidence in the project. I think, like most things, the people who are closest to it have the least confidence in it."

But that doesn't mean he's lost confidence in restoring old New England structures, making do with the fact that New England is too poor to generate extensive new building.

Ten years ago, when I first got going in this business, we could do a new apartment unit for the elderly — a typical HUD [Department of Housing and Urban Development] unit, six hundred and twenty-five square feet — for well under twenty-five thousand dollars. Now you can't touch it for under thirty-five thousand.

Now, in Central Falls [Rhode Island], we're doing an old mill building right on Main Street — housing for the elderly. And it's a beautiful project because what we're going to do is have hydroelectric power there. When we got going on the Lowell job, we got really interested in alternative sources of energy. Everybody talks about solar, but they're way off base, at least for this part of the century. The solar power industry is totally embryonic at this point. However, there are two hundred and seventy sites in New England that are appropriate for water power. We went out looking for one. We found our own developers. And we're just about complete with the housing, and we're going to be doing a hydro power project. Low-head dam. The water drops thirteen feet. It will be the first federally assisted housing project development which has a good portion of its energy met by hydro power. We have two hundred and some odd thousand dollars in grants. It's a very exciting project.

We're talking about doing a new building for ourselves, for an office. We'd much prefer to renovate a building if we could find one. But Boston's running out of buildings to renovate. For sure! The best ones in terms of physical condition, layout, neighborhoods, are done first. It's a limited resource like anything else.

Lots of New England was built before the invention of the electric light. The mill buildings are therefore narrow — fifty, fifty-five feet wide, because everybody had to work in natural light.

That's a tremendous amenity for housing, big windows. The mill buildings built before the light bulb are the best ones for renovation.

As New England faces its future, Cott is not the only one who is finding that a nation built in a simpler century has some advantages. Boston, for example, has put a lid on the number of parking spaces built in the city, thus forcing people onto rapid transit or into the use of their feet. As a result, people are finding that Boston was built on a human scale, with everything close to everything else, back when that was the only kind of scale there was. If the automobile were to disappear tomorrow, Boston would hardly find it as crushing as would Houston or L.A.

In fact, the argument has been made that New England's future lies in its being fully depreciated. Unlike newer regions, New England's mortgage is paid off. In Denver, for example, the future is going to pay for the present. Growth there is demanding new roads, new water, new sewers, new pollution controls, new firemen, policemen — services of all sorts. If Denver were paying for all this as it went along, the taxes on each newcomer would be staggering. What would happen, in the classic checks-and-balances fashion, would be that the boom would slow, because the cost of doing business in Denver would suddenly soar. The last thing Denver, or anyplace else in the South and West, wants to do is slow the boom. So Los Angeles, for example, went into debt to build freeways. In Houston, the plan was to avoid financial obligations by not building any new freeway for years. But in both cases, citizens of the future will pay the price. In Los Angeles, taxes at last have caught up with financial realities, as these debts became due. In newer Houston, the evening rush hour, now over four hours long, will continue to lengthen until new transportation facilities are built, or the population becomes so outraged at the inconvenience of getting around the place that people begin to leave.

By contrast, New England sports almost four centuries of capital expenditures, built to last, as the restoration architects are discovering. Blessed with great geographic diversity in a very compact area — Massachusetts is three and a half hours wide and forty-five minutes deep – New England's transportation needs are less formidable than, say, those of Texas. And many of the solutions are in place; public transportation has been a tradition since well before the automobile was developed. Unlike most of the West, New England has a wealth of water, and though municipal sewer systems may be falling into disrepair, at least they already exist, which is more than you can say for the new, high-growth areas. Housing, education, recreation, and cultural facilities are all there right now.

And almost everything that it was possible for New England to lose — jobs, industry, money, power — is already gone. This area went through the agonies of decline decades ago. Survival was hardly a picnic, but what's left is a paid-for asset.

Thus, even Jim Howell, senior vice-president of the First National Bank of Boston, who readily concedes he prefers the go-go business methods of Kansas City to some of the tight economic circumspection he sees among Yankees, discerns some advantages to New England's position.

The difference between us, now, and the Great Lakes is that the Great Lakes region has got a wage structure that is probably thirty, forty, or fifty percent above ours. Wage structure levels get set by the dominant industry, and the dominant industry in the Great Lakes has been automobiles. The dominant industry here has been low-wage industries — textiles, apparel, leather. So our wage structure right now is highly competitive even with the South, because in the South, wages have risen.

The difference that may help us is that the decade of the eighties is going to be one of critical labor shortages. Skilled labor. Blue collar. Because everybody wanted to be a white-collar worker in the fifties and sixties. All you have to do is look in the working-class bars, and the people are all old.

Howell points to the considerable tradition in the ethnic communities of New England of working with your hands as precision instruments, either in the jewelry business, or the textile business.

That's why we're building on a strength. It's unusual to have a policy option that actually addresses a major problem . . . that builds on something you're pretty good at.

And I think that's why the high-technology industry is here to stay. [Building computers] involves literally thousands upon thousands of people that turn widgets. You go visit these plants, and the only difference in the textile and the electronics area is that you're working with something metal, not cloth. It involves the same sort of skill and dexterity. There are twelve thousand people working under one roof in Western Electric's North Andover plant. All are doing something with their hands.

High technology. That seems to be New England's future. It started as early as the 1940s, with the education centers of Cambridge leading the way into the new frontiers of digital electronics and solid state physics, which produced the computers that changed our lives. A lot of the speculative work that mushroomed in the post-Sputnik era came from right here. Commercial spin-offs of the advances in high technology began to litter Route 128 — the beltway that circles Boston. Now, New England is a center of one of the hottest areas in electronics — the assembly of minicomputers. The biggest employer in the Lowell area now, for example, is Wang Laboratories. Makers of small computers and small word-processing systems, it employs three thousand, is building a high-rise in the heart of Lowell, and is buying up ancient, unused textile mills for manufacturing and warehousing. Dr. A. E. Wang, who got his Ph.D. from Harvard in 1946 in applied physics, has been in business since 1952, and really saw his affairs take off when he made a major breakthrough in the electronic calculator field in 1964. In part of the valley of the Merrimack — the river that originally powered the mills of Lowell — the other big employer is Raytheon.

In fact, at one point, if somebody came to the First National Bank of Boston to ask for money, and he had a government contract associated with a high-technology scheme, the loan officers had standing orders: No matter how crazy either this person or his idea seemed to be, neither could be turned down without authorization from a senior vice-president.

The man credited with convincing the appalled banking community that such aggressive support of high technology was bound to pay off big was Peter Brooke. Now an independent venture capitalist, he sees New England's future this way:

New England is still an area that smart people like to go to. I think it's the climate of intellectual ferment. To me, Boston is the best of the American cities. We've got a first-class symphony, first-class art museums, and the places of interest are small, attainable, well run. For a certain kind of person, it is a nice place to be. You're easily mobile, and you've got all these interesting things . . . the mountains, the seashore. I think it may be mature economically, but I think it may be even more mature philosophically. It doesn't have the hazard of meaningless pace. You don't find people rushing toward some goal without thinking about what it is they're trying to achieve. We live on less. We're like the British in that regard.

And smart people have a way of lasting. They always generate new ideas.

If that is true, Peterborough, New Hampshire, in turn, has discovered that new ideas have a way of making money, and that some of New England's underdevelopment can be its greatest strength.

Peterborough, near the ski areas of Mount Monadnock, is achingly quaint. Just up the road from the requisite, perfectly proportioned Congregational church, with the delicate, graceful white spire, is a quite large, stately, red-brick building, complete with four white pillars at the entrance, labeled the American Guernsey Club Headquarters.

Guernsey cows, like all aspects of New England agriculture, not being the hot item they once were in southern New Hampshire, the club rents out much of its building. And it is here that, to the scream of circular saws, workers are building partitions out of natural wood, cut at the obligatory diagonal, in order to expand the offices of *Byte*.

Byte, or, to be more precise, a byte (pronounced like what you do to a hamburger), is a unit of information in computer babble. It is also the name of the first, largest, and fastest-growing magazine directed to the home-computer owner in America. Every month, it contains 250 or more glossy pages, in perfect binding, with a full-color, graphically intriguing, heavy-stock cover. Many, many of those 250 pages are high-rent advertising from the giants and would-be giants of this booming field. Circulation is pushing two hundred thousand as of this writing and is regularly outstripping the audit reports. A second magazine, called *onComputing*, aimed at less technical-minded computer dilettantes, has been started up so as to bracket the market fully. It is expected that *onComputing* will soon dwarf *Byte* in circulation.

Publishing giant McGraw-Hill has just bought into the whole shebang.

All of this out of the American Guernsey Club Headquarters in Peterborough.

I'd come to talk to *Byte*'s founding editor, Carl Helmers, but he didn't want to keep the appointment in his office, having just jet-ted back from the West Coast, so I found myself driving behind a young lady who'd said that when she'd been hired a year before, she was the twenty-fifth employee, and now there were sixty. I was following her because she seemed to be one of the few people senior enough to know the way to Helmers' home.

(Digression: New Englanders are incapable of giving directions. They do not know the names of streets, nor do they remember the numbers on major highways, nor do they have the foggiest idea how far one place is from another, nor can they tell you which way is north. Their street systems are so Old World and convo-luted that they can find their way around only by feel. If their surroundings begin to look familiar to them, they attempt to find their way by an intuitive process as mysterious as that which leads the swallows back to Capistrano. Under no circumstance can they describe this process in a simple declarative sentence. When a Massachusetts taxi driver was asked for directions to a nearby museum, his response was "Gee, that's hard."

Their spatial confusion is matched only by their reluctance to travel at all. One man from Dixie who was working for a major Boston corporation marveled at how his colleagues considered Worcester, forty miles to the west, "the frontier." It was the edge of civilization, beyond which was nothing but barely explored un-pleasantness. Conversely, for children traveling such a distance from the hinterlands to the great metropolis, mothers pack lunches and ask if they think they can make it all the way back the same day. The only place with a sense of space similar to this is West Virginia, and West Virginia at least has the excuse of hav-ing mountain roads with sheer drop-offs that make automobile travel a genuinely scary experience. The one thing equally fright-ening about New England is its insane drivers. The only way a stranger ever finds anything in New England is through a process in which the native tries for several strangled minutes to give directions on the phone and then says: "Oh hell. Get as far as the Howard Johnson's and call, and I'll come and get you." It was exactly this process which led me to be following the young em-ployee from *Byte*.)

Helmers, it turned out, lives off a dirt road, in a comfortable, practically new, if rather conventional home set among ever-greens and tall birches. In it, he had just installed a Vermont Castings wood stove. He considers both the house and the stove temporary measures.

"I'm going to build my own house sooner or later," said the

bearded, mildly rotund bachelor, who, in his early thirties, looks like the semi-grown-up version of the kid in your high school who always went around with a slide rule dangling from his belt — the one who called it a "slip stick."

This is a temporary measure. I have fifty acres on the other side of Hancock. It's a very nice fifty acres, covered with pine. If I were to log it flat, I probably could pay for it out of the wood value. But I'm not going to do that. It's where I'm going to get firewood for the next year. I know enough people who want free firewood who'll cut it down for me. The main reason for the Vigilant [the wood stove] is not to be noble and save energy. It's a fine stop-gap in case the power fails. But then I'm going to get rid of that. I'm hoping to get installed, before the winter comes, a propane-fired five-kilowatt generator for my standby electricity, in which case I don't really need the Vigilant.

My land has a nice stream flowing across it that, in the driest part of this year — like two months without significant rain — was still flowing at fifteen kilograms per second, and it flows down fifteen meters across my property. That works out to about fifteen hundred watts, which would charge a lot of batteries. And that's just at leanest flow, and that's if I intercept the whole stream. A week ago, when we'd had five inches of rain in fifteen days, it was flowing as much as when the snow run-off was happening.

That I can roughly estimate at three hundred or four hundred kilograms a second, which works out to be about fifty kilowatts. That's a lot of power. The technology involved is getting an impulse wheel and putting an automobile alternator on it and running it to some batteries, and charge them up and have semiconductor inverters on them. The semiconductors are the same technology as is involved in my computers. The whole system will not save money. It's done primarily as a neat thing to do.

Was forming a serious, high-technology-related publishing empire in Peterborough also primarily a neat thing to do?

You can publish a magazine anywhere. It's an idea industry. I camped out in Boston [working for a firm called Intermetrics, which designs space-ship brains] for four years, looking for an economic excuse to live in New Hampshire. That was my explicit philosophy when I moved to Boston. I had friends who lived in New Hampshire, and I liked it. I just thought it was a neat place to live.

There are a number of advantages right around here. First of all, you have a very large back-to-nature group, hiding out in the hills. Same thing could be said of [Ecotopian] Sonoma County in California. You have to pick and choose among these people and find the ones who really will work. But because of the fact that you're the only jobs around, and the place has so much psychological boost to it, in order to be here, people are willing to work for a slightly lower wage scale. Not drastically lower, but it more than compensates for other costs.

Byte is written by authors all over the continent, who mail their work to Peterborough, where it is edited. The copy is then typeset by a local printer, although computer-driven machines so unexotic as to be familiar to any college newspaper will soon bring that manufacturing operation into the Guernsey building. When the pages are ready for the offset camera, they are shipped, via overnight air cargo, to Wisconsin, where they are turned into a magazine by a publishing firm there. Any questions are dealt with by telephone and telecopier. A new printer, also Wisconsin-based, will soon arrange things so that the master pages will travel only as far as Boston, with the press plates made there. "Thus," Helmers pointed out, "if the plane gets trashed, you can always make some more plates. There's hardly any way camera-ready copy can get wiped out in an automobile ride to Boston."

In fact, the copy doesn't even have to be edited in Peterborough. A very senior editor, one of the magazine's earliest employees, "has informed us that he is going to go off on the road," Helmers said. "He and his wife are buying a tractor-trailer. They're going to have a contract with Mayflower, and be hauling things back and forth. Look at him. He's on top of the world, he's in his twenties, there's no way he can make the money he's making [at *Byte*]."

But, it turns out, his wife has always had a burning desire to drive a tractor-trailer.

"So he's quitting in January or so. And he has this vision of having his Apple computer in the cab of the truck while his wife is driving. He's got an inverter for it to power it off the truck and everything. He has visions of doing fifty pages a month as a quota of editorial copy preparation, which is what he's been doing. The computer will be used for more than just word processing. He'll test certain programming ideas in the articles too. And then he'll give me a disc [computer memory device], and I'll print it out on my own computer. I'll show you the computer. Come upstairs."

There are two computers upstairs, as it turns out — each about the size of a generous wastebasket. The computer that is about to see North America is hardly the more fascinating.

It's the New England Digital Able/6o attached to what appears to be an organ keyboard, two speakers, a television set, and a typewriter that's the real eye-catcher.

The musical keyboard is a Synclavier synthesizer, also made by New England Digital. Helmers steps up to the keyboard, switches it on, red lights flash, and he tinkles away at a little Bach. The computer sorts out what he's doing at the keyboard, and out through the speakers comes a little Bach.

Far out.

"Oh no, you haven't heard the far-out part yet."

Helmers makes some adjustments, different red lights come on, and the ditty he's just played on what sounded like an organ is again coughed out by the computer, but this time sounding as if it were being played on a harpsichord.

"Or . . ."

Now it comes back at us, memorized by the computer, sounding like pipes.

"Or . . ."

Now it's chimes, and with the twist of a dial it's been slowed down to 645/1000ths of its original speed.

"And if you get tired of that, you can always . . ."

What's now coming out of the machine is the beginnings of an orchestra. The sounds of different instruments, all of which have been given their voice by the computer, blend and pour over each other.

"Here, let me play it back."

Same notes, but now each instrument is different. The high part, which had been calliope is now violin, and the part that had been chimes is piano.

What the hell, I say, what is this?

He explains that his next step is to rig the computer to a television screen so that when he plays a tune, not only will the tones come out of the speakers, but the computer will automatically write the score on the screen. Not only that, but each instrument stored in the computer will have its own color on the screen — the tuba notes may be purple — so that an entire symphony can be written on one score by one person simply playing each instrument's part on the keyboard.

"This is definitely *not* a toy. This is going to be a *very* commercial product. I'm starting a little company on the side."

And — let me see if I've got this straight — when you finish building your house, your color-coded symphony-writing computer will be fired up by your water wheel?

"Isn't doing electronic music in the woods fun?"

Well, I thought to myself, it isn't Dickens Street.

Dickens Street is in Pawtucket, Rhode Island, which was the

first town in North America to have a factory; the first town in
North America to have a polluted river next to the factory.

On Dickens Street, in a cramped living room the dimensions of
which are made no larger by the presence of a twelve-string guitar, a six-string guitar, a classical guitar, an electric bass, a television, a videotape machine and camera, four tape recorders, a
record turntable, an amplifier, a sound-mixer, speakers, pillows,
and a terrarium housing hermit crabs, the talk is about the quality of life in New England for the voluntarily poor.

Take the mailroom at the *Pawtucket Times* [says Paul Brissette, thirty,
who likes to refer to himself, ironically, as a derelict]. Now, the mailroom [that's where the papers are sorted and bundled for distribution]
you *know* is considered the armpit of the newspaper. We're looked down
on by everybody else in the building. But we have a lot of guys who are
college-educated or going to college or who only have a high school di-
ploma but who are very intelligent, very well read.

The other people in the building would avoid us because we were
scum. Yet we'd go out as a group to see Bergman or Fellini movies. Or
we'd pick out a classy German or French restaurant in Providence. We
used to look forward to it — every couple of weeks. Of course it took us
a couple of weeks to save *up* for this, but . . . The hours in the mailroom
are short. You start twenty-five cents above the minimum wage. You can
live on it in New England. I was living on the third floor of a tenement
in Central Falls paying twenty dollars a week, but I moved to the second
floor, so now I'm paying twenty-five.

One of the guys is very articulate, very thoughtful, and here he is,
working in the mailroom, because it's a part-time job, which doesn't in-
terfere with his photography, his art, his writing. I'm the same way. I'm
thirty years old; I have a wife and a kid. I do a paper route. I'm a ne'er-
do-well. I admit it. I don't care. I'm a year away from a B.A.

Paul is from a family of fourteen children who grew up on Dickens Street. He and five of his brothers are bright, educated, and
enormously talented musically. Their speech is studded with
phrases like "soothing, low-frequency rumble" to describe the
sound the freight trains made as they lulled the boys to sleep at
night, passing right by the back door. Perhaps because of their
abundant sense of absurdist humor and their chronic inability to
see money as an end in itself, none of them has ever been happy
in a conventional job.

Rob Brissette, in his mid-thirties, the man whose apartment
this is, has left his job as a puppeteer because of what one of his
brothers describes as "a personality clash with the puppets."

Now, he says, "I'm just working. Working in a mill. Weaving — like chain mail — for watch bands. It's just work. Let's not talk about it."

Nights, he plays guitar in smoky clubs, and he's good enough to make up to $100 a gig.

Aime, also in his mid-thirties, with a degree in music, is working for the city government, counseling the long-term unemployed. "Lord knows I'm *qualified* for this job." He laughs. "Experienced. Nobody wanted to hire me because I had a five-year gap in my work record." The gap occurred when he ripped up his back, working as a manual laborer because there were no jobs for music instructors.

Charlie, in his twenties, has abandoned his paper route to attend the prestigious Berklee College of Music in Boston.

Buzz has left for Los Angeles. He'd had it with playing rhythm guitar in trashy Woonsocket clubs for $25 a night. No matter how many songs he wrote, he figured, that's no way to become a star. So now he's delivering papers for the *Los Angeles Herald-Examiner*. But he says that he's about to turn the corner in his musical career, and he keeps sending copies of his demonstration records back east.

Buzz's going-away party was held in the tired old Knights of Columbus hall on Japonica Street. The music came from man-high speakers wired to a maze of microphones, amplifiers, guitars, and keyboards, accompanied by a thicket of drums, all bought on time from the Ray Mullins Music Company. The fact that all their equipment is acquired in a dollar-down, dollar-a-week fashion, and is rarely paid off, amuses the brothers. Off the crooked ceiling tiles of the low, dark, crowded room bounced the loud Rolling Stones question: "What can a poor boy do, save to play in a rock and roll band?"

Cheap, fresh, exquisite-tasting local clams were steamed, dipped in melted butter, and their nutty sweetness chased by long pulls on Narragansett Lager Beer, the local brew, which, if not exactly Michelob, was at least cold.

Licking butter off their fingers, and keeping an eye on the Red Sox game on the television set over the bar, the revelers did not talk about a California where there are no tenements demanding expensive heating oil. It wasn't a day of pining for a better, more middle-class life. The talk was of old schemes and new songs.

Said one of the brothers of a plan with some unusual economic ramifications: "We were going to have this band called Ricky and the Rockets. We were going to have one guy dressed up as Ricky, playing the harp [harmonica], making an appearance now and then. He wasn't even going to be in the band. We were going to have three different pictures with all different personnel. There were going to be two members of the band that were in it all the time. And the rest of it would be floating, just to see if the club owners would catch on. *Spread the work around . . ."*

It can be argued that free spirits like the Dickens Street bunch exist everywhere, and that is true. But nowhere else in North America are they part of as old and distinguished a tradition as in New England.

Outside Concord, Massachusetts, in the 1850s, a man lived for two years and two months, heating with wood in the winter, watching birds in the spring, and considering where material wealth and civilization intersected.

The men of Dickens Street are familiar with his thoughts, for, being New Englanders, they read.

None can be an impartial or wise observer of human life but from the vantage ground of what we should call voluntary poverty [he agreed] . . . I do not speak to those who are well employed, in whatever circumstances, and they know whether they are well employed or not; — but mainly to the mass of men who are discontented, and idly complaining of the hardness of their lot or of the times, when they might improve them . . . I also have in my mind that seemingly wealthy, but most terribly impoverished class of all, who have accumulated dross, but know not how to use it, or get rid of it, and thus have forged their own golden or silver fetters . . .

However mean your life is, meet it and live it; do not shun it and call it hard names . . . The fault-finder will find faults even in paradise. Love your life, poor as it is. You may perhaps have some pleasant, thrilling, glorious hours, even in a poor-house. The setting sun is reflected from the windows of the alms-house as brightly as from the rich man's abode; the snow melts before its door as early in the spring. I do not see but a quiet mind may live as contentedly there, and have as cheering thoughts, as in a palace. The town's poor seem to me often to live the most independent lives of any. May be they are simply great enough to receive without misgiving. Most think that they are above being supported by the town; but it oftener happens that they are not above supporting themselves by dishonest means, which should be more disreputable. Cultivate poverty like a garden herb, like sage. Do not trouble yourself much to get new things, whether clothes or friends. Turn the old; return to them. Things do not change; we change. Sell your clothes and keep your thoughts. God will see that you do not want society . . .

Why should we be in such desperate haste to succeed, and in such desperate enterprises? If a man does not keep pace with his companions, perhaps it is because he hears a different drummer. Let him step to the music which he hears, however measured or far away.

On a warm summer day, when children ride in the swan-shaped paddle boats in Boston's Public Garden, and, in the evening, hundreds gather on the Esplanade to hear a free Boston Pops symphony concert, this New Englander's words echo across the decades. This is also true next to a salt marsh near Brunswick, Maine, as a man shows off the house he built himself, cheaply and with great beauty, out of planks salvaged from an ancient barn. And, of course, even in the high-decible world of the Japonica Street Knights of Columbus Hall, thoughts turn to him.

For New England is continuing to learn his lesson, especially as it was stated by Ralph Waldo Emerson. Emerson was talking about his friend Henry David Thoreau. Thoreau wrote the words quoted above on the banks of Walden Pond, out beyond what is now Route 128.

"He chose," said Emerson, "to be rich, by making his wants few."

THE FOUNDRY

"Oh-ho say can you see . . ."

Dull green with yellow tips, the hefty cranes up on towers cluster, sporting the markings of Bethlehem Steel. Amid them, incongruously, are nestled the white-tipped black yardarms of a three-masted sailing ship, the U.S.S. *Constellation.*

"By the dawn's early light . . ."

From the top of a rise in the lush park, the eye slowly pans the horizon. The park is on a sharp point of land guarding the harbor, which surrounds it on all sides. The view is of brick smokestacks and white and black water towers. Across the harbor over to the left, a tall, blocky gray tower with the look of a grain elevator is actually a storage place for concrete. LEHIGH CEMENT, it says on the side. A real grain elevator, its tall cylinders bound together like a monstrous six-pack, looms in the other direction, dwarfing the crab apple trees of Fort McHenry.

"What so proudly we hailed . . ."

Actually, dozens of cranes spike the horizon, a closer examination reveals. The Maryland Shipbuilding and Drydock yard over to the right has its collection, as does the Dundalk Marine Terminal, and many more belong to industries even lifelong residents can't readily identify from this perspective. The Francis Scott Key Bridge, a businesslike crisscross of steel, carries the Baltimore Beltway over the wide water. The smoky black, coal-dust-covered pier, much the worse for wear, belongs to Consolidated Coal. It had once helped fuel the industrial behemoth that was the envy of the world — the gritty cities of North America's industrial Northeast. Now, the pier needs a lot of work.

"At the twilight's last gleaming . . ."

The Continental soldiers march with great precision, in their blue swallowtailed coats with red trim and gold buttons. Their pants and leggings are as white as the George Washington wigs under their three-cornered hats. Pennants are layered as thick as palm fronds over one of the flags they carry. The pennants say things like CENTRAL BURMA, 1945. Where and why, exactly, was the battle for central Burma? The wool costumes look hot in the bright June sun. The fireboat for the inner harbor fires tall jets of high-pressure water into the cloudless sky. Tarnished red and silver trailer boxes lie nearby like so many building blocks for a colossus, stacked and waiting for the containerized ocean freighter that is riding high in the water of the Chesapeake Bay as it heaves to.

"Oh say does tha-hat Star Spangled . . ."

The crowd in the park listening to the contralto belt it out is an extremely diverse lot. Orientals. Blacks. Surprising number of redheads. Uncommon quantities of adults under five and a half feet tall, with pinched smiles and gnarled hands. Virtually the entire history of the migrations that have made up North America is written on their faces. The neighborhood just behind Fort McHenry is Locust Point. Surrounding the Locust Point Marine Terminal, it is the classic northeastern ethnic enclave. The front stoops of the row houses are polished white, gleaming from repeated scrubbings on hands and knees with soapy water and a stiff brush. "These Germans and Polacks here in Locust Point," the mayor of Baltimore had said earlier, "they think they're independent of the city. They're not poor. They have a lot of pride. You don't do anything down here without asking them. It's a pain in the ass."

"Ba-NER-her ye-het wa-ha-ha-have . . ."

Over the star-shaped old squat brick fort, a replica of an old flag was being raised. In the Indian summer of 1814, in retaliation for North Americans torching Toronto, British imperial forces had burned the White House in Washington, forty miles south of here, and were then zeroing in on the crucial fledgling industry of the port city of Baltimore. The commandant of the fort that stood between the fleet and the city was casting about for a very specific symbol of defiance. "It is my desire," he wrote, archly, "to have a flag so large that the British will have no difficulty in seeing it from a distance." So he ordered a banner sewn thirty feet hoist by forty-two feet fly, spangled with fifteen five-pointed stars, each two feet across, and fifteen stripes. Its exact duplicate, being raised this day, is one huge flag.

"O'er the la-hand of the FREE . . ."

The p.a. system screeches on the word "free." It always does. There doesn't seem to be a p.a. system made that can deal with that high E flat. The British today are having no difficulty seeing this Star Spangled Banner. Nor are the Hungarians, the French, the Vietnamese, the Italians, the Jamaicans, the Lithuanians, the Ecuadorians . . . The British, as a matter of fact, are out in force this fine Flag Day. In a park on the shores farther into the harbor, they are holding a Celtic-Scandinavian ethnic festival. Other flags are flying there — from the yellow cross on the blue field of Sweden, to the fierce red dragon of Wales. In fact, the harbor was again being invaded, but this time it was by forty-foot serpent-headed long boats, their Viking crews brandishing padded swords. Swedes, Norwegians, and ethnic Finns attacked; Scots, Welsh, and Irish defended. When the warriors got thirsty, they drank a sweet, cold, potent pear wine imported from England.

"And the home . . . of the . . . BRAAAAAVE."

Bravery, as it happens, was the topic of discussion later in the day, as William Donald Schaefer toured his city in the long green Fleetwood with the license plates that simply said MAYOR. In addition to his driver, he traveled with Gary Mitchell, a double-knit aide who looked like an administrative assistant and sometimes functioned as one, but who really was there on special detachment from Baltimore's Tac Squad — the equivalent of a SWAT team. Formerly with the elite police helicopter branch, in which he had thrown spotlights into bleak alleys from the safety of the air, he now traveled with a .38 under his plaid-jacketed shoulder, and the knowledge that the mayor of a northeastern city wades into some fairly strange crowds.

Actually, the conversation was not about bravery per se. It was about windows.

In the Union Square neighborhood, where H. L. Mencken, "the sage of Baltimore," once lived, there is a "shopsteading" program. Shopsteading is a spin-off of Baltimore's "homesteading" plan. In northeastern urban homesteading, gutted aged townhouses, which are in no condition to support decent human life but whose sturdy brick walls are still so structurally sound that it seems a shame just to bulldoze them, are sold by the city for a dollar and some promises. The homesteaders who acquire these charming old shells, which today would cost a fortune to build from scratch, agree to fix the houses up — they frequently have to replace the plumbing and heating systems, the plaster, and sometimes even the roof — and then actually live in them for at least a few years.

The houses are available for a dollar because their previous owners have abandoned them — been scared off — and they've fallen into the hands of the city in a tax sale.

The deal, when it works right, usually boils down to this:

The city marks out a neighborhood that it thinks ripe for resuscitation. It attempts to stretch its overtaxed social services so that the entire neighborhood can be turned around by these homesteaders. It knows from bitter experience that only one or two rehabbed houses in a block won't do the trick. The whole block has to be attacked for critical social change to occur. So the designated neighborhood, at least in Baltimore, gets an extra dose of police protection, and the city code inspectors make a special effort to lean on property owners who are not bringing their places up to the new standards. Street fairs and ethnic festivals are encouraged, with the city providing bandstands and roping off streets to automobile traffic so that pedestrians can wander.

In exchange, a young couple with no chance of being able to afford a more conventional first home in a tight, spiraling real estate market, promise to invest their sweat, and possibly risk their personal safety, rehabilitating a row house in a tough, but presumably not hopeless, part of a city that suburbanites and people who have moved to Oregon have generally written off as irrevocably declining.

There is no question that the neighborhoods involved are tough. The edge of the rehabbed areas, where they fade off into hard-core slums, is commonly referred to as the "frontier." If the neighborhood once again becomes livable, and an adjacent area becomes newly attractive to homesteaders, the process is referred to as "pushing back the frontier." The nastier inhabitants on the wrong side of the frontier are called "the Indians."

Obviously, a certain number of these phrases are blatantly racist code words. But by no means is that the whole story. A good number of the people who get these $1.00 houses and fix them up are themselves black. Furthermore, since the people who homestead have committed themselves actually to living in these neighborhoods, they're betting their bodies that a pluralistic, northeastern urban society can be attractive, profitable, possible, and fun.

Now, in the Union Square shopsteading program, for $100 folk get not just a row house, but a two- or three-story building, the top floors of which offer lavish living area as well as the ground floor for some mom-and-pop retail establishment. When the work on the structure is completed, theoretically the couple wind up with both a place to live and a place in which to earn their living.

On West Baltimore Street, holes have been drilled in the middle of the sidewalk, with steel posts firmly cemented into them. From the posts are hung chain-link fencing, mean-looking barbed wire, and a sign saying all this is the work of William Donald Schaefer, mayor, and the city of Baltimore. Behind this makeshift fort, offering night protection from the Indians, dozens of shopsteaders hammer and buzz-saw away, hauling out wheelbarrow after wheelbarrow of rotted timber and powdered plaster.

A word about Schaefer: A bachelor in his fifties, Schaefer lives with his mother, Tulula, although "lives with" is somewhat misleading, since his city hall office includes a much-used cot, and he spends inordinate amounts of time, nights and weekends included, personally seeing after his city. Schaefer is a blond, freckled teetotaler of German extraction with almost transparent green-blue eyes. He has a permanent battle with his waistline, made infinitely more difficult by the ethnic festivals his city sponsors at which he finds pressed on him endless crêpes, perogies, and lasagna.

Schaefer is an up-front admirer of the late Richard J. Daley and of Frank Rizzo, the former bosses of Chicago and Philadelphia, respectively. As he indefatigably prowls through the city in the back seat of his limousine, he whips out multisheet forms that are labeled "Executive Action Memos." At the top of each sheet is printed the list of the perhaps thirty people at the heights of the city's administration. There is a little box next to each name. Whenever Schaefer sees anything in his city that frosts him, he checks off the name of the department head who will soon wish that he had seen it first, and then scrawls in longhand, as the car tools on, a description of, for example, the grafitti on an overpass that Schaefer wants to see painted over, and yesterday. He then checks off how long the department head has to respond to the memo. The longest period is two weeks, and frequently he checks the box next to "Immediately." When he gets back to city hall, these memos are logged, numbered, and shipped to the offending executive. A copy is retained by an old Prussian, who is a retired utility engineer. His job, for which he is paid next to nothing, is largely to make sure that if an action memo demands a response in two days, by the beard of St. Nicholas, a response is produced in two days. The habits this kind of system instills in city workers can be awesome to behold. At ten o'clock one Saturday morning, a mayor's aide received a call from the organizers of a dedication ceremony at a neighborhood "multiservice" center. More people were showing up at the festivities than had been anticipated, and there were not enough folding chairs. The aide made one call. At 10:56, one yellow truck, number 2737, Department of Public Works, Bureau of Operations, showed up at that center on North Dukeland Street, two miles west of city hall, in the predominantly black Rosemont neighborhood. It had two workers in orange and yellow reflector vests, who worked with a will to unload and set up a hundred more blue folding chairs.

In some northeastern cities on a weekend morning, you can't call 911 and get the *police* to show up in fifty-six minutes flat, much less get a hundred folding chairs and a work crew. And, unlike some of the old-line mayors and Maryland politicians he admires, Schaefer has never been accused of corruption; moreover, he seems to exercise his capacity for repressive totalitarianism only on political allies, opponents, and newspaper reporters — all of whom probably can be considered fair game. Across the pillars of the rehabbed Rosemont neighborhood center marked by clean new plate glass, sandblasted and repointed turn-of-the-century brick, and marvelous old turrets, hung a banner whose message seemed to be heartfelt (in 1979, Schaefer ran without significant opposition). In the city's colors of black and yellow (not very different from the black and orange of the city's beloved baseball team, the Orioles), it read: WELCOME MAYOR SCHAEFER.

Anyway, this Saturday afternoon — after attending the neighborhood multipurpose center dedication, the Celtic-Scandinavian festival, the Flag Day ceremonies at Fort McHenry, and yet other activities, such as the French ethnic festival, a rummage sale at the 125-year-old Light Street Presbyterian Church, and a south Baltimore street fair in which he responded to a man who wanted to help keep the city clean by issuing an Executive Action Memo directing a city department to deliver the fellow a broom — Schaefer had thoroughly exhausted the men twenty years his junior who had tried to keep up with his pace. Now, the mayor, a nondrinker, found himself on West Baltimore Street in the Union Square neighborhood inside the New Deal Bar.

"My goodness," he said. "I never thought I'd live to see the day that I'd find myself inside the New Deal Bar."

Joann Whitely, a thirty-six-year-old with dark hair and dirt smudges on her face, showed the mayor the work she, her husband, and their renovation crew had done on the bar they'd recently bought. She nearly burst with pride. Here were the murals they were preserving. "During the forties," she explained later, "a man came into the bar and could not pay, and in lieu of funds, he painted the murals. It took him almost a year. Apparently he'd run up an extremely high bill."

The long-forgotten alcoholic genius had painted what he saw around the bar, and what he saw was so raunchy that Whitely carefully steered the mayor away from some of the more colorful paeans to pimps and whores. *Baltimore* magazine in the late seventies, before Whitely took it over, conferred on the the New Deal Bar the awesome title "The Worst Bar in Baltimore."

"During the war," Whitely said, "the servicemen were barred from going on the premises. It was really that bad. It was the place where narcotics were trafficked. There were some murders in the New Deal. There were rapes. Yes, within the last few years this all happened. In fact, when we first bought it, one day I walked toward the back of the bar and these two guys were firing up right outside the bathroom. Yes, shooting up. Heroin. In fact, the liquor board would not allow us to use the name New Deal Two. They just wanted the name New Deal completely gone from the memory of everyone in Baltimore. So we're going to call it Heathen Days, after one of Mencken's books."

Whitely proudly showed the mayor the long oak bar she and her husband had discovered and moved in, and the fine brass rails on which the future would place its feet. She discussed the oak ice box with beveled mirrors and ornate brass trim that was coming in next. She mentioned that the couple will have sunk $105,000 into the bar by the time it reopens. She pointed out the "amenities," like the fireplace halfway up the wall, and the carefully carved wooden detail along the roofline. "Where else could you get detail like that?" she asked.

I looked out at West Baltimore Street. I was glad I was traveling not alone, but with the mayor — and Mitchell, with his concealed .38. There was a faded arrow labeled "Eddie's Lunch." An old barber shop sign hung half off its hinges, its twirling glass completely smashed. Al's Billiard Supply was boarded up, its sign flaking. Citywide TV Sales & Service sat there with its front covered by grilles of steel. M. Hess Luncheonette was abandoned. Drifters ambled past with no particular place to go.

"Doesn't this neighborhood ever *scare* you?" I later asked Whitely.

"Not really."

"Aren't you afraid of being raped?"

"No. I can't explain it, but I feel a closeness to this entire neighborhood. Union Square is very special to me, because when I was growing up I saw a neighborhood — West Fayette Street — die, and I think within me there was a psychological need. We saw a neighborhood go from a solid one to a ghetto. A lot of the families moved out after the war. It became a tenant area. It integrated too quickly; then the state and the city started condemning properties for the expansion of the University of Maryland. Buildings began to be boarded up. And once that started there was no return.

"The crime rate increased. Everything started to fall apart. My father died on West Fayette Street, the six hundred block, in nineteen sixty-six. The day my father died, it was unbelievable, because here was this little house that was set back with fig trees and roses in the front yard. And then the state came in and took over, and today the new dental school stands where my home was."

And now Whitely is in the middle of the West Baltimore Street shopsteading area, attacking the worst bar in Baltimore with a crowbar. She paid considerably more than the token $100 to the city for her building, because, as much as the cops might have wished it, the New Deal had not been abandoned. But all around her, up and down the block, carpenters and masons who had made such a deal were at work restoring storefronts that would soon become an ice cream parlor, a unisex hair salon, a quickie printing shop, a self-service laundry, a silk-screen shop, an upholsterer's operation, a delicatessen, an architect's office, a tax consultant's, a constructions firm's.

In the course of conversation, Whitely casually mentioned the burglaries, robberies, muggings, and lootings that occur from time to time on West Baltimore Street. "I'm not afraid to live here," she said. "A lot of people can't understand that, but Baltimore Street is the last frontier to be conquered out here. Until Baltimore Street is turned around in terms of physical appearance and being a viable business corridor, we'll never make it."

She really wanted to tell the mayor about the pièce de résistance of the new bar, and this is how the subject of windows and bravery came up. "They say windows are dead in Baltimore," she told Schaefer. "They're wrong." And she went on about the ultimate architectural statement she and her husband intended to make with the newly christened Heathen Days.

They were going to tear out the bricked-up front of the building and replace it with glass. Plate glass. Not even rockproof. And without steel bars.

Several weeks later, I found myself in Hamtramck, Michigan, talking about Whitely to David Olko. Olko is the part-owner of the Second Precinct Lounge there, and we'd been talking about Amori's Party Store on East Jefferson in Detroit, several miles south. Amori's is across the street from Renaissance Ford, a dealership that is, in turn, practically in the shadow of the new downtown Renaissance Center, which is supposed to typify the resurgence of downtown Detroit. Amori's has a lot of glass, too, only the glass is an inch and a half thick and bulletproof and *inside* the liquor store, separating the operators from the customers. Olko agreed that he'd never seen a *bank* with that kind of security, although he allowed that he'd seen a bar outfitted similarly. His Second Precinct Lounge had been burglarized just the week before, and they'd gotten not only his cash but the guns he keeps handy. The day before that, his cottage up by the lake had been burned. Arson. And a lot of bars were closing around him in Hamtramck, now that the Chrysler Dodge Main plant next door had been shut down permanently, throwing thousands out of work. But Olko wasn't pessimistic about his future, and he said he felt he knew where Whitely was coming from. "Yeah," he said. "You just gotta be tough."

And tough is what defines North America's nation of northeastern gritty cities in a multitude of ways.

Gary. South Bend. Flint. Toledo. Cleveland. Akron. Canton. Youngstown. Wheeling. Sudbury. London. Hamilton. Buffalo. Syracuse. Schenectady. Pittsburgh. Bethlehem. Harrisburg. Wilkes-Barre. Wilmington. Camden. Trenton. Newark.

The litany of names bring clear associations even to the most insulated residents of other regions. These names mean one thing: heavy work with heavy machines. Hard work for those with jobs; hard times for those without.

When columnists speak of managing decline, this is the region they mean. When they speak of the seminal battles of trade unionism, they place their markers here. When they write of the disappearing Democratic city political juggernauts, not for nothing do they call them machines, for this is where they hummed, then rusted.

When television presents the concept "Archie Bunker," it locates his neighborhood here, for the four boroughs of New York that are not Manhattan are part of this nation.

In an ironic way, this place is the real New South, for it received the vast internal migration of job-hungry blacks fleeing the once-overworked land of Dixie, and now it is the warehouse of their discontent. North America's Gulag Archipelago, it's been called; the continent's chain of urban prison camps.

Its capital must be Detroit, the birthplace of the assembly line, but its spiritual center is bankrupt Cleveland. Its hope may be Baltimore, but its shame is Cicero, the northern town whose hatred broke the heart of Martin Luther King, Jr.

This is the nation of the Foundry.

A foundry, in which molten metal is cast into forms, historically represents one of the most basic and ancient technologies known to man. "If you want to use your imagination a bit," says Sheldon Wesson, of the American Iron and Steel Institute, "one would guess that the first foundry was born when primitive man saw this reddish crud melting around his campfire, and this hot stuff trickled down into the sand, and when it cooled, it assumed the shape of the area in the sand where it had trickled. It didn't take much of a leap for him to realize that he could produce a form to his own specifications. I've seen foundries today so primitive that you wouldn't believe it. Just wet sand on the floor of the factory. A guy comes along with a hand ladle and pours hot metal pretty much as it was done a million years ago."

Well, not a million years ago, but in the case of copper, at least three millennia before the birth of Christ. Iron is mentioned in the Old Testament eighty-six times, and steel, three.

And historically, the nation of the Foundry served as basic and time-honored a role in the development of North America as the facilities after which it is named. In fact, especially for the hundred years ending during World War II, North American industrial history and the history of the Foundry were close to being the same thing. But even before that, during the 1770s, around the eastern Pennsylvania iron deposits, "iron plantations" were formed, the largest at Hopewell, Pennsylvania, with twelve hundred inhabitants, casting and forging arms, shot, and cannon for the Revolution. The most famous of these plantations, among the many destroyed by British troops trying to weaken George Washington's armies, is Valley Forge.

Early in the 1800s, water power, which had driven the air bellows to create the high temperatures necessary to melt metal, was replaced by steam power. This was an important advance for several reasons, not the least of which was its timeliness, as the demand for boilers, locomotives, rails, and bridges surged with the accelerated western movement of a rapidly growing continent.

But it was also important because it freed the industry geographically from its dependence on locations next to East Coast rivers, flowing rapidly down from the Appalachians, and facilitated its move closer to its supplies of raw materials, most of which were in, or west of, the mountains.

It was in the mid 1800s that a system was invented that would make the production of steel so cheap that the much stronger material could compete with iron — the Bessemer process. In 1864, at Wyandotte, Michigan, on the Detroit River less than ten miles from the Dearborn that Henry Ford would put on the map half a century later, the first North American commercial pour of Bessemer steel was made. From these ingots, North America's first steel railroad track was made in 1865, at the North Chicago Rolling Mill.

Steel from the nation of the Foundry changed the face of the continent. Barbed wire allowed the building of fences in the treeless Breadbasket, transforming it from rangeland into farmland and promoting the creation of towns. On May 10, 1869, at Promontory Point, Utah, steel rails linked the Central Pacific and the Union Pacific railroads, and thus the coasts. The "Chicago school" of architecture changed the ways cities would look and function by pioneering the steel skyscraper in the 1880s and 1890s.

Meanwhile, steel was changing the geography of the Foundry itself, the interior of which found itself ideally situated in the middle of a triangle of the three resources basic to both iron and steel:

• High-quality iron ore from northern Michigan and, after the completion of the Sault Sainte Marie locks linking Lake Superior and Lake Huron in 1855, the Mesabi Range of Minnesota.

• Bituminous coal, to be baked into the high-heat-value coke of almost pure carbon, found in virtually the entire eastern mountain range, but mainly in the valleys of Pennsylvania, West Virginia, and Kentucky.

• Limestone, which is the shells of prehistoric crustaceans squeezed into rock, used to remove impurities in the iron and steel. It can be found in deposits miles long and thousands of feet deep all over the Northeast, especially in New York, Pennsylvania, Indiana, Ohio, Michigan, and Ontario.

But best of all, the water-rich Foundry was laced with navigable waterways ranging from the Great Lakes to the Ohio River to the Erie Canal, and, to this day, water is still the cheapest way to move heavy, bulky items.

So industrial towns grew next to ports. Pittsburgh, the home of United States Steel and Pittsburgh Plate Glass, and the third greatest headquarters city in the United States, is located where the Monongahela and Allegheny rivers merge to create the Ohio River. (It's no accident that the football Steelers play in Three Rivers Stadium.)

Cleveland is located where the Cuyahoga River — famous for once being so polluted that it burst into flames — meets Lake Erie — also famous for once being so polluted that it was incapable of sustaining marine life.

Detroit is on the western edge of Lake Erie, as is Toledo.

Buffalo is on its eastern edge.

You can still get from Buffalo to Albany via the 1825 Erie Canal, and from there to New York City on the Hudson River. It was that barge canal, linking New York City and the Great Lakes, and along which the cities of Utica, Syracuse, and Rochester were built, which was the beginning of the end for Boston and New England as the primary industrial region. It transformed New York City from a second-class seaport to the East Coast's commercial center. It helped make New York the Empire State. Today's Interstate 90 roughly parallels that canal.

Chicago, Gary, and Milwaukee are on Lake Michigan.

Toronto is on Lake Ontario, and as recently as 1959, that was making an enormous political and economic difference in North America. Nineteen fifty-nine was the year that the St. Lawrence Seaway was completed. As noted above, it's not that the Seaway connected the Lakes and the Atlantic for the first time. What the Seaway did was allow all but the largest oceangoing traffic (for example, supertankers) into the Lakes. Prior to 1959, Québec's Montréal was functionally the end of the line for large craft, and, not coincidentally, Montréal was the financial and commercial hub of Canada. In the last twenty years, that title has passed over to inland Foundry Toronto, and to this day you can find presumably paranoid Québecois who view the Seaway as nothing but an elaborate Anglo plot to screw the French-speakers once again.

Be that as it may, the point is that these cities would not have evolved, or at least evolved the way they did, had they not been strategically located to wrest wealth efficiently from the very dirt of the planet. These cities were well positioned to have the various earths shipped inexpensively, via the abundant waterways, to central locations. There, they would be thrown together at high heat to make metal and other extremely basic nineteenth-century industrial products. In this process, they attracted wave after wave of cheap immigrant labor — first the wave of Europeans, then the wave of southern blacks, recently the Hispanics. Not for nothing did they call it the Melting Pot. How many people have "melting pots" in their kitchen? That's a Foundry term and concept.

Diego Rivera, the celebrated Mexican muralist, made this point explicitly in the Garden Court of the Detroit Institute of Arts in 1932.

An idealistic Marxist and champion of the working class who believed in individuals laboring for the good of all, Rivera was fascinated by economic and industrial development. When, in California in 1930, he met Dr. William Valentiner, then the curator of that art institute, "he wanted to hear all that I knew about industry in Detroit," Valentiner wrote. The staggering capitalist achievement of "the Rouge" — the Rouge River industrial complex of Henry Ford — intrigued him. Here, within one two-thousand-acre industrial "city," raw iron-laden earth came in one end, and Model As came out the other, with virtually every other industrial process associated with the automobile (the making of glass, for example) integrated in between. "In all the constructions of man's past," wrote Rivera, "pyramids, Roman roads and aqueducts, cathedrals and palaces, there is nothing to equal these [skyscrapers, superhighways, and machines] . . . the best modern architects of our age are finding their aesthetic and functional inspiration in [North American] industrial buildings, machine-design, and engineering, the greatest expressions of the . . . genius of this New World."

Charging $100 per square yard, which ended up costing Detroit art patron Edsel Ford $20,889 — a handsome sum during the Depression — Rivera painted twenty-seven panels on the four walls of the museum's skylit, bungalow-sized Garden Court, in the ancient Roman water-color-on-fresh-plaster fresco technique.

In striking, bold colors, lines, and metaphors, Rivera impressionistically but accurately depicted over fifty major operations of the Rouge, from Power House No. 1, to the blast furnace, foundry operations, and open-hearth steel mill, through the stamping operations, welding, painting, and final assembly. The end result — the automobile — was of less interest to Rivera than the process. The only completed car that appears in the murals is a tiny speck, way in the distance at the end of the final assembly line.

Of far more concern to Rivera were the basic raw materials — men and earth. Looming over the busy north and south panels that depict the guts of the plants are four quiet, reclining nudes — Caucasian, Oriental, American Indian, and Negro. In their hands, they offer, respectively, lumps of limestone, sand, iron ore, and coal, the races and substances Rivera saw as analogous "in their . . . quality of color and form, as well as by their historic [North American] functions."

Conventional thinking about the Foundry today combines an odd combination of memory and amnesia concerning what the Foundry once meant to North Americans.

On the one hand, it's possible to forget that to artists like Rivera and Charlie Chaplin, who, in the film *Modern Times* (1936), showed man becoming merely a cog in a societal machine, the Foundry was a metaphor of the future. A world in which everything that moved was measured in tons, and humans were dwarfed by their inventions, was the ultimate statement of both hope and despair. Detroit and the cities like it were to their time what Houston, Los Angeles, and the cities of the MexAmerican Southwest are to this generation — visions of wonder that both amaze and appall.

On the other hand, especially to residents of the Foundry itself, who, like all North Americans, are capable of their own parochialism, sometimes memories of what *was* are confused with what *is*. In the days of Rivera, the Foundry was the linchpin of North American development. In fact, to most, the Foundry — "back east" — *was* North America. The United States portion of the Foundry *was* the United States. It is of Baltimore that the United States national anthem sings. Henry Ford, who had his own air force of Ford Tri-motors, his own navy of Great Lakes freighters, and certainly his own army of tens of thousands of workers, was as towering a figure as any president or premier. The same was true of Morgan of U.S. Steel and Rockefeller of Standard Oil.

The problem with this memory, if you look at North America today from the perspective of Nine Nations, is that it has become a misleading metaphor.

The Foundry is still the most populous of the Nine Nations. It has approximately ninety million people of the perhaps three hundred million living in the area described by this volume, or 30 percent.

It still controls the majority of the continent's basic — in the sense of late nineteenth- and early twentieth-century — industry. It's difficult to quantify the Foundry's gross national product precisely, as it obviously does not have customs barriers around its borders, and thus statistics are not usually gathered along the lines this chapter describes.

But, for example, Illinois, Indiana, Ohio, Pennsylvania, Michigan, and New York produced sixty-four million tons of pig iron in 1977, which was 70 percent of the United States–Canadian total. And that's not even counting the production of Ontario, West Virginia, Delaware, New Jersey, and Maryland, whose total production the iron industry's statistics perversely make difficult to assess.

Similarly, if you take the above six states and this time throw in Ontario, you discover that that portion of the Foundry produced 106 million tons of raw steel in 1977, which was 75 percent of the United States–Canadian total. And that's again not counting leviathans like the Sparrow's Point plant in Maryland, whose production is considered something of a trade secret. Nor does that include New Jersey's Roebling Works, producer of the steel rope used in building the Brooklyn Bridge.

If you examine the automobile assembly numbers for the appropriate portions of these twelve states and provinces, you discover that in 1978, 9,288,527 cars and trucks were finished there, for 64 percent of the United States–Canadian total. And, of course, that doesn't reflect the component industries — the factories that produce the parts that Motown and Company bolts together.

In a walk along the vast assembly line at the Rouge Works in the summer of 1980, just before destitute Ford shut down public tours for the first time in fifty years in order to save the $2 million they cost, I watched barely recognizable hunks of gray metal come together in a stately waltz that ultimately resulted in gleaming, strongly hued Mustangs and Capris being spit out once every forty-eight seconds. And I got a lesson in industrial geography.

For sure, the car doors hung in racks labeled "Return to Ford Bordeaux." France. The piece of cardboard hanging from the transmissions was labeled "Lanfkarte. Pallet Tag. Carte Suiveuse." And carpets were labeled "Troy Mills, Troy, N.H."

But the overwhelming majority of the curiously shaped pieces of metal and plastic that sat in wire bins, waiting to be precisely placed on the slowly passing hulks, had clues to their origin like these:

"Return to Warner Gear Division, Muncie, Indiana."

"Kalamazoo Stamping and Die Co., Kalamazoo, Michigan, Producers of quality dies and metal stampings."

"The Akro Corp., Canton, Ohio."

"Midwest Rubber, Deckerville, Michigan."

"Federal Screw Works, Romulus, Michigan."

"Yale Rubber Manufacturing Co., Sandusky, Michigan."

"RB & W Metal Forming Division, Mentor, Ohio."

"Jim Robbins Co., Black Cowl Panel, Troy, Michigan."

"Manchester Plastics, Manchester, Michigan."

"Rockwell International, Chelsea, Michigan."

"Rockwell International, Logansport, Indiana."

"S&S Products, Wheel Cover Assembly, Wyandotte, Michigan."

"American Hose Corp., Winchester, Indiana."

"Huron Plastics, St. Clair, Michigan."

"Sashaban Products, Clarkston, Michigan."

"Stant, a Purolator Co., Connersville, Indiana."

"Huron Tool & Manufacturing, a U.S. Industries company, and that makes a world of difference, Lexington, Michigan."

Unquestionably, the Foundry is still a formidable place, one that can make a world of difference. The danger lies in our continuing to view it as a metaphor of the future — seeing it as the only place in which North America's tomorrows are being hammered out. By the turn of the century, it may not even be the most important segment of North America. That role may well be assumed by the MexAmerican Southwest, all by itself. Already, the continental population is shifting to a southern and western majority, from northern and eastern. The largest bank in North America is not in New York. It's in California — the Bank of America. If energy deposits are destiny, the Foundry's future is by no means assured. Although its coal reserves are fantastic, they are deep beneath the mountains, and are mined by men still scarred by battles with exploiters that occurred half a century ago. Being a United Mine Worker is an emotional allegiance, as is being a United Auto Worker, a Rubber Worker, a Steel Worker.

The problem with the Foundry is that it is failing. Its cities are old and creaking, as is much of its industry. It is still struggling with its historic role as the integrator of wildly different personalities and cultures and ethnic groups, and there is no assurance that the sociological battles that it has been assigned will end in victory.

But the Foundry is *not* North America, despite what the continental news media — most of which are headquartered there — may lead you to believe. The Foundry is the only one of the Nine Nations that can be said to be on the decline. The other eight are, at worst, economically stable (for example, Québec and New England), in the sense that a plausible balance between quality of life and modest growth rate make for stability. And others are generating wealth and growth so fast that their biggest problem is controlling the boom.

This is not to say that other nations do not have problems. They do. Water is as crucial to Tucson's future as race relations are to Baltimore's. It is not even to say that the rest of the continent does not share some of the Foundry's problems. Many of Dixie's cities are at least as old as the Foundry's. Refitting steel mills and assembly lines to meet the challenges of Japan are concerns in the Breadbasket — even in Ecotopia — not just in the Foundry.

The error, as this continent matures, is in our unquestioningly equating the inevitable decline in the Foundry's dominance with an inevitable decline in the world position of the United States or Canada. What's happening in the Foundry today is perhaps comparable to the wrenching realizations Europeans were subjected to over the last five centuries: not only does the sun not revolve around the earth; the earth does not revolve around London. Yet, somehow, Western civilization survives — even prospers.

Defining the borders of the Foundry is an exercise in human, rather than geophysical distinctions. Each of the nations of the Breadbasket, the Foundry, and Dixie is a mixture of agriculture and industry. There is significant corn production in Ohio, just as there is significant automobile production in Oklahoma. The view along the New Jersey Turnpike is so appalling that Dixie planners specifically mention that state as what they don't want to see their world become. Yet the largest stretch of wilderness in the East is in New Jersey — the Pine Barrens of the southern part of the state. The Delaware River, along its west, is the biggest wild river in the East. The rural scenery twenty minutes north of Trenton is breathtaking, and, by the same token, there are portions of Kansas City, the capital of the Breadbasket, that are pretty wretched.

But this hardly means these nations are the same. There are sharp differences in history, attitudes toward the land, prejudices, economics, and futures among these nations, and it's how these differences come together that defines their boundaries. Thus, the Foundry, for example, is a place that is thoroughly described by man and what he's done to the mountains and rivers and plains in the course of trying to get ahead, more than it is by mountains or rivers themselves.

Cities are the Foundry's dominant physical characteristic. There are lots of them. They're not terribly far apart, by the standards of most of the continent, and they are crowded places. As a result, there is no trouble pointing to the Foundry's heartland — its megalopolises. The boundaries are less distinct where the area is less urban. A tour around the border of the Foundry helps explain.

As noted in the chapter on New England, the southwestern third of Connecticut is part of the Foundry, because it is tied by television stations, commuting highways, and suburban values to New York.

Manhattan itself is so unusual on this continent that it is dealt with separately in the next chapter. But its suburbs are not, and thus the border town between the Foundry and New England is New Haven.

To the west of New Haven is Fairfield County, with its bedroom communities like Bridgeport, Darien, and New Canaan, which would shrivel up and die without New York. To its east is New London, which is clearly part of New England. An important part of the New London–Groton–Mystic area is its relationship to the open Atlantic. Nuclear submarines, built at the Electric Boatworks, the Coast Guard's training vessels attached to its academy, and historic whaling tall ships all call eastern Connecticut home.

The line, therefore, must be drawn between these two different worlds, and New Haven is inviting. On the one hand, it has a distinguished institution, Yale, on which to base its claim as a civilized place. On the other hand, it has very little else on which to base a claim as a civilized place. Providence is more charming than New Haven.

New Haven's politics also demonstrate the predictable confusion of a town straddling two nations. It has all sorts of anomalies, not the least of which is its enormous ethnic Italian-American population, which votes Republican because, years ago, the Irish had locked up the Democratic Party.

New Haven is also where the East Coast megalopolis kicks north up toward Hartford, rather than continuing along Long Island Sound. This is important to the way a Foundry–New England border is perceived by a casual visitor. A tourist driving up to New England from anywhere south of New York, for example, starts tensing up at about the intersection of the New Jersey Turnpike and the Garden State Parkway, well below New York City.

That's the point at which one starts shushing the kids, because daddy needs to pay close attention to his driving lest everybody get lost or the car gets stacked up on the southbound. The tension doesn't end until New Haven. After New Haven, the traffic thins out, it's possible to start admiring the scenery, and you can start feeling as if you're on vacation.

Down along the Foundry-Dixie line, Annapolis is a border town. To its north is Baltimore. But across and below the long Chesapeake Bay Bridge is the Eastern Shore of Maryland, which, with its chicken farms and insulated, isolated rural poverty, is clearly old-line Dixie. Annapolis itself is a graceful place, a good place to walk around in, a town even someone accustomed to the beauty of Charleston, South Carolina, or Savannah, Georgia, could love. But it's also the state capital of Maryland, and has seen so much good old big-city political corruption that it makes Trenton look clean by contrast.

Moving west along the Foundry-Dixie line, we come to Washington, D.C., which, like Manhattan, is so consumed by itself that it is dealt with separately in the next chapter. It should be noted, however, that its wealthy suburbs, like New York's, are definitely part of the Foundry. They're certainly not Dixie. In the Virginia state capital, Richmond, suburbs like Fairfax are viewed with awe and disbelief. The voters up there have all manner of reprehensible Yankee notions. You can find people in northern Virginia who are not only actually in favor of the government subsidizing mass transit and abortion, but in favor of controlling handguns. The majority of Virginians look at anything that goes on north of the Rappahannock River with suspicion.

Out past the Blue Ridge Mountains (you know why they look

blue from a distance? They're so covered with trees that, in the course of photosynthesis, they exhale resinous hydrocarbons that create their own natural haze) is the Shenandoah Valley.

Songwriter John Denver has it wrong when he sings about the Shenandoah Valley being in West Virginia, rather than Virginia, but he was right about its being almost heaven, and it is not part of the Foundry. The pace of affairs at the Southern States Farmers Co-op is the tip-off: if you wish to buy a screwdriver, for example, you first pause, mention the weather, remark on the price of seed, joke with the girl behind the counter, and *then* ask for the tool. Brusquely and impersonally attempting to slap down money and leave with your merchandise marks you as an outsider. Even the industrialization is not what you'll find in the Foundry. This picturesque sheep-and-orchard valley is the sort of place that is offered clean, lucrative factories, like the Adolph Coors Company's eastern beer-brewing plant. This is the sort of job creation that planners will kill for, and it is a plum that is reserved only for places with a high quality of life. But this happened in far northern Dixie, and was received by the valley people with a skepticism unusual for the South. Being near the border of the Foundry, they have seen so much industrial devastation in Pennsylvania, Maryland, and West Virginia that even the value of jobs like these are questioned, because of the change they'd bring.

Northern West Virginia — Morgantown, Parkersburg, Wheeling — especially its northern panhandle, which follows the Ohio River south from Pittsburgh, is clearly part of the Foundry. The Monongahela and the Ohio are loaded with industry that turns water strange colors and brings texture to the air. Coal-fired electric plants split the hills with high-tension lines. Steel, glass, and industrial chemical plants bring worrisome jobs — jobs that are not only dangerous and difficult, but are hit first in a slackening economy.

Southeastern West Virginia is problematic. It is at all times isolated by its mountains. Similar terrain in the Empty Quarter at least has the good grace not to be populated. Charleston, West Virginia, is by no means the most rugged part, yet its airport can inspire respect in *good* weather. In search of enough horizontal space for a runway, its planners sheared off the peak of a mountain. That leaves no margin for pilot error. The grandly named West Virginia Turnpike, meanwhile, is two lanes, undivided. West Virginians typically have a very limited spacial horizon. It's common to find some who have never been to a town fifty miles away. They consider that a long drive, and they're right. The roads in Alaska have fewer twists and more guard rails. Some folk here especially avoid driving on holidays, like the Fourth of July. These roads are hard enough without a driver's having to cope with traffic. It's uncanny, the way smashed cars decorate West Virginia front yards like lawn ornaments. In good times, southeastern West Virginia can be considered an isolated part of the Foundry. In bad times, it is an isolated part of Dixie.

The good times are when coal is running strong. This has not been recently. The coal is high in sulfur, which makes it difficult and expensive to burn without causing pollution. It is often in deep mines, which requires the work of a lot of high-priced men operating in conditions in which they can, and frequently do, die. Deep-mining coal is still the world's most dangerous industrial occupation. Where the coal is near the surface, and can be strip-mined, it's generally on a slope so steep that the operation destroys the environment. There's a theory that holds that an increase in the severity of spring floods in these parts is connected to strip-mining practices. The hills just can't hold the rain as well as they used to. With Washington pushing coal as an export item to Europe, coal may soon again be king here, despite all this. But if it is, it will almost undoubtedly be accompanied by an increase in labor unrest. The UMW started off as a cause, dissolved into a racket offering its leaders cushy lives, and now, pathetically, the union's reformers seem incapable of leadership.

So much bad blood was built up during this process, and so much good blood spilled, that unionization is a fiercely polarizing topic here yet, long after labor and management in other parts of North America have managed to confront the issues with other than a quasi-religious, gunfire-punctuated fanaticism. This is why in "good" times this area is part of the Foundry.

In really bad times, when there isn't much work at all, the way folk hunker down in their hollows for the long haul is pure Dixie. After all the years of infusion of antipoverty money, the opportunities for education, health care, adequate diet, and having one's horizons expanded are better than they were. But it's still not something that has caused abandonment of a century-old pessimism about the inevitability of progress. There is still a devotion to the land here, no matter how unyielding it is (and there is virtually no commercial farming in West Virginia).

From Huntington, West Virginia, to Cincinnati, the border follows the Kentucky side of the Ohio River. Some scholars have contended that U.S. Route 40 — the old "national road" — is the dividing line between Dixie and the Foundry. It runs from Wheeling, West Virginia, to Ohio's capital, Columbus, and on to Richmond, Indiana. They traced substantial differences in food, architecture, the layout of towns, and music to either side of that highway.

That probably was once a useful distinction. There is still a taste of the culture of old Dixie in southern Ohio. But the fact that it is referred to as the U.S. 40 line, instead of the Interstate 70 line (70 now parallels 40), tells you how old the idea is. Both the Foundry and Dixie have gone through a lot of changes in the last fifty years.

Be that as it may, the Ruhr-like industrialization and pollution of the upper Ohio River Valley now is the fact that controls. Cincinnati and Dayton are definitely part of the Foundry.

Dayton, in fact, was referred to in Richard Scammon and Ben Wattenberg's *The Real Majority* as "the typical American city." While this chapter contends that the Foundry is typical of nothing except itself, it's interesting to note that *The Almanac of American Politics* tells us that Dayton is the home of Richard Nixon's vision of the typical United States voter: a housewife whose husband works in a factory and whose brother-in-law is a cop. Dayton is middle-sized and middle class. It is losing population and has a black mayor. The substantial growth has been in the suburbs. And it has given birth to such phenomena as the Wright brothers, Erma Bombeck (the suburban muse), and "The Phil Donahue Show."

Cincinnati, meanwhile, is so Germanic that it is beyond imagination that some fan would become so undisciplined at a Reds game that he might throw a beer cup into the outfield. Cincinnati is the home of Procter and Gamble, which is certainly next to Teutonic godliness. Cincinnati is so straight that you used to have to cross the river into Kentucky to have a good time. The Beverly Hills Supper Club, until it burned in a tragic fire in 1977, attracted first-rate Las Vegas talent. It was in, of all places, Covington, Kentucky, just south of Cincinnati. In fact, that part of Kentucky had long been considered a mini-Vegas, in which thoroughly illegal prostitution, gambling, and vice had also flourished.

As the Ohio River flows into Indiana, the national boundaries get complicated. Here are the facts:

Northern Indiana — Fort Wayne, Elkhart, Gary — are unquestionably part of the Foundry. Notre Dame football teams are full of hulking Slavic Pennsylvanians who did not wish to spend the rest of their lives in a steel mill, but who nonetheless feel right at home under South Bend's cold, yellowish-gray clouds.

Southern Indiana — the scenic hills that start below Indianapolis and tread through the Hoosier National Forest toward Evansville — is definitely part of Dixie, and has been ever since the Copperheads (those Northerners who sympathized with the Confederacy in the 1860s).

As you move on to western Indiana, you find it impossible to ignore the corn, in more ways than one. Big-acreage, big-dollar, full-time farms influence politics and culture so strongly that that area is neither Foundry nor Dixie. It's the start of the Breadbasket.

Smack in the middle of this is Indianapolis, the largest city in North America with so few natural advantages. It is not on a river of any moment. It is not on a sea. It is not in an area of compelling beauty. It's not warm in the winter or cool in the summer. It is not near great mineral wealth. In fact, it's not near much of anything. Its detractors refer to it as Indian-no-place, and decry its lack of character. Cincinnati, such people cruelly claim, is veritably awash with character by contrast.

But these critics are ignoring Indianapolis' great strength. It is a border town. It is the crossroads town where three nations meet: the Breadbasket, Dixie, and the Foundry. No city in North America, save the far vaster border town of Chicago, is the intersection of more interstate highways. The compromise view might be to call it a place to be in on your way to someplace else.

Where, then, does one draw the line through Indiana between the Foundry and Dixie? Perhaps Interstate 74 from Cincinnati to Indianapolis. And the line between the Foundry and the Breadbasket? Interstate 65 between Indianapolis and Gary.

Especially in the area surrounding Indianapolis, it is important never to underestimate the regional significance of a major highway. Don't think of it as a road. Think of it as something like $30 million a mile transferred from the taxpayers to the construction and land companies. Think of it as a spectacular accelerator of real estate values, especially in a rural area, where the plopping of an exit on this man's land, versus that man's, is often a fairly arbitrary (and hence easily influenced) exercise. Think of it not as a link, but as a divider. To the left of the highway, back when it was proposed, were interests who wished to gain, and on the right were other interests with similar, if conflicting, ideas. The final location of the highway was an extraordinarily political decision that balanced forces like this against each other and also against the forces that wished to get a direct route from city to city. An interstate can be an eloquent statement of political balances.

In northwestern Indiana, the spoor of the Foundry is not subtle. The Montréal-to-Milwaukee megalopolis, far longer than the one from Boston to Washington, takes the corner around Lake Michigan wide and outside, lit by the otherworldly flares of the refineries of Gary. The smell is the same as that of Elizabeth, New Jersey. The particulate matter belched from the stacks of its steel mills was once so great that it affected the weather. Moisture-laden clouds coming in from the west would pick up this stuff over Gary and become so heavy that they would precipitate out whatever they held a few dozen miles east, which is roughly where LaPorte lies. LaPorte was regularly the rainiest or snowiest place in Indiana.

Welcome to Chicago. Richard J. Daley, Mayor. I know. He's gone. But it will be a generation before the billboards equating the city with his pug face fade from the mind. Its slogans about itself — the City of Broad Shoulders, the Windy City — stress Foundry themes, like toughness.

Chicago, "The Second City," a fundamentally eastern city compared to the real West, like Salt Lake City, is, in its relationship to New York, the Foundry model for the urban competitions one sees all over North America. Tulsa–Oklahoma City, for example. Dallas-Houston. Anchorage-Fairbanks. Montréal-Toronto. The first city claims to be the "New York" of wherever it is, the more glamorous pacesetter. The other, peeved, but not capable of dismissing the claim, responds by suggesting it is more down to earth, more "real." More into making money than making trends, perhaps. It will be a long time before Chicago lives down its fame as the "city that works."

West of "Chicagoland," as the radio stations like to call it, as if it were a theme park, is the Breadbasket, where distances between major population centers begin to get excessive. Conveniently, and not coincidentally, Chicago is North America's greatest transportation hub, linking the great "Out There" to its west with the industrial heartland to its east, and both to the world by rail, road, pipeline, ship, and air (Chicago's O'Hare Airport is the busiest in the world). The spider webs of trade routes ending in Chicago are dense and impressive.

North of the city, the Foundry continues past Milwaukee to Green Bay. There's a fast-food plaza on the New Jersey Turnpike named after the late Green Bay Packers coach, Vince Lombardi. Green Bay is definitely Foundry. It shares patron saints.

This far north, with all due apologies to the folk in western Ontario, cultural boundaries become a little thin, since there are too few people to make cultural distinctions about. But we press on across Lake Superior. Sault Sainte Marie is Foundry both because of its grittiness and its iron interests. Thunder Bay, the eastern shipping terminal for Canadian wheat, is Breadbasket. Sudbury is the staggeringly ugly, bombed-out portion of the globe where the astronauts were brought so that they could get an advance idea of what the moon looked like.

The line of the Foundry curves east to include the Lake Huron provincial parks, which are the playgrounds for Toronto and Ottawa workers. There is no question that southern Ontario is Foundry. It is the most densely populated, most industrialized, and, until recently, the dominant part of Canada. Its primacy is undergoing major challenge from the Canadian portion of the other northern five of the Nine Nations. In fact, because Canada is the most loosely confederated Western democracy, Ottawa having nothing like the internal power Washington does, the distinctions among North America's nations can be seen with the greatest clarity north of the 49th parallel. Not only does Ottawa face a separatist Québec, but the energy-rich environs of Alberta in the Empty Quarter show repeated determination to set their own course, refusing to be treated like a colony with oil reserves to be exploited. These provinces are separated by the Breadbasket nation, which includes much of Saskatchewan and all of Manitoba, and which resents being victimized by high-priced energy and industrial goods from its partners to the east and west. And Ecotopian British Columbia, like the New England-ish Maritime Provinces, are so different from the central provinces that they periodically and seriously debate whether confederation was a good idea, after all. This is the implied threat behind Québec separatism: Why stop there?

Meanwhile, southern Ontario is so commingled with the United States portion of the Foundry that Windsor, for example, is actually south of Detroit. The most direct route between Detroit and Buffalo is really through this portion of Canada, over the north shore of Lake Erie, not the long way around, by way of Cleveland. Canada's auto industry, which is centered in southern

Ontario, is inextricably linked to that of Detroit via the Autopact, which is, in effect, a common market agreement that makes the United States–Canadian boundary transparent to the movement of components and finished products in exchange for an allocation of jobs.

Despite extensive Canadian attempts to exert sovereignty over its economy, according to *The Financial Post* in 1978 the number one corporation in sales in Canada was General Motors of Canada, Ltd., headquartered in Oshawa, an hour east of Toronto, and perhaps eighty miles across Lake Ontario from Buffalo as the snow flies. One hundred percent of it is owned by GM in Detroit. (As much as 80 percent of some Canadian auto-factory production is destined for the U.S. market.) Canada's number two corporation was Ford Motor Company of Canada, in Oakville, less than an hour west of Toronto and even closer to the United States. Eighty-eight percent of it is owned by Ford in Dearborn. Number three was Imperial Oil, Ltd., Toronto. Seventy percent owned by Exxon in New York.

Conversely, Canadian firms are the largest foreign investors in U.S. metals and machine manufacturing. Canadian investment in the United States overall is higher, per capita, than the other way around. The *New York Times* estimated the 1979 total, direct and indirect, to be $20 billion.

The Foundry, then, finally ends north of Ottawa, at the Ottawa River, on the other side of which is another industrialized nation, but one that is unique in North America, in that most of its population does not speak English: the emerging and defiant nation of Québec.

•   •   •

The central issues in the Foundry, both in human and financial terms, revolve around questions of investment. Enormous quantities of time, sweat, and money have been invested in making this region what it is, and the Foundry's future will be determined by the extent to which North Americans decide they should, or will, walk away from that.

Questions of reindustrializing aged facilities, revitalizing crumbled cities, and recommitting political will to ease the results of racism, are all intertwined.

For openers, the whole point of living in the Foundry is work. It has been argued that the Protestant work ethic never really caught on in North America to the extent that its p.r. would suggest.

"The work ethic," Daniel T. Rodgers, a University of Wisconsin professor, has written, "has always been a minority phenomenon in American life.

"The idea that hard, self-denying labor is the *summum bonum* of life never cut deeply in the South. It was violated in scores of 19th-century frontier settlements and in rich men's ballrooms . . ."

But it's tough to maintain that position in the Foundry. No one, for example, ever lived in Buffalo for the climate. Or in Gary for the scenic vistas. Or in Camden for the recreational opportunities. Or in Wheeling for the beach. Blue-collar workers may drink to oblivion, or load up their Winnebagos for a weekend in northern Michigan, but they do so in response to their work. Welfare is an emotional issue in these highly taxed Foundry cities because its recipients don't work.

Work is so central to this experience that when people are thrown out of it, they literally go crazy.

M. Harvey Brenner made a detailed study of the effects of unemployment under the auspices of Congress's Joint Economic Committee. His professionally well-regarded calculations are that, historically, for each 1 percent increase in joblessness in the United States economy, the direct result has been 38,886 deaths, 20,240 cardiovascular failures, 494 cases of death from cirrhosis of the liver attendant to alcoholism, 920 suicides, and 648 homicides.

In May 1980, the state of Michigan was suffering from automobile-industry layoffs that yielded an unemployment rate of 14.4 percent, the highest rate reported since the records started being kept. Six hundred and twenty-five thousand people were out of work. (And the unemployment numbers went even higher in succeeding months.) But on the basis of those May figures, which accounted for 0.5 percent of the 7.5 percent U.S. unemployment rate, Michigan used Brenner's study to arrive at the conclusion that shortly the state was going to see 460 more suicides, 324 more murders, and so on.

And sure enough, as Oscar Paskal said to me in Solidarity House, the Detroit headquarters of the United Auto Workers, "Watch television tonight. See what's on the news." What was on the news was a horrifying report about snipers who were driving around and, apparently, taking random pot shots at children. "It won't be long before you get the standard man-goes-berserk, barricades-self-inside-house, opens-fire-with-deer-rifle," Paskal said. "In fact, it's already started."

Right again. The day before, on the front page of the *Detroit News*, an article appeared headlined SLUMP BREEDS MENTAL ILLS.

"Some stare silently for hours at walls," it read. "Others over-eat or drink heavily. Some feel tired constantly, even though they may sleep hours. All of these are common symptoms of the depression among Michigan's growing number of unemployed . . .

"In recent weeks, several newly unemployed persons have barricaded themselves with shotguns inside their homes. One east side Detroiter, who lost his job and his wife within the last two years, shot at two of his neighbors and then killed himself . . .

" 'These are not mild cases of the blues,' " said Mel Ravitz, director of the Detroit-Wayne County Community Mental Health Board in a colossal understatement. " 'Unemployment for a prolonged period of time attacks the very core of a person's identity and self-perception. Their frustration and feelings of worthlessness in turn threaten the entire fabric of the family. These people can't deal with all the problems and complications . . .' "

The very core of a person's identity and self-perception.

Ask these people who they are, and before they say man, woman, Methodist, Catholic, American, Canadian, Democrat, Republican, black, white, or brown, they'll say, for example: steelworker.

It's this which brings the dry abstractions of the steel industry's bleats about foreign competition down to human scale.

At the end of World War II, North America produced the majority of the world's steel. The United States' share alone was 48 percent in the 1948–1952 period, and its share of exports was 25 percent. By the mid-seventies, the U.S. share of world production was down to a mere 18 percent, and its exports down to less than 5 percent.

What was happening during that period was that every part of the world was recognizing steel production as basic to its development. Today, one of the first things an emerging nation does is go looking for an international loan to build a steel mill. It's an even more basic drive than that toward energy independence. And appropriate, too. The world's second largest iron-ore reserves, for example, after the Soviet Union, are in Brazil.

Furthermore, war-ravaged industrialized countries, notably Japan, were creating a vast internal market for new steel needed to rebuild themselves. And they met that demand with the latest, most efficient technology. There are obvious advantages to being forced to start again from scratch.

In 1948–1952, Japan produced less than 3 percent of the world's steel. By 1975, that had grown to 16 percent. But more important, Japan increased its share of exports from less than 5 percent in 1950 to become the world's leading exporter, shipping over 35 percent by the mid-seventies.

Meanwhile, by the mid-seventies, the United States had begun to import as much as 12 percent of its steel — more than Europe, more than the Communist bloc. In many ways, what had happened to New England's textile industry decades earlier has been happening to the Foundry's steel. It was being transferred to other parts of the world, where the costs were lower. Steel-making is no longer an awesome technology. It doesn't begin to compare in complexity with the manufacture and assembly of semiconductor computer devices. And that manufacture, in turn, will someday be eclipsed by the now-fledgling genetic-engineering industry, with its industrial creation of new forms of life — little microbes, for instance, that are custom-designed to eat copper ore and spit out refined copper.

It's going to be a while before the technology of 256K semiconductor memory chips and genetically altered microbes are commonplace in Bulgaria, but the manufacturing of steel is no mystery there now. The point is that some of the Foundry's steel industry's overseas markets were drying up — being better served by home-grown industry. And those newly industrializing nations had an advantage over the older steel centers, in that they frequently started from scratch, so they could invest in the most efficient new methods then developed. The Foundry, meanwhile, had an enormous investment in, for example, antiquated openhearth furnaces that perhaps should have been rapidly scrapped but weren't.

Moreover, a Foundry location was becoming less important for steel. Steel today is made in thirty-five U.S. states. Some of the largest post–World War II steel facilities built in the United States, such as the Fairless Works of U.S. Steel, built in 1953, were not built inside the Great Lakes resources triangle. Fairless is in the Foundry, but it is north of Philadelphia, with a straight shot at the Atlantic. At Fairless, you can see why: great mounds of various portions of the planet lie about, in their characteristic colors. Venezuelan iron-laden dirt is more reddish-brown than iron-laden Québec dirt, which is more a glinting metallic gray. As the global reach of the steel industry has grown, it has responded by rethinking its locations.

The only new steel mill to open in North America in more than a decade, the $1.2 billion job at Nanticoke, Ontario, eighty miles west of Toronto, is owned by the Steel Company of Canada. Ironically, even its Lake Erie location, directly across from aging steel towns like Youngstown, Ohio, reflects the new realities. Apart from the traditional reasons for locating in the heart of the Foundry, Stelco had new, more sophisticated imperatives. A spokesman for the company admitted it didn't see a location in the dirt-poor, thinly populated Atlantic Maritimes market as much of a bet. Neither was it eager to further its investment in nationalistic, French-speaking Québec. But at the same time, its growth market, according to company executives, is seen as the Empty Quarter environs of Alberta, which will need everything from high-rise steel buildings to Stelco's wide-gauge steel pipelines. If one assumes that a competitive steel mill must be built with access to cheap water transportation, then it comes down to the Great Lakes or the Pacific coast. Cheaper to ship west, across the flatlands of the Breadbasket, than try to lift this stuff east over the mountains from British Columbia, Stelco feels.

The North American steel industry today says it has been dealt dirty by the governments of the United States, Canada, and Japan. The United States and Canada, the industry says, have slowed revitalization by forcing the corporations to invest billions of dollars in environmental equipment to clean the water and air of the Foundry — billions that, they say, should have been spent on increasing productivity. The Japanese industry, by contrast, they say, is in bed with its government, which is true. But the more serious charge is that Japanese and other exporters are dumping — shipping steel across the Pacific for less than they can afford to make it in order to keep their furnaces blasting at full capacity and to retain advantages of scale and penetration of market.

There are enormous arguments over this. Critics of North American steel companies say that they have simply made tremendous blunders in not modernizing more quickly. These complacent old leviathans, the critics charge, were more interested in maintaining profit margins than in plowing back the billions of dollars that would have been necessary to maintain technological parity with Japan.

But some part of this argument is moot. One steel mill after another has been shut down. Plans to build new ones have been indefinitely delayed, because the offending company concluded that steel is simply no longer a growth industry in North America.

When, in 1979, U.S. Steel shut down facilities it called "marginal," throwing one Foundry town after another into turmoil and depression, the corporation averred that it was simply doing what it had to do in order to avoid the near-bankruptcy that plagues Chrysler. If Chrysler had backed out of the product it had been traditionally associated with — big cars — as quickly as U.S. Steel was backing out of steel, it wouldn't have been so troubled, the corporation argued.

And there is a certain merciless logic to that, from the market perspective. A corporation naturally wants to make money, not necessarily steel. If there's more money in making chemicals . . .

And it's true. North America is a maturing continent. The Foundry itself is a mature region. That limits how much steel the continent needs. It's not like the turn of the century. A lot of skyscrapers are already built, for instance. Furthermore, the biggest market North American steel has — the automobile industry — is backing out of steel as quickly as it can in order to lower the weight of its cars. Aluminum, graphite, and plastics are performing all manner of structural and decorative functions that used to be performed by steel. The cars are getting better gas mileage as a result. Meanwhile, the automobile industry itself is, as of this writing, in a terrible slump, as high interest rates, toughened credit availability, soaring costs, and unpredictable fuel supplies not only end North America's proverbial "love affair" with the car, but threaten even to end the marriage. And all this continues to drive down the demand for steel.

It would perhaps warm the hearts of free-market Adam Smiths. But the problem is the enormous social cost the shift entails.

Youngstown is the classic example of what has been invested in a steel town.

On the Ohio-Pennsylvania border, about seventy miles south of Lake Erie and halfway between Cleveland and Pittsburgh, Youngstown is a grimy and cheerless burg where well-meaning would-be gourmets point a visitor in the direction of the Italian dishes at the Holiday Inn. It has a city population of 140,000 and dropping, and a metropolitan area population of about half a million.

If it were located elsewhere, those numbers would put Youngstown in most other nations' lists of their ten largest cities. But in the Foundry, it's only number five in *Ohio*.

The point of Youngstown, traditionally, has been the making of iron and steel, much of which has been consumed by nearby associated industries, such as the modern, automated GM plant at

Lordstown, a few miles west. (Lordstown once achieved a degree of notoriety as a result of studies that demonstrated extreme levels of boredom and alienation among its young workers. Lordstown also served as the model for Fernwood in TV's "Mary Hartman, Mary Hartman." But I digress.)

Starting in 1977, three major steel mills in a row folded in Youngstown, starting with the Campbell Works of Youngstown Sheet and Tube, followed by U.S. Steel's Ohio Works, and its McDonald Works.

They were just a few of the hundreds of major plants that have closed in the Foundry in the past decade as industries moved south or west, or were unable to meet foreign competition, or phased out obsolete facilities.

Shortly before Youngstown's Black Monday, September 17, 1977, when the first mill closed, throwing four thousand out of work, Bethlehem Steel laid off thirty-five hundred workers in Lackawanna, New York, a suburb of Buffalo, and another thirty-five hundred in Johnstown, Pennsylvania. Bethlehem also halted work on a new steel mill in Johnstown. Three thousand workers were out of a job in Conshohocken, New York, when another steel company declared bankruptcy. In Akron, Ohio, twenty-one thousand jobs in the rubber industry have disappeared since 1950, twenty-five hundred of them in 1978 alone. New York state lost three hundred and twenty-seven thousand jobs in the first seven years of the seventies. Michigan figured that plant relocations alone cost thirty thousand jobs in that state between 1970 and 1974, and Ohio figures that plant closings alone cost it fifty thousand jobs between 1970 and 1977.

The Bureau of Labor Statistics, gathering numbers that cover what is basically the United States portions of the Foundry and New England, says 1.4 million industrial jobs have been lost there in the thirteen years from 1966 to 1979, and clearly, the bulk of that impact has to have been in the Foundry.

Youngstown's triple closings — the elimination of nearly ten thousand high-skill, high-pay, high-status jobs, the holders of which have known no other life — alone produced a ripple effect that has ended up costing the taxpayers hundreds of millions of dollars.

The closings, in effect, were a manmade disaster equivalent to a killer hurricane or a tornado. The "ripples," in fact, were monstrous waves, touching every resident, from the department store clerk to the gas station attendant.

Youngstown was special. Unlike the citizens of other communities that quietly accepted their fate, Youngstown's civic, religious, and union leaders banded together to investigate the re-
vival of the mills as worker-owned enterprises. David Smith and
Patrick McGuigan of the Technological Development Corporation
in Boston gathered these studies together in a tract called "Towards a Public Balance Sheet: Calculating the costs and benefits
of community stabilization."

In the first three years after the closing of the Campbell Works [says the
introduction], it was estimated that the tax-supported public sector
would bear costs of $60–$70 million in adjustment assistance, unemployment compensation, revenue reduction and increased government expenditures. These costs are imposed by the Lykes Corporation's decision
to close its facility, but they do not show up on Lykes' balance sheet.
Reducing these public costs to $50 million or even to zero would bring
no additional return to Lykes, or reduce its loss. However, it would represent a significant gain for the taxpayers' balance sheet. Put another
way, had this $60–$70 million in public funds been invested *prior* to the
Campbell Works' closing in a successful effort to keep the mill open, taxpayers might well have ended up with a positive rather than negative
return.

Actually, it can be argued that the figures in "Balance Sheet" are
conservative. For one thing, they were gathered after the first mill
went under, before the second and third followed suit. Then, too,
there are the medical costs associated with Brenner's estimates of
an attendant rise in heart attacks, suicides, and the like. What do
a thousand heart attacks cost?

And apart from these human costs, there is the investment in
urban facilities that Youngstown represents. No one has ever calculated exactly what a city that size embodies in terms of capital
investment. But Youngstown has dozens of schools, endless miles
of sewers, roads and street lamps, municipal buildings, art museums and sports fields — not to mention hundreds of thousands
of housing units. What did they cost?

Conventional analysis says that in a free market, firms act to
maximize profits; mobile capital seeks the highest rate of return;
steel mills, like Youngstown's, that are less efficient go out of
business; and there is a competition among regions for investment capital such that a plant reduction or closing reflects an
area's basic inability to cut it.

The theory goes, then, that the Foundry has priced itself out of the market, with high-priced unionized labor, high land costs, high energy costs, high pollution-control costs, and so forth.

The liberal National Center for Economic Alternatives in effect asks certain questions, however: Are we really going to do this? Are we really going to walk away from these Foundry cities? Are we really going to try to build them all over again in MexAmerica and Dixie? Do you have any idea of what that's going to cost?

The center and its ideological soulmates have carried out yet more extensive studies that show that Youngstown, for example, should be an excellent place for heavy investment in certain kinds of steel facilities. In order to gain support for the granting of government seed money for the revitalization of Youngstown's steel industry, they've trotted out analyses purporting to show that Youngstown's location is an advantage, not a disadvantage. One of the more technologically sophisticated ways of making steel — the electric-furnace method — requires enormous quantities of scrap as a basic item. Where would be a better place to put an electric-furnace mill, this argument goes, than on a rail line in the middle of more junkyards than any in the dreams of a mean dog: Youngstown? This analysis states that relatively cheap power can be generated from the region's coal, and that a savings of perhaps $40 a ton could ensue.

Yet the reports have done little save give rise to a few headlines and then gather dust. One analyst cynically suggested that Youngstown will have to wait until the Japanese read these figures and locate a North American plant there.

Meanwhile, the Foundry continues to decline.

In Hamtramck, Michigan, an incorporated city completely surrounded by Detroit, United Auto Workers Local 3 is preparing to shut down.

In 1910, Hamtramck was a sleepy, German-American village of less than four thousand. But Chrysler changed all that. Dodge began car production in Hamtramck in 1914, and thousands of workers moved into the sparsely settled town. Many were young men without families, living in overcrowded rooming houses and dingy hotels, where each bed did twenty-four-hour service. By 1920, Hamtramck's population had bulged to forty-five thousand, making it the state's fastest-growing boom town. It became the Polish "capital" of Michigan, absorbing wave after wave of eastern Europeans and Ukrainians hungry for work. By 1930, 58 percent of Hamtramck's population was Polish-speaking.

Ethnic pride found expression in organizations like the Polish

Workers Local 187, one of the earliest UAW bodies in the city. To this day, on Chene Street a little south of Hamtramck, there's a wonderful Polish restaurant called The Round Bar, formerly Zosia's. It has a massive bar on the first floor that can seat a hundred people, although it happens to be rectangular rather than round. Shots of 100-proof Wyborowa vodka line up next to water tumblers full of Stroh's draft beer. Above the rows of liquor bottles are bowling trophies. The ceiling over the bar — gilt-painted stamped tin — is two stories up, and the bar is ringed overhead by a second-level balcony displaying proud white-on-red Polish eagles and tinsel rope left over from Christmas. The restaurant on this second-level balcony has plain wooden chairs and white tablecloths covered by clear plastic. Near the cash register, elaborately crocheted and taffetaed dolls are on display. On the back wall, a poster advertises the St. Hyancinth parish picnic, in Warsaw Park, featuring polka dancing. A Wayne County Community College poster announces UCZMY SIE! That's pronounced *Uchimi che*, it was explained to me, and means *We're learning!* The menu offers *pierogiz mięsem* — perogis, tasty fried meat dumplings — for $2.60. *Pieczen wieprzowa*, a roast pork dinner, costs $3.30, and is the most expensive thing on the menu. *Naleśniki z powidłami* turn out to be prune blintzes. *Maślanka* is buttermilk.

But The Round Bar is nearly empty. For on January 4, 1980, without much warning, after seventy years Chrysler shut down its Dodge Main plant in Hamtramck, with annual payroll and benefits of $120 million, throwing 2925 people out of work. A factory of five million square feet, on eight floors, over 120 acres, which used to produce as many as 511,000 Plymouth Volaré and Dodge Aspen automobiles a year, now stands derelict.

At the once-bustling union hall, there is now only a trickle of people walking in, keeping their unemployment and retraining benefits current. They are a subdued lot.

James S. Bryant, a heavyset black man in his early sixties, tells about coming to Detroit in 1946, right after the war.

I was born and raised in Alabama. In Birmingham. Tarrant City, really, just outside of Birmingham. When I got out of the service, all my folks had come up here. It was a question of better working conditions. Back in Birmingham, I had a job in the steel mills. I quit. I didn't go back to it. I had a better opportunity here. I had a chance to advance myself. I couldn't advance in Birmingham, see? I could not, in them times, you know, because I was black. I was fixing the track for the switching engines. Maybe five or six years I could have gotten a better job down there, but I wasn't going to stay there, no way. Yeah, there were millions of us with the same idea, I'm sure. I figured I'd start out at anything up here and work my way up, which I did. I started off in the foundry. Really hot job. Shaking dust off the castings. Did that about three years. It was a bad job. I would say so, yeah, that was the kind of jobs black people would get. There weren't any white guys doing that job. Ninety-eight cents an hour, though, and that was good money back then. When the Dodge Main plant finally closed, I was a paint repairer. If a car came through the line and there was a scratch or something, I had to repair it before it went to final inspection. Paint repair, now, that's a good job. That's skilled. Almost top [pay] scale. In my department that's almost the top job. Ain't no discrimination now. I got that because I had thirty-three years' seniority. You get the job you want, you just got no problems. Repairing paint is a good job because you don't work on every car, the way I see it. Sometimes you only get every third car. You don't have to bust your butt. Good job. Good pay. About eight dollars and something an hour.

I've been out of work now six months. Longest I'd been out before was on strike, a hundred and five days. I been piddling around a lot. Painting, working around the house. Doing little odd jobs. The first month, it seemed like [model year plant] changeover. But after that, it gets on your nerves a bit. You just don't get used to it that quick. You work around hundreds and hundreds of friends, you don't get used to leaving them that quick. You can't just walk away from a group of friends of thirty years and you don't see them no more and you be happy about it. The mill is just like your home.

The United Auto Workers' contract has a "thirty and out" clause, which allows men to retire after thirty years of service. Men who start work at eighteen, then, are eligible for a pension at forty-eight. Bryant hadn't planned on retiring yet, but with Dodge Main shut down, he sees no choice for himself except to spend the rest of his days at home. "My wife," he adds with a grin, "what with me being retired, sometimes she says, 'I'll be glad when you go.' "

Dominick Roy, in his early fifties, a pudgy white man, doesn't have Bryant's option of retiring. He'd worked at Dodge Main only since 1953.

"I was a miscellaneous sprayer when I was laid off. Putting the black-out in the front and the back, and under the hood. The job wasn't too bad, but the paint can get to you. I was in the wheel room for twelve years until they shifted me into trim. I was lifting the wheels — not the tires, just the wheels — onto a conveyor belt.

"My hometown is Hazard, Kentucky," he said in an almost TV-parody hill twang that he still hasn't managed to shake. Hazard is a notoriously tough coal town, only one county away from "Bloody Harlan," the Kentucky coal center renowned for its pitched battles between workers and mine owners. "My father was a coal-miner. He's been retired for twenty years. I didn't even think about staying in Hazard and becoming a coal-miner. Just figured back then that there were a lot of jobs up here, and I came and just got established here."

Roy believed he had enough seniority to get a job at Chrysler's Jefferson Street assembly plant, which in a few months was to start building the small, fuel-efficient, front-wheel-drive "K" cars that Chrysler was betting its future on. "Don't know if I'll get the same job over there. Ain't never been inside Jefferson," he said, betraying a touch of anxiety. "Don't know if it works the same way. You ever been in there?"

Nagi Kaid also was worried. Kaid is from North Yemen, an Arab, like so many auto workers in Detroit. Detroit has the largest concentration of Arab-Americans in the continent.

I came over in 'seventy-three [he said], and I've been working at Dodge Main since a month after I got here. I don't know what I'm going to do. I don't think there are any jobs here in Detroit. You can look for a job all day and you can't get one. Not even small things. I have a wife and children back in Yemen. I support them. I've been back there twice in the seven years. If the situation stays bad like it is now, maybe I go back to Yemen. I thought about bringing my family here, but if there is no job, how are you going to deal with your family here? If I go back to Yemen, I can be a farmer, I guess. But I left Yemen because my brothers were here. Five of them. They wrote, saying it was good. When I came, you could find a job if you looked. But now, maybe I go to the West Coast. I maybe go to California.

Kaid's situation is similar to that of many recent Arab immigrants in Detroit. "They worked hard," said one union official. "Never turned down a minute of overtime. Maybe sent seventy-five percent of their salary back home." Now, unfortunately, there are many who do not speak English well and feel very reluctant to leave the security of Detroit's Arab community, striking out anew in a strange continent. Kaid himself said that the only place in North America he'd been to other than Detroit was New York, and then only for a week.

When I asked him whether he'd thought of looking for work in Houston or some other town much better off economically than depressed Detroit, he answered the question vaguely, with an unmistakable lack of clarity about where Houston was. It was outside his world, at any rate.

Douglas Gulock, twenty-five, however, had discovered Huntsville; he had already spent some time there. He was born and had grown up in Detroit, but he and his wife were gearing up to move to Alabama.

We build all the electrical parts for the Chrysler Corporation down there. Electrical ignition, the [computer-controlled] lean-burn engines, starting right from scratch. When I go down there, they're going to send me to school for soldering. I figured in the Detroit area, I wasn't going anywhere. I figure, you know, they're all going to move south. And to be in a newer plant there'd be more chance of the plant sticking around. I don't know a soul in Alabama. But after the first week, I really started liking it, and that was the turning point. The people are friendly. The work is a lot more interesting. There's more to it. More of a challenge. If you go to school you can really make a career down there. Move yourself up. They got a few trouble-shooter jobs there, and you gotta have two years of electronics. As soon as I get settled down there, I want to get into school, and, because it's job related, Chrysler will pay for part of it. I'll go to college at night . . . Couple more years and I'll at least be eligible for some kind of pension. I can just go down there and wait for the right job to open up. I don't think I'm going to miss Detroit. The only hard part is like my parents and my in-laws maybe. My whole family is up here. But when it comes down to missing *Detroit* . . .

Gulock said that the Chrysler Corporation had offered much of the Dodge Main work force the opportunity to move out of state to other Chrysler plants, but that many of his buddies hadn't even signed up for transfer. They were looking for other jobs in the Detroit area, "in steel mills, in meat-packing plants, whatever," and some had taken big pay cuts — "five, six dollars an hour."

"Everybody gets set in their old ways," Gulock said. "Even the young guys, although for some, it may have been their wives saying no. They got family here, and they don't want to uproot their kids. But I think I've been thinking about the future more than they have. I have to make a living for myself. I figure that if Chrysler makes it, they're going to shut down a lot of the old plants up here and move south."

Gulock said that of the twelve people in his group whom Chrysler flew down to Alabama to show the opportunity there, only five finally ended up taking Dixie jobs.

"The guys who didn't take it were more or less black. I guess they were content here, all their friends and everything." But he allowed as how he thought that most of them just saw no way they were going to move to a small town in Alabama, with all the historical and emotional baggage that entails. Actually, there's some irony in that. A lot of the young southern blacks I talked to when I was preparing the Dixie chapter saw no way that they ever wanted to go north. They saw the North as a worse place for blacks than the South.

Yeah, the blacks who were educated down there now have a different way of thinking than the guys who were educated up here [said Ernest Carmack, a muscular black man who had taken retirement from Dodge Main]. I came to Detroit from Alabama when I was ten years old, so I know both sides. The guys in the South get a better education than the ones up here, I think. It's the New South. A lot of people still don't believe that. The guy who's really in trouble is the guy between the ages of thirty-five and forty. Maybe he's been buying a home for ten years. Not enough seniority to stay in a plant up here.

But he's assumed responsibility. Has a family, two or three kids, maybe. It would be a b***buster for him to start all over again in electronics. The longer he's been out of school, the harder it is for him to pick it up. This is what I'm thinking.

Carmack said he'd been planning his retirement for twelve years, ever since his kids grew up, and that he'd wound up buying two four-flat apartment buildings. He figures he'll spend his time maintaining them. "And I have personal things that I do every day. It's not illegal," he explained, in refusing to divulge what that is, "but it's personal, and it keeps me occupied."

Said Joseph P. Elliott, the financial secretary of the soon-to-be defunct local:

Yeah, all a guy has to do is, when he's retired, go somewhere for eight or nine hours and do *something* each day. Just like you punching a time card. Go do something interesting for eight or nine hours. Then come home. At least you keep active. Even if it's voluntary work. As long as you go somewhere five days a week. What happens to a guy who retires. His wife don't want him home. She's got her way of doing things during the day, and he's following her around. They get on each other's nerves, two people in a house.

I've seen cases down here when the wife doesn't even want to see her husband retire at sixty-two, sixty-five. They don't want them home. They call, see if we can't keep the old man in the plant longer. The real problem is with the poor guy who had to retire when Dodge Main closed who had had a lot of kids, a lot of sickness, and never was able to save anything up. He doesn't have a pot to piss in, and now he's retired. Well, he can't do nothing. Health probably gone. Soon he starts boozing too much.

Elliott himself wasn't sure what he wanted to do. He'd thought about writing a book about the union. "The politics, you know; just putting down my thoughts." He also mentioned, dreamily, that he still had his papers as an able-bodied seaman, from when he worked on freighters, starting at the age of sixteen. "Freshwater and saltwater. They're almost forty years old now, but I like the sea. I used to go San Francisco to the [Hawaiian] Islands on the freighters. That's not hard work. Four hours on, four hours off." But he thought he was probably getting too old for that life. He wouldn't want long voyages away from his family.

Meanwhile, across the street, David Olko, the part-owner of the Second Precinct Lounge mentioned earlier in this chapter, was surveying the traffic.

"Last Friday night, we played ball outside. And at eleven o'clock on a Friday night, there were two cars that went by in fifteen minutes. Two cars in that period of time. It's like a ghost town. Then a bus went by with only two people in it. Listen now. You can hear what traffic there is. None. There used to be traffic all the time, and there were people walking by. It's a scary feeling."

• • •

At some point in working on this chapter, I began to wonder how much of the Foundry's decline was strictly logical, as opposed to emotional. One premise I start from is that historical trends are finally realized by millions of small, individual decisions taken over time. No corporation wakes up one morning and says, okay, we're going to abandon South Bend; San Diego, here we come. Instead, individual decisions are made as questions come up concerning markets, replacement costs, and new opportunities. Studies are made of possible answers to narrow questions, and presumably a logical decision is made as to where the corporation's self-interest lies. Individuals operate the same way. There may be a few people who just decide that they are not going to live through one more Cleveland winter, pick up the kids, and head south, without any idea of where they're going to live, or how. But they are in the extreme minority.

The far more typical dynamic is for a person to arrive at some natural breaking point — like losing a job, retiring, graduating from school, getting out of the service, getting married, getting divorced, or having the kids grow up — and then examining one's options. It's at that point that one starts calling around, talking to friends, to figure out what to do next. And it is then that one entertains thoughts about getting out of wherever he or she is and moving on. It is these individual decisions that form the flow of a future, a flow of money, people, and power — a flow of history.

It is in this context that it seems important to look at the emotional baggage the Foundry carries with it. Sixties-style northeastern urban renewal, which concentrated on bulldozing whole city blocks and starting all over again, often produced disastrous results. The problems didn't go away; they just moved to a different, previously healthy neighborhood.

It has been suggested, however, that the war-on-poverty, gung-ho approach to incipient decline represents more than an unsophisticated economic analysis that refused to recognize the investment in money and energy even a dilapidated neighborhood of brick row houses represents. It may have been an emotional response to stubborn, interrelated problems that confronted would-be saviors of the Foundry. Rather than grapple with complex issues, and possibly be defeated by them, the planners simply decided to try to obliterate them.

In Trenton, New Jersey, in the early seventies, a group of young architects facetiously came up with an elaborate plan for that venerable city; it involved setting bonfires on its borders to serve as markers for precision bombardiers inside B-52s. The idea was that this would be Trenton's share of the "war bonus," which was supposed to be forthcoming when Washington finally stopped spending money on Vietnam and instead turned to the "problems of the cities," that is, the Foundry.

What would be left after the prolonged air raid, these architects suggested, would be a new Trenton, restored to the way George Washington knew it when he defeated the Hessians there on Christmas Eve, 1776.

Of course, as Freud pointed out, there is no such thing as a joke, and the interesting thing about the architects' idea is the level of frustration it reflects. In saner moments, these men were the ones who labored mightily to restore beautiful old Victorian homes that had seen better days, and tried to revive the state capital's weary downtown. What does this "plan" tell you about depression?

There are frequent newspaper headlines that suggest strongly that the Foundry has had first crack at some of the great North American mistakes — but the question is whether an analysis of this news would help shed any light on the decline of population and investment in the region.

There are almost a hundred nuclear reactors on this continent, for example, but only one went haywire, raising a profoundly emotional response from the world, and it was in the Foundry: Metropolitan Edison's Three Mile Island, just outside Harrisburg, Pennsylvania.

There are an estimated fifty thousand chemical dump sites in North America, and some of the worst of them are in Dixie, but the continental symbol of the revolt of the mutants is in the Foundry: Hooker Chemical's Love Canal, near Buffalo.

There are an untold number of flashy, "stunt"-architecture high-rise buildings in North America, but the most telling examples of fortress architecture, with no windows, or windows that are mere slits, are in the Foundry. Even Detroit's Renaissance Center, with its all-glass cylindrical and hexagonal towers, is built behind thirty-foot-tall medieval earth embankments. It's not easy to *walk* to the Renaissance Center. It clearly was meant to be arrived at by car, through checkpoints.

All of North America has pollution problems, the Houston Ship Channel among the worst. But only the Cuyahoga River actually burst into flames; only Lake Erie toyed with dying; it is mainly in the Foundry that acid rain has made dramatic inroads, killing off mountain-stream fish populations.

All of North America is confronting the energy crisis, but some of the most trenchant continental memories of deprivation came in the winters of '77 and '78, when much of Ohio, Pennsylvania and New York was immobilized by cold; the Ohio River was clogged by ice, thwarting coal-barge shipments; and, on top of that, factories closed for lack of natural gas. How many people are there who wouldn't respond in a thought-association quiz to the challenge "snow," with the city "Buffalo."

And, of course, if racism is bred of fear, with what part of the continent does North America associate black ghettos?

The question is how much of this is in the slightest rational? In pursuit of an answer, I started calling journalistic colleagues, asking them for suggestions as to the worst ghettos in North America in order that I might pick one to take a closer look at. I ended up with an interesting suggestion from Warren Brown, who works for the *Washington Post*, is black, and has been around. "Academy Street in Trenton," he insisted. "There are a lot of slums that are bigger, and some that are more bombed out, but Academy Street is not only poor; it doesn't have any life. You can go to North Philadelphia, and if you're reasonably careful, you're safe. In fact, you can have a pretty good time. Somebody might come up to you and warn you that hey man, you're in the wrong neighborhood, but if you're cool, you're okay. I mean, look at Harlem. But I've never seen anything like Academy Street. It's the most depressing slum I've ever been in."

"Oh Warren's full of crap," replied Bob Joffee, of the *Trenton Times*, who is white and who, as part of investigations, has lived on Academy Street for extended periods. "Academy Street's not that bad. It's just the human condition. Come on up. I'll show you Academy Street."

Over excellent prime steak, pasta, and good wine at Lorenzo's — to my mind, one of the East Coast's superior restaurants — across the street from the Trenton train station, and perhaps eight blocks from Academy Street, Joffee explained his view of Academy Street.

What interested me, what I wanted to do, was look at urban poverty as if it were a foreign country, expose myself to it, and see what I learned about it. I think the reason I've been able to persuade the paper to let me do this is that the issues I deal with on that beat are the central issues of liberalism today. What does the government do to intervene in the lives of the poor, and does it work from a strictly humanistic point of view? How are individuals, lots of them, affected by what government does? What I think I've found is that the liberal intention notwithstanding, liberal government programs tend to have, by and large, a harmful impact on the people they are trying to help. Social workers are people who, with some sort of academic training, are believed to be equipped to intervene somehow in the lives of the poor and make them not quite so bad. Do the feds hand out three-thousand-dollar-a-year day-care slots to the children of working women? Yes, they do. And yet the child care of choice for most working women turns out to be the extended family. And so it turns out that the feds, to my way of seeing, are handing out this money without any compelling argument that this is a useful social service with a broad impact on society.

Or, for example, look at foster care. Foster care is what purports to be temporary round-the-clock care for otherwise homeless children in private homes, subsidized by the government. It has evolved as the principal means by which government intercedes to protect children it perceives to be in danger, because they've been abandoned, beaten, neglected, or abused.

But what's commonly perceived as neglect is simply some middle-class social worker labeling poverty as somehow a manifestation of parental irresponsibility.

Okay, say I'm a social worker. I walk into a home because there's a kid in the hospital who's severely injured. The doctor says there may have been parental abuse. I go to the apartment. It turns out the kid fell out the window. I call it parental neglect, because I'm the hypothetical social worker. After all, a decent parent wouldn't allow his kid to be exposed to the incredible danger of a rusted-through iron railing five stories above the pavement, or whatever. But any practical person would say, "That's simply what slum housing is like, you stupid m**********r." What the social-welfare industry likes to call parental neglect is just a fancy new way of justifying intervention by the state in the lives of the poor. What happens is that it is a way for a bunch of middle-class people with degrees in the social sciences to end up finding work.

What happens to the poor? Their families live under the additional stress of having their families divided, and children shipped off to foster homes. What my examination of abuse and neglect in New Jersey has led me to, politically, is that it's turned me into an anarchist. I think that if we shut down the state agencies that intervene in cases of alleged abuse and neglect, infant-mortality rates in New Jersey would not be perceptibly worse. The problem would be that the social workers would be out of work.

I mean, I've been looking at specific cases. There's this one woman I met on Academy Street, when I was trying to see what life was like in the slums. Over a period of some three years, I saw how her life and the lives of her children were really affected or unaffected by the intervention of all these agencies. And on balance I can see no change whatever. They're still living in a lousy slum apartment; the children are still doing poorly in school, are still subject to the dangers of sexual molestation that accompany any situation where children are unsupervised in a lumpenproletariat neighborhood. The prognosis for improved stability or self-sufficiency is just as bad as it ever was. I mean, one cannot find any tangible improvement in the life of this family as a result of all this. One can see that intervention has led the woman to be completely distrustful of these people who purport to be trying to help her. The bottom-line threat to her has been all along that if you don't cooperate with us interveners, we will ship your kids off to foster homes. And what happens? Sometimes these kids end up in foster care for the rest of their minority. It can be argued that growing up in a slum is fraught with danger, but so is growing up in a state-supported private home with people who are told to love the kids — but not too much, because we can take them away from you at any time. And these people are convinced they can raise kids on two hundred dollars a month from the state. Maybe even have a little left over. By contrast, momma may be drunk, but at least it's momma. I guess, actually, I'm not persuaded that the kid is necessarily worse off because of the intervention of the state; just that I can't see where the kid and the family are better off. Intervention by the state in their lives has not been on the balance beneficial, other than that it employs a lot of middle-class people, and these middle-class people are allowed the delusion that they are not completely neglecting the poor.

On Academy Street, the next day, my inclination was to agree instantly with Warren Brown's assessment of the place. The only thing worse than the smell of urine in a hallway, it turns out, is the smell of urine and Lysol in a hallway. Abandoned row houses, with all their windows broken and their doors blown off, are littered with the broken glass from bottles of cheap, sweet Swiss-Up wine, which methadone users reportedly are partial to. A group of street people stand just outside the Urban League office, smoking and jiving, and one lady yells out at me, "Oh, you've got such pretty red *hair*! I just love red *hair*!" I try my best not to make my smile look queasy. In the Urban League office, they laugh at the attention I've attracted. Right; they giggle. It must be your beard. Couldn't be your freckled white skin. The Urban League has been trying to convince homesteaders to move into Academy Street but, so far, hasn't had much luck. Under government programs, they've tried to use street people to fix up abandoned homes, but there are complications, like their plumbing trainee getting taken up on murder-one charges after a fight with a buddy. And the copper plumbing keeps disappearing, taken off in a professional manner, they say, by people who clearly know what copper is worth. We get into a cynical discussion of slums that goes into the well, what the hell, hookers, addicts, and boosters (thieves) have to live somewhere, don't they? A direction that is markedly unproductive.

Joffee, meanwhile, is enjoying himself. He knocks on a door and drags me into the tidy apartment of a Puerto Rican family. They show me the velvet map of Vietnam, where one relative served, and the citizenship awards from grade school of another son, and they pull out slightly-out-of-focus snapshots of the fine-looking home they are building back in Puerto Rico with the money they're making working in the States, and show me the cap and gown another kid will be wearing to fifth-grade graduation in the afternoon.

Joffee drags me out of that apartment and down the street, where a barefoot man with gnarled black toenails insists on bringing us into his apartment to show us the improvements he's been making. Brand-new bright red checked linoleum is on the floor of the room that serves as his kitchen, living room, and dining room. It doesn't quite match the bright, and equally fresh, rose and brown paint on the wall, but it's a nice try. He climbs over the couch with the hole spewing stuffing and beckons me to follow him. It's blocking the door to the cramped bedroom and bath. They are, he says, with great pride, what he wants to attack next.

A white-haired woman, with a perky blue scarf and pants that are dirty and frayed at the cuff, latches on to us and says that she wants to write a book about all the experiences she has had running rooming houses on Academy Street, and Joffee assures her that there are nothing but interesting stories on Academy Street.

We pass a bunch of older men, in the center of which is a body stretched out on a mattress, unconscious, asleep perhaps, oblivious of what's going on around him.

Joffee clearly loves Academy Street. It is not clear that it loves him back. He gives the big hello to one little white girl, and she withdraws, refusing to speak. "She's mad at me for something," he muses.

At the vestpocket park, which used to have an inflated dome over the basketball courts, until the vandals put a fifteen-foot, irreparable hole into its side, another crowd surrounds a small building scarred by arson. They're painting it. It's a group of neighborhood people who, they say, went from door to door, begging half-empty cans of paint to try to make the park into something. No, the city had nothing to do with it, they tell us. What can the city do? It is too poor to replace the nylon dome. As the salsa music plays, they show us the big Puerto Rican flag they have painted on one wall, and the map they've made with paint and stones in the circle where a tree tried to grow and failed. It is clearly labeled: ARECIBO. GERONIMO. PUERTO RICO.

We stop by La Lareña café, which, Joffee is delighted to see, someone is rebuilding. It used to produce terrific pork, roasted right out back on a spit, until the fire spread from the pig to the back of the building one night.

I ask who lives in the white-haired lady's rooming house, and

Joffee says, "Let's go find out," and charges up some steps into a hallway and starts banging on doors at random. Nobody answers. "I guess nobody's home," he says, as I encourage him to get back out on the street.

We end up in the apartment of a woman whose young son Joffee has become fond of. He takes the kid out for ice cream, or to a quarry to swim, along with some of the kid's friends. "I guess I just like kids," he says. The kid is supposed to be in that fifth-grade graduation at one-thirty. Joffee asks the woman if she wants a ride to the school. The woman is drunk. It's eleven in the morning. Joffee gives her a hard time, saying he'll bring coffee when he comes around to pick her up, and until then she's to lay off the sauce. Out the open window over the fire escape in this third-floor walkup, you can see backyards of trampled dirt, without even any weeds. Broken windows. Houses that need paint. Brick chimneys leaning at a precarious angle, garbage in the street, and people in their finest clothes leaving for the graduation ceremonies.

We repair to Speckle Red's Soulfood Restaurant for lunch. "Nobody ever leaves Speckle Red's hungry," Red boasts, and is that ever the truth. The menu offers stewed chicken, fried chicken, pork chops and fish (together), roast spare ribs, lima beans, mashed potatoes, macaroni and cheese, collard greens, corn bread with margarine, and yams. And that's for *lunch*. Breakfast includes fish, grits, and eggs. One plateful of all the above.

And over lunch, Joffee confronts me with my own racism. "You were scared out there, weren't you?" he asks.

"Yes," I say, meaning it, "I was scared."

"Would you have been as scared if you were in a white Appalachian slum? They're just as capable of violence there as anybody on Academy Street."

"Well, hell," I bluster. "I mean, look, how often does a white man show up on Academy Street? And when he does, who is he? He's a cop or a social worker or a college kid trying to deal dope. Whoever he is, he doesn't mean any good to the people who live there. They'd be completely justified in doing a number on my head first, and asking questions later.

"It's the reverse fruits of racism. It's perfectly reasonable for me to be afraid."

But the short answer is:

No.

• • •

Forty feet long, and weighing four tons, the skelp slab rumbled by on rollers, beneath our feet. Late on this warm summer afternoon, this orange-hot hunk of metal, being shaped and formed by huge blocks and cylinders at the Fairless Works of U.S. Steel on the Delaware River in Pennsylvania, was on its way to becoming continuous-weld pipe, as small as half an inch in diameter. It would wind up as plumbing in someone's house. A humble end result for this industrial colossus covering two thousand acres and employing seventeen thousand people.

Earlier in the day, Dave Hankins and Jack Thompson had started trying to educate an ignorant reporter on the basics of making steel. They were good teachers. They still held their subject in awe, and rightly so. At the coke ovens, these mighty barns full of roaring hot coal being purified, they pointed out what they called "Fairless rain." The coke is so hot that when it is quenched in a valley of water, a cloud of steam erupts; as it cools, several thousand yards downwind, it turns into droplets on a car windshield. It creates small ponds. The guides say they're clean. They are, in fact, being enjoyed by a host of wild water birds. A woman stands by the business end of the coke oven. At least, Hankins says it's a woman. There was enough roll to the hips of the worker's walk to make his statement plausible. But with the worker's helmet, face mask, heavy heat-resistant jacket and pants, and Li'l Abner steel-lined safety boots, it's an open question. Streams of yellow sulfur escape before the refractory bricks expand to seal the coke oven doors tight.

At the blast furnace, where manmade winds of four-hundred miles an hour hold the ore, coke, and limestone being worked in midair, in defiance of gravity, flaming red molten iron pours out of the bottom constantly, like milk from a jug.

The soul of the primitive open-hearth steel-making furnace can be viewed only through dark green smoked glass, Hankins and Thompson say, as they hand over a rectangle of it. It's like looking into the sun. You'll sear your eyes from a hundred feet away if you glance at it directly. As overhead cranes maneuver giant hooks the size of battleship anchors, which hold the ladles carrying hundreds of tons of the molten stuff of the core of the earth, they give a machine operator a hand signal, and the doors swing, and there, an eerie green, through the looking glass, are flames so intense that there should be another word for them. If Dante could have only seen this . . .

Much farther down the line is the forty-inch mill part of the roll shop, where the aforementioned skelp slab is being elongated like an angular squeeze of toothpaste. Inside a steel mill, one sees remarkably few humans. In fact, from the catwalk over the unearthly large rollers and binders, we could see only one. He stood with a sledgehammer, on the business end of which were raised numerals. As the slabs came by him, cooled to gray but still soft enough to take an impression, he tensed and wanged them a resounding blow. And they were thus branded with a code that would later tell a metallurgical engineer the precise characteristics of this piece of steel. Late sunlight streamed through the open sides of this structure, which, if one called it a hangar, wouldn't convey how big it really is. A steel mill is actually a very beautiful place, in its own way. Even the pale red plumes of particulate matter coming out of the stacks, having managed to escape the environment-mandated scrubbers, are a lovely color against the blue sky. The shadows and lines are cubist. The workers are all hidden inside air-conditioned control blocks sprinkled along the lines.

"Jesus, it's hot!" exclaims the reporter, with sweat pouring off his safety helmet, into his goggled eyes, his torso dripping inside the heavy green safety jacket, as he stands a few dozen feet above the radiating 2100 degree Fahrenheit slab.

Jack Thompson, who has worked for U.S. Steel for twenty-seven years, twenty-two of them as a roll grinder, turns to the piece of steel and smiles. He throws back his head, eyes half-closed, spreads his arms, as if basking in a tropical sun, and stands there on the catwalk, in cruciform pose.

"I love this heat," he says. "I love it. It's where my paycheck comes from."

ABERRATIONS

On FORTY-FIFTH STREET in Manhattan, there is a transvestite disco called G. G. Barnum's.

For ten bucks, its patrons get two unwatered drinks, the opportunity to exercise as many kinks as they can conjure up, and — unusual even by the standards of midtown — an air show.

The ceiling above the dance floor is perhaps thirty feet high. Just over the heads of the paying customers, cargo netting has been strung from wall to wall. Above the cargo netting are trapezes. Also, shiny chrome vertical and horizontal bars. And gymnast's rings.

Performing, on this equipment high above the dancers, are half a dozen people of indeterminate sex, wearing perhaps more costume than would be expected, considering the diversity of entertainment available in this part of New York. But the clothing does what nakedness could not: it offers a multitude of possibilities for the imagination to consider. The outfits are made of black leather. And studs.

To the thunderous dance beat, the paid talent contorts vigorously, and not without a certain amount of premeditation. Actually, it's rather startling. Olympic competitors may never know just how many athletic postures can be achieved with the help of trapezes, rings, bars, cargo netting, and the consent of two or more adults.

In fact, the evening I conducted my research, the boredom was relieved when I was nearly decapitated by a flying G-string. What happened is that a trapeze broke on its upward arc, catapulting its occupant into the balcony where I was taking notes. The landing was pinpoint — right into the glass of Scotch belonging to the black gentleman at the next table. It scattered shattered glass, Scotch, and black man in all directions as the gold-lamé-clad far below danced on. Never missing a beat. Or even looking up. This place is so cool that management even refused to buy the patron a fresh drink.

Outside this dance hall, with its décor of torn linoleum, scarred paint, and much-kicked stackable plastic furniture, in what passes for the quiet of the city's streets, stalk the joint's own police force. They're in uniform, and they carry guns.

It's too hard, at three in the morning, to figure out all the possible reasons why these folk feel the need to carry pistols on their hips. There are, for example, too many possible combinations of people who might have to be separated forcibly. There are the people inside versus the people inside. Or inside versus outside. Or outside versus outside.

On the marquee are displayed a collection of quotes from various awed journalists who have visited Barnum's. One of them addresses this point:

The most bizarre thing is the absolutely unique mix of customers — every conceivable stratum of class, ethnic and religious origin, age and even gender. The sheer diversity is overwhelming.

I, for one, was most overwhelmed by the look on the face of the most surprised black man in New York City when the trapeze artist landed in his drink. But I understand what the reporter was trying to say. The range of exotica, like the air show, was three-dimensional, revolving from three-piece suits to cowboy shirts to very little to Carol Channing look-alikes.

I'm here to tell you that it's not like this in Oklahoma City, ever. In Oklahoma City, it's almost impossible to get barbecue after 9:00 P.M., and that's a fact.

I mention the above by way of conceding that there exist some exceptions to North America's rules. Not only are there places that refuse to act in ways their location and resources would predict. But their behavior is viewed as being in the weird-to-incomprehensible range by the standards of the rest of this diverse continent. When viewed from the perspective of Nine Nations, they can only be described as aberrations.

New York City is clearly one of these aberrations.

The fact that there are such places as New York City that just don't fit, however, is not the fault of the Nine Nations. It merely explains why some key parts of the continent are screwed up. Schizophrenic.

Take Washington, D.C., for example.

For almost two centuries, Washington was content to accept a fate dictated to it by circumstances. Less was it a nexus of any great import than it was a sleepy border town between the Foundry and Dixie, inauspiciously located in a semidrained swamp. John Kennedy said it best: Washington had all the charm of a northern city, and all the efficiency of a southern one.

Earlier in this century, pre-air-conditioning, the Congress evacuated the fetid city during the summer, and sometimes didn't bother to return until after the November election, if then, and the affairs of the Republic rumbled on. This was back in the days when United States citizens demonstrated that they cared who was president by voting in percentages so large as to be unthinkable today.

Admittedly, those were not the most democratic of times. Racism was institutionalized in the South, eastern industrialists could manipulate their work forces as they pleased, farmers were at the mercy of their banks, and the West was held hostage by railroad interests. It was in this context that men of good will came to the conclusion that only the conjuring of a powerful federal presence could offset these evils.

So rose the current welfare state, with its mighty regulatory tentacles. Its goals were undeniably worthy — uplifting the poor, protecting the environment, shoring up the cities. Unfortunately, it had a founding flaw: it didn't have much faith in democracy, either. Despite rhetoric to the contrary, it assumed that the citizenry was too stupid or too greedy to manage its own affairs satisfactorily, and thus had to be protected from itself.

Although this assumption is by no means insupportable, it has led, inexorably, to fundamental contradictions. A former Agriculture Department official has described the federal role today as "usually that of a martinet teacher toward a dimwitted pupil. It is executed in the most narrow, nanny-like and suspicious manner possible. In fact, with some programs, such as those of the Department of Health and Human Services, the rules are generally so strict and the surveillance so intense that you wonder why HHS doesn't just do the job itself."

It's beyond the scope of this book to detail why the idea that gathering continental power in one place, where it could be wielded by the educated and the enlightened, was once considered reasonable, possible, and in the best interests of the majority.

But that it has gone awry is undeniable. Washington today is an imperial capital. Its interests and those of the people whom it is supposed to be of, by, and for are commonly divergent. Only the residents of Washington, reaping the benefits of being at the center of the Imperium, fail to view this as bizarre.

Washington revels, for example, in the fact that the bigger the problems in the rest of the continent, the greater its growth.

During the war on the Depression, the population of the Washington area grew by three hundred thousand. During the war on the Axis, another half-million were added, doubling the population of the city itself. Even greater growth was seen during the periodic recessions of the Eisenhower years. But the truly astonishing jump was during the most turbulent decade in recent history — the sixties. With both the doctrine of the "best and the brightest" and the air-conditioning revolution in full flower, eight hundred thousand new inhabitants flocked to Washington.

Growth during the seventies was a "mere" 12 percent, the metropolitan population leveling off at just under three million. But that was the decade that saw Washington truly become a metropolis of the wealthy. That was the decade in which suburban Fairfax County and Arlington County, adjacent to the District of Columbia, began to rank among the richest, per household, in North America.

This came as a direct result of Washington's affairs becoming increasingly incomprehensible.

It's not the paychecks of the bureaucrats that caused Washington real estate prices to double in five years. While hardly what you'd call niggardly, they don't pay for the great castles on Foxhall Road.

It's the subsidiary private industries spawned by the existence of the bureaucrats that have made the *average* home worth $100,-000 in the District, at a time when $35,000 buys a fine house in Kansas, and $70,000 buys a palace in Indiana.

The three biggest industries in the Washington area, after government and tourism, are the government code-breakers: lawyers, communicators, and consultants. Depending on how you define consultant, that industry may actually be bigger than the federal government which spawned it.

The purposes of the lawyers are straightforward. They are supposed to understand, manipulate, and beat the purposes of the government. When they focus on the welfare of one particular client or economic interest group, they're called lobbyists, and, according to an executive research firm, each typically earns over $50,000 a year. Contrary to popular belief, they rarely resort to plying congressmen with bimbos and booze. Their most potent tool is information. On Capitol Hill, it's a truism that the biggest single problem faced, day to day, is figuring out exactly what the nature of a problem is, and then figuring out what the results of a proposed plan of action would be.

A successful industry lobbyist is capable of bringing far greater resources to bear on the researching of a narrow question than can the beleaguered staff of any one congressman or committee. An oil lobbyist, for example, has access to invaluable proprietary corporate information that the Congress does not. In the case of the impenetrably technical tax code, a well-argued case for the addition or deletion of a few words, slipped to a sympathetic legislator, can save a company millions of dollars.

Consultants, meanwhile, don't like to be called consultants, because it's become pejorative. "We never refer to ourselves as consultants. Never," Earle C. Williams, president of BDM, a major Washington federal contractor supplying technical expertise, research, and development, was quoted as saying. The preferred term is "professional services firm." The common term in Washington is "Beltway bandit," after the circulatory highway on which their shiny new office buildings are constructed. Due to politically popular lids on the hiring of more bureaucrats, they are contracted to perform government studies, write government pamphlets, translate government documents, hold government hearings, develop government specifications, and, critics say, make government decisions.

They cluster around their clients — life-sciences consultants, for example, locating near the Food and Drug Administration and the National Institutes of Health. And they analyze, experiment, test, design, research, and otherwise manipulate information in areas including defense, energy, communications, transportation, environment, and public policy.

In fiscal 1979, the Department of Defense handed $24 million to the aforementioned obscure BDM for its services. If the role of the consultant is unknown to most North Americans, it's because, as the vice-president of one such company candidly pointed out, "in this business, anonymity is an asset." If you don't know it exists, you can't cut its budget. Meanwhile, in the 1970s, government hiring remained stable while the federal budget increased $350 billion.

Finally, there is communications. The very first thing done by any medium-sized newspaper newly determined to prove its worth to its readers — in yet another noble attempt to figure out what's really going on — is to open a Washington bureau. The same can be said of any number of foreign news organizations. The size of some of these bureaus can be astonishing — larger than the entire staff of many dailies. And not without good reason. There are always more reaches of the Imperium than there are reporters. The *Washington Post* is the largest private employer in the District, and it routinely amazes itself by missing important stories.

Commercial television and radio are similarly garrisoned. Public broadcasting, of course, is headquartered in Washington. The Government Printing Office itself is the largest publisher on the continent, and somebody has to write all the stuff it prints.

In addition, the city is loaded with highly specialized newsletters — some of them dailies — providing tiny audiences in industries like banking with "inside" information, charging up to $1000 a year for the privilege. Most North Americans have never heard of one of the most influential and imaginative magazines commenting on politics and policy in Washington — *The National Journal.* A subscription runs almost $400 a year.

Sports Illustrated has suggested that news organizations are to Washington what organized sports teams are to the residents of other cities, and that's a defensible position. In how many other places do you ordinarily find self-described "media junkies" — not in the profession themselves — who readily and with sophistication discuss the styles and careers of reporters they've never met. Elsewhere, such effort is lavished on quarterbacks.

Each of these industries pays very well by the standards of any other city's major industries. That they should all be grouped in one place explains certain Washington truisms that have become casually accepted.

The Washingtonian magazine categorizes as "moderately priced" any restaurant you can get out of for under fifty bucks per couple.

Washington's hotel growth is tilted toward the self-described "luxury" range, the cheapest room pushing $100 a night.

The hottest race in retail trade is among outlets catering to the superdiscriminating, such as Neiman-Marcus, Bloomingdale's, and I. Magnin's.

The *New York Times* culture pages periodically ask, in bold headlines, CAN WASHINGTON LURE THE ARTS FROM NEW YORK?

The local papers routinely celebrate the city's uncommon appetites — for Japanese raw fish, or cocaine, or adults roller-skating from one *boîte* to another.

Washington supports twice as many psychiatrists, per head, as any other North American city.

Don't get me wrong. It's a good life. Cosmopolitan trappings serve London and Paris well, too.

Washington's *aberration* is in its categorical refusal to recognize itself as an aberration.

"He realized, after two and a half years here, how isolated he'd become," one of Jimmy Carter's advisers told the *New York Times* of his boss. The occasion was an interview shortly after the then-president had announced to the world that "Washington, D.C., had become an island," unresponsive to the nation's needs — a characterization that, predictably, left Washington steaming.

"He had become an islander," continued the adviser, thoughtfully munching his breakfast at McDonald's on his way to work. "He had fallen prey to the same things he had talked about when he was running for president." Himself paying close attention to the details of Washington ritual, the adviser granted the interview only on an anonymous, "background" basis, apparently fearful of the explosive nature of his insights. Carter felt "in a mystical way," he said, that Washington "is out of tune with America.

"People here don't live the way the rest of the country does. Here, people are all relatively rich, and more or less equal. Leaving aside the black poor of the city, this town has the highest per capita income of any city in the country. And yet it's not a few billionaires that account for it. The money is spread more evenly. What kind of twisted idea does that give you about what the rest of the country is like?"

Apparently, the idea it gives you is not Copernican. There is simply no convincing Washington that the universe does not, in fact, revolve around it. Heretics who suggest otherwise are not even regarded as amusing, much less worthy of being burned at the stake. They're just quaintly uninformed.

This tallies with the suggestion that Washington's foremost pursuit is "rat calculus." The observation is that Washington has become such a parody of its own institutions that the techniques of running through its self-created maze have become far more important and interesting than asking whether the maze does any good. Broad, unquantifiable speculations as to whether the lot of the citizenry is being enhanced by certain actions, in this context, are considered at best naïve. Even relatively straightforward considerations, like whether there'll be enough heating oil in New England to last the winter, are instantly subsumed by calculations professionally carried out to thousandths of a point as to the question's impact on the president's chances in the New Hampshire primary.

But actually, a calm, distant examination of this situation can demonstrate that there's a bright side to it all.

Serious and learned have been the lamentations that Washington is beset by paralysis. The president can't get a damn thing through Congress. Congressmen are quitting because of the inhuman strain put on them by constituents' demands. Agencies point with alarm to the way their initiatives are gutted by special interests. Citizens grasp at panaceas devoted to getting Washington to "work right." Constitutional amendments are offered to balance the budget, limit the terms of politicians, and — my favorite — to move the capital entirely to some presumably less polluted location, like Fargo, North Dakota.

The flaw with these proposals is that they are meant to render the federal government more efficient. Few seem to recognize the ominous implications of an efficient federal government. If the population rebels at the thought of the power the anonymous feds wield now, think of the horrors that could be perpetrated if the Imperium ever ran lean and mean. The last time Washington "worked," in the sense of its various appendages pulling in more or less the same direction, the United States ended up with half a million troops in Vietnam.

As a matter of fact, it can be argued that Washington's dilemmas and alarums are demonstrations of a smoothly functioning, generally benign, if unorthodox system — another proof of the political ingenuity of North America. Aware voters and perceptive private enterprise have sent high-quality representatives to Washington to ensure that power can be exercised there only in the negative. Nobody can get anything accomplished. Success is measured in terms of what horror has been *blocked*.

This has created a vacuum into which local government has stepped. Many state governments are now running a budget surplus. Legislative initiatives are coming almost solely out of local government. "Sunshine" laws, which force public decisions to be made in public, were first enacted by state legislatures. So were "sunset" laws, which require that a law be rendered automatically defunct after a certain number of years unless it is actively renewed. Even currently hot topics in the Imperium, like budget-cutting, never would have penetrated Washington were it not for local initiatives, such as California's Proposition 13.

There's a lot to be said for this federal paralysis. A reasonable portion of miscreants continues to tread that much more lightly for fear of being bankrupted by a mindlessly interminable battle with Environmental Protection, Occupational Safety and Health, or Securities and Exchange. The truly innovative, meanwhile, are freed to direct their energies to local problems and solutions.

Granted, this benefit is at the formidable expense of feeding the coffers and power fantasies of the Imperium. But a close examination of the virtues of government deadlock, and the grouping of the most aggressive lawyers, lobbyists, journalists, and other practitioners of rat calculus in one geographic location, where they can do only limited harm, and then mainly to each other, offers a most consoling thought.

We've ground the bastards to a halt. If government that governs least governs best, the United States seems to have triumphed in crafting the best government money can buy.

• • •

Alaskans — whose judgments about anything must be measured against their decision to live in a place where tomatoes won't — think that theirs is a separate nation.

They go to elaborate lengths to burnish this theory.

Practically by the time a newcomer gets from the baggage-claim area at the Anchorage airport to the taxi stand, he's picked up the local habit of referring to the rest of the world as "Outside," as if coming into Alaska were a hitch in Vietnam.

Since Alaskans wallow in their apparatus, and the number of Anglos living in Alaska who were actually born there is virtually nil, one keen-eyed administrative assistant in Juneau has considered marketing an immigrant's kit. No banker wants to look like anything except a bush pilot, so the kit would include the requisite twelve-pound insulated boots for the walk from the office to lunch. Bumper stickers proclaiming the local theologies — such as WE DON'T GIVE A DAMN HOW THEY DO IT OUTSIDE — would be part

of the package. As would the small-bore cannon with the elaborate telescopic sights, suitable for bringing down grizzly bears,
avalanches, small aircraft, whatever. That's something for the
Fairbanks lawyer to carry into the supermarket when he picks up
a quart of milk.

Nonchalance in the face of exotic circumstances is worshiped.
In Alaska, the ultimate expression of professional detachment is
displayed by what you attempt to carry on board a regularly
scheduled commercial jet as under-the-seat baggage. A white-
eyed, inscrutable, Asiatic dog used to be good. But not since every
Eskimo with half a brain recognized that snow machines work a
lot better than a sled team. Mining equipment still humming and
beeping remains solid. But I liked the short, squat Native patiently standing in line, eyes down, for a Wien Air Alaska flight
out of Anchorage with a substantial Evinrude outboard motor
digging into his shoulder.

Yet none of this commends Alaska as a nation. If it were one, it
would not stand as — hands down — the most conflicted and confused place in North America. Alaska is this continent's most en-
dearing aberration.

The only really predictable thing about Alaskans is that they
will disagree about anything — politics, religion, economics, history, sex . . . They can't even agree on what constitutes "good"
weather.

We're so polarized up here [said Alaska governor Jay Hammond], that
one end of the spectrum has got half the people saying that we should
secede from the Union, and anything less than that is an unacceptable
capitulation sell-out to the federal government.

The other end of the spectrum is insisting that Anchorage be returned
to wilderness, or it's unacceptable environmental degradation. Really,
there's no middle ground.

It really is astounding why anybody is ever elected, to say nothing of
being re-elected, under those circumstances. Everybody ends up shouting
in high decibels. Frankly, I wouldn't vote for anybody, including Hammond, if I believed half of what I heard and read. It's just terrible. I
wonder how anybody survives it.

In Alaska, uncommon political alliances are commonplace. The
far right is so far right that it has been known to link up with the
left on some issues (although for completely antithetical reasons).
Private possession of marijuana, for example, is legal. Conserva-
tives allowed as how the hippies ought to have the complete right

to poison their bodies as long as they didn't ask the taxpayers to pay for the consequences. (The only two Libertarian Party members in North America elected to state office live in Alaska.) Similarly, the titular left has been known to side with the right-wingers when it comes to property ownership. Homesteaders wanting the opportunity to settle a piece of land have sided with the oil companies — against environmentalists — on the issue of opening up federally owned wilderness.

But apart from that, Hammond is right in pinpointing the decibel level of all arguments as the most identifiable Alaskan trait. It's all the way up. Every time. The moral and emotional energy expended on any controversy is pause-giving.

The reason is simple. Alaska is the land over which three nations are warring, and it's entirely too soon to know which, if any, is winning. The three nations are the Empty Quarter, Ecotopia, and that of the Trans-Polar Innuit (about which more shortly).

Most of Alaska, in terms of physical geography, is part of the Empty Quarter. Picture Alaska as a man's face, looking left. Subtract the throat, from just south of Anchorage to the capital, Juneau. That's the relatively temperate area, where it rarely gets much above 70 or colder than 5 below. The rest has a continental inland climate, like Wyoming, only worse. (In Fairbanks, the temperature range is from 90 above to 40 below.) It is also desperate for water.

You may have a mental image of Alaska as lush and green when it isn't covered with snow, but that's misleading. The hundreds of thousands of lakes manifest in the summer of the far north are the result of only four inches of moisture a year — less than that in the Sahara. They collect because the earth, from eighteen inches below the surface to a depth of about two thousand feet, is permanently frozen, so the water does not percolate. Similarly, because at the very top of Alaska it is never really warm — not even in August, as I can personally testify — evaporation is impeded.

So you end up with enough water to sustain caribou and small bands of Natives, but when man decides to do something exotic like build a large Native village (Barrow — population, twenty-five hundred) or a large Texas village (the oil camp at Prudhoe Bay — population, two thousand) on the shores of the Arctic Ocean, the first thing he runs into is water problems.

All over Alaska, of course, there is mineral wealth of such magnitude that it brings tears to the eyes of geologists. From gold to molybdenum to petroleum — it's all there.

To make the Empty Quarter credentials perfect, the land is rugged, vast, and short on people. The question of scale is a constantly disturbing one in Alaska. Observing a simple operation like widening a two-lane road to four lanes, a visitor, aswim in the cavern of a full-sized American sedan, is dwarfed by the Caterpillar construction equipment far more appropriate to mining than to road work. The wheels are taller than the car. The cab is the equivalent of an attic on a two-story house. Yet these trucks seem pitifully inadequate to the job of moving all the rubble being blown off the side of the mountain for the right of way. At the same time, the scar man is making on the mountain with his dynamite is a mere scratch on these structures, which offer scale to the clouds. Both photographically and metaphorically, it's tough to pick your lens in Alaska. A wide-angle, which gets it all in while losing detail? Or a telephoto, which dwells lovingly on the particular without offering a sense of how untouchable it all seems?

In Alaska, it's easy to succumb to the urge to make a mark on the land, just to prove that you exist. Otherwise ordinary young people own a ten-wheel flatbed truck. Or a crane. Or a wide-blade bulldozer. You never know when they may come in handy. It makes you wonder what the frontier West would look like today if the pioneers over a hundred years ago had had Cats instead of Conestoga wagons.

It's exactly this thought around which the argument over Alaska's future gains volume. All sides view Alaska as perhaps the last place left in North America where fresh opportunity is available — where the mistakes of the twentieth century can be forgotten. It's what constitutes a "mistake" around which the controversy swirls, for everyone here is trying to invent his or her own Alaska.

Due largely to the most expensive and concentrated political effort continental environmentalists have ever brought to bear, less than 1 percent of Alaska's land is in private hands. Some belongs to the state of Alaska, and a great deal is assigned to the Native tribes, but the bulk is operated by the notorious federal government, which has banned hunting, homesteading, mining, logging, drilling, and even motorized travel in blocks so huge that envious Alaskans charge that the bureaucrats *couldn't* have realized, by looking at a map, the size of the areas they were talking about.

To some who see Alaska as a last opportunity to practice self-reliance, escaping the mistakes and madnesses of civilization —

the crowding, the powerlessness, and especially the slavery to a nine-to-five paycheck — this is a dream-crusher. Visions of being part of a special breed, which measures human worth against a harsh but essentially rational nature, evaporate in a real estate market where, in the midst of unthinkable emptiness, a five-acre homestead five hours south of Anchorage can cost as much as it does in the Blue Ridge Mountains, less than two hours west of Washington, D.C.

Advocates of this arrangement say they were blocking a different mistake. They were saving fragile and pristine natural wilderness from depredation, taking advantage of the last chance for North America to protect entire natural habitats from the twentieth century.

They claim that the rights of Alaskans must yield to the rights of future "Outsiders" to the "unspoiled." They don't get too worked up about the plight of the inhabitants, saying that the majority of Anglo Alaskans are essentially transients, anyway. Not only were they not born there; they will not die there.

The average age in Alaska is the lowest on the continent until you get to Mexico. The adventurers it attracts are young; the environment is too harsh for the old. Few Alaskans retire there — they head to warmer climes after one too many winters has seeped into their bones. (For that matter, there is a brisk traffic in air tickets to Hawaii among even the young and hardy.)

This argument points, with justification, to the mess that most Alaskans make of any habitat they touch. Even John McPhee, in his sympathetic, astute, and best-selling study of Alaska, *Coming Into the Country*, points out that the authentic Alaskan landmark is a dump. Rare is the Alaskan home outside which is not a pile of weather-ravaged junk, saved because "it might come in handy."

The view from the ocean side of the Top of the World Motel in Barrow, three hundred miles north of the Arctic Circle, is of the town's pile of derelict hardware.

The locals don't apologize for that. The ground is frozen, so the stuff is impossible to bury. And because of artificial freight tariffs, it's far more expensive to haul out the junk than the value of the scrap would return. If any extra funds are available, they say, they will be spent on schools and sewage systems before they're spent on trash removal.

In fact, the only really tidy settlements to be found in all Alaska are in the oil fields of the North Slope. Sohio, British Petroleum, and Arco are the only enterprises wealthy enough to cart their detritus out. During the few weeks when the Arctic Ocean ice floes recede from the shore, oceangoing vessels rush in gear far too bulky or heavy to fit into even the ubiquitous air freighter. On the return trip — and at the same extraordinary freight rates — machines ruined by their exposure to the elements are hauled out.

Of course, Sohio, BP and Arco are also the only enterprises that have to cope with the never-ending — and justified — surveillance and suspicion devoted to oil companies. They are so conscious of their image that they hire a few dozen teen-agers in the summer to pick pieces of paper off the tundra, to the amazement of the Eskimos. The Natives never cease to be astonished by some of the tribal rituals of the white man.

It's a fact that the most eloquent distillation — or parody — of television-standard North American culture you'll ever want to see are those Sohio–BP and Arco installations at Deadhorse, near Prudhoe Bay.

It's not just the existence of toasty swimming pools this far north. Nor the carefully sealed-off world of saunas and the jogging tracks and the basketball gym and the volleyball court and the universal exercise machines and the first-run movies amid the caribou.

It's not the videotapes for the eighty-five-inch-screen television sets. Nor the T-bone steaks cooked exactly medium rare and the three fresh vegetables and six fresh desserts — free to all comers, and seconds encouraged. Nor is it the garden at the Sohio–BP installation, in a two-story tall atrium, in which flowers are carefully tended thousands of miles north of their natural habitat.

It's not just the people who joke about how much easier it will be when they're asked to drill for oil on the far side of the moon. There'll be no wind there, they point out, and no ice and no environmentalists. Transportation in and out couldn't conceivably be much more difficult.

And it's not even the creepie-crawly moon machines that they use right now to move — intact — entire apartment buildings, prefabbed in California, into place. Similar gigantic tracked vehicles are used in Florida to shlep Saturn V rockets slowly around.

Nor is it that these apartment units are placed high above a man's head, on pods locked into the ice of the permafrost, and that they look a great deal like the set for a science-fiction movie.

These buildings look perfectly capable of flying. (After all, how *else* did they get way the hell up here?)

It's not even the RCA communications dish that completes this all-time macho technological fantasy. Designed to make telephone calls to your girl friend in Texas a routine matter, this dish antenna is so far north that in order for it to link up with a satellite hovering over the equator, it must be aimed almost flat at the horizon, its beam barely clearing the mountains, skewing your sense of which direction is "up."

The statement this all makes is really one reflective of an entire Anglo world view. The assumption it makes is that no right-thinking, sane human would do it any other way. *How else would you live?*

The Natives, of course, have considered this question closely for several thousand years. And have come up with spectacularly different conclusions.

The Natives of the North — ranging from the Innuit (which is what most Alaskan Eskimos call themselves and other Eskimos; it's their word for "people") to the Anathapsa to the Métis to the Cree — offer a vivid reminder that Sohio's is only one vision of humanity. The world does not end at the limits of *The Rand McNally Road Atlas*. There are tens of thousands of people up here, beyond the white man's highways. And, as Willie Hensley says, "the Eskimo's foremost character trait is the ability to survive."

Willie Hensley's thoughts on the subject are not to be ignored. *Time* magazine may have got it right, for once, when it declared this Innuit, in one of its typical presumptions, one of America's fifty leaders for tomorrow, or some such designation. He is a leader of NANA, the Northwest Alaska Native Association, one of the most successful Native corporations. These corporations were established in the early seventies to help clear the claim the Natives had to the state's oil wealth. That settlement, ultimately backed by the oil companies because without it they couldn't build the Alaska oil pipeline, also ceded great tracts of land to the Natives, and a lot of money. Hensley, from remote Kotzebue, is young, George Washington University–educated, smashing in his Pierre Cardin suits, and the chairman of an $80 million Native-owned bank.

I hope he's right about the Innuit surviving. The twentieth century has certainly screwed up a lot of Indians, as reflected in the question of a Fairbanks Anglo who amiably asked me if I wanted to go down to Second Avenue "to watch the subsistence hunters swing on the parking meters." There are a lot of burned-out, drunk Natives on Fourth Avenue in Anchorage, too, and in most villages, sad to report.

But I like the Innuit, if for no other reason than that I find enormously appealing the Trans-Polar Innuit Conference, one of the more clever regional political consolidations around.

The Trans-Polar Innuit Conference was designed to unite all the people at the top of the world who share the Native language, culture, and problems (that is, the white man in general and the energy companies in particular). Those people aren't just Alaskans. They live in Canada, Greenland, and even the Soviet Union, and their ancestors were there millennia before these national distinctions were established. In fact, the Trans-Polar Conference could easily be the tenth nation of North America if it did not include so much of Europe and Asia.

But it does, and I have to cut off this regionalization process somewhere, and here is where I so choose. I simply am not going to get involved in explaining how the Greenland Innuit used this Trans-Polar Conference politically to block Danes who wanted to trap them into entanglements with the European Common Market that were not in their interest.

But nonetheless, the conference exists, and it is centered in Barrow, the largest Eskimo village on earth and the capital of the North Slope Borough, whose fifty-five hundred Natives occupy eighty-seven thousand square miles of territory (just a tad smaller than West Germany), most of it just lousy with oil. Its mayor, until his recent death, was Eben Hopson. Hopson delighted in driving white men crazy.

Undoubtedly, the late mayor's associates would object to that assessment. Their position is that establishing a historic preservation district in the middle of what the casual observer might characterize as godforsaken tundra merely shows reverence for their traditions. They would maintain that their act is no less sacred to them than preserving the Alamo is to those damn goat-roper Texan oilmen.

They would further maintain that the fact that the rezoning would block the construction of those Texans' multibillion-dollar gas pipeline was the sheerest unfortunate coincidence.

They would say that they were surprised and grateful that the pipeline company began paying a great deal more attention to their opinions about how many Eskimos should be employed in the construction after this brush-up. They would certainly deny that it was anything other than coincidence that they dropped the rezoning idea shortly after they and the energy company began to see eye to eye. They might even try to deny that had the pipeline company not capitulated, the borough would have taken them all the way to the Supreme Court, after hiring the best lawyers money could buy, and after raising the property taxes at the Prudhoe Bay oil bases to pay for them.

Whatever the real story, the North Slope Innuit have an unassailable point, which for once has stood the test in the white man's courts: they were here first. It's murky, exactly what rights that now gives them. And it's unkind to suggest that they have exploited that murkiness for all it's worth, promulgating laws and taxes first and asking questions later.

Be that as it may, Barrow is a fascinating laboratory. While nothing like the typical tiny Native village, it still contains many who consider it obvious that walruses have spirits that must be treated with respect, and who continue to hunt the whale for meat. All have been shaped by the experience of seeing uncountable clouds of waterfowl fly over the spit on which they have pitched a summer camp. It's in Barrow that unusual accommodations with the twentieth century are being formed.

Barrow, like much of Alaska disturbed by humans, is covered in the summer with a fine talc dust. It's blown up from the glacial gravel that, in this town, makes up the streets, the sidewalks, the yards, the parking lots, the runways, and the Arctic Ocean beach.

There are two kinds of buildings: those that, in the words of Governor Hammond, point up the relative affluence of Appalachia, and those the borough built. The latter look more grand the longer you think how hard it was to scrape together the scraps to build the former, given how close to the Pole you are.

There are a lot of white men around, considering that this is an Eskimo capital. A lot of them hold jobs of high responsibility in the borough government, which infuriates some of the younger Innuit. The whites respond by referring to the young Turks as the "Red Guard."

The Red Guard is fundamentally in opposition to the U.S. Army National Guard, which, believe it or not, is the white institution that acculturated many of the older Innuit who are now in power. Eben Hopson held rank in the National Guard. He, like many in the village, traced a portion of his ancestry to European whalers who used Point Barrow as a port in the late nineteenth century.

The Anglos working for the village, though slightly embarrassed that there are not more Natives in middle management, would have you believe that different cultures operate in different modes. White culture, they claim, thinks that making beds and cleaning rooms is a bad job, and so pays what the Eskimos consider a lot of money to have the Natives do it. Eskimos think that being chief of police is a bad job, so they pay whites a lot of money to do that.

Young Eskimos say that that's a crock, and that it reflects racism on the part of older Eskimos who don't think their people can do the job.

The older Eskimos, who over the course of the last few years have figured out that they don't have to pay an undue amount of attention to what the younger Eskimos think (times may have changed, but not *that* much), end the discussion with the observation that any chief of police native to Barrow, one time out of three, would be put in the position of arresting somebody to whom he was related, which would be culturally inconceivable.

But that doesn't mean there isn't a lot of on-the-job-training (OJT) for Eskimos in Barrow. The "Beluga building" is referred to by one sympathetic white as "another of our $80,000 OJT mistakes." The Beluga building is an enormous inflatable dome, so named because it resembles the white whale of that species. It was erected without a floor, because who needs a floor on frozen ground. Unfortunately, when heated, the balloon building melted the permafrost underneath it, and the vehicles meant to be garaged inside sank irretrievably into the muck.

Similarly, there's the high school at Anaktuvuk Pass that ended up costing $7 million. Serving no more than some handfuls of students, it is one of the few educational facilities in the world that included as part of its construction budget the creation of a full-length jet airstrip. Every nail of that building was flown in on a C-130 Hercules. It's so remote, said one of its planners, "that we almost had to fly in the water for the swimming pool."

Expensive?

"We spend fourteen thousand, seven hundred, and eleven dollars a year per pupil on *operating* costs," I was told. "That *doesn't* include construction costs.

"For that kind of dough we could give these kids first-rate educations any place they wanted Outside and still fly them home for duck, whaling, and caribou season."

This last was a very impolitic remark. One of the reasons the Innuit no longer fly the children out is that, several years ago, an entire generation was lost when the plane they were riding to their schools Outside piled into the Brooks Range.

But the remark is also a Prudhoe Bay way of looking at things. Prudhoe Bay, culturally, is incapable of operating without T-bone steaks and eighty-five-inch television screens. The money it spends on making its people feel at home is orders of magnitude more than what the Innuit spend.

Yet Prudhoe would no more question the wisdom of shipping entertainment — or, for that matter, fresh broccoli — from Southern California to the Arctic Circle than it would question the wisdom of endangering a few marine mammals that some Innuit still believe are sacred.

It's a study in the contrast of cultures to realize that the oil companies are boggled by the idea that these Innuit are interested in very expensive systems to ensure running water, sewage disposal, central heating, electric power, and modern schools — while continuing to live in the Arctic. They hold the Innuit up to ridicule for their ideas. But the Innuit persevere. Ninety-eight percent of the money raised to pay for these new conveniences comes from the oil companies anyway, as property taxes to the North Slope Borough. For that, Arco is entitled to its opinions.

It's the poor, embattled Ecotopians of Alaska whom the Innuit really drive up the wall. The apparent irreverence with which Natives are capable of indiscriminately blowing away the wildlife with the latest in twentieth-century firepower doesn't square at all with the Anglos' intellectualization of the Plains Indian concept of "walking lightly on the land."

Ecotopians are appalled by the idea of a gut-over-the-belt desk jockey in Anchorage whose tour of duty isn't really complete until he's "killed one of everything." On that, they have an internal consensus.

But they go into paroxysms when, after all they've gone through to get the International Whaling Commission to stop the Japanese from spearing the endangered bowhead whale, some university-educated, reasonably well-off Eskimo announces that he has to go "subsistence" hunting for that very species.

The Innuit respond by trotting out Jon Buchholdt, their Anglo mouthpiece.

All the villages in the Arctic [he explains with great force], are strategically placed to go out after the walrus or the whale, or whatever. They're there because of the traditional interaction with an animal or two. They will always exist. I don't think we can do anything to put a stop to that.

Questioning this has become offensive to the Eskimos. Kind of like asking somebody in Iran why she has returned to the *chodor* — complex reasons behind that, and probably none of them defensible in your frame of reference. And the social and cultural conflicts are apparent right in the question. It's as though you were going into an agricultural area and trying to get the farmers to leave to build a Levittown. They just don't want to talk about it.

This has to be understood as casting aspersions upon the legitimacy of religion. Subsistence hunting has to be understood as a religious act, insofar as religion or religiosity distinguishes one culture from another. It's sacred. It's bound up and inseparable from all of the other sacred institutions of the [Innuit] society. No other political or social situation can compete at all with the sacredness of what we're talking about. And everything you see around [Barrow] would gladly be given up tomorrow if it had to be traded off for subsistence.

(Long pause.)

"At the risk," I stumbled, "of asking a, a . . ."

"An irreligious question?"

(Laughter.)

"Ah, this works pretty good at nailing the white liberal guilt feelings about Indians right between the eyes, too, doesn't it?"

"Un-huh! Un-huh! The attack upon the subsistence hunting in the Arctic, or its displacement by oil and gas development, has to be seen as a continuity of a rather shameful American tradition of killing Native people."

And you wonder why the debates are so raucous in Alaska. Try to explain the above to the Oriental who's losing his whaling job, or to the Anglo Alaskan for whom hanging a freshly stuffed walrus head on the wall of his den is an extremely serious felony.

While I don't deride the Ecotopian reverence for earth consciousness, I wonder if it's any accident that the stiffest concentration of Ecotopians in Alaska — in Homer — settled in a region that is not only wooded and hilly and water-surrounded and beautiful.

It's completely devoid of Natives.

• • •

It's really not fair for me to characterize Hawaii as a North American aberration.

Hawaii is as much an Asian aberration as it is a North American aberration.

This is not to say that "paradise" is what you'd really want to call screwed up. Although the potential is certainly there. Its development pace is exceeding that of Southern California; most of the high-rise construction that is now choking Waikiki came not only after statehood in 1959, but in the late seventies, after the introduction of jumbo jets that could dump 350 tourists from North America and Japan at a clip. Hawaiian prices are astronomical by North American standards. It's 92 percent dependent on foreign oil for energy. Crime is on the rise, although it still lags well behind the Mainland, especially in terms of violent crime; the *aloha* spirit isn't dead yet. (By the way, CBS notwithstanding, Hawaii Five-O doesn't exist.) It has a restive, and rightfully so, Native population that keeps threatening violence. (The U.S. military, meanwhile, continues to practice its aerial-bombing techniques on islands the locals consider sacred; the U.S. judiciary and Congress flatly refuse to compensate the Polynesians for allegedly stolen land in amounts commensurate to what they pay the Eskimos and Indians.) And the phones have an annoying habit of not working right.

But when it comes to schizophrenia, Hawaii's got it.

Isolated cultures always develop in distinctive, idiosyncratic ways, and Hawaii is as far from any continent as it is possible to be in the northern hemisphere. It's a good twenty-four hundred miles to either the coast of California or Alaska. As the attack on Pearl Harbor demonstrated, it's not that much farther to Japan. Its eight major islands are the beginning of an archipelago that finally peters out in dots of uninhabited rock two thousand miles to the northwest.

But Hawaii's schizophrenia lies in such things as priding itself in its cultural diversity while harboring racial tension. It lies in being utterly dependent on the Mainland for goods while harboring the hope of becoming totally energy independent. It lies in having the wettest spot on the planet, Mount Waialeale, which garners 486 inches of rain a year, while many spots in the islands, surrounded by vast ocean, thirst for freshwater. It lies in being the only state in the West to vote Democratic in the 1976 and 1980 presidential elections. But most of all, it lies in a future in which, as Joni Mitchell sings, you "pave paradise / put up a parking lot."

Hawaii is a place of Ecotopian possibilities, with MexAmerican growth values and limits, run by Asians.

It's an aberration.

The main reason it is not widely perceived that way on the

Mainland is that, as Robert W. Bone put it, "As delightful a destination as are the islands for an upbeat vacation, many Hawaii-philes who return year after year still feel that you *can* get too much of a good thing — that there is an enervating surfeit of surf, sun, sand, and somnolence which is fine for a vacation but not conducive to efficient and productive living on a year-round basis. Some call the disease 'Polynesian Paralysis.'" This affects journalists too. So the word doesn't tend to get out.

Hawaii is the first place in modern North America in which residents of European stock are a distinct minority, both numerically and in terms of political power.

It is thought that before the turn of the century, Anglos may well become a minority in California, outnumbered by Asians, Hispanics, and blacks. (The lack of Anglos is already a pressing concern in the Los Angeles school system. Its busing plans are plagued by there simply not being enough Anglos to go around.)

The ancient Spanish culture of New Mexico may soon be reinforced by enough Old Mexicans to make it a third.

But right now, Hawaii is the first and only place in the United States and Canada where not only are Anglos a distinct minority (as in Québec and Puerto Rico), but where people of Asian descent are in the majority.

Asians and Asian-Americans comprise more than two thirds of the permanent population of Hawaii. Almost all the rest is English-speaking Caucasian, usually called *haoles*, although this has begun to take on a somewhat derogatory overtone. (The number of Hispanics and blacks has risen from negligible to very small, the Hispanic population growing the faster of the two.)

As of this writing, the Hawaiian congressional delegation is studded with names like Inouye, Matsunaga, and Akaka. (The fourth is Cecil Heftel, a Mormon.) The governor's name is Ariyoshi. Senators Daniel K. Inouye and Spark M. Matsunaga fought in the most decorated and wounded American military unit in World War II. It was the Nisei 442d Infantry Regimental Command Team. *Nisei* denotes second-generation Japanese-American in Japanese.

The lieutenant governor, the president of the state senate, the speaker of the house, the president of the University of Hawaii, and most school principals and state judges are also of Japanese descent.

While the haole population is slightly larger than that of the Japanese-Americans — each comprises a little over a quarter of the population — the Japanese-Americans represent a far larger proportion of the registered voters — 42 percent.

You can get into a raft of arguments trying to describe the pecking order in Hawaii, especially because there are large cultural chasms between the first, second, and third generations of any ethnic strain. To use the Japanese-Americans as an example, those who were scarred by the shameful racial backlash of World War II obviously have different perceptions from those who did not. For that matter, with Hawaii's 30 percent racial intermarriage rate, figuring out who is what is not always easy.

Hawaii's unusual economic triad of tourism, the military, and agriculture, to complicate the picture further, is suffused by absentee money that can come from anywhere. Australians, Japanese, and Canadians are among the non–United States citizens that are thought to have $600 million invested in these small specks of land. When you then factor in the persistent reports that *pakalolo* — Maui Wowie, marijuana — has become Hawaii's number one cash crop, passing pineapple and cane, who knows where the ends of the economic strings pulled on these islands are.

But one thing can be said for sure. While corporations still control a staggering amount of Hawaii's land, the days when five great Anglo companies divided unquestioned control are gone.

The resident haoles, it can be argued, are a close second in power to the Japanese-Americans. Then come the Chinese and, farther down the line, others from the Asian mainland, such as Koreans and Vietnamese. Next to last are the more recently arrived Filipinos and Samoans, to whom is relegated much of the scut work. At the very bottom, as always in North America, are the Natives — the Polynesians whose land and pride has been taken from them at every opportunity.

The result is more a mixture than a blend. Hawaii is by no means distressed Haiti, where a vacation can turn out to be downright depressing. But it is a mistake to think that the leis and grass skirts of the ancient Polynesian culture with which one is confronted at the airport is reflective of any modern reality other than a savvy tourist industry. The Kamehameha School, which accepts only students who are at least partially of Hawaiian ancestry, until recently refused to teach such aspects of the Hawaiian culture as the hula, on the grounds that it was an antiquated obstacle to assimilation.

What the tourists don't see are the Marines who from time to time get beaten to a pulp — even killed — by locals, especially of the lower classes, who resent the presence of armed guards keeping them from military recreational facilities and beaches. Also not publicized is the fact that a lot of Anglo schoolchildren tend to stay away from classes on the school year's last day, which is affectionately referred to as "kill a haole day." Nobody actually dies, but nobody on the receiving end considers the experience pleasant. It hardly mitigates things that similar festivities exist aimed at "Japs" and "Flips."

This is not meant to paint an unrelentingly bleak portrait of paradise; merely to indicate that Hawaii is not just the land of four-colored brochures. Real people live here in some very strange circumstances.

Actually, the best news on these islands, torn between the realities of late twentieth-century North America and other distant places and times, is that there is more local control and vision when it comes to the islands' problems than you find in some parts of the continent.

The most hopeful example is energy. Right now, there is no part of North America more dependent on imported oil than Hawaii; continuous tanker landings from Indonesia are needed to light Honolulu, refrigerate food, and fuel the all-important airliners.

Though long-term contracts for adequate supplies exist, nothing is forever. Meanwhile, the islands contain no oil, gas, or coal, and nuclear power is impractical in a land with power demands that are relatively small and scattered.

What the islands do have are prime conditions for virtually every kind of "exotic" energy development. If ever there were a place where solar energy was practical, Hawaii is it. The same goes for geothermal; Hawaii is, after all, a volcanic chain, the geology of which as a matter of course generates great quantities of free steam. Hawaii will probably be the first place on the hemisphere to see an army of industrial-sized wind machines on its mountains and ridges. Little is more dependable than the trade winds, which prevent smog from building up despite Honolulu's plethora of internal combustion engines. The waste from this fecund tropical garden is perfect for conversion into alcohol. Finally, there's ocean thermal conversion — generating electricity by exploiting the difference between the sun-warmed water on the surface and the chill ocean depths. Hawaii is the location of the first large-scale experiments.

John Shupe, dean of the University of Hawaii's College of Engineering, sees in the near future a society on the islands that other parts of North America really would consider paradise. He sees the day when Hawaii's energy imports will be cut in half, and the lucrative and exportable technology for generating exotic energy will be a bigger industry than sugar.

"Of course," he says reassuringly, "oil will be important to us for many years. But I believe the islands can be self-sufficient within this generation."

•   •   •

This gets us back to New York. New York City, for the purposes of discussing aberrations, does not include the six or so million people jammed into the Bronx, Queens, Brooklyn, Staten Island, and Harlem. Those places are perfectly well understood as part of the Foundry.

"New York" is Manhattan south of Ninety-sixth Street on the West Side and south of Eighty-sixth Street on the East Side, with a few major colonies scattered throughout the suburbs.

That's the area the rest of the continent views as the alien and dangerous headquarters of such fabled, insulated cliques as the Wasteful Unions, Profligate Politicians, Surly Help, fast-talking jive artists, subway spray-painters, sin merchants, Foreign Policy Establishment, Banking Establishment, East Coast Liberal Media Establishment, and so forth. That's the area the commentators are talking about when they suggest that "New York" be allowed to float out to sea.

New Yorkers accept the same geographic demarcations, but to them they define the unmatchable glory of charged ideas, dazzling talk, money, art, beautiful faces, and high-quality all-night delicatessens that make the garbage, violence, power blackouts, cramped apartments, and great expense all worthwhile.

New York is an aberration because, though, in the dark ages, it would seem to have been a logical place for a border town between New England and the Middle Atlantic civilizations, it's been clear almost from the start that that is hardly the role it had any desire to play.

If New York was going to be the border town between anything, it would be between North America and the rest of the planet (read Europe). In the course of this pursuit, it acquired such muscle at the expense of the rest of this continent that it convinced even Chicago to refer to itself as the Second City, which seems an odd point of pride.

Washington at least always paid lip service to caring about what went on west of the Potomac. New York never dreamed of such hypocrisy. Civilization ended at the Hudson. If it hadn't happened in New York, it hadn't happened. In the sixties, what started as an in-joke among literary barflies ended up, as these things do when the self-anointed start talking to no one but each other, as a semiserious campaign: New York City should become the fifty-first state. The logic was impeccable. It's the least that could be done. The whole world, after all, was divided into New York and not–New York.

Thus, the greatest psychic jolt to New Yorkers was the attempt to wipe the civic sneer off their face as the city's bankruptcy loomed in the seventies. It's hard to judge what came harder: turning to the rest of the continent to beg, hat in hand, for bailout money, or having to launch the "I Love New York" campaign to explain to the ignorant damn rubes why they should be grateful New York existed.

The classic New Yorker's mental map was drawn by Saul Steinberg for *The New Yorker* magazine. It looks west and carefully labels 8th, 9th, and 10th avenues. Then there's the Hudson; a thin strip labeled New Jersey; an only slightly less thin strip labeled Texas, Utah, and California; the Pacific; and then China, Japan, and Russia.

It's almost self-parody that this map, blown up to poster size, should hang in the cramped offices of Bobby Zarem, "superflack." Zarem, like so many New Yorkers, has a hard time explaining exactly what he does for a living that results in so many other New Yorkers showering him with money and adulation. But what he does, essentially, is figure out what perceptions people hold toward his client and alter them, favorably, and usually through an intuitive process. He was the perfect person to promote the "I Love New York" campaign, which he did.

Zarem, who is very spacy (his conversations are punctuated by long silences as he sorts through his skull, attempting to come in for a landing on the same psychic plane that you're on), is from Savannah, Georgia. But he is now wildly a New Yorker, and he defines that in the term most real to him: fantasy.

I have lived in New York, as many people have, for practically nothing. I was doing some graduate work at Columbia and I was living off about two hundred dollars a month. I found cheap theater tickets; I found inexpensive or free concert tickets. There's very little I didn't find a way of doing. I used to stand at the opera twice a week. It wasn't very comfortable, granted; one can't do that for life. But it sure as s*** can give some meaning to life and it sure can lift you the f*** out of the day-to-day sort of rough, irritable aspects of life.

I don't mean to sound like some Pollyanna, but every once in a while I stop to think, oh my God, I'm building a life off nothing very concrete. I don't own any property; I don't have a lot of cash. I'm building a life on fantasies. My own and other people's.

New York is once again what it always was, which is a hubbub of energy and excitement and tension and creativity and hard work and results. I mean New York is all the things right now that it ever was. I don't know if it's permanent. I have a feeling that it could be. I don't know much about the financial side of things. I never did figure out why the city was bankrupt; how it got back the money to continue functioning. I don't know if it's out of the woods now or not. I just know that by reinforcing those very, very positive, wonderful things that New York always was, we were very, very effective in helping to stem the tide and turn it around.

Everything's relative. When I was eight, I used to go to Atlanta just to go to the opera and the theater, but it was still only a cheap substitute for New York.

I could go to Atlanta because there was a train that took seven and a half hours and was twelve dollars round trip and I had four hundred relatives there. My mother would put me on the train with a chicken or egg salad sandwich and I'd go to Atlanta and I went up to see anything I could. I went to Atlanta as a child to see Joan Blondell in some f***ing play. I didn't even give a s*** the name of it, screw what it was about, who wrote it; I just wanted to see anybody I could see on the road. But I was still aware that what I was seeing was not the real thing. It was a travesty. It was almost depressing, that I had to go to *Atlanta* to see Joan Blondell and that Joan Blondell had come to *Atlanta* to perform it.

In my mind, in any case, whatever it was, it wasn't the real thing. I belonged to New York. I've never liked Atlanta. Sure, Atlanta's hot now. Look at sleazy Jerry Rafshoon [Jimmy Carter's dogged former public relations man]. I mean, come on, he has a business there. Anybody that sleazy who could have a business in Atlanta, I could have had five times the business. He's a cheap copy of what's coming out of New York.

I came to New York for the good, not for the bad. I did not come to pull some deal over people's eyes and make a fast million. I did not come to New York because you can pick up hookers every night two blocks away, or to f*** little boys or anything. I did not come to New York for that, although all those things are fine.

I didn't give a f*** about them. I came to New York for the uplifting aspects of the town.

New York as a fantasy is interesting in the study of regionalism. One of the central ideas involved in thinking of North America as Nine Nations is that power is being dispersed as the continent matures. Now, so the theory goes, you can plausibly fantasize about making an important dent in the world from Los Angeles or Houston or Dallas.

Bobby Zarem is the perfect New Yorker to the extent that this idea has no meaning to him whatsoever. When he saw New York at what he calls "the all-time pits rock-bottom low," when the Stock Exchange was talking about moving to New Jersey, when the advertising agencies were going to move to Bayonne, he said, "If you guys move out of the city it is the final step for any of the creative processes that also have a commercial value. The ad agencies go, writers and directors and whatnot for the commercials go, it's the exodus of the last remaining heavy industry here. And I sat down and wrote letter after letter . . ."

This was a time when the garbage was piling up, the subways stuck, the newspapers struck, and the only surprises left were what bizarre new urban way there was to die, like being firebombed in a telephone booth by a stranger.

But it clearly never occurred to Zarem to leave.

It never occurred to him that New York might be a bad idea, that it might be caving in under the artificiality of its existence. What was life without a thousand Chinese restaurants? Where did the concepts civilization and Denver intersect?

New York had habitually soaked up the cream of so many different regions that it seemed there could be no other way. For it to be else was for there not to be a New York. It was inconceivable that Georgia might oppose bailing out New York as a revenge among nations. It was shocking that Atlanta might cheer the *New York Daily News* headline FORD TO NYC — DROP DEAD.

But sure enough, New York pulled it off again. With what is always described as a "massive infusion of federal funds," New York, as we've defined it, has come back strong. (The Bronx is still a bombed-out moon base, and Puerto Ricans are moving back to San Juan because it looks so good by contrast, but those are details, details.)

As *Fortune* magazine authoritatively described it:

New York City these days has the look and feel of a boom town. Cranes hoisting girders for new office buildings and hotels hog the sidewalks of Manhattan, snarling traffic. And the acres of office space vacant only a few years ago have been settled upon by international banks and others. Office rents have almost doubled. Apartment prices are going through the roof, bid up by foreigners flush with dollars and by the growing number of two-income families who can afford the high costs of city living.

All this is a far cry from the dolorous days of the early seventies, when the real-estate market was on the skids and corporations were making their publicized exits from the city . . .

The half-mile [of Madison Avenue] between Sixty-first Street and Seventy-second has become a brilliantly cosmopolitan urban shopping center, with far-out window displays, exotic merchandise, and celebrities as customers . . . Even the upstairs shops draw the smart set, from River Oaks [megabucks Houston], Bogotá [drug-wealthy Colombia], and show business.

The article goes on to mourn the flight of manufacturing from Manhattan, but who cares? The point is that New York continues to do what New York has always done best: *find the angle.*

Eddie Epstein understands the real thing when he sees it. Eddie Epstein is the New York supermarket maven. He's the consultant Coca-Cola comes to when it's having trouble pushing its bubbly into your shopping cart.

And Eddie, despite the fact that he's a New Yorker, can see some possibilities in regionalism.

What you're doing, he told me, is segmenting the market — repackaging America.

Repackaging America?

Yeah, he said, that's what you always have to do to extend the life cycle of a mature product. America is just like Coca-Cola.

Like Coca-Cola?

Yeah, people get bored with the same old thing. They know Coca-Cola, and they like it, but they come to the supermarket and they say I want to try something different. Live a little. They've seen the ads for Doctor Pepper, so they say I'll try a six-pack of that.

So what do you do about it? Well, it's a problem. See, this is how it's like America. You can't up the name recognition. Everybody knows Coke; everybody knows America. Everybody knows what they think of both. Very difficult to get anywhere in terms of name recognition.

You also can't reformulate. If it were detergent, you could come up with New! Improved! Tide!

But New! Improved! Coke? What's that? Apart from all the people in Atlanta who would slit their throats before doing something like that, what would you end up with? Something that ain't Coke.

So whaddya do? You repackage. You have the twelve-ounce

bottle. You add eight-ounce, sixteen-ounce, twenty-four-ounce, thirty-two-ounce, sixty-four-ounce, and tank truck. You put it in six-packs, eight-packs, cases. You put it out in plastic, metal, and glass. You put it out in returnable and nonreturnable.

And what do you get? In Texas, you sell lots of returnables. In Texas, the four cents means to them. They care about the money. They've also got houses big enough that they accumulate thirty, forty empty bottles; it's no big deal. People usually wash the bottles, stack 'em up, sooner or later they shlep them back in their station wagon.

In New York City, returnables die. You live in New York, you've got bigger problems than worrying about the four cents. Also, you add a six-pack of empty bottles to a New York apartment, and that's the final straw. You have to sleep in the bathtub. There finally is just no more room in the bedroom.

Eddie Epstein leans back in his swivel chair in his home office, an aerie thirty feet above his swimming pool and tennis court, half an hour from the City, paid for in the classic New York way — finding the angle.

Repackaging America, Eddie muses.

I like it. I think it would sell. You and me we go on the convention circuit together. This could sell a lot of Quaker Oats.

DIXIE

In Hinds County, Mississippi, in a dark-paneled reception room brightened by striking orange Scandinavian furniture, on a mahogany pole, stands a Confederate battle flag.

As recently as ten or fifteen years ago, there would be nothing remarkable about the presence of the flag in this, the deepest of the Deep South, just below the state capital of Jackson. In fact, if it were standing alone, it might not attract any attention today. But this particular, full-sized, gold-fringed symbol of a certain time and place stands in a row of four. The first flag is that of the Union. But the second is the flag of the Federal Republic of Germany. And the third, snuggled up against the Stars and Bars, is a flag whose design is centuries older than the War Between the States. A stylized white castle above which floats a Maltese cross against a blue shield, it is the battle flag of a place called Ravensburg. Ravensburg, a small town seventy miles south of Stuttgart in southern Germany, was once home to a man by the name of Erwin Gross. Gross, whose wife's name is Hildegard, and whose secretary's name is Helga, is a brand-new Mississippian.

Andrea, his sixteen-year-old daughter, speaks English with a southern drawl complicated by a slight, if startling German accent. A blow-dried blond heartbreaker in tight jeans and cinched shirt tails, she looks remarkably like the stereotype of an Ole Miss sorority belle. The Grosses' rambling ranch house, complete with swimming pool, is decorated with dried-flower arrangements that include fluffy bolls of Delta cotton grown just a few counties to the west. Somehow, the talk turns to guns, and Erwin jokes that "I am not enough of a Mississippian yet to own a Luger."

Yet Mississippian Erwin is, in perhaps the most basic way it is possible to be these days. For Erwin has brought 135 high-paying industrial jobs to Hinds County. He's the director of the Hawera Tool Manufacturing branch plant here.

Hawera makes what connoisseurs call the Cadillac of carbide-tipped drill bits for punching holes in concrete. They cost $60 to $70 apiece retail, and come in a film of fine machine oil, like a high-quality rifle barrel. If, for some reason, you had a block of concrete six football fields long that you wanted to drill a hole through, you'd ask for a Hawera bit because the six hundred meters of concrete will give before the bit does.

With two thousand employees worldwide, Hawera's companies do about $300 million worth of business annually, with perhaps 30 percent of their drill-bit sales in the United States. When Hawera decided to service the North American market with its first factory located here, it analyzed place after place. Seven bound volumes comparing states — monuments to what Gross likes to think was a methodical, unemotional, and culture-free approach to the siting procedure — sit in his office to this day.

"We made a real professional research," said Gross in his rapid-fire English, the fluency of which is a triumph, considering that he took his first eight-week crash course in the language only two years ago. "We checked everything which was important to us: electricity, transportation, wages, skills, property price, tax . . ."

The choice came down to Mississippi.

So today, in the heart of the state many North Americans still think of as far and away the most backward — behind stylishly architected brick and unfinished-concrete walls — stand Mississippians working state-of-the-art machines from Switzerland, Sweden, and Germany, making up to $8.00 an hour, which is more than a lot of newspaper reporters get. The shop's typical wage would be on the order of $5.00 to $6.00 an hour, considered good money here. The working conditions are antiseptic. The benefits package is sound. About 30 percent of the work force is black, which is comparable to the racial make-up of the county and the state.

As for Gross, his cathedral-ceilinged house is nearly three times the size of the one he lived in in Germany, but it cost less. He says there are more cultural opportunities in Jackson than in

Ravensburg. (The night I visited with his family, the kids were in a hurry to catch the new show at the planetarium.) And he still can't get over how many people to whom he's never been formally introduced wave to him on the street and say, "Hi, Erwin!"

And by God, Erwin has become proud. Proud to be a Mississippian.

If you talk to people in the Norse [says Gross, who has the charming habit of referring to his new-found region as the Souse], they just don't know what Mississippi is. They just don't know *where* it is, sometimes.

I'm logical and objective. I'm not saying they're Yankees. I'm saying they're stupid. You travel around over there. They ask you, "Where do you come from?"

"Jackson."

"Jackson, where?"

"Jackson, Mississippi."

"Blaaaah," they say. They just have a negative.

But if you ask them, have you been in Jackson? they say no. Do you know where it is? No. Do you know where Mississippi is? Ya, I know, down in the Souse. How many people live there? What's going on there? They don't know anything. But they have opinions. I don't know where they get their information from. Maybe twenty years ago, thirty years ago, it was a certain way of life here, and they still believe it. Like some people still believe fairy tales, like the stork that brings babies. They really don't know that the Souse has changed a lot!

Indeed, the South has changed so much in the past decade or two that change itself has become Dixie's most identifiable characteristic. Long a region identified with stagnation — backward, rural, poor, and racist, a colony of the industrialized North, enamored of an allegedly glorious past of dubious authenticity — Dixie is now best described as that forever-underdeveloped North American nation across which the social and economic machine of the late twentieth century has most dramatically swept.

The Southern Growth Policies Board — easily the most sophisticated regional economic pressure group in North America — casting about for a learned analogy from which to analyze Dixie, picked post–World War II Germany and Japan. In fact, in an almost impenetrable hardbound volume entitled *The Economics of Southern Growth*, it flat-out says that "1965, the year by which both the voting rights and civil rights act had been passed, was for the South what 1945 had been for Germany and Japan."

The board, created as the research and lobbying arm of the

southern governors, in effect compares 1965, when "the ancient disputes about what racial policy should be were finally settled with a defeat of the Old South by the rest of the country," with the liberation of Europe and Asia by the Allies.

It straightforwardly compares the economic effects on ingrown, nationalistic, totalitarian regimes suddenly opened to the effects, good and bad, of Western, liberal, social democratic realities.

This, they say, is the condition which now defines the South. If that is true, it makes the task of defining the new borders of Dixie somewhat less formidable.

Sociologically, climactically, historically, politically, topographically, and racially, Dixie is a quilt. Rigid analysis of what constitutes Dixie can lead one to believe that it doesn't exist, and never did. It's not hard to make the case that the heavily black coastal lowlands of the Carolinas are very different from the mountains of Tennessee. Louisiana Cajuns are very different from Ozark hillbillies. You can take a state like Alabama and confound those who would describe it as monolithically Deep South by pointing out the historically pro-Union counties at the southern tip of the Appalachians. Atlanta, undeniably, is the capital of Dixie. The authentic southern experience is changing planes in the just expanded, but until recently unutterably vile, concrete-block bomb shelter of an airport there. Yet all over the South you can find people who will flatly, and wrongly, assert that Atlanta has nothing to do with the "real" South.

It's amazing, considering the variety of sage distinctions that can be made about Dixie, that people refer to themselves as "Southerners" at all. Considering that being a "Southerner" is the most fervent and time-honored regional distinction in North America, it almost makes you wonder if ordinary people know something that the academicians do not.

Perhaps what most folk realize is that Dixie's boundaries are defined more by emotion than any other nation. Like New England, Dixie is an idea that has been around for a long time, and people have had a lot of time to savor it, curse it, love it, and leave it.

In fact, one of the best ways of identifying the South is by listening for it in casual conversation. I don't mean drawls. I mean constant calculations — like shop talk in a factory or office — about where the place has been, where it's going, whether things are getting better or worse than the excruciatingly well-remembered past.

There is such a multitude of threads to the fabric called Dixie that official organizations draw boundaries enclosing anywhere from nine to seventeen states and call the place "the South." (And this doesn't even get to the question of what constitutes that spurious idea called the "Sunbelt.") "Dixie" is the classic example of a place that eludes definition by conventional political geography.

As a result, I like the interesting intuitive grip displayed by teen-agers and small-town merchants when it comes to defining the South.

The teen-agers have an exquisite sense of where, geographically, displaying an ancient defiance by flying the Stars and Bars from their radio aerials will rile the grownups. The merchants have finely tuned ideas about where it is that calling their establishments the Dixie Bar and Grill, or Rebel Auto Sales, will help them make money.

Drop back a county or two from the northern- or westernmost meaningful collections of these displays (both of these groups notoriously overreach), and you're within shouting distance of the Dixie line.

(There are many theories, and no unanimity, about how the South came to be called Dixie. However, my vote for the least plausible explanation seriously propounded goes to the learned gentleman who said he'd traced it all back to a Dutchman, name of Dixye. This Dutchman allegedly decided to grow tobacco in Harlem. When, with absolute predictability, this turned out to be a terrible idea, old man Dixye reportedly sold off his slaves to a guy in South Carolina, who did not treat them at all well. This led to the slaves composing songs in which they wished they were back in Dixye's land, and the rest, look away, is history.)

At any rate, Dixie starts on the midcontinental Atlantic at about Ocean City, Maryland. Ocean City, socially, is to Washington, D.C., as Prince Georges County, Maryland, is to the capital, suburbanly. Prince Georges and Ocean City are those places which, unfavored by the high and mighty, tend to attract first-generation money — both black and white — to whom the very idea of living in a place called a "condo" — or, for that matter, a "suburb" — is rightfully perceived as a miracle of upward mobility.

As resorts go, Ocean City is more like Myrtle Beach, South Carolina, than it is Surf City, New Jersey. In Myrtle Beach, a mayor who opposed billboards was denounced not only as a communist, but as a "Yankee." Economic observers only half-jokingly refer to this response as a triumph of modernism. They're grateful the mayor didn't end up in the swamp.

From there, as described in the Foundry chapter, Dixie cuts across the chicken farms of southern Delaware to include the Eastern Shore of Maryland, eastern referring to its location relative to the Chesapeake Bay. The gracious capital, Annapolis, is a border town between Dixie and the Foundry. The boundary carefully skirts Washington's wealthier suburbs and drives up through rural Virginia, north of the Shenandoah Valley, to swoop down the western edge of the worst of the southern Appalachians, splitting off chemical-factory-laden West Virginia river counties like Mason, Jackson, and Wood. There are those who would argue that Ohio counties like Scioto and Adams, across the Ohio River from Kentucky, are still southern. Similarly, Covington, Kentucky, across the river from the industrial presence of Cincinnati, is not southern. But by and large, the Ohio River is a meaningful border until you hit Indiana, the rolling hills of which, north of Louisville, are economically and emotionally part of Dixie.

Actually, some would say South Bend, on the Michigan border, is the northernmost penetration of the Confederacy, but that's an exaggeration perpetrated by Northerners who like to dwell unfairly on the Klan marches that were occurring there in the sixties.

(For that matter, Louisville makes a fetish of claiming it is not part of the South. That's ridiculous. It may well have been a Union bastion over a century ago, but that's nothing on which to base Southernness today. I don't see any move on the part of Louisville to pry the evil influence of mint juleps from the minds of its young during the Kentucky Derby.)

Indianapolis is the boundary where the Foundry and Dixie part company. From Indianapolis on, the distinction to be made is between the South and the "real" Midwest — the Breadbasket — another very old idea in America, which, despite industrialization, communications, and travel, retains great power.

Near the Illinois boundary, Terre Haute has been a dividing line in Indiana dialects, politics, and values for over a hundred years and still is, and as a result is another good border town.

As many as thirty-one counties, below a line roughly from Terre Haute to East St. Louis, have from time to time been identified as part of Southernillinois (pronounced by natives as one word). Route 50, from Vincennes, somewhat farther south, has also been suggested as the border, although Illinois political correspondents reply that it's "common knowledge" that Southernillinois "is ten miles beyond wherever you're standing."

But what all these descriptions refer to is the area at the heart of which is the flat plain where the Mississippi and the Ohio rivers come together, locally called Egypt. Its capital is Cairo (pronounced KAY-roe), one of the meanest burgs of its size outside Oklahoma. The memory of pitched and repeated racial battles in this shabby Dixie river town is not dimmed.

The news generally is not bright in this crescent, which has the disadvantages of southern problems in a state whose prosperity is built on decidedly nonsouthern solutions. Divisions between industrial and agricultural interests — divisions between the Foundry and the Breadbasket — get far more attention in Illinois.

East St. Louis, Illinois, is one of the grimmer slums on the continent, with no appreciable tax base from which to attack its problems. Like St. Louis, Missouri, it is an outpost of Foundry-like third-generation problems, made worse by its being an island, and a border island at that, between regions that don't understand and don't want to understand. Both the Breadbasket and Dixie are afraid that what St. Louis and East St. Louis have got — congenital urban decay — is contagious.

The only good news out of southern Illinois, where jobs are not plentiful, is that, like the rest of the state, it is resting on a thick bed of coal. The university town down there, in fact, is named Carbondale. Other parts of Illinois consider the chewing up of prime farmland preposterous. Southern Illinois is grateful to be one of the most heavily strip-mined lands east of the Mississippi.

Missouri is a state of great conflicts and paradoxes. It was admitted to the Union as a slave state, but did not join the Confederacy. Instead, it waged a particularly virulent internal civil war over these issues. The southeast "boot heel" on the Mississippi River is thoroughly Deep South. The southwest corner is the Ozarks, which, in their mountainous isolation and great beauty, are like eastern Kentucky and West Virginia. The rich soil of northwest Missouri that the last glacier left behind is so thoroughly a part of the Great Plains that Kansas City is the capital of the Breadbasket. The center of the state is called "Little Dixie."

The politics and history of this kind of mishmash have been so confused and tangled for so long that Missouri's boast is its pugnacity: "Show Me" is its motto, and Harry Truman, a native son, its pride.

Missouri makes such little sense as a state that even the Federal
Reserve Board has Kansas City and St. Louis as capitals of separate regions. Untangling this skein is complicated enough to explain why most observers just call Missouri a "border state," and
then don't actually try to draw the border.

But the Breadbasket-Dixie influences begin to balance out in a
fashion such that the boundary probably should be drawn
through St. Louis and on to Columbia. Dixie's influence does extend north of that line — as has been observed elsewhere, Mark
Twain might still recognize his beloved river town of Hannibal —
but it is leavened by those two cities. St. Louis, one of the dozens
of places it's possible to call the "gateway to the West," is almost
Foundry in its mixture of ethnics and blacks, machine politics
and liberalism, heavy industry and tenements. Columbia, the
capital of Little Dixie, is the home of the University of Missouri.

From Columbia, the Dixie line curves down to include the
Ozarks. John Gunther, in his seminal *Inside U.S.A.*, charmingly
assessed the Ozarks of the forties as "The Poor White Trash Cita-
del of America. The people are underdeveloped, suspicious, inert.
There are children aged fifteen who have never seen a tooth-
brush."

The last thirty years have brought such amazing southern-style
change that the Ozarks should definitely be considered part of
Dixie, despite their historic antipathy toward the Confederacy. To
be sure, there are hollows in this highland Missouri-Arkansas-
Oklahoma region that still hold poverty worse than southern Appalachia. But Arkansas, like West Virginia, has had as governor a
Rockefeller who understood the value of throwing other people's
money at poverty to help make it go away. And the politicians
who followed Winthrop Rockefeller have been striking examples
of the new young, mediagenic, non-Neanderthal southern politician, one of whom was briefly president in the seventies.

The sure sign that social work has had impact on the Ozarks is
that folklorists have descended on the region in droves to record
the quirks of the white trash "before it is too late" and they all
become well fed and uncolorful.

But more important than the VISTA workers to the Ozarks has
been the "quality-of-life" revolution, started in the sixties. The
Ozarks in the past suffered from having little that would respond
profitably to the assault of a dragline or an exploratory well or a
Tennessee Valley Authority or DDT. The Ozarks have had precious little going for them except beautiful mountains, restful
lakes, peaceful small to medium-sized towns, and cheap, avail-

able, if rarely horizontal, land. Thus, "progress" passed it by. In the latter half of the twentieth century, as it turns out, that very lack of "progress" was of enormous attraction to retirees, vacationers from the cities that ring the mountains, young people who, fancying themselves "homesteaders," wished to apply their urban educations to the problems of going "back to the land," and light industries that could locate anywhere there was an interstate highway and a WATS line. The influx of people like that, for better or for worse, has whiplashed, if not Future-Shocked, the Ozarks. That phenomenon — being Future-Shocked or the threat of being so — is, in the 1980s, what ties the South together.

So the boundary toddles down through the thin northeastern edge of Oklahoma, which is part of the Ozarks, only to broaden and head west as it hits another Little Dixie, even more enduring than Missouri's.

Unlike the Ozarks, Oklahoma's Little Dixie is marked by how little things have changed despite all attempts. Oklahoma always has demonstrated a singular resiliency to outsiders' notions of what is socially acceptable behavior. Little Dixie, which lives up to its name by being poor but proud, is champion in its articulation of a private sense of what constitutes murder.

Mark Singer, in a marvelous *New Yorker* magazine disquisition on one Gene Stipe, who remains Little Dixie's "Prince of Darkness," observed that "in Latimer County, one of the three counties in Stipe's legislative district, the smartest thing that someone accused of a felony could have done between 1949 and 1974 would have been to request a jury trial. That quarter of a century slipped by without a single verdict of guilty."

Singer continues, " 'Let's say I pick up a Smith & Wesson double-action .22-calibre revolver on a .32 frame with a four-inch barrel and plant one right between your eyes,' a man in Latimer County once said to me, in what I decided to regard as an utterly speculative and friendly tone of voice. 'Now, if I've got a brain in my head, all I need to do is drop the gun and borrow a dime and call Gene Stipe. And I'm pretty sure he can find me a jury of my peers that believes in the good old "Judge not, that ye be not judged." ' "

Couple this with cavernous brush country that to this day can conceal dangerous outlaws and even a couple of renegade circus elephants with complete thoroughness, despite massive searches, and you have a sense of the challenge Little Dixie is capable of offering to the forces of assimilation.

Somewhere, perhaps below Durant, Oklahoma, we cross the Red River, leave Little Dixie, and are in Texas, on the last lap of the boundary tour.

The problem here is that, as in Indiana, three nations come together, in this case, Dixie, the Breadbasket, and MexAmerica. In Indiana, the lines of force are tough to define because Indianapolis is the place where three nations peter out. Here, however, it's tough because the values of three nations have been and are coming together and clashing with great force and many fireworks.

Here are the facts. East Texas near Louisiana is pure Dixie of loblolly and slash piney woods. Not only is it unlike the rest of Texas by being moist and densely forested; it is poor, it is black and "peckerwood" white, it is isolated, it is suspicious, and it has been so for a long, long time.

South Texas near Mexico is dry, hot, and Spanish. Climatically, geographically, and historically, it belonged to Mexico, and at the rate the Spanish-speaking population is making itself felt, it may again. In the vast King ranch south of Corpus Christi, Hispanic workers do not say they work "for" the man; they work "with" him. It is MexAmerica.

The West Texas hill country is where the chaparral starts. This is the land of Lyndon Baines Johnson, and "outlaw" country-and-western music star Willie Nelson. It is cattle and, farther north into the Panhandle, cotton and wheat. And it is very Anglo.

It is the real home of the great Texas myths about plain-spoken square-shooters. It is the most colorful part of the Breadbasket.

These three nations are competing for influence over a triangle approximately 250 miles on a side defined by Dallas and Fort Worth in the north, Houston in the southeast, and San Antonio in the southwest.

Historically, Dixie had the upper hand. Although well into the Plains, Dallas, the cosmopolitan merchant town then at the end of the railroad line, was long considered southern. Not only did it have merchants, gamblers, and prostitutes; it had "society" and "good families" and a fixed sneer for its sister city, Fort Worth. Fort Worth was separated from Dallas by only a few dozen miles and the Balcones Fault, a geological fault of more interest to natural historians than anyone else, but Fort Worth always was either "where the West begins" or "a godforsaken cowtown," depending on who was talking. Breadbasket towns have always suffered from the theory that they're hick.

Meanwhile, Houston, right on the edge of the pines, and only inches above sea level, is a swamp of heat and humidity only an air-conditioner repairman or an oil engineer could love. Dixie had a hold on it because of the climate, location, and opportunity it offered to both poor blacks and whites.

Yet San Antonio was always part of MexAmerica. It has one of the largest Hispanic communities of any city well north of the United States border, and certainly one of the best organized politically. In Mexico, there are a lot of folk who literally think that San Antonio is the most important city in the States.

With the rise of Houston and Dallas as cheerfully, obnoxiously arrogant world capitals of glass, steel, and money, the Anglo Plains culture is clearly now dominant in this crescent.

But it's still tempting to draw the Dixie line right down the middle between Dallas and Fort Worth — smack on Runway 17 Left, the main north-south slab of concrete of that improbable megastructure, the Dallas–Fort Worth International Airport. From there, the boundary heads toward Houston and the Gulf of Mexico.

Houston is the biggest draw for opportunity-seekers of all colors and classes this nation has seen since Los Angeles. Some of the richest and most powerful men in America call the western suburbs of Houston home. But while their presence is at the top of Houston's image, it's by no means the whole story. Almost literally in the shadow of the tall buildings at Houston's core are black slums straight out of the heart of Mississippi. They are so antiquely southern, they're not even urban. They're shotgun shacks — propped up on blocks and with a front door and a back door, through both of which, when they are open, a 12-gauge can be fired without hitting a thing.

But Houston's blacks are not all poor and powerless. The community is numerous, and it votes. Barbara Jordan, with Andrew Young of Atlanta, the first black elected to Congress from the South in the twentieth century, was from Houston. The city can not only look and feel southern; it can act it.

The Dixie line follows the extraordinarily vile liquid in the Houston Ship Channel the fifty miles to Galveston, and on out into the Gulf of Mexico. At the eastern edge of the Gulf, half a continent away, is southern Florida, which also isn't Dixie. Like the border town of Houston, Miami is a land of great promise in the eyes of a lot of people who don't commonly use the language in which this book is written.

One major difference between these two parts of the Gulf is

that the Hispanics of South Florida are so commonly first- and second-wave Cuban immigrants of the sixties, which is to say middle class, which is to say in possession of a heritage of education and skills such as entrepreneurship. Unlike the poor, rural Mexicans who have begun to ring Houston, living in houses that don't look like slums until you realize that four families are trying to live in one little bungalow, the Cubans have exported a whole world with them to Florida. In the words of songwriter Jimmy Buffett, they don't have to buy any secondhand American dreams.

One of the more interesting lessons to be drawn from this tour is economic. Despite the South's reputation as a place of great growth, almost all the truly spectacular development of the so-called Sunbelt phenomenon has occurred on Dixie's boundaries: the wealth of the Virginia suburbs of Washington, D.C., is as marginally "southern," as is the boom along the Dallas-Houston corridor or the population influx to South Florida.

What you see in Dixie is great *change* — social, emotional, even architectural. Change so amazing to Southerners that sometimes it seems that all they can do is marvel over the recent past. This change, of course, is epitomized by attitudes about race.

I watched a white man from Philadelphia, Mississippi, turn seriously purple from lack of oxygen, his mind trying to force his reluctant body to utter the word "nigger" in front of a reporter.

Philadelphia, Mississippi, is noted for little save the murders of three civil rights workers in 1964 — murders that led to a scorched-earth policy on the part of the U.S. Justice Department, which guarantees that, no matter what happens elsewhere, the very last hamlet on the face of this earth to be de-integrated is going to be in Neshoba County.

This fellow from Philadelphia, who presumably had nothing to do with the proverbial "racial disturbances" in his home town back then, is now the manager of a chemical plant elsewhere in the South, and to this day, he can't bring himself to refer to his non-Caucasian employees even as "Negroes" or "blacks." He calls them "minorities." As in, "The older minorities try to call me Mr. Jameson or Mr. Jim [neither his real name]. I tell the minorities that 'Mister' was my father's name. I insist the minorities call me Jim."

The way he got into oxygen deprivation was by attempting to explain to me how it was that his plant, which is currently high-paying, modern, and reasonably hygienic by the standards of the industry, came to have about 80 percent of its line workers black.

Well, he explained, back in 1961, when this factory was built, before OSHA, before EPA, before unionization threats, and before he was out of knee pants, the particular kind of chemical manipulation that it requires was performed in an un-air-conditioned, grueling atmosphere highly charged with toxic dust. Absolutely refusing to be tape-recorded, he said, "At that time, at this place, it was viewed as minority work." Realizing how ridiculous he sounded, he struggled to spit it out. "It was . . . was . . . view . . . viewed . . . as . . . nig . . . nig . . . nig . . . nigger work," he finally croaked, with visions of his future as a corporate manager flashing before his eyes, his career gone up in smoke for his candor.

I didn't get to belt back a few bourbons with this guy and find out how he feels about "minorities" deep in the recesses of his soul. But I do conclude, from his verbal tick, that, at the very least, he will go to his grave believing that, as a Southerner working for a major corporation, if he doesn't appear to be the very model of modern race relations, he's cooked.

Now, that may not be liberty and justice for all, but it is neck-snapping social *change*, and it is what I think is important to distinguish from economic *growth* in the South. Since growth and change have arrived in the South virtually simultaneously and, of course, have fed off each other, it's easy to think they're one phenomenon. But they're not.

You can have growth without change.

Tupelo, for example, in the hills of northeastern Mississippi, was mercifully by-passed by conflict and violence during the civil rights period of the sixties. Now a thriving industrial city — which is still not what you call common in Mississippi — in the late seventies, a resurgence of the Klan made the place look like a remake of *The Birth of a Nation*, complete with cross-burnings and a black boycott of white stores.

The International Chemical Workers made the bold move of trying to organize a chicken-processing factory in southeastern Mississippi in the seventies. They have been unsuccessful in coming up with a contract, even though there is a standing joke that the factory has done more for race relations than every federal civil rights law ever written. "[The boss] didn't treat nobody different, no matter you black or white," one worker was quoted as saying. "Ever'body who worked there was treated like a nigger."

And you can have change without growth.

Neither New Orleans nor Birmingham is setting any records, economically, yet both elected black mayors in the late seventies.

At the same time, Floyd McKissick, famous in the sixties for being among the first to call for black power, was seeing his dream of creating a "new town" in the hills of North Carolina crippled. Soul City was supposed to have eighteen thousand residents by 1979, according to the plan. When the year came and went with a total of 135 people living there with great faith, but no industry, the federal government pulled the financial plug.

Growth in Dixie is a many-level thing.

On the more or less negative side: the Sunbelt is a misleading confection. Dixie's growth rate, though twice the national average, is far different from that of the Southwest and of southern Florida. Of the top ten cities in rate of population increase in the southeastern United States in the first half of the seventies, only one was in Dixie proper. And that was Fort Smith, along the Arkansas-Oklahoma line, which was eighth, reflecting the Ozark quality-of-life revolution and a strong military presence. Far more typical in the list were places like Temple, Texas, on the outskirts of the Fort Hood Army base, or the West Palm Beach–Boca Raton–Fort Lauderdale strip just north of Miami. None of those places can be considered Dixie. In terms of absolute population increase, there is only one non-Texas, non-Florida southern city in the top ten: Atlanta.

Some of Dixie's growth is artificial. One of the South's favorite urbanization techniques is annexation. When a rural area that may have taken three decades to become densely populated enough to be called a suburb is viewed as being wealthy enough to be profitably added to a city's tax rolls, bang, it suddenly finds itself within the new, revised city limits. This is a useful way of ensuring that a city doesn't atrophy. But it distorts the sense of growth you get from statistics. It's not the growth that has occurred instantaneously; it's the change in borders.

All of Dixie's growth has been catch-up. There is still not one southern state with a per capita income that matches the United States average, and as of 1977, the states that are wholly within Dixie were behind by at least 14 and as much as 29 percent.

A lot of the growth has been of dubious quality. In North Carolina, for example, vast numbers of industrial jobs have been created, but the majority of them are still in minimum-wage industries, like cut-and-sew shops, textiles, furniture-making, and food-packaging. What those jobs amount to are people trying to make things cheaper than the Taiwanese can. And succeeding.

Growth associated with high pay has not always been welcome. The Miller Beer Company, paying more than $9.00 an hour, wanted to locate a $100 million brewery, employing five hundred, in Raleigh, North Carolina. The Chamber of Commerce figured, accurately, that workers making a third of that in other shops would flock to such jobs. In order to keep their most highly skilled people, other industries might have to raise their pay. Rather than have that happen, they ran Miller out of town on a rail. It finally located in Eden, North Carolina, far from competition.

Philip Morris wanted to build a huge cigarette plant in Concord, North Carolina. Concord is in Cabarrus County, the least unionized county in North America. It is also the home of Cannon Mills, the textile firm that feudally dominates its company town of Kannapolis. Not only would Philip Morris offer starting pay that, at $5.25 an hour, would be more than a dollar above what the county was used to as average pay, but Philip Morris was accustomed to having unions in its plants elsewhere. The "Welcome to Carrabus County" vote in the executive board of the Chamber of Commerce ended in a tie. And *that* came after people started picketing in the streets with signs that said CALL FOR PHILIP MORRIS.

Erwin Gross, the German industrialist mentioned earlier in the chapter, acknowledged that, despite his plant's relatively high pay, "a little bit of politics was involved" in the decision of his company to locate in Mississippi. "We hoped and we still hope that it will take a certain time until the unions move slowly down from the North to the South, and the farther down you are, the longer it may take," he said. "A lot of industry wants out of the North because of the high labor problems, because of people living together crowded in big cities — aggressive people giving problems to factories. We said to ourselves, it will not take very long. It's getting as crowded in North Carolina now as it is in Chicago. We said, okay, just go down, ya? You will have ten, twenty, twenty-five years more time till you got the same trouble. It gives you more room to maneuver. It was one of the major points."

And a lot of the growth looks like hell. Because of the South's historic poverty, for example, there was a dearth of decent housing even before the emigration ended and the immigration began. To accommodate the new growth, Dixie has embraced the mobile home. Trailers are becoming the most typical southern architectural form. Granted, they're affordable and reasonably practical (when they don't blow over in a high wind or burst into flames from one dropped cigarette). But there is no getting around the fact that they are ugly. The only thing worse than a plain one is one that its makers advertise as "French Provincial."

As Stephen Suitts, head of the Southern Regional Council, puts it, "Southerners don't have any rich relatives. God was a Northerner. Without a heritage of anything except denial, Southerners, given a chance to improve their standard of living, are doing so, and they do it largely without concern or perception of ultimately whether it's good or bad. To not have the problems of your parents is to not have problems."

On the more positive side, the growth is more evenly distributed than in many parts of North America.

To be sure, as some cities grow, they begin to chain up, like the Washington-to-Boston megalopolis or the Montreal-to-Milwaukee one. Take the more-than-200-mile-long strip from Raleigh/Durham, North Carolina, to Greenville/Spartanburg, South Carolina, for example. Once a string of, at best, sleepy mill towns like Burlington, Greensboro, Winston-Salem, Kannapolis, Charlotte, and Gastonia, it has now been grandly christened the Piedmont Crescent. There's serious talk of the need for high-speed rail transportation in this corridor, like the New York–to–Washington Metroliner.

Similarly, it probably won't be long before the Gulf Coast, from Pensacola, Florida, to Galveston, Texas, clots. Pensacola is anchored by its world-without-end naval air station. Mobile, Alabama, already isn't hurting as a port. If the unforgivably expensive Army Corps of Engineers' plot to connect the Tennessee and Tombigbee rivers is ever completed, linking the Appalachian coal fields with the sea, Mobile will be the prime beneficiary.

Biloxi, Mississippi, is the home of the cost overrun. Biloxi is represented on Capitol Hill by one of the last of a dying breed — John C. Stennis, the extremely senior senator from Mississippi (first elected, 1947; re-elected in 1976, at the age of seventy-five, without opposition in the general election and with 85 percent of the vote in the primary). For some reason, on the tiny bit of beach frontage in the home state of the man who was chairman of the Senate Armed Services Committee from 1969 to 1980, there is a very large Litton Industries shipyard that makes amazingly expensive war boats.

If a small megalopolis is possible, that's what New Orleans–

Baton Rouge, at the mouth of the Mississippi, has become. Its economy is still based on port facilities that, if taken all together, rank as the number one tonnage-handlers on the continent. The operations range from those of the huge grain elevators, where the dust explodes from time to time, to the chemical plants, which send out loaded freight cars that periodically fall off the tracks, "forcing massive evacuation," as the newspapers always put it.

But in New Orleans proper, that marvelous collection of sleaziness and peeling paint that only an 88 percent humidity (the annual 6:00 A.M. average) can produce, the primary industry is now tourism. Jim Chubbuck, the savvy administrative assistant to the mayor, says that the town is closely watching the increase in European tourism in the United States — which is now a bigger deal than U.S. tourism in Europe. He figures that Europeans will be as unsophisticated about the United States as Americans were about Europe thirty years ago. What do they know from Boise? They'll go to four places, he figures: New York, Washington, San Francisco — and New Orleans. Similarly, he would like to steal some of the South American action from Miami. He knows how much Venezuelans spend.

New Orleans certainly has the climate to be a Caribbean town, I said. Does it have the drug money? (As will be discussed in the Islands chapter, drugs are becoming important development factors in many places. There is only so much in the way of profits that can be plowed back into yachts, jets, and exotic personal habits. The money has to go somewhere. So people buy office buildings and shopping centers and stuff.)

No, Chubbuck said, like everything else in this town, drugs have been locked up by the establishment since the nineteenth century. In this case, the Mob. (This is as good a place as any to note that Dixie is the only North American nation contained entirely within the United States.)

Lafayette, Lake Charles, Port Arthur . . . The Atchafalaya "River" is so called because it is a narrow body of water deep enough that trees will not grow in it. That is how you distinguish it from the swamp that pervades Louisiana west of the Mississippi. What constitutes "land" versus what constitutes "not land" is a matter of great debate in this part of the world, where you are wise to build your hunting cabin on stilts, and where ATVs — all-terrain vehicles, which essentially are boats with wheels — are big sellers. But urbanization is rapidly consuming even the

Atchafalaya Basin. The U.S. Fish and Wildlife Service is trying desperately to save this fertile and beautiful refuge from vigorous drainage efforts. Locals respond by saying, in effect: "Let me see if I've got this straight. You think there's a serious threat that southwestern Louisiana might be joining civilization?" Amazing as it may seem, the answer is yes.

Beaumont, Texas, is part of this Gulf growth sphere. There's an off-color Aggie joke (the Texas version of a Polish joke) that has a woman suggesting to the Aggie that he perform a lewd activity upon her person "where it's dirty and nasty." The punchline is "So he drove her to Beaumont."

High Island, Texas, which gets its name from being several feet, rather than inches, above sea level (it's on top of a salt dome), is where a great number of pipes come ashore from the Gulf's oil wells. It's also where Vietnam-era helicopter pilots, skimming over four-foot seas in almost horizontal rain, with zero visibility, turn to their obviously panic-drunk passengers, grin, and say, "If we keep on this heading for twenty-eight minutes and the rig isn't under us, we're lost."

And Galveston is at the mouth of the Ship Channel, which makes inland Houston the third-largest port in tonnage in North America.

Offshore oil, shipbuilding, ports, commercial fishing, resort development, and tourism are bringing strip development, trailer parks, office towers, traffic jams, and other signs of progress to what was recently and quite literally the backwaters of North America.

Conversely, there are still places like Terrell County, Georgia (one county south from the town of Plains), where black people still make a point of getting off the downtown streets before sundown. A black out-of-town newspaper reporter, who didn't know that until he felt it was almost too late, kids feebly that he was terribly glad to be down there with a New York Jewish lawyer, since that's the one person he could think of who would be less popular than his own swarthy self.

And there are places like Tallahatchie County, Mississippi. (Remember the song about Billy Jo McAllister dumping a mysterious parcel off the Tallahatchie Bridge? Same place.) Delta poverty is so grueling that it's tough to imagine how it could get worse. Yet the seemingly impossible is occurring. Tallahatchie County is suffering from a *decline* in manufacturing jobs.

But by and large, the growth that has occurred in the South

has been pretty well spread around. The feeling Southerners have that they can see it "everywhere" is borne out by the Southern Growth Policies Board. On its economic map of Dixie, the pale green of growth — more people making more money — speckles the region so thoroughly that it's far easier to point out where it is not taking place — northern Louisiana, southern Arkansas, western Mississippi — than to attempt to catalogue all the places where it is.

Statistics show that urban and rural growth have been pretty well balanced, too. This means that economic improvement is being felt by a broader range of people than if it occurred just in Montgomery or Savannah, for example. It also spreads out the problems associated with growth, like clogged roads and visual blight. Theoretically, this allows them to be dealt with more easily. They don't overwhelm simply one locality, like Detroit or Cleveland.

Evan Brunson of the board analyzes the dispersal on several levels. First and most obvious is that the less industry a town has, the more likely it will be to have land and labor that can be bought cheap. Second, the poorer the area, the more hungry it is likely to be. If a locale in Dixie wants your factory badly enough, the taxpayers will frantically fund an industrial development board to woo your company, and will issue revenue and general-obligation bonds to finance your land, buildings, and equipment. The locality will train workers expressly for your tasks, at your site, at their expense, without even guaranteeing jobs to the trainees, thus making it easy for you to screen applicants. And then it'll waive your property tax for a few decades. Third, no matter where the town is, it's getting increasingly difficult for it to be more than an hour away from an interstate or a commercial airport linking it to whatever's needed in the way of critical parts or technicians if an emergency should arise.

But finally, Brunson thinks, you can't underestimate that mysterious thing called southern quality of life. It's this simple: when a plant is being sited, no matter what the beady-eyed bookkeepers come up with in terms of economic justifications, the decision-makers are going to get to the point where it dawns on them that there are some among them who will literally have to live with this choice — go down to run the place and raise their kids in this town. Survey after survey has shown that most North Americans, given their druthers, would like to live in a small, stable community, where they can get to know their neighbors. And, of course, that's precisely the South's long suit.

Contributing to this quality-of-life theory is the federal government. I had started off with a notion that the Environmental Protection Agency in the 1980s was going to become the most hated arm of Big Brother in Dixie. It, I figured, would be getting in the way of a whole lot of growth to which Dixie was religiously committed.

But now I'm not so sure. The EPA's existence allows an Alabama mayor to say to a developer "Now Fred, you know how much I'd like to let you dump your purple widget waste right into the drinking water here, and if it were up to me, Lord knows we could work something out, but it isn't. You know those damn boys in Washington would be all over me."

And there's no way the industrialist is going to be able to say "Well, in Arkansas, they told me different." What Alabama can say is that we don't put any *additional* environmental restrictions on you. That's something that Ohio, for one, can't say. Because of the density of its current development, and the age of many of its factories, Ohio has existing air- and water-quality problems that force it to put an additional squeeze on new operations.

Thus, ironically, environmentalism aids in bringing industrialism to places it's never been seen before. But at the same time, the new factories are of intrinsically higher quality than those built decades ago in the Foundry. Because of national environmental laws, a new paper mill, for instance, though still not something you'd want to have on the village green, is not the thoroughly outrageous polluter and exploiter it was twenty years ago. They literally don't build them like they used to.

And, ironically, another plus is that Dixie is not, in fact, growing as fast as Houston or Boca Raton or Denver. Moderate growth has a lot of advantages. It allows time to plan. On as basic a level as trying to figure out what a town will need five or ten years down the road in terms of sewers or schools, Nashville has a pretty good chance of having today's estimates bear some relationship to tomorrow's realities. That's simply not true in Tucson. In a boom town, the decision you make today looks ludicrous when implemented two years from now. You thought that you surely couldn't possibly need more than five new cops. Instead, you need fifty.

Finally, analyses of what growth is doing to Dixie are forced to make comparisons mercifully unnecessary elsewhere. Gene Patterson, now the editor of the *St. Petersburg Times*, won the Pulitzer Prize when he was at the *Atlanta Constitution* during the civil rights era for his editorial stand on the side of the angels. But when it comes to industrial development today, he cautioned me, "Remember, about a lot of what you're going to see . . . It beats the hell out of pellagra."

Pellagra is a disease that comes from subsisting on a diet totally lacking in essential vitamins. It can result in insanity. Like hookworm infection, which children get from dirt contaminated with excrement, and which can cause anemia, stunted growth, and heart attacks, it was so common in Dixie until recent times that the memory of it is fresh in the minds of many of the people making decisions today.

●   ●   ●

With a singular history, and with growth and change so much on the mind of Dixie these days, the dark side of its development, to me, is how few people have any idea where the region should be going. If anyone has a clear and compelling vision of Dixie's future as a special place, he is hiding his light under a bushel.

The chorus to which I became accustomed whenever I brought up the subject of the future of Dixie was "Have you read John Egerton?"

John Egerton, of Nashville, Tennessee, is the author of a book called *The Americanization of Dixie*, which eloquently suggests that in return for the mess of pottage represented by the proliferation of modern McDonald's stands, the South is trading its birthright — the ineffable that once created a Faulkner.

The South as a land of grace and violence [writes Egerton], as beauty and the beast, had an irresistible fascination about it. It was evil and decadent, but it also bred heroes and dreamers, and it yielded a tenacious sense of hopefulness that kept the world from going home. It still has qualities that could make the world come back for another look. But it is well on its way to a surrender of its distinctiveness, to amalgamation in the nation, at a time when the nation is still groping, after two hundred years, for a society in harmony with the principles on which it was founded.

In the Americanization of Dixie — and in the Southernization of America — the South and the nation seem in many ways to be imitating the worse in each other, exporting vices without importing virtues; there is no spiritual or cultural or social balance of payments. The South is becoming more urban, less overtly racist, less self-conscious and defensive, more affluent — and more uncritically accepting of the ways of the North. And the North, for its part, seems more overtly racist than it had been; shorn of its pretensions of moral innocence, it is exhibiting many of the attitudes that once were thought to be the exclusive possession of white Southerners.

The South is now closer to being like the rest of America than it has ever been. The mobility of people and the diffusion of cultures through television and other media have advanced the process of Americanization to a new level. The lesson of the historians is that the South has never made a practice of learning from the mistakes of others or from its own: if it remains true to form, it will keep on going through the open door into the Union, emulating unquestioningly the values and venalities of the big house.

This view demands special attention, not only because of the power inherent in it, but particularly because it appears to have become the majority view of the thinking Southerner. It is a view that seems to be gaining the status of Gospel. And it has some implications that may very well be accurate, but that are no less disturbing for that.

For one thing, if assimilation is Dixie's future, does that suggest that once again it's bucking history's tide? A hundred years ago, most of the continent realized the advantages of federalism: armies to confront Spaniards, Indians, and other obstacles to conquest; a treasury to raid for crucial public works; an industrial base to crank out tools for dealing with savage conditions. This, of course, is exactly when Dixie chose to rearrange the architecture of Fort Sumter, for its own good and sufficient reasons, and the ultimate result was a century of underdevelopment.

Today, North America would appear to be maturing. One region after another discovers itself to be strong, distinctive, and capable of having interests and solutions neither dependent on, nor congruent with, other regions. Places like the Pacific Northwest, without a tenth of the history and pain of the South, are forging very original and highly idiosyncratic responses to challenges. So, I would submit, are the other nations of which this volume speaks.

But what, then, if Dixie is in fact becoming "Americanized," would the response of the South seem to be? Apparently, the answer is to pack it in. Forget the music, the dialects, the tales, the violence, the beauty, the humidity, and everything else that always made Dixie the most distinctive nation. Obviously, that has nothing to say to the future. General Sherman may have started the process, but General Electric, with its air conditioners, is going to finish it. The South will become little save the happy hunting grounds of Holiday Inn.

Does this sound plausible? Well, yes, if you concentrate solely on what the South today is *not*. It is no longer predominantly poor. Nor rural. Nor agricultural. Nor apartheid. If it is not all these things that once set it apart, then it is logical, perhaps, to see it as embracing all things plastic and homogeneous.

The trouble I have with this theory is that if it is true, it would seem to me to imply that there was nothing about the South in all these years that met three criteria: being special, being capable of surviving a complicated, industrial world, and being good. The implication seems to be that if the South throws out all the bad, it throws out all that's uniquely southern.

That may be true. It could be that the well was poisoned for so long that it will never flow sweet. If it's not true, then I guess the obligation is to show what will be tomorrow's South.

And there appear to be a few interested in embracing this task.

In a walk around Durham, North Carolina, you can begin to see Egerton's point. The place still smells like Dixie. The home of Liggett and Myers, the scent of ripe tobacco fills its air. Durham smells like a fresh package of Chesterfield Kings. If you look closely at the brick of a warehouse wall, you can still see the faded paint, which reads DRINK LEMON-KOLA. It's an ornate script that swashes out from the bottom of the *K*, and then loops to return to link up with the word LEMON. It's a style that survives in the Coca-Cola logo, Coca-Cola, interestingly enough, being both a symbol of world homogeneity and its birthplace: Atlanta, Georgia. Lemon-Kola itself is gone. I wonder what a lemon cola tasted like.

Beyond Elliot Street is the standard, poor, black neighborhood. A lot of tin roofs that need paint. A ramshackle "cash grocery" with steel grilles over the windows and chain-link fencing around its entrance. Mt. Giliad Baptist, with its inevitable blue and white bus. Endless rows of porches. A few have curved tubular-leg kitchen chairs on them, and occasionally you'll see a comfortable-looking stuffed chair with a rip down the middle of its vinyl. But overwhelmingly, the porch furniture is molded-metal armchairs and love seats that glide back and forth on rails, all with identically patterned perforations on the back and seat to let cool air through. Somebody made a fortune selling molded-metal porch furniture in Durham years ago.

But these are traces of what used to be. They're not how you'd describe the town now to a stranger. Durham now is Duke University and the C'est La Vie Disco and Dinner Lounge in the rehabbed brick warehouse. The downtown has been totally face-lifted. Trees have been planted, fountains added, and modern, geometric street lighting installed. Of course, all the diagonal-to-the-curb parking spaces have been eliminated in the process. That just irks the hell out of the locals and probably explains a lot of the empty storefronts downtown. Urban renewal has been going great guns for at least twenty years. You'd think by now they'd be able to get it right.

The North Carolina Mutual Life Insurance Company building is one of those high-rises that appears to float on walls of glass. The Northwestern Bank, Home Security Life, and even the First Presbyterian Church Day Care Center are basic corporate modern, and are linked by flowing concrete highways that swirl through and around the downtown in brand-new, graceful, if enormously confusing patterns. In the wealthier residential neighborhoods, porches are rare. Somebody else made another fortune in Durham more recently, punching holes in old walls three feet wide, two feet high, and five feet above the floor. Where the air conditioner goes.

(Digression: A woman in Arkansas told a man that her life had been changed by three things: television, air-conditioning, and rice. Rice? he asked. Yes. Television gave her a reason to come in off her porch. Air-conditioning made it physically possible to do so. But when the fields were flooded in order to grow rice, the mosquitoes came, and now she can't go back out to spend the evening chatting with her neighbors and watching the passing parade, even though she has a mind to.)

Heading out toward the University of North Carolina along the Jefferson Davis Highway, one gets a view of what Egerton might agree is becoming the "real" South. Route 15–501 to Chapel Hill is solid strip development. Shiny chrome and glass cubicles that dispense gasoline, cigarettes, and beer. Acres of concrete parking lots. Shopping centers. Massage parlors featuring adult entertainment. All the modern conveniences.

I almost blew right past that vision of an adaptive future, the Southern Cooking Carolina Style Eat In, Take Out Restaurant. Surrounded by a parking lot, with a garish back-lit sign that tends to blend in with the forest, and fronted with plate glass, it's a very studied, if not entirely successful, attempt at looking like a cookie-cuttered Franchise Fast-Food Heaven. But it messes up the details. For one thing, right out front it indicates the availability of Brunswick Stew, Pinto Beans, Hot Biscuits, 6:00 A.M. to 9:00 P.M.

For another thing, although the cramped foyer in front of the counter where you place your order had four booths, close examination reveals that they are not machine-made. They are heavily covered with enamel paint to make them look like plastic, but they are definitely not the real thing. They're made of wood. Another thing is that you can't be too fat, and you have to snuggle real close to get four people into the booths. They do not meet Standards.

The pecan and banana cream pies are another failing: they do not look commercial. They taste homemade.

Under the part of the menu on the wall labeled "Biscuits," there is a category "Fatback." Fifty cents. I ordered two. The fat came crispy and golden, with a rough, salty bacon taste to it, and very hot. The biscuits were piping, and I could be wrong, but I could swear they were made by a human. It took me four minutes to be served. And seven hours later, when the day's first splash of bourbon hit my stomach, the lunch revealed itself to be still there. That's value. That's stick-to-your-ribs. I was a satisfied customer.

Driving up through the Mississippi River Delta along Route 1, one gets a very different vision. The road is four feet above the surrounding fields, just to get it out of the mud. The land is absolutely, precision-ground flat. Far flatter than Iowa ever dreamed of being. And it's empty. You can drive for miles without seeing a building or a farm implement or another car on the road, even though this is some of the richest cotton and soybean country in the land. The scale of agriculture here goes to thousands of acres per operation — ten thousand, twenty thousand in some cases — far grander than Nebraska ever dreamed. They're still called plantations. And this is still the poorest part of Dixie.

Without even going off into the back roads, you can see many a shack with a crack-back roof beam, barely supporting rusted-out plates of tin that hang off at an angle. The porch sags, wallboards are missing, and a blowout patch covers a major hole in the side. Cardboard covers broken windows; the door hangs off one hinge — and you think oh God please don't let there be anybody living in that; please let it be abandoned. But a line of laundry flutters out back. Or a stick-ribbed, evil-looking, spavined cow stares at you from out front. Absolutely isolated in the middle of a field, a weathered church stands next to a fresh grave, lavishly covered with colorful wreaths and flowers.

As with everything in Dixie, there are two ways of looking at this wretchedness, about which foreign correspondents reach for comparisons to Bangladesh or Arab refugee camps. On the one hand, you can be amazed that it still exists after all these years, after all that work, after all that federal money. On the other, you can, like Phil Carter, the former editor of the *Greenville Delta-Democrat Times*, be amazed at how little of it is left after less than one generation of war on it.

For driving into Greenville is not unalloyed misery. As common as the shacks, are well-painted green aluminum roofs supported by steel beams and no walls, under which stand row after row of tractors, combines, and trailers with wire-mesh sides from which hang flecks of cotton. Brightly colored and obviously well taken care of, this John Deere equipment stands, some of it with four, man-high, rear flotation wheels; hundreds of thousands of dollars' worth of equipment, all alone, ready to go. In the middle of another cotton field, you'll see a brand-new, two-car-garaged, brick ranch house so fresh and new that the scraggly young shrubs in the front haven't settled into the earth yet. The most obviously expensive brand-new suburban homes have pillars in front of them. (In many parts of the South, the long, low, California-style ranch house has had a second story tacked, incongruously, above the foyer, in order to allow two-story pillars to be placed in front.)

Coming into Greenville on the inevitable strip-development highway, one sees, just after the Country Club Estates, the intriguingly named Mainstream Mall. Bright, shiny, and utterly interchangeable with any shopping center in North America, it has a Baskin-Robbins 31 Ice Cream and a place called the Dutch Country Family Restaurant. Folk in the Delta will tell you that the name Mainstream Mall is a reference to the Mississippi River, and has nothing to do with its place in society. If that's true, it's the most colossal commercial Freudian slip I've run across.

The architects have even gotten to downtown Greenville. Phil Carter's father, Hodding Carter, who won a Pulitzer Prize in 1946 for his stands in favor of racial moderation (Hodding Carter III, Phil's brother, was a spokesman for the State Department on television during many international crises, including Iran, in the late seventies), once wrote a book called *Where Main Street Meets the Levee*. It was a collection of tales mostly about newspapering in a small southern town, and is still read by folk who realize how important a task that was in a land noted for ignorance. The title is a reference to where the newspaper office once was. It's no longer there. The paper has moved out near the by-pass, next to the new Uncle Ben's Converted Rice factory, which represents growth that people are excited about as far away as Jackson. Main Street, meanwhile, has been turned into S-curves. The wide avenue, in which I'm sure a horse-drawn wagon once could easily have turned around, has been planted with mounds of trees and bushes, such that the traffic pattern now is very narrow, and swings from the left curb to the right curb to the left curb to the right curb. Presumably, the thought was to add shade to the street while making it difficult to speed. The plan did not take into account the southern drunk, of which there are few drunker. From time to time some old boy late at night forgets that they've put curves in Main Street and takes it straight in a four-wheel-drive pickup, clipping off saplings, left and right.

Mercifully, the bulldozers haven't gotten to Greenville, though. Architecturally, it's still a Dixie town of two- and three-story façades, with shops below and offices and living quarters above, punctuated by the occasional grand old public building, like the massive stone bank. It's very pleasant to sit up on the second floor of one of these places, sipping something cool and telling lies, letting a breeze come in from an open window, watching the people below stroll late at night. Mr. Egerton seems to be right in thinking that the days of such buildings are numbered. People don't seem to know what to do with these old shops. They're not big enough for most modern emporiums. It's considered eccentric to want to live above one of them, if you've got a car and the ability to live out in the suburbs. When you put a high-rise Hilton or Federal-Building-Post-Office in among them, they start to look downright rural.

By contrast, the question of abandoned railroad stations in Dixie has been thoroughly examined and conquered. I should have expected it, but I did not. The old Columbus and Greenville Railroad Company station is the site of the Clone Bar of Greenville, Mississippi.

It's not really called the Clone Bar. That's just an idea that has stuck in my mind ever since a friend took me for a drink in Washington at yet another joint that is referred to as a "watering hole." He began speculating on the factory that must exist to grind out prefabricated trendiness. In nature, he figured, there are only so many ferns. Only so many spider plants. Only so much macramé from which to hang the ferns and the spider plants. For sure there is no way that the nineteenth century ever produced as many mirrors, on which are painted colorful and baroque advertising slogans for spirits, as there now exist on the walls of these clone bars. Where the hell did all these long, carved wooden bars with brass foot rests that just ooze character come from? The stained glass?

The twist on this in the South — it may happen elsewhere, but nowhere else is it so ubiquitous — is to ensconce the clone bar in the abandoned railroad station. The station is inevitably of solid construction, near downtown, cheap, and of fabulously period design, complete with gingerbread. All that needs be done is blow out the interior walls, expose the beautiful brick and beams, and then — in the touch that is always considered a stroke of genius, no matter how often it's done — roll up a boxcar, and maybe a caboose, and rehab them too (!), connecting them permanently to the station (!).

As these things go, the Clone Bar of Greenville is a very classy execution. It's multilevel, and red and white banners hang down from the ceiling. The seating is rattan and red plush. It has circular butcher-block tables. The wine racks above the bar are natural wood. The boxcar room is perfect. At its entrance is the legend:

Home Shop for Repairs

Do not load Rule 1.

CAPY 110000XM

LD CMT 119100

LT WT 57900

But the best part isn't the station itself. Nor is it the shacks to the side of it, which used to serve as dorms for freight-car workers, long ago, and which now have also been rehabbed and plate-glassed and house tiny art galleries.

The best part is that this whole thing is the project of an outfit called Delta Enterprises. Delta Enterprises is a black self-help organization encouraged by the Ford Foundation to turn to capitalism to help relieve poverty in the Delta, in the Mississippi once referred to as "The Closed Society."

Well, think I, casually examining the leggy, long-haired blondes at the bar, and feeling far more dazed by the whole experience than can be accounted for by the whiskey. It's working. This place is packed. It must be making a fortune. Mr. Egerton would be proud.

But, then, if Dixie is being Americanized, what in blazes do Southerners have against Atlanta? Surely, the airport was long an abomination in the eyes of God, and naturally, any capital city will evoke envy. But what I was hearing, I felt, was more thoughtful.

For example, it came from the Chamber of Commerce factotum of a small, decidedly non-Georgian town about as far away from Atlanta as you can get and still be undeniably in the South. I had dropped in on him for some statistics, unannounced and in a hurry to make another appointment. Of course, the visit provoked a prolonged tale about the development of the town, its new schools, its new industrial park, its bright future . . .

With the new north-south crossroad coming through, he said, we should really take off now. (Pause.) It kind of scares me, he seemed to surprise himself by admitting. I sure hope we don't become like Atlanta, he sighed, ignoring the obvious impossibility of his city going from a population of twenty thousand to a population of two million any time soon.

I took a sudden new interest in the man's ambivalence. Why? What's the matter with Atlanta? Well, he fumbled, it's the quality of life, falling back on the line he'd read somewhere. What do you mean? I asked. What have you got here that you don't have in Atlanta? Well, he said, when I drive downtown here, I almost go off the road because I have to use both hands to wave at friends.

Again and again I ran into this strange antipathy toward Dixie's largest city, matched by similarly unsatisfactory explanations. A certain amount of it was mixed with pride, but it was part of a great-place-to-visit-hate-to-live-there attitude. And this came even from transplanted Northerners, that species which is becoming so common in the South.

Could it be the crime reports? I asked myself. Atlanta from time to time is labeled the murder capital of the United States. But not for lack of competition. It regularly trades the title with New Orleans and Houston. Each of the three cities is far more bloody than Detroit, New York, or Washington. And New Orleans is more the home of quadruple apartment locks than Atlanta. Yet I didn't hear people badmouthing New Orleans and Houston.

Could it be the transportation? The freeways of Atlanta are a mess at rush hour, but, again, no more so than in most cities, and Atlanta has brought **MARTA**, the subway system, into operation, freeing thousands of commuters, a fact that had been widely reported and hailed. And, of course, the airport has been rebuilt. It's now the continent's largest.

Could it be that the city government is run by blacks? How likely could that be when the economic structure is still firmly and obviously in the hands of whites? For that matter, it's been a

long time since black city governments were a rarity in the South
or anywhere else. Why pick on Atlanta?

The mystery deepened for me when I got there. By any reasonable urban standards, this is a swell city. It's got a well-developed
fabric of 118 neighborhoods, most of them with their own local
neighborhood association. It's got excellent older housing stock
that lends itself to being spruced up and made fashionable. A lot
of the neighborhoods are amazingly close to downtown — easy
bicycle distance, even walking distance. The prices are right.
Maybe high by the standards of Paducah, Kentucky, or Trenton,
New Jersey, but a steal by the standards of desirable living in
Washington, Baltimore, or Philadelphia. It's an easy place to get
outdoors. (The jogging population is absolutely obnoxious.) It
may not be what you'd call integrated, especially when it comes
to redneck neighborhoods versus poor black neighborhoods. But
in the more middle-class areas, there are white enclaves in the
black west side and a thin but significant black presence in the
white east side. The fact that there are a hundred thousand or so
members of the black middle class within the city limits is a sta-
bilizing influence most big city mayors would die for. This is,
after all, the city of the Ebenezer Baptist Church, of Martin Luther King, senior and junior. That's always been an essentially
middle-class congregation, even if its Auburn Street neighborhood — "Sweet Auburn," as it's locally known — has seen better
days as a commercial strip.

For that matter, it's the home of the chain of black colleges
anchored by Morehouse, the most prestigious in the world. Atlanta's loaded with schools, Georgia Tech and Coca-Cola–
endowed Emory among them.

Still within the city limits, but to the north, there are twenty-
five solid square miles of nonstop mansions, weaving in and out
of the creeks and valleys of the foothills of north Georgia. If there's
a larger collection of quarter-million-dollar-and-up homes within
a major city's limits in North America, I don't know where it is.
When *this* neighborhood goes downhill, there won't be enough
stiffs in all of North America to justify turning all these places
into funeral homes. Even if some were made into small hotels —
a perfectly plausible use — it wouldn't take up all the slack.
There are not now, and never in all of history were, as many Co-
rinthian columns in Greece as there are along Paces Ferry Road in
north Atlanta. Even the neighborhood movie house is called
Loew's Tara.

The downtown, admittedly, is a bit much. Atlanta has given in to the proverbial edifice complex. "Megastructure" is the by-word in downtown Atlanta. A local architect who is nauseated by the competition to build bigger, glitzier, more stunt-laden buildings has devised a plan that, he is convinced, could make him Atlanta Architect of the Year.

He wants to put up a building ten or so stories taller than the Peachtree Plaza, which now tops the city at seventy stories, and then crown it with a ferris wheel. He's positive it would make him a civic hero.

He's right in observing that Atlanta seems to love inducing vertigo. Among the clichés no hotel would be without is the glass-walled elevator, whether it offers a view or not. Multistory atriums are very big. (Newspapermen whisper about the indoor suicide leaps right into the indoor dogwood trees.) Fronds of plants trail from space frames that support acres of skylights wherever you go. Indoor ponds are fed by indoor waterfalls. Restaurants rotate, walls are carpeted, ceilings are mirrored, banners hang everywhere, and it seems to be a crime against the profession to build a right angle, or design a shop with a simple, flat, nonmultilevel floor.

I think this vertigo may have something to do with the reason a lot of Southerners who used to rail against New York have now focused on Atlanta.

One crowded Saturday afternoon, in the Omni International — the home of every distracting environmental stunt that architecture has ever devised — a wise Georgian and I spent some minutes watching a teen-age girl watch an escalator. She stared at the sharp-edged, slatted blades of steel emerge from the floor and march up the ramp, and she watched people step on them. She watched how they held their bodies; she swayed as if to catch the rhythm with which they stepped off the floor and onto the moving stairs. She was with three younger children, and clearly she was attempting to figure out how the four of them were going to get up this escalator. She finally took a deep breath, faced the escalator — and took off her shoes. As in touch with the situation as she was ever going to be, she leaped on. Arriving successfully at the top, she started hollering directions down to her charges.

From the hollering — which, as a habit, is perfectly ordinary in a rural setting, but is quickly dropped when folk start getting used to cities — my friend analyzed the situation as one of south Georgia culture shock.

Later, I was pointed toward a bar called Harrison's as a place to study why "they" hate Atlanta. It's a clone bar, albeit one of

the biggest I've ever seen. It's where former presidential assis-
tants like Ham Jordan and Jody Powell hung out back when all
they were was ambitious, and it's probably where they hang out
now. It was jammed with slinky young women in velvet and
floppy hats, and with blow-dry-coiffed, square-jawed young men
in the standard southern uniform of three-piece suits all buttoned
up even well after office hours. I was trying to take notes on this
discreetly, still not certain what I was supposed to be understanding, when I was picked up by the girl from Tennessee. She was
from a small mountain town and had left there "to look for a
change." She had tried living in Washington, but had come to
Atlanta to work for a federal grant program, "giving away money,
you know?" She said she didn't really like Harrison's "because
the guys won't even talk to you, they're just looking around, you
know?" although she objected to characterizing the place as a
meat rack, pointing out that here, at least, it was possible to come
without getting molested. She gave me a big brave smile as she
continued her slightly cracked urban hustle, which she had never
learned in Tennessee.

It finally clicked. I got to wondering what her daddy did, and if
he knew the kind of urban insecurity his daughter had accepted
in trade for leaving her small town. And then I thought about the
late Dr. Andrew Young, Sr., the New Orleans dentist who was
the father of Andrew Young, briefly our ambassador to the UN
after serving as one of the first black congressmen from Dixie in
this century. Dr. Young, born in 1896, was a frail thoughtful man
near the end of a long life when I talked with him. When he spoke
about Dixie, he repeatedly came back to the point that, in his
opinion:

The South has always been a better place to live than the North, even
during segregation. You always *knew* where you were. The South has
always been better because you've had less chance of being embarrassed.
In the North [in the pre–civil rights era] you could go into a store, or a
tavern, but they'd serve you when they felt like serving you. In my opinion, it was better not to be able to go into a store at all than face that
kind of humiliation. Now, in the South those unjust old [segregation]
laws don't exist. They can't hide behind those laws. In the North you
still wait. In New York, just recently, we were in Lord and Taylor. I sat
there, my wife walked around, and nobody came up to her at all. It was
humiliating. Here in New Orleans, they meet you at the door.

This sense of knowing where you are and who you are — in the
best, nonracist sense of the phrase, quite literally knowing your

place, both geographic and your position in it — might be the elusive factor that is southern and good and possibly capable of surviving.

The suggestion is rooted in the South, more than any other region, being a patchwork of small cities and towns, and likely to remain so for the foreseeable future. It is one of the few places where economics are matching social goals. Small cities and towns are where people want to live, and small cities and towns are where industry wants to go. Since the South is an industrial frontier, nothing is there to stop it. This suggests that the forces of nature are working to prevent exactly what the residents fear: the Atlanta-ization of every comfortable town.

The importance of this comes down to the hackles on your neck. People who grew up in the Foundry or New England may find it difficult to believe, but it's possible to have a stranger wave and say hello on the street without that person being a Moonie or a bum. In Charlottesville, Virginia, being waved at by people you don't know is a warm and enduring part of life in a southern town. It's considered poor form to respond to it by averting your eyes, shortening your neck down into your shirt collar, and quickening your step.

People who do that remind me of the *Wall Street Journal* reporter who recently asked me of my travels: "Is Mississippi still scary?"

In Mississippi, drivers go so far as to wave automatically to strangers in a raised two-finger salute from the top of the steering wheel as they speed past. It's part of living in a world that people understand and feel that they can control.

It even helps to bring the apparently inexplicable into focus. As one Atlantan put it:

Crime in the city is tremendously threatening — the bizarre things that happen. But you know, it's not that things are more bizarre. It's that you don't know the person. You don't have any idea where he or she came from, and it's just crazy to you. For example, the guy who walked up and shot the secretary in broad daylight. There were two million people in Atlanta who didn't know that fella, and it just seemed awfully bizarre.

Well, I recall about seven years ago, somebody went into an old woman's house over in Greenville, Mississippi, and sat down and just sort of began the game of shooting her. Shot her in the leg, then shot her in the arm, and then, well, he killed her.

Well, that was horrible. But folks knew him. "Now you know," they'd whisper, "his family, they were never really quite . . . You know his uncle. He always would get . . ." They could somehow make it all fit. Terrible, but it fit. It's not just crime in the newspaper.

Yet there are many who argue that a vision of an industrialized, wealthy, dispersed, friendly South, freed by foresight and intelligence from having made the mistakes of the North all over again, is a joke.

A bunch of southern liberals, called the L. Q. C. Lamar Society, in 1972 published an extraordinarily depressing book entitled *You Can't Eat Magnolias*. First it argued the importance and inevitability of economic development. Then it listed just about every single thing that could go wrong in the process. Then it attempted to suggest solutions. The reason the book is depressing is that the solutions often read like the same ones that have been defeated everywhere else. Like schemes to limit suburban sprawl by the government intervening and buying up land. If the solutions don't sound likely to be adopted, then you're left with the list of problems; and believe me, it is long.

I wasted more than a hour of the time of Blaine Liner, the director of the Southern Growth Policies Board, in the manicured monument to that immaculate miracle of industry, Research Triangle Park, North Carolina. I kept on talking at cross-purposes with the man. He discoursed about growth. I kept asking, "What's southern in all this?" Finally, he blew up at my ignorance.

"What the hell do you want from us?" he asked. "Twelve-inch-wide pecan floorboards on our airports? Do you want to spend two days slopping from Raleigh to Durham on roads that aren't paved? I can fly to Birmingham, get my work done, and fly back the same night. I don't know if that's southern, but I like it."

It wasn't until I talked to Terry Sanford, the former governor of North Carolina, former presidential candidate, and guiding spirit behind the founding of the board, that I realized quite how confused I'd been. When the board was first founded early in the seventies, its very slogan was "Southern Growth Without Northern Mistakes," and I thought that still was where they were coming from. I didn't pick up on the repeated reference to the slogan being "that old cliché." Sanford finally explained it to me. Around the middle of the seventies, people stopped taking the idea seriously because the politicians involved couldn't come up with a specific consensus on what a northern mistake was.

Even Stephen Suitts, whose Southern Regional Council attempts to continue the work of the civil rights movement, referred ironically to some of his old ideas as "foolish."

I've always held that quixotic notion [he said], that the South's potential for what Martin King called a beloved community — and what I hope is an integrated community — has always been much greater than in any other region. And I've always thought that was important not only in terms of equality and freedom, but in terms of productivity for your region. It influences everything.

I thought the South had more potential than anyplace else. So what's happening is, I'm seeing the welfare of some Southerners increase, and the potential which I've always thought the region had, being slowly but surely diminished.

There was good reason ten years ago to speculate that the South could well be the region where anybody and everybody would want to live. But those of us who were speculating on it are finding the South less attractive to ourselves. That potential is just not being grasped.

When the weather in the South becomes the major factor in talking about why people live in the South, you know that it's become an accident of geography, rather than [a product of] human enterprise.

•   •   •

If writing about Dixie has been a growth industry for the last two hundred years (which it has; there is little more daunting than facing the libraries and libraries published about Dixie), then declaring a portion of southern history "New" is the South's most time-honored literary trap.

By my calculations, there have been at least six major, widely hailed New Souths since Lee's surrender to Grant, not to mention the minor, trial-balloon New Souths that the sad surplus of southern journalists float from time to time (everybody's gotta eat).

Few have not taken a lick at the notion. Faulkner, in *Absalom, Absalom!*, had one of his characters, a Canadian, upon hearing a particularly lurid tale, remark: "Jesus, the South is fine, isn't it. It's better than the theatre, isn't it. It's better than *Ben Hur*, isn't it. No wonder you have to come away now and then, isn't it."

W. J. Cash, in a much-honored work called *The Mind of the South*, published in 1941, says in the preface that his New South — which I believe is about three New Souths ago — "now, indeed, save for a few quaint survivals and gentle sentimentalities and a few shocking and inexplicable brutalities such as lynching is almost as industrialized and modernized in its outlook as the North."

(This is the same preface in which the author feels compelled to address the question of whether "white trash" are really genetically incapacitated. After considerable discussion, the author cautiously generalizes that the answer is no.)

So it's always dangerous to talk about change in the South, and undoubtedly even more dangerous to fixate on Opelousas, Louisiana.

But west of the Atchafalaya Bridge, which is where, they say, real Cajun country starts, and on your way up toward Evangeline Parish, north of Opelousas, there's a place called T and D's Groceries and Apartments. It's right on the cement-tar road there, just a block from a house where a family is keeping four young steers in the side yard — you never know these days about beef prices. The Sears Service Center is across the street.

T and D's offers state-of-the-art hot boudin, which, kept warm in a slow-cooking electric pot, is a fat gray sausage with rice in it and a spiciness that kind of sneaks up on you from behind when you're not looking. T and D's also offers cracklin's, which are pieces of golden fried fatback, packed in a little plastic bag, convenient for snacks. Also tasso (for gumbo), crawfish tails, and duck meat.

Back of T and D's, through the mixture of rural and suburban housing that plants a five-house brick subdivision next to trailer homes up on blocks, emerges a broad, football-field-sized expanse of lawn surrounded by a chain-link fence topped with barbed wire, beyond which is a cluster of buildings identified by a small sign: FMC.

FMC is a twenty-nine-division conglomerate, into everything from food-handling to solid rocket propellants. This plant was built in the sixties to make insecticides. It produces carbofuran, which is marketed as Furadan, and what Furadan does is get poured into the ground of Dixie by tractors, and then taken up into the root systems of corn, tobacco, peanuts, rice, sugar cane, Irish potatoes, sorghum, and millet. It then proceeds to do terrible things to the corn-root worm, the tobacco worm, and nematodes.

There's a guy who lives next to this FMC plant who also claims, in a very large lawsuit, the likes of which is also becoming very Dixie, that Furadan has done terrible things to his horses, which graze a few feet from the plant's fence. Also typically, the plant's management vigorously, and thoroughly, refuses to discuss this.

The FMC plant is worth studying in other ways. Its pay of $5.00 to $6.00 an hour for line employees is considered an 8 on the local 10-point wage scale. It's in a place with a convenient "surplus" of labor. Unemployment ranges from 8.5 to 11.5 percent. Taxes are low. Unions are few. Its location is twenty-four miles from the nearest interstate, although it is serviced by two other major divided highways. Navigable water is nearby; the airport is being expanded.

And it employs Agnes Stelly.

In 1965, Opelousas, faced with the civil rights revolution, attempted to counter demands for integration of the schools by offering "freedom of choice." Anybody could register for any high school they chose.

Agnes Stelly, one of a family of seven black children born on literally the wrong side of the tracks, had a vague sense that she might be able to get a better education if she got out of her segregated environment. So she chose to sign up for the white high school.

She remembers those years as very lonely. A few months into the school year, she concluded she'd made a terrible mistake. There were so few blacks that she refers to herself as part of "one half of one percent."

As for the whites, well, when I asked her if interracial dating was a problem, Agnes said, "It wasn't a question of interracial dating. It was a question of interracial hello-saying." Yet the thought of going back to her old life, and admitting that she couldn't handle her decision to face the new, seemed even more humiliating. So Agnes stuck it out in the white high school for four years. The year she graduated was the year the freedom-of-choice plan was shucked and the Opelousas schools were thoroughly, and mandatorily, integrated.

But meanwhile, Agnes had gone on to the University of Southwestern Louisiana, in Lafayette, to study chemistry. Despite her father's skepticism about the cash value of higher learning — after all, look at schoolteachers — all seven of his children went to colleges ranging from USL to Southern University to Xavier to the University of New Orleans.

And now, all seven young Stellys have found their place in the world. Two are middle-management executives — one in Los Angeles and one in Flint, Michigan. Another is a sales rep in San Francisco. (Agnes particularly admires him. She can't get over that he's gotten into something as risky as sales and has actually made it.)

Two are in New Orleans — one working for the federal government and the other a reporter for the *States-Item*. (The latter is the one the elder Stelly points to as proving his point about the dubious cash value of higher education.) And one is a bookkeeper in Houston.

But Agnes has returned to Opelousas. Her early twenties were turbulent. At a certain point, Agnes had had so many chemistry courses that she could have screamed. She left school short of a degree. A marriage, a child, a life in Houston, and a divorce were mixed in there, before she decided to come back home and sort out her life.

That's when FMC came to get her. Bill Williamson, the manager at the plant and her boss, keeps saying, "She's worth every penny. She's worth every penny."

Agnes is using her chemistry background to be the head of quality control for the plant. In her lab inside the firestone-brick office building at FMC, in front of the huge gray cubes of aluminum that make up the plant itself, she is surrounded by things like her Hewlett-Packard 5730A gas chromatograph. It's attached to the 5701A isotherm oven and the 3380A computer. A Mettler H51 balance for weighing things to five digits right of the decimal point is somehow associated with the microscope, the centrifuge, the pipettes, and the sulfuric acid.

Agnes is making plans. FMC is willing to pay for her to take courses leading to the completion of her degree, and she intends to take the company up on the offer.

She doesn't want to stay in Opelousas forever, although she admits the money is good, and she's putting away every nickel she can, and they are many.

Williamson, when asked about Agnes' salary, takes a deep breath. She's making a lot of money, he says. Compared with those line workers whose wages are described as 8 on a 10-point scale? Oh hell, she's making a *lot* more money than them. She makes more money than a schoolteacher. Why, he adds, she's making a lot of money by the standards of a man!

And that remark may reveal why it's logical to suggest that we're heading into a kind of seventh New South, another step, perhaps, in the Americanization of Dixie.

In 1956, Agnes' father, a bus driver, was approached by the city fathers and asked if he would accept a special task. Times were changing, they explained, and Louisiana had to change with them, and would Philip Stelly be willing to take a job as one of the first two black police officers of Opelousas? He describes those years as so long ago that "it was before they made the streets one-way." And he doesn't remember them as being easy. First it was a struggle to get a patrol car allocated to a black man, and then it was a struggle to get a patrol car that wasn't a hand-me-down from a white man. But time moved on, and Mr. Stelly moved with them.

And now FMC has turned to Agnes and offered her a job, and it admits that it recruited her for reasons of social justice. But not because she's black. This plant, surrounded by homes the front yards of which, even in the 1980s, can still be found littered with geese and goats — in a Dixie deeper than which it's damn tough to get — has been integrated for years.

Bill Williamson even looked confused when I asked him whether he'd hired Agnes because of her race.

Of course not, he said.

I hired her because she's a woman.

THE ISLANDS

ABOUT THREE MILES into the heart of the city, but at a point where the Miami River is still wide enough for a small ocean freighter to just squeeze through, the denizens of the Gunkhole were trying to figure out why the Coast Guard was on their case.

The officers had been through earlier that day, rapping on hulls, waking people up well before noon. The twenty-fourth of the month, they kept repeating. The twenty-fourth. They wanted to make sure everybody knew, because they were coming back then, and with extreme prejudice.

The river rat lounged in his bathrobe near the newest blowout patch on the deck of his fiber-glass twenty-eight-footer. It was now near sundown, the hour that, along the river, made the sober acutely aware of their condition, setting them off in search of a cure. Near a banyan tree, one of the ubiquitous rusting fifty-five-gallon drums bore empties of the universal solvents: Myers's Rum, Beck's Beer, Tropicana Orange Juice, and 80 W 90 gear oil.

The river rat was the one who had christened with the name Gunkhole the largely commercial anchorage in which he and his cohorts lived on their boats. Actually, what he'd said was that there were two ways to go with boats: Merrill Stevens and Gunkhole, and this wasn't Merrill Stevens.

Merrill Stevens is a drydock and anchorage at the southern edge of Miami, on Dinner Key, in Coconut Grove. Its view is of Key Biscayne, the superwealthy island to which Richard Nixon used to retreat with his pal Bebe Rebozo. Merrill Stevens' customers wear starched whites, own "yachts," not "boats," and hire cleaning ladies for them while they are in port. The sterns bear the names of cities from Montréal to Panama. Merrill Stevens believes in hulls with many layers of fine lacquer, accented with metallic gold pinstripes. It does fine work. Its customers do little at all.

The Gunkhole, by contrast, is very different, but just as much Miami. Halfway between downtown and the airport, it's a somewhat trashed oasis. The Miami "River" is actually more of a crooked canal. It's lined with docked craft ranging from cabin cruisers to rustbuckets over a hundred feet long that haul, between islands, TV dinners or whatever. The open water between hulls on one side and hulls on the other, in fact, is less wide than a swimming pool is long.

It's nonetheless been so repeatedly dredged that, as you sit under the Gunkhole's banyan, in a salvaged leather seat from a ship's cockpit, amid the dead batteries and crapped-out motorcycles, sipping beer, you can look out and see what appears to be the penthouse of a small apartment building drifting past, towering over the palms. It's actually a cargo ship improbably heading upriver, guided by two tugs being careful, very careful, not to scrape somebody's paint job.

Though the Gunkhole is hardly the antiseptic world of Dinner Key, there is little purposeless junk around it. A rusting pile of steel is being miraculously transformed into a fifty-eight-foot sailboat. A young blond Viking who barely speaks English is working with an acetylene torch, great precision, and the help only of a grizzled old man, to produce the hull's graceful curves, angling flat piece of metal to flat piece of metal.

Under a kerosene lamp, the woodworking "shop" of the aforementioned river rat stands on the bank, covered only by some sheets of plastic and a few lizards. Power cords off a jerry-rigged patch box lead to a jigsaw and a grinding wheel, next to a paintbrush and a can of epoxy. An old dory that's been painstakingly sanded down and caulked lies upside down on some logs. Shorn of its paint flakes and marine growths, the boat's timber shows its fine grain. Examined closely, this utilitarian cork is something of a work of art. Tiny white flowers bloom nearby.

Overhead, planes with exotic markings scream in low, drowning out the conversation, as they do all over Miami. The sport in the Gunkhole is to attempt to determine their cargo and origin by their sound and looks. Engines protesting their need of a tune-up as they angle their craft into the glide path are assumed to be from islands where the fine points of twentieth-century technology are considered optional. Ditto jets that, while over a populated area, jettison excess fuel so that their wings won't break off on landing. The airways of the islands continue to harbor virtually every make of commercial aircraft ever built, no matter what its age. A Super Constellation, the triple-tailed prop job made obsolete by the first 707s, rumbles by, its nose at an odd angle to the runway. Nobody believes that anything legal is carted in the hold of the unmarked DC-3 that follows.

A Coast Guard *environmental* inspection? asked the pirate in cutoffs from the sloop docked nearby in the Gunkhole. He watched the soap suds trickle illicitly into the river from the open-air shower on the bank. Use of the shower constitutes indecent exposure. But more to the point, the soap pollution is the kind of thing the Coast Guard seemed to be upset about.

Any kind of law enforcement in the Gunkhole was considered a marvel. The evening was full of idle curiosity about what, exactly, moved the Coast Guard to attempt to tighten up on the laws against flushing toilets into the water.

Maybe it was the snake drills. Maybe that's what got to them. From time to time, it seemed right to throw a length of hose into the river, yell "Snake!" and everybody open up with shotguns, Magnums, semiautomatic weapons, whatever was handy on the boats. Apart from being fun, it established that the Gunkhole was heavily armed and crazy, which was all to the good. You wound up being able to leave your tools out on deck and go for a beer and come back, and nobody had messed with your stuff.

Maybe it was the dope. But no. For one thing, drug-smuggling is South Florida's number one industry — ahead of tourism. It would be preposterous to think of a pollution check as the pretext for a bust. "Fishing" boats whose nets had obviously never touched water plied the river all the time. It would take at least the Navy to put even a dent in the traffic. Besides, it was no big secret that the Gunkhole had no reason to be holding cargo. The multimillion-dollar shipments of marijuana bales were off-loaded at the seafood store up the way.

Maybe it was the 220-volt line to the radio's illegal linear amplifier that had brought the Coast Guard. That idea aroused great jocularity. When that radio was fired up, they explained, lights dimmed all over Miami, television along the river displayed unseasonable snow, and you could ship-to-shore with Colombia. But the antenna had been broken for several weeks. No, that couldn't have been it.

The pirate allowed as how he thought he would just pull out to sea until this inspection nonsense blew over. The IRS and he had failed to communicate for some time now, and he saw no reason to risk his streak of luck by talking to the Coast Guard. Not about anything.

Unfortunately, there was a problem with that. It would lead to a hassle with the damn state of Florida, since the boat, which he'd built from scratch, suffered from an utter lack of title, registration, running numbers, tax payments, and so forth. The river rat in the bathrobe thought he'd hang around. He was fairly sure that he could find something more current than the expired registration sticker displayed on the bow.

Besides. There was a bright side to all this, he said. If you put five gallons of crankcase oil into the bilge of the neighbor's tugboat and got it pumping out just as the cutter hove into view, the Coast Guard would take one look at the slick on the water and hit the tug's captain with at least a $5000 fine.

The Coast Guard just can't take a joke about oil slicks, pointed out the river rat, warming to his idea. They'd lead that old bastard away in handcuffs. Probably impound the boat. Serve him right, just for the time he steered two hundred feet of concrete-post-laden barge through a yacht basin up by Hollywood. Get him out of the water once and for all.

I've been waiting for a chance like this, said the river rat. I've been patient too. And that's the answer right there. Five gallons of black oil on the twenty-fourth.

Between jets, the noise of the city streets that surround the Gunkhole could barely be heard. The anchorage is almost totally separated from that world by land, difficult to find, accessible only via twisted gravel back alleys, lushly shaded by tropical foliage, opening up only at the very end to the clearing, where a square-nosed barge had, improbably, been made over into somebody's idea of living quarters.

I think I know why the Coast Guard is prowling around here looking for cracked toilet seats, mused the pirate. I think it's really pretty simple. I think they're just trying to figure out what the hell they've got on their hands here.

•   •   •

The first railroad didn't discover what it had on its hands in Miami — that "tangled mass of vine, brush, trees and rock," as the site on which it was to grow was then described — until the turn of this century. That was decades after the rails had reached California, at a time when Frederick Jackson Turner was prematurely declaring the end of the North American frontier. It was almost four hundred years after the Spanish discovered Florida, only to decide that it apparently hadn't been worth the bother.

The railroad was built by a former partner of John D. Rockefeller, one Henry M. Flagler. His vision was to offer one of the few places on the mainland decidedly below the frost belt to the leisured wealthy with whom he was accustomed to associate. As regionalist Neal Pierce notes, he had already "made" Palm Beach to the north, with a sumptuous new hotel, The Breakers. In a kind of winter Newport, private railway cars of the ultrarich crowded the Palm Beach sidings, and large private "cottages" clustered near the hotel. "In the evenings," historian Marjory Douglas recorded, "the music from the hotel ballroom mingled with the rustling of palm fronds, glittering in moonlight, and the winds of the sea."

The only hitch with Palm Beach was that it still was not reliably Caribbean enough to guarantee the rich a permanent haven from the cold. So Flagler built farther south, ultimately pushing his railroad even past Miami, out into the water. Seven hundred men died laying steel, island by island, until "Flagler's Folly" got to Key West in 1913. Flagler's next stop, literally, was Havana, and for a while a car ferry plied between Key West and Havana. But he wanted to build a railroad bridge to the Cuban capital, a goal the state of Florida actually began to implement in 1934. This plan might have had an awesome effect on the region's twentieth-century history, had it not been for the hurricane of '35, which wiped out forty-one miles of railroad track and trestle and forced the abandonment of the Havana bridge.

It's important to note Flagler's dream, because it was the first of the many that have washed over South Florida in waves, each different, each ultimately receding, but each leaving its mark at the high-water line.

Every one of those dreams continues to exist here intact — unassimilated — captured by the promise of the sun. Because they are dreams — visions of a kind of perfection leaving old problems behind — they do everything they can to ignore each other.

The yachted aristocrats, in their dream, had not envisioned an invasion of pensioners wishing to live cheap where the slush does not grow. The white-haired from a homogeneously Anglo-German Great Plains, meanwhile, were rather taken aback that large numbers of blacks and some crackers, as they are still locally called, considered Florida an extension of Dixie. The crackers and blacks were amazed that the Mafia considered South Florida a vacation spa, meeting place, retirement goal, and place to invest their ill-gotten gains in legitimate business. Then the Mob found itself in the midst of a cultural, economical, demographic, and political island on the land, transformed by "a piece of Manhattan which floated 1,000 miles to the south, warmed by the waters of the Gulf Stream," as one professor put it. Miami had become a dream to northeastern Jews, too.

What these dreams have had in common is that they belonged to the inhabitants of the mainland. Miami looked in one direction for its future. North. Real estate and tourism were the driving force of the economy, the source of riches. The money that came in, came in from the cold.

Despite their considerable differences, the newcomers shared a certain background so fundamental that they took it for granted. They all spoke English, for one thing, and they acknowledged certain continental Anglo ideas, not the least of which was that this was a white man's world.

This is why the geographic reorientation that South Florida has undergone in the last decade has been the most sweeping of any not caused by war in North American history. The economy and culture have turned completely around, and are now facing due south. They now look to Cuba, Puerto Rico, Colombia, Venezuela — even Argentina — for their future. As Liberty City rioting showed in 1980, black dreams have been dashed. Anglo dreams, though still alive, have become a little irrelevant.

"Jaime Roldos, the then-president-elect of Ecuador, said it best at the trade fair here in 'seventy-nine," said Maurice Ferré, who ought to know, he being the mayor of Miami. "He made a beautiful speech and then the key line was 'Miami has now become the capital of Latin America.' "

In 1959, Fidel Castro altered the history of North America in a way he undoubtedly hadn't intended. When he stepped out of the Sierra Maestra and into power, Cuba was one of the wealthiest islands in the Caribbean, as well as the largest. Unfortunately, it was also only marginally sovereign — an economic colony of the United States. There were gross inequities in the distribution of income. The Batista regime Castro overthrew was corrupt. Havana had become an anything-goes playground for foreigners in which prostitution, gambling, and vice flourished. And the large underclass suffered from vast gaps in education and health care.

In the course of attacking these problems, however, Castro discarded civil liberties and democratic reforms as bourgeois baggage. Property not only of the oligarchy but of the middle class was seized; class consciousness turning the poor against the well-off was encouraged; and, ultimately, enemies of the regime and their families were threatened, imprisoned, and killed.

The result was refugees. Hundreds of thousands of them, fleeing by boat and airplane, from repression. But these refugees of the sixties were different from most who had arrived on the North American mainland; they assumed that they would soon be returning home. They were not refugees, but exiles. It was clear to them that the Castro regime was a temporary, if not inexplicable, aberration; it would soon fail under the burdens of its own contradictions. The masses would rise and overthrow him.

So first they settled nearby, and South Florida is the nearest-by to Havana there is. Second, because they viewed Florida as a temporary refuge, they made no excessive effort to integrate themselves into the existing social structure. (To this day, Cubans do not participate as vigorously in Miami elections as they could because many still have not applied for United States citizenship. That would be to concede that they're never going home.) And third, they plotted.

They plotted compulsively, and with the skill peculiar to their circumstances. The Cubans who left the island, understandably enough, were those who stood to lose the most by staying.

Doctors, lawyers, accountants, bankers — professionals of all kinds who were less than enthusiastic about being forced into the fields to hack away at the sugar cane — made up an extraordinary proportion of the exiles. As Ferré has said, an entire class — an entire nation — was uprooted from Cuba and dropped into Miami. Neurosurgeons who did not speak English took jobs in Florida hospitals changing bedpans. Distinguished jurists whose training was useless in a legal system totally different from the one they knew loaded bundles of the *Miami Herald* onto trucks.

And they learned about the dark side of power. With the highest patriotic motives, they turned to the small clique in their midst accustomed to clandestine activities — the irate mobsters of Havana who had also skedaddled at their first opportunity — to raise money, purchase arms, train cadres. Small boats began to run raids, shelling coastal oil and sugar refineries. Guerrillas were secretly landed in Cuba to attempt the counterrevolution.

Men disappeared from Miami for months at a time. Later it would be discovered that they had been on huge, isolated Central American ranches, conducting maneuvers, training for the Bay of Pigs.

The Cubans' new environment was totally supportive of this underground. Not only was the Miami Mafia on cordial terms with their cousins who had run the lucrative Havana casinos and brothels, but Washington egged them on. The new young president of the United States who would soon organize the Green Berets was eager to explore new methods of dealing with insurgencies. The Central Intelligence Agency was delighted to help organize a small war against communism. These troops were *motivated*.

It will doubtless never be known exactly how much this unholy alliance changed the course of history. But conspiracy theorists, for example, are convinced that John Kennedy would be alive today, a graying elder statesman in his sixties, had it never existed. Castro, they say, enraged at the repeated clandestine attempts on his life ordered by the CIA and subcontracted to the Mafia, was behind the assassination of Kennedy.

The one thing that can be said for certain is that Miami was transformed into the intrigue capital of the hemisphere, reinforcing the dissimilarity between South Florida and the mainland to which it was only physically attached — an island very much like Hong Kong.

Even now, although the Cuban community has become far more interested in legitimate enterprise than in retaking the island — has become middle class and more involved in prosperity than exotic poisons — the pattern of operation the CIA pioneered persists.

Secrecy punctuated by tall tales envelops aspect after aspect of Miami. A reporter attempting to get at a description of the internal workings of the place is tempted to throw up his hands. "Those that know don't say, and those that say don't know," I was repeatedly told, even about the affairs of publicly held multinational corporations whose Latin American operations are headquartered in Miami. And the tales one does hear are so hairraising — the "snake drills" mentioned earlier are an excellent example — that one is tempted to write them off as macho b.s. baked too long in the sun.

Yet there are certain undeniable facts and sober estimates about the place:

• "There is an unusually large number of gun dealers here," says Bob Nunnery, special agent in charge of U.S. Customs operations here. "A lot of the trade is legitimate," but when Central and South American political operatives need equipment on the sly, "they tend to come here also." It's routine news — the papers don't make a big deal out of it anymore — when a Salvadorian diplomat is nailed smuggling high-powered weapons out of Miami, or a quarter of a million rounds of illegal ammunition is discovered stashed in a shipment of air conditioners. "There's a huge traffic in weapons," says Dave Tucker, director of the Treasury Department's local Alcohol, Tobacco and Firearms division. "You can triple your money by selling in Central and South America. We really just touch the surface of this."

• Companies like Focus Scientific and Electronics openly advertise as CIA equipment stuff ranging from infrared nightscopes to antibugging devices to phone scramblers.

• As many as nine deposed Central and South American heads of state have been counted living in the Miami area at one time. When Anastasio Somoza was ousted as the ruler of Nicaragua — and before he moved to Paraguay, where he was killed — Miami is where he, his henchmen, and his money fled.

• The Federal Reserve has noted that in 1979, an excess of 5.4 billion more untraceable cash dollars — much of it in $100 bills — arrived in Florida banks, from other parts of North America and the world, than left. The Fed assumes that this currency, which is an amount on the order of the United States balance-of-trade deficit in some of the 1970s, constitutes payoffs to the underground economy. California, which also has its share of tourism and crime, by comparison, showed no such surplus.

• Murders linked to the drug trade are averaging more than one a week in the Miami area.

• Plane crashes associated with attempts to fly in under coastal radar defenses, without lights, in order to land marijuana at isolated dirt airstrips, also without lights, have mounted to as high as one a day.

• When the Nixon administration went looking for talent to break into the Democratic National Committee headquarters in the Watergate, it went to Miami and recruited CIA–trained Cubans.

• When DINA, the Chilean secret police, sent Michael Townley, a thirty-five-year-old North American Anglo, to murder Orlando Letelier, Townley also sought out militant Cubans to aid him in his scheme. Orlando Letelier was the former Chilean ambassador to the United States during the leftist Allende administration, which was overthrown by the CIA. The goal of the four Cubans, one of whom was the head of an outfit called the Cuban Nationalist Movement (CNM), was to trade their involvement for permission to set up a government-in-exile in Chile under its present military dictatorship. Admittedly, these Cubans who helped bomb Letelier's car in the streets of downtown Washington were from the Cuban community in New Jersey, not Florida. But Armando Santana, the man who became head of CNM when its former leader went to prison over the Letelier murder, and who denies vigorously the FBI conclusion that he is also head of a terrorist group called Omega Seven, told CBS's "60 Minutes": "I'm not criticizing the old generation, but everything in history evolves. The new generation takes over, okay. That's common history. But the tactics of the old generation are concentrated on waiting for the green light from Washington, and waiting for the Marines to solve their problems; the CIA to solve their problems for them. And we don't believe the American government and its interests are ever going to concord with our interests. If we're going to wait for the Marines to liberate our nation, I'm going to be buried here in the United States."

But by the same token, the presence of half a million Cubans has transformed the legitimate business world of South Florida. The *Wall Street Journal* coyly refers to the Cubans as the Phoenicians of the Caribbean. The only thing I ever heard them called in Miami was the Jews of the Caribbean, often by Cubans themselves and usually in an admiring tone.

(Digression: For some reason that I can't imagine, the Cubans seem to have become the first immigrant group in North America not to have acquired a derogatory nickname. Other immigrants have been known as wops, micks, canucks, greasers, chinks, whatever. The only way outsiders have discovered to register their disapproval of Cubans is to use the standard four-letter salute, in its participial adjective form, as in "those f***ing Cubans.")

At any rate, the Cuban economic miracle has been so great that the luring of pasty-fleshed tourists is no longer the number one industry in South Florida. (Drugs are number one.) Tourism is not even number two. Trade with the rest of the hemisphere is. Because Miami is now basically a Spanish-speaking community, multinationals have flocked to neighboring Coral Gables as the base of their Latin American operations. Latin American businessmen come to Miami to export northward their textiles, apparel, crafts, beef, and coffee. And the new middle class of the Americas comes to Miami to purchase consumer goods, ranging from videotape recorders to surfboards, that are either too expensive or unavailable in their own lands.

But although tourism is now number three, that's not because it hasn't burgeoned. Latinos have revolutionized that industry, also, opening up the hitherto-dead summer season to vibrant activity. J. C. Penney now even stocks fur coats in Miami in August to appeal to the tourists from south of the equator who arrive during their own winter.

Miami is the only place in the United States [says Mayor Ferré], that's going to escape major recessions, and the reason — you really have to be honest about it — goes back to two things: the drug cash flow that comes in and impacts the whole community. And number two, the increased centralization of trade, commerce, and banking in Miami toward the Caribbean and Central and South America. This is *the* place to do business. And so, you no longer go to New York like it used to be ten years ago.

Ten years ago, Miami was not a trade center. Why was it not a trade center ten years ago and why is it a trade center today? [asked Ferré, who is himself Puerto Rican and has a Latin habit of conducting an entire dialogue by answering his own questions].

The availability of a tremendous amount of money — most of which comes from drugs, but not all — and the availability of a tremendous Spanish-speaking infrastructure. Hospitals. Engineering firms. Real estate. Lawyers. Banks. You can go from the cradle to the grave and make a lot of money in-between in Miami. In Spanish.

South Florida has been opened up as an intersection of myriad worlds. While once tied to the land, at the mercy of whatever destiny wandered down the peninsula's railways and interstates, now its avenues of the future are the seas by which it's surrounded.

"You and I look out there," said one Key West lawyer, waving vaguely in the direction of Cuba, "and all we see is water. The Conchs [Key West natives] look out, and they see streets."

If South Florida itself has become an island — with three of the fastest-growing North American cities in it, Fort Lauderdale, Miami, and Palm Beach, it might even be called a fantasy island — its rightful place is in the nation of the Islands. And that nation properly begins at Jupiter Inlet.

Jupiter Inlet is a major cut in Florida's barrier islands that allows oceangoing craft to enter the shelter of the East's Intracoastal Waterway. Just above Palm Beach, it is the northern end of South Florida's east coast — that wall of condominiums, hotels, and marinas that, shoulder to shoulder for over a hundred miles, make this strip of the Atlantic the most valuable per linear foot in the East, with the possible exception of Manhattan.

It is where the Gulf Stream makes its closest approach to the North American mainland — under ten miles. And it's where the climate changes. The Weather Bureau issues its forecast for South Florida "from Jupiter Inlet to the Dry Tortugas" (the islands out beyond Key West that Mr. Flagler's railroad didn't reach). Jupiter Inlet is the point where the balmy southerly winds of the Islands tend to give way to the more southeasterly winds, which yield the climate of Dixie.

Just east of Jupiter Inlet starts the first of the Islands' three chains. So thoroughly guarding southern Florida and Cuba from the Atlantic that the gaps between them are called "passages" — Crooked Island Passage, Mayaguana Passage, Silver Bank Passage — are the Bahamas. Almost three thousand islands, only about 1 percent of them inhabited, the Bahamas start so close to Florida (about fifty miles) that people waterski from point to point. In 1979, Diana Nyad swam the distance. Those fifty miles between Grand Bahama and the mainland is one of the longest distances between island steppingstones from Florida to Venezuela.

The Bahamas extend 760 miles straight southeast to the Dominican Republic. Smack in the middle, four hundred miles almost due east of the Keys, is San Salvador. On October 12, 1492, Christopher Columbus set the tone for the ensuing history of the Islands by declaring that spot the conquest of far-off interests. Only in the last two decades has the Islands even begun to break that pattern.

Dividing the Bahamas from the third, chain are the Greater Antilles, the only four sizable islands of the Caribbean. Cuba is far and away the largest, stretching, as it does, the distance from New York to Chicago, or Los Angeles to Eugene, Oregon. Castro has made great gains in literacy and public health among his people. His island's economy, however, is still essentially agricultural, depending heavily on sugar and tobacco, as always. Fluctuations in international markets for these goods, and the ever-present threat of crop disease, continue to make the economy of the island fragile and the possibilities for social unrest high. In fact, the 1980 Cuban refugee flood was triggered by such conditions. Cuba is a member of Comecon, the eastern European common market, and Castro's critics like to point out that without Soviet aid, which totals millions of dollars a day, the island would collapse. Unfortunately, the same could be said of the relationship between the United States and Puerto Rico.

Puerto Rico, the smallest of these four islands, is also now the wealthiest, with a per capita income approaching $3000. Unfortunately, that's still less than half the rate in Florida, and not even within shouting distance of impoverished Mississippi's, which is $5000. And of that total, almost a quarter of it is tax dollars transferred from the United States in one form or another, such as food stamps. Spanish-speaking Puerto Rico has a commonwealth association with the United States, an association about which few feel completely comfortable. Its residents are American citizens, but though they can vote in presidential-preference primaries, they can't vote in the general election. They are exempt from U.S. income tax, but have no voting representation in Congress. Puerto Rico has about as much self-rule as an American state, but that's nothing compared to the autonomy of, say, a Canadian province. Puerto Rico is no longer "the poorhouse of the Caribbean," as it was once known. Industrialization programs arising from Puerto Rico's special tax relations with the United States have created so many jobs that Puerto Rico is now witnessing more immigration — much of it in the form of Puerto Ricans returning from mainland cities — than emigration. But the price has been air and water pollution unmatched in the Islands, a pollution so bad that it's now killing crops. In the early eighties, Puerto Rico is scheduled to conduct a plebiscite to determine whether it should remain a commonwealth, become an independent nation, or be the fifty-first state. The creation of a 98 percent Hispanic state — in effect, a declaration that you don't have to speak English to be a full United States citizen — would have enormous continental implications. The point will be dwelt on at greater length in the chapter on MexAmerica.

The island separating these two is Hispaniola, divided into the Dominican Republic on the eastern, Puerto Rican side, and Haiti on the Cuban side.

Haiti is, hands down, the most miserable place in the Caribbean. Of every ten people, only one can read and write. The language is Créole, a corruption of French, which virtually nobody elsewhere understands. Most men don't live to see fifty. The practice of voodoo is widespread. The government, such as it is, is in the hands of the Duvalier family, as it has been for decades. In 1980, hundreds of black Haitian refugees started flowing into South Florida each day. Anglo officials, with no idea of what to do with these people, who had practically no skills appropriate to the twentieth century, urged that they be deported. They're not political refugees, the argument went. They're merely starving.

The refugees' supporters replied that in Haiti starvation *is* political, and thus they are legitimate refugees; justice demands that they be rescued and settled.

This is an interesting doctrine. The Haitians arrived in South Florida by overcrowding tiny boats and then floating them north. Because the Bahamas are so tightly packed, the Haitians were able to break the seven-hundred-mile trip into ten-, twenty-, and fifty-mile chunks, manageable during calm weather. In 1980, when multiple crop failures caused repeated social unrest in Cuba, mainland Cubans pulled thousands of refugees a day off the island with relatively inexpensive pleasure craft. Open outboard runabouts as small as eighteen feet made the 180-mile round trip between Key West and the port of Mariel without compasses. Larger craft, such as cabin cruisers commonly used in deep-sea fishing, made it in six-foot seas.

The point is that there is no place in the Islands that cannot be reached by these methods, and the corollary would seem to be that there is no place in this watery nation that cannot easily export its hungry to the wealthy capital of the Islands, South Florida. If this reality is going to be accepted, then South Florida suddenly has a very keen financial interest in the affairs of despots like Jean-Claude "Baby Doc" Duvalier. It would appear that if Miami doesn't want these refugees, its only option is to start taking an active hand in the affairs of the regimes under which they're starving. Either that, or push the boat people back out into the water to drown, which seems unlikely, although that's been the answer in other parts of the world.

Just below Cuba, and to the west of Haiti, is Jamaica. English-speaking, also black, and blessed with substantial bauxite deposits, it nonetheless suffers from perhaps the most crippled economy in the Islands, with, in the seventies, seven straight years of negative economic growth. Its former radical socialist prime minister, Michael Manley, claimed Jamaica was the victim of imperialist exploitation. And, as a matter of fact, bauxite-ore refineries, which make valuable aluminum, creating jobs, are scarce. Much of the refining is done in the far more wealthy — and secure — U.S. Virgin Islands, and the attendant money stays there. As a result, many Jamaicans have also emigrated — quite a few to Great Britain, since the island has commonwealth status in the United Kingdom. That's caused enormous racial unrest in England, which is not accustomed to its colonial past coming back to haunt it in the form of dark-skinned citizens from the West Indies. Meanwhile, international financial institutions, like the International Monetary Fund, have made it clear that the island will see no more development loans until the government stops spending at a rate almost twice that of its incoming tax revenues.

These four Greater Antilles are the northernmost barrier of the Caribbean Sea; to the northwest, Cuba almost touches Mexico's Yucatán Peninsula, separating the Caribbean from the Gulf of Mexico. Just to the east of Puerto Rico begins the third island chain, the Lesser Antilles, starting with the Virgin Islands. (The Virgin Islands were named by Columbus after the virgins of St. Ursula — who some consider the patron saint of sailors — for reasons probably too unsavory to speculate on.) This third archipelago curves out into the Atlantic and then back in toward the mainland of Venezuela in the shape of a horseshoe on its side. The northernmost are called the Leeward Islands; the southernmost, the Windward. The islands double back on themselves in such a way that they end farther west than they began — in the Netherlands Antilles. Almost touching Venezuela, the Netherlands Antilles are the most mysterious international banking and corporate haven in the hemisphere. Only the Bahamas come close in the race to harbor North American cash flows beyond the scrutiny of the Internal Revenue Service.

The question of which beaches in the Islands are the most spectacular is debated endlessly, heatedly, sometimes drunkenly, but never idly. The economy of much of this nation, after all, is still tourist-dependent.

But should you wish to search out the widest, softest, most deserted sands . . . Or carefully calculate which waters are the closest to the temperature of amniotic fluid, lacking only the fetal tha-thump-thump, tha-thump-thump to force total withdrawal from whatever you once thought was important . . . Or spend your days searching for words to describe the color of the sea — unnatural blues from ice to indigo; greens that would be repulsive, comparable to the color of an algae bloom, were they not so clear and beautiful . . . Should you care to study sunsets the strata of which drive observers literally and unself-consciously to applause . . .

Start with the Lesser Antilles, perhaps in Guadeloupe or Martinique — halfway through the chain.

Then spend the rest of your life working your way out.

Ahhh.

Where was I?

Venezuela. Yes.

At the extremities of North America — both at the Arctic Ocean and the Caribbean Sea — boundaries become debatable. The southern rim of the Caribbean, for example — Venezuela and Colombia — are unarguably on the mainland of South America. Yet equally unarguably they are part of the southern sphere that has Miami for its capital.

Venezuela, for example, not Saudi Arabia, invented OPEC, the Organization of Petroleum Exporting Countries. (The original idea was, believe it or not, basically ecological. The world, so the theory went, should not waste its resources and pollute its air and water. A cartel would be able to enforce conservation and husbanding. It has, too.) While Venezuela's oil is the property of the government, its development has produced a relatively large upper middle class. The oil may belong to the people, but the pipelines, the housing for the workers, and the Pepsi-Cola bottling plants to quench their thirst, were put up by local private enterprise, at a profit that often finds itself reinvested in Miami.

Enormous quantities of marijuana, cocaine, and methaqualone pills (known familiarly by their trade name, Quaaludes) are being produced or transshipped from Colombia, just west of Venezuela. The *Wall Street Journal* calculated that if the multibillion-dollar under-ground economy were ever taken into account, the United States would be revealed as a net agricultural *importing* country. The value of the vast exports of corn, wheat, and soybeans to fill bellies would be more than offset by the imports of vegetables that bend minds. Most of that trade is brokered in Miami.

Central America can also legitimately lay claim to this nation. It's geographically proximate. (Remember, the Panama Canal is *east* of Miami.) The *Miami Herald* circulates its Latin American edition there. Costa Rica, Nicaragua, Honduras, El Salvador, Guatemala, and Belize share much historically and politically with the Islands. They all are struggling with the passing of an old order marked by tightly held oligarchies that controlled tremendous land and wealth to the detriment of the *campesinos* — the peasants who worked the land. Their future is very much up for grabs. They could come down anywhere in the political spectrum from revolutionary communism to social democracy to iron-fisted military dictatorship. Meanwhile, whoever loses in these internal struggles seems unerringly to take refuge in Miami.

In Florida, meanwhile, the western border of the Islands starts at the Gulf of Mexico city of Fort Myers. Fort Myers is a bit north of an area called the Ten Thousand Islands. That would be an appropriate name were it not an undercount. This underdeveloped area really is less full of islands than it is an extension of the tufts and hummocks of the Everglades. The difference between them and the swamp is that they're surrounded by enough water to permit navigation by craft larger than an air boat. They've been a smuggler's paradise since the days of Spanish gold, and there are tales that just below their surface you can still find caches of rum lost during Prohibition. A line drawn from Fort Myers to Jupiter Inlet, under the orange groves that surround huge Lake Okeechobee, also happens to approximate the boundary of the U.S. Customs District of South Florida, which is appropriate. When a Florida official was asked whether the drug-runners of Colombia had annexed this part of his state, he replied, thoughtfully, "No. But they *have* declared it a free-trade zone."

It's obviously possible to overestimate the importance of the drug and intrigue industries of the Islands. Millions of its citizens, after all, go about their business every day without knowing a joint from a shuffleboard cue. But ignoring the dope presence in the Islands is like trying to ignore oil in Texas. The U.S. Senate Permanent Subcommittee on Investigations estimates that approximately $52 billion are spent on drugs in the United States each *year*. That's equivalent to the annual sales of Exxon, the world's largest corporation. And the undeniable capital of that trade is Miami.

Trying to get a straight fix on the impact of this money on the community is difficult. Both the smugglers and most law enforcement operations are prime sources of the macho b.s. mentioned earlier. They love to tell cops-and-robbers stories about plane chases and gunshots on the high seas. And they're good stories, too. But they tend to be isolated views, skewed to make the bad guys look bad, and the good, good, depending on the teller's perspective.

The least mouth-foaming, most thoughtful interview I had on the subject was with a top official of the Florida State Attorney's office, who asked to remain anonymous. He started by acknowledging that his outfit was simply not even trying to shut down any major segment of the industry.

We're not even keeping up [he said, with an ironic chuckle]. Tell you what we do. Like with the Sting [his office's major 1979 antidrug operation]. The Sting was a big case. We ran twenty-two wires [wiretaps]. We charged a hundred and twenty people. Got another hundred that we may charge before it's all over. Created a big flash, a lot of publicity. Well, the action just shifted from here over to Fort Myers. And as many as we divert, there are still more drug operators in Dade County [Miami] than we can handle. Yeah, we're pissing against the tide. There's no question about it.

The thing about DEA [the federal Drug Enforcement Administration] . . . There's no question that narcotics is a huge, major industry in Florida. But the truth about those figures [such as the ones quoted by the Senate] is that DEA doesn't have any idea *how* big it is. They keep saying that so much is being taken down, so much is not being taken down. They say law enforcement is getting seven, eight percent of the narcotics coming in. They just don't know.

And that's the overwhelming thing to me. Here's this huge national agency doing all of this stuff, and they just haven't been very effective. This is economic crime. This is big business. Seizing narcotics is simply a cost of doing business to the smugglers. The profits they're making . . . A seizure is just a negligible cost.

I'm very concerned about the whole value structure. What's happening with police agencies. Last year, this office, in conjunction with the Internal Review Agency of the Miami Police Department, made cases against fifteen police officers in one year. Fifteen! And we could do the same thing with PSD. [The Dade County Public Safety Department is the largest police force in South Florida.] Morale is so low there . . . I'm afraid we're going to lose PSD. We've had a couple of employees — one we made a case against — selling files out of *here* a couple of years back. One last year quit before we got a chance to fire her. She was living with a cocaine importer. It's something you've constantly got to be worried about.

Hell, there are lawyers in this office who use Quaaludes, cocaine, and marijuana, but they're very careful about it. I've told everybody here that if I can ever make a case against them, I'm gonna bust their ass. But a lot of them are University of Miami Law School graduates, and it's just part of the culture. So instead, all we do is get to bust cops.

My belief is that there is a group of very rich, very large-scale narcotics people who conduct proactive infiltration [of law enforcement agencies].

In other words, they're going after information actively. They're not sitting back and taking what comes. They're hiring ex-policemen to work in things like security firms, working with narcotics importers.

They have people like "Monkey" Morales. Ricardo Morales. He's a Cuban fellow who fought with Castro, then turned against him, worked for the CIA for years, was a major or something in the Venezuelan secret police. Very sophisticated. We arrested Monkey at a narcotics scene, unloading bales of marijuana. He had with him a radio to monitor all law enforcement radios — federal, state, maritime. And he had with him a book in which all the law enforcement bands were written down. So he could flip to them as he wanted to. Of course, those bands are supposed to be secret. He didn't just have a scanner. He knew exactly where to go. Morales is a very suave, sophisticated man. A golden man. Yeah, I guess it *is* nice to be able to have respect for your adversaries.

There are banks that we can point to that are out of line. Not that many, but they exist. Many other banks are used without their knowledge. The effect on the real estate prices is just killing us. So much money. So much money. Powerful and respected people have relationships with people who are well-known narcotics types. I'm just terrified, with the kind of money that is involved with banking, real estate, other kinds of things, about what's going to happen to the political situation over the next fifteen or twenty years.

Those security agencies they're creating. These people are putting on uniforms, and there's a hundred of them, and these people may be ex-police officers, ex-Batista officers, and they work for the smugglers, providing protection. They're a private army. They fight other narcotics people, they protect themselves, they conduct extortion, provide a political force in the community . . . Hell, what did they do with private armies in old Havana?

Most murder is really second-degree. Neighbor kills neighbor, a family dispute, a traffic dispute. Especially in a community like this, with everybody armed. But our true first-degree murder — a planned, premeditated killing, cold-blooded . . . a majority of that, far and away, is drug-related. Because our murder rate is so high here, because we've got so many other kinds of problems, no way we can keep up. If you want to commit a whodunit, you're best off doing it here now. We just don't have the investigative time.

We're drawing the battle line at trying to maintain the integrity of institutions. If we can maintain integrity in political and police and other institutions — some of our large financial institutions — we'll be ahead of the game. I would be ecstatic if we could do that. Because there's so much *money*.

The revised standard cops-and-robbers of the drug industry in the Islands goes like this:

Since about 1978, when the Mexican government's efforts to put a lid on its own marijuana-growers by bombing the fields with herbicides started showing real results, the drug capital of the hemisphere has been the Guajira Peninsula, on the Caribbean side of Colombia, which supplies about 70 percent of the North American market. Stretching from its long and irregular Caribbean coastline into the rugged and isolated ravines of the Sierra Nevada de Santa Marta, the peninsula is remote and underdeveloped. Thatched huts are common, and not even Bogotá is nearby. The broiling climate and the mountain soil combine to yield plants fifteen feet tall — three times as big as standard North American home-grown — and loaded with powerful resin. Marijuana generally produces a mild, relaxing euphoria that somehow focuses the user's attention on the finer points of music, graphic arts, and conversation, according to reports. Some of the Colombian stuff, however, is so strong that it rolls home movies on the inside of your eyeballs. Just like coffee, which is another Colombian export, the best product traditionally came from the mountains. But such innovations as irrigation, tractors, careful pruning, and the introduction of Asian seeds and carefully nurtured hybrids, have attracted the interest even of connoisseurs to the marijuana grown in the plains. A Colombian government official, outraged at the talk that 25,000 acres of his country were devoted to the drug, made a "strict calculation" based on helicopter observations and came up with the figure that *250,000* acres — ten times the original estimate — were under cultivation. *Time* magazine calculated that "such fields have a potential of producing six billion pounds of marijuana, each pound worth $600."

Of course, multiply that out and you've got $3.6 trillion worth of marijuana out of this little corner of the planet; that's almost twice the gross national product of the United States, and obviously a completely wrong figure. But it helps explain where some of the more commonly accepted, but still fabulously high figures come out. One percent of *Time*'s figure would be $36 billion, which is the traditional low-end-of-the-scale estimate of the worth of the entire North American drug industry.

Cocaine generally does not originate in Colombia; it comes from the Andes of Peru, Bolivia, and Ecuador, where the coca shrubs are grown. Colombia is the place where it's refined into fine dust and fitted into the transportation pipeline. Cocaine produces a tremendous sense of power — you feel that your mind and body are a delicately tuned machine of the gods; that you're

smart, beautiful, and tough enough to tackle anything successfully. It was made in heaven for lawyers and other control-
junkies, which explains why the allegations that it was being used
by the White House staff — though apparently utterly ground-
less — were credible.

Because of the pipeline, Colombia has become a manufacturer
of millions of Quaalude pills, almost as an afterthought. According to my Miami psychopharmacology adviser (his motto about
pills: "If you don't know what they are, never take more than
three of them"), Quaaludes produce an inhibition reduction akin
to that felt after the consumption of two or three six-packs of beer
(at half the price), while leaving the user with a comparatively
clear, if extremely twisted, head. Very popular with the younger
set, who, in the past, were the only ones who would dream of
drinking beer to get drunk in the first place.

As of this writing, little heroin, if any, is attached to the Colombia trade. This comes at a time when the use of heroin — the
only genuinely addictive narcotic in this list — has declined
markedly in North America from the level of the 1960s, although
it's edging back up. All other categories of dope, with the possible
exception of LSD, have boomed.

I've heard a dozen conflicting accounts of how the economics of
all this works. Lord knows which one is accurate. But, since U.S.
tax dollars paid for it, I'll give you the DEA's version:

Cocaine goes through six transactions between the grower and
the user. In four of them, its value doubles each time. In the first
and last, it increases by at least a factor of ten or twenty times.
The South American peasant sells 500 kilos (half a ton) of coca
leaves for about $250, which is pretty good money in a country
like Peru, where the average person makes only about $500 a year,
total. Step two: the leaves are reduced to about two and a half
kilos of paste, which sells for $5000. Step three, that paste is pro-
cessed into one kilo of cocaine base, worth $10,000. Step four, the
base is crystallized by a Colombian lab, and that kilo sells for
$20,000. Step five: it's smuggled to Florida, where it brings $40,-
000. Step six: it's cut to wholesale strength by distributors, increasing its value to $80,000. Step seven: it's cut to retail strength,
about 12 percent (although it can be as low as 5 percent), and it
becomes worth $800,000. Note that we're talking about something
the size of two cans of coffee, which can also be dissolved in
harmless-looking liquids like perfume, or compressed and packed
into any orifice imagination can devise.

It's something of a miracle that any of it is intercepted at all. Several runners, or "mules," were discovered to be smuggling only after they dropped dead. They'd swallowed small bags of the stuff, hoping to regurgitate them after they'd cleared customs. Unfortunately, some of the bags had burst. Note also that the real money is all made after the stuff is smuggled in, which also suggests the profits are largely spent in continental North America.

But marijuana, although nowhere near as costly per kilo, is the really lucrative product. Not only is the market much larger, but marijuana requires no processing. Dry it, bale it like hay, wrap the bales, and it's ready to go. Of the ultimate wholesale price, which is currently about $400 a kilo, according to DEA, the grower again gets only about 1 percent. But that's still much more than he could get scraping corn from the land. After transportation costs, the rest is gravy — much of which also stays up north. Of course, because it is so bulky, it doesn't pay to razzle-dazzle it past the customs agents in small quantities. So it's shipped in multiton lots, and this is where the excitement begins.

Getting marijuana out of Colombia is not the major logistical hassle. The drug industry has produced an unprecedented $4 billion positive balance of trade for Colombia. But since that's in dollars, the government has to print pesos to buy them, and that's produced a 30 percent inflation rate. So the current regime, alarmed at the disintegration of order in its economy, has sent its Army out to try to crimp the *trafficantes*. But bribes are effective, and the territory to cover forbidding.

An innocent-looking yacht, or for that matter, even a suspicious-looking freighter, can easily duck into corners of Colombia's extensive coast along what was once called the Spanish Main. Untold numbers of airstrips have been hacked out of the shrubbery, marked only as memorized coordinates on a map. (Flying by coordinates is not for amateurs, which is one reason people end up seriously dead from a case of landing at the wrong airstrip. Or just simply crashing. It also explains why there are so many well-trained Vietnam-era pilots in the business. This kind of enterprise is only for those who actually get off on fear.)

Blending into the heavy interisland traffic is also not the major problem. The way the United States law is written, Colombian seamen could fly the flag of the seven-leaved marijuana symbol from the poop deck and still not be eligible for arrest as long as they remained outside the twelve-mile limit and displayed no intent to enter it. Landing the stuff is the test.

Florida is, on average, the flattest place in North America, which is convenient for airplanes. It's so convenient that one of the dope planes — unloaded and abandoned — was discovered by a former governor of the state, much to his outrage, on an isolated portion of his ranch in the deserted interior of the peninsula. Pilots getting $25,000 for twenty-four hours' work have been known to put cargo planes down in a field marked only by the headlights of two pickup trucks, one at either end of the target.

As mentioned earlier, coastal radar and air-traffic controllers are often evaded by pilots flying in over the treetops. But recently, authorities have experimented with the use of Airborne Warning and Control Systems planes. These are military 707s whose radar and computers can actually look down from considerable altitude. They were designed, appropriately enough, to command and control everything off the ground in a complex theater of war. Unfortunately, such aircraft are so rare, and their use so expensive ("For once," said Commandant John Hayes of the Coast Guard, "we have something more sophisticated than smugglers can buy"), that not even governments can afford to use them routinely. So, much gets through. Drug-running is so lucrative, for that matter, that it's been calculated that four planes out of five could be nabbed — ten times the current level of success — and the one flight that got through with its three-quarters-of-a-million-dollar-a-ton cargo would still make the effort superbly profitable.

An entire industry, in fact, has sprung up in South Florida to provide ancient and expendable aircraft to the drug trade. For $10,000 or $20,000, under the table, cash, tax free, fixed-base operators with a legitimate cover provide untraceable old gooney birds. They are often abandoned after only one flight in order to frustrate lawmen. In one case, a DEA source told the *New York Times*, smugglers "landed their small plane, unloaded the dope, climbed back in and headed back out to sea, set it on automatic pilot, and parachuted out, leaving the plane to fly until it ran out of gas and crashed in 500 feet of water." If the fixed-base operator has real guts, he then reports the plane as stolen and collects the insurance on his smashed plane, in addition to the payoff. The smugglers write off the craft as a very minor cost of doing business — more expensive than the price to the peasant of growing its cargo, but cheaper than the pilot, and worth maybe 2 percent of the wholesale value of a ton of marijuana. And a DC-4 can carry seven and a half tons.

But the latest twist in the seagoing trade is what has authorities really demoralized. They had tried monitoring the dope from space. They negotiated the use of surveillance satellites to track freighters from Guajira, across the Caribbean, around the Windward Passage near Cuba, up the Santaren Channel to Florida. They succeeded in zeroing in on specific ships, all the way, and as soon as the vessels entered coastal waters, they were nabbed, much to the amazement of their crews. But this led to a practice of mother ships steaming up the coast, outside territorial water, while their crews heaved waterproofed marijuana bales out into the ocean. In order to avoid suspicion on the part of coastal radar operators, they didn't even slow down. Shrimping vessels out of Key West, after waiting a decent interval until the freighter was over the horizon, then showed up at the predetermined point and hauled in the "square grouper," as the bales are picturesquely known, and brought them into dock.

Some of the ships are now sporting electronic rigs costing $250,000 each in order to make the connection precisely. The equipment beams in on a navigational signal that fixes position on the featureless sea with a margin of error measured in feet. Ironically, the signal is beamed from a cousin of the machine that started this dance in the first place — a military satellite.

The tales can go on and on. An FBI spokesman told me reverently of a twenty-van parade full of dope that trooped up Interstate 95 with communications wagons fore and aft, and air support looking for police up ahead.

But the question remains: What is this traffic doing to the Islands?

Charles Kimball angers a lot of Islands people who don't like the implications of his analyses, but no one questions his expertise when it comes to the make-up of the South Florida real estate market. Kimball is an economist whose fanatic devotion to researching arcane real estate transfer records has led him to conclude that 40 percent of all sales over $300,000 in the Miami area are paid for with money that smells.

His work shows that the Islands has evolved a highly sophisticated banking system that unites otherwise widely disparate entrepreneurs, everywhere from Venezuela to South Florida to Central America, in one common cause: getting around the financial laws of the dozens of places in the Islands that make the mistake of trying to act as if they have sovereign governments.

In order to follow his logic, you have to understand that the

United States has gone to great lengths in its tax law to make sure that a citizen of one country, investing in some other country, is not clobbered by taxation from both countries. Originally written to allow U.S. corporations investing abroad to remain competitive with home-grown companies, the tax law now also allows the citizens of Colombia, for example, to buy and sell shopping centers in South Florida without paying any capital gains tax on the transaction there. The theory is that such investors will ultimately have to pay taxes back home in Colombia, just as Floridians investing in Colombia have to pay their native tax. This is all completely legal.

However, scattered all over the globe, there are various tiny specks of land that have, improbably, become international finance centers because of the peculiarities of their laws. In Europe, these include Liechtenstein and the Isle of Jersey. But the major collection of havens are in the Islands — notably, the Netherlands Antilles, near Venezuela; the Bahamas, near Florida; the Cayman Islands, south of Cuba; and Panama; although there are others.

In the Netherlands Antilles, particularly, corporations are allowed to maintain complete anonymity. There is no legal way to compel the representatives of corporations domiciled there to reveal who their major stockholders are, or where their money came from, unlike in the United States. Roughly speaking, it's the corporate equivalent of a numbered Swiss bank account.

Furthermore, the laws of these places are such that transactions in exotic currencies can be accomplished with far more ease than they could in the United States. So-called Eurodollars, for example — U.S. dollars that are exchanged as a kind of world currency in all parts of the globe, but obviously without the monetary controls of U.S. agencies whose jurisdictions do not extend overseas — are readily handled in the Bahamas. If these dollars changed hands fifty miles west, in Palm Beach, they would be open to a barrage of probing questions as to their origin, destination, and tax obligations.

So, because of the tax laws, the anonymous corporations, and the currency laws, what it comes down to is that you can work all kinds of scams out of the Islands.

If you have just sold a DC-4 full of dope, for example, you now have four shopping bags, weighing a total of about ninety pounds, loaded with slips of paper six inches long, two and a half inches wide, on each of which is a portrait of Benjamin Franklin. And you've got a problem. What do you do with four and a half million dollars in cash?

(How do you know you've actually received all the $100 bills to which you are entitled? Either you've fed them through your automatic money-counting machine, which, at a rate of $150,000 a minute, or $100 every .04 second, still would take half an hour to total up the bucks; or, if you're in a hurry, which happens in this trade, you would simply weigh them. One hundred million dollars in $100 bills goes you almost exactly a ton.)

Obviously, walking around with shopping bags full of money (this is literally done because there is so much money involved in drug-dealing) is not the most convenient way of operating. Apart from the physical problems of the weight and bulk (these are real considerations), a very sophisticated law enforcement agency may be able to follow your cash through its various transactions and back to you. Even if they can't lay a finger on you for drug-dealing, they may try to buck the new privacy laws that make this difficult by hitting you with tax-evasion charges, as they did to the mobsters in the thirties.

What you do, then, is ship the money to the anonymous corporation your lawyer has set up for you in the Netherlands Antilles. You can accomplish the transfer in one of two ways. You can fly it to your extremely discreet bank in the Cayman Islands, right next to you on the first class seat you've bought for it. But again, while this is sometimes done, it's inconvenient.

Or you can bring it to a downtown Miami bank, for electronic transfer.

Now if the Miami bank is operating legally, it will routinely report to the authorities that you've made a large cash transaction. If you don't like the kind of attention this may bring, you buy a company like a dress shop or U.S. auto dealership, which can become a regular customer of the bank, thus becoming exempt from the cash-reporting law. Or you can buy the bank, replacing the board of directors with people who see things your way. Outlaws used to rob banks. Now they buy them. This happens. The wife of your basic Class I felon picked up a South Florida bank for $4 million recently, which is less than you, hypothetically, have in your shopping bags. A standard parlor game among Miami journalists is figuring out which banks are knowingly operating illegally and which are simply being used without their knowledge.

Once the various banks have accomplished the transfer of your money to the control of your offshore corporation, this money suddenly becomes the property, in the eyes of the law, of a Netherlands Antilles entity, eligible for all the tax benefits accruing to a foreign investor. So when you want to buy a shopping center in South Florida with your drug money, you'll find the money treated as clean foreign cash. It is also not taxed in Florida, because presumably it is being taxed elsewhere. But since nobody knows that you're behind this offshore corporation, and nobody can find out, you can keep the various tax men of various regimes confused for a long time.

But okay, suppose you're by no means a drug-dealer. Suppose your money was made in a perfectly legitimate fashion. Say you're a Pepsi-Cola bottler in one of the Islands. Now, if your island is poor and slightly Marxist — or if it is merely poor and under a lot of heat from the International Monetary Fund — it probably has laws against your taking profits out of the country. Your leaders undoubtedly figure that it's your patriotic duty to reinvest the dough in the island where your profits were made. If you don't agree, they can and will, with some justification, brand you as an imperialist exploiter of the masses and throw you in the slammer.

But suppose you don't see it their way. It could be that you figure that you risked your own capital and used your own ingenuity to make these profits, and it's your money, so you should be able to do with it what you see fit. You may be concerned that your local government is showing signs of being overthrown in a coup, or it may be showing signs of nationalizing your business without offering you what you consider fair compensation. Or, for that matter, you may simply be appalled at the staggering inflation rates common in your part of the world, and want to shelter your money in South Florida, where the inflation rate is only double-digit, not triple-digit.

Again, what you do is ship your excess cash out to your anonymous Netherlands Antilles corporation, where it is suddenly transformed into clean foreign cash, indistinguishable from the drug-dealer's. You either smuggle the actual cash out of the country, or, more likely, you bribe a government official to ignore a wire transfer.

In this case, you are not breaking any United States laws; merely those of the country in which you made your money. And furthermore, there are a lot of Miami bankers and lawyers who would not dream of getting involved with black dollars — with drug money — who would love to help out you and your gray money because they see restrictions on the international flow of capital as a sin. They see your country's laws in the same way you do — as a crime against everything free-market economies stand for — and they are proud to strike a blow for the unrestricted international flow of capital. They're great friends of deposed dictators.

Finally, you could be a Venezuelan who's made a lot of money on government contracts. Your country has no laws against your shipping out your money, but if the government leaders find that you're doing it, they may interpret that as a vote of no confidence on your part in your country's future, and they may retaliate by not giving you any more business.

So you, too, have a motive for masking your South Florida investments by going through an anonymous offshore corporation. This transaction is completely legal; but again, the object of the game is to deceive your government.

There are a very few utterly legitimate reasons for using Netherlands Antilles' anonymous corporations. The most commonly cited is the case of an industrialist who is attempting to hide his true worth lest his family attract the attention of terrorists seeking ransom money. But there isn't a law enforcement agent alive who thinks that there are enough terrorists in the whole world to make such considerations alone the reason remote islands have become major world finance centers.

This system, of course, works for money that comes in from outside the Islands, too. Politically alarmed Italians, sophisticated Germans, and determined members of the Québecois mob all use these arrangements. But what's special about the Islands' underground economy — apart from its enormity — is that every important element of the infrastructure is right here, from the seed money to the offshore shelters to the highly trained cadre of professional people skilled in ignoring dozens of widely disparate legal systems to the end market of South Florida real estate.

Once you see it the way the people who use the system do, the whole arrangement acquires a great grace and beauty. It's a finely tuned instrument designed to circumvent the historically wrong, sociologically misguided, and petty considerations of babbling bureaucrats trying to intervene between simple tradesmen trying to make a buck and the multitudes who only want a Pepsi-Cola or a snort of cocaine or whatever. If the Islands were half as good at distributing necessities to the bottom 50 percent of its population as it is in facilitating the exchange of wealth among the top 5, it could really bring paradise to paradise.

In the meantime, of course, the system is shredding the institutions theoretically committed to other economic and social
goals and standards of morality. Professions founded on trust,
such as banking, accounting, and the law, are thoroughly com-
promised. The *Miami Herald*, in 1980, ran an entertaining but
mind-numbing six-part series in which it painted the entire economy and system of government and justice of Key West, from the
police to the city attorney to the state's attorney to the fire chief
to bankers, builders, real estate agents, merchants, jewelers, car-
dealers, boat manufacturers, and fishermen, as part of a matter-
of-fact system dedicated to importing drugs. "It's a legitimate,
illegitimate business," they quoted public defender John Keane
as saying. "The law becomes a nullity when it's laughed at by so
many people." Folk openly sport bumper stickers that say WHEN
MARIJUANA IS LEGALIZED, I WILL BE ON WELFARE. That one is allegedly circulated by the "Key West Pharmaceutical Shipper's Association." But the president of the Key West Business Guild was
quoted as saying, "I'm sure it's our biggest industry. I don't really
care. I don't know what's bad about it."

Well, for one thing, such an underground economy, which obviously pays little in taxes, drives up the levies on those who do
participate in the legitimate portion of the economy. It also adds
significantly to negative balances of trade, driving down the value
of the affected currencies, like the dollar. That helps fuel inflation.

Sam Nunn, former chairman of the U.S. Senate Investigations
Subcommittee, said, "These narco-dollars may have an economic
impact that is similar, in character if not size, to the more infamous 'petro-dollars,' both in terms of inflation and on our balance of payments. Every narco-dollar that is paid to a Colombian
pot grower or hidden away in a numbered foreign bank account
is lost to our economy, just like a petro-dollar spent for one gallon
of imported gasoline."

Of course, Charles Kimball's calculations indicate that Senator
Nunn may have a bigger problem than he thinks, because it appears clear that these dollars are not staying "out there." Like
petro-dollars in the hands of Arabs buying up properties in the
western hemisphere, these dollars are coming home.

In 1979, said Kimball, who adds that his figures are so tight
that they are admissible as evidence in court should the need
arise, a hundred thousand housing units worth $7 billion changed
hands in the South Florida counties of Dade (Miami) and Bro-
ward (Fort Lauderdale). Almost $5 billion worth of commercial

properties were sold. Zeroing in on one quarter — the last of '79 — and merely the most expensive properties — those over $300,000 in worth — Kimball says that 42 percent of the sales — almost half — were made to foreign-controlled entities or investors.

Of those sales, 54 percent — more than half — were carried out through the anonymous offshore corporations. "This is the stuff to be really worried about," said Kimball. "The offshore anonymous corporations outnumber the other legitimate investors I could find. Every one of those is suspicious. I would say at least eighty percent of these sales are crooked. Are very bad." He then pointed to a chart on which he traced in percentage terms things like "direct investments of major drug-dealers," "investments of international swindlers," "bribes, embezzlements, graft," "income tax evasion," and so forth.

The foreign investors, many of them narcotics financed [Kimball has testified], have huge cash resources so that when they are competing against legitimate investors who want to buy a property, they are quite willing to make larger downpayments, quite willing to bid up the price so that the real yield, for example, on a large building in Coral Gables would be about one percent.

You can see that no [ordinary] investor would be prudent to compete in the present financial market. If the doctor has to pay more for his office, or a warehouse in which brooms are kept has to have higher rent, because of this type of inflation, you can begin to see the impact on every citizen. And in some areas we see virtually all shopping centers in large metropolitan areas, virtually all office buildings, going into the hands of foreign investors.

• • •

Right where Arthur Godfrey Road from the mainland meets Collins Avenue, the main drag of the island of Miami Beach, stands the Crown Hotel. One of the last two all-kosher hotels on the Beach, the Crown for years has catered to nothing but the most dedicated practitioners of the Jewish faith. From sundown Friday to sundown Saturday, it chains its driveway, because it is forbidden to the devout to travel on the Sabbath. The hotel will only take emergency telephone calls on Saturdays, because phone calls on the Sabbath are taboo. Its front desk is staffed by young men in crocheted yarmulkes. Its veteran director of food services explained to me at great length the effort the hotel goes to to make sure that, for example, no tiger's milk somehow gets slipped onto the breakfast tray. Not being knowledgeable about such things, I was confused. You mean Tiger's Milk, the stuff that comes in powder form that health nuts and body-builders use as a diet supplement? I asked. What's wrong with that? No, he explained with a straight face, tiger's milk. The stuff that comes out of the females of those big mean cats if you hold one down and pull on its teats. Tiger's milk isn't kosher. Neither is camel's milk. We have rabbis to make sure that the milk we serve is strictly kosher. It comes out of nothing but cows. Or goats. Goat's milk is kosher. Never from tigers or camels.

The Crown deals with all kinds of problems not frequently encountered in other hotels. Some of its male patrons, for example, refuse to enter the swimming pool out by the beach if there are women in it. That would be a defilement. So these people have to swim in shifts. Jerry Pinault, the assistant general manager, is given fits trying to juggle reservations because some guests won't take rooms on high floors. Using the elevator, you see, would be a violation of the Sabbath. And then there are the extreme devotees of the laws of Moses for whom he has to provide pre-cut toilet paper. There's something about tearing it off the roll that appalls them.

But the most unprecedented hassle the Crown Hotel had gone through in some time was occurring the day I was there. Management was trying to figure out where to put the dart board. On that spring day, the hotel, which normally would be getting ready to shut down for the season, was, instead, girding for an invasion of thousands of vacationers from Britain, who would be arriving at the hotel all through the summer. The Crown had applied for a liquor license for its tea room, figuring that the Brits would probably want a pint of stout from time to time.

But they had little idea where to go from there when it came to creating a pub and making their Gentile foreign guests feel at home. After considerable debate, it was decided that a dart board was absolutely necessary, and it had been acquired. But then came the discussion of how large a free-fire zone one had to clear between it and a drunken limey with a clutch of very sharp objects in his fist. No one had a clue.

All over South Florida, calculations such as these are being made as the region adjusts to the declining importance of trade with the rest of North America, compared to trade with other parts of the Islands, South America, and Europe. The Crown Hotel's British invasion came as a result of some sharp-eyed tour-promoter's observation that a family from London could holiday for two weeks in Miami Beach cheaper than it could in Paris — even including air fare.

In the Columbus Hotel, meanwhile, on waterfront Biscayne Boulevard in downtown Miami, the newsstand offers *Penthouse*, the skin magazine — *"La revista internacional para hombres"* — in its Spanish edition only. *Selecciones del Reader's Digest* is also there. The newspapers available do not include the *New York Times* or the *Wall Street Journal*, but the stands do stock Caracas' *El Universal*, Bogotá's *El Tiempo*, and Buenos Aires' *El Nacion*.

Even the *Miami Herald* comes wrapped in *El Miami Herald*. *El Herald* is a daily Spanish-language newspaper with its own staff of reporters and editors that comes as an insert to the *Miami Herald*. Not merely a translation of the English-language paper, it functions as a quasi-independent voice, catering to its own readership. If the *Herald* is leading the paper with a particular story, *El Herald* may pick it up and make the news judgment to rewrite it or re-report it, but it may not. The same is true in reverse. The papers are read by two different worlds. Thus, the decisions about what constitutes news are not routinely congruent, although the various journalists involved in this process are somewhat schizophrenically sitting right next to each other. The *Herald*, meanwhile, is running daily Spanish lessons on its comics page. *El Herald*, however, does not run English lessons.

Up the street at the Everglades Hotel, a sign asks patrons to *"perdonen nuestra apariencia"* because the hotel is being carefully remodeled in indirect light and dark wood tones, accented with chrome and black strips that somehow look rich and well-executed as they reflect the wood.

In Miami, you can wander around for an hour without once hearing a word of English, but unlike portions of other cities in North America, such as Chicago, New York, and Los Angeles, which have far larger Hispanic communities, the Cuban dominance in Miami has resulted in an accent on wealth.

Downtown Miami has become the shopping district for the upper class of the Islands. Latino visitors to Miami, statistics show, spend two and a half times as much a day as Anglo visitors do. And the shops along the street named for railroader Flagler demonstrate that. Expensive *cosmeticos* are sold in chic nooks, as are such exotic goods as a *bomba de achique*. Which is a sump pump. For your yacht.

El Cowboy Ideal sells Hereford brand belt buckles, Texas Imperial boots, embroidered western shirts, and posters of frolicking colts, all at *precios especiales para export*.

Maurice Rizikow, whom many point to as the driving force behind a renewed downtown Miami, started as a Latino Horatio Alger. He came here in 1965 from Argentina, speaking broken English, and began selling imitation-fur coats out of a one-room shop on the fourth floor of a rundown building. Today he is the Miami connection for some of the freest spending the city has ever seen. His Electro Florida Corporation peddles $1700 videotape decks and chest-high stacks of matched Pioneer audio components at prices that "the common man can afford," as the sign says in his window. In Spanish. Only in Spanish. He now owns the downtown Galería Internacional, with its forty-five shops, and is making plans to build a $38 million hotel aimed, as are all the downtown Miami hotels, at the Latin trade.

Granted, there is an economic explanation to the fact that virtually every store in downtown Miami either carries, or is next to a shop that carries, mammoth, hip-high suitcases convenient for only one thing: loading expensive goodies for a long return trip to Central and South America and the Caribbean.

"Look at it this way," Rizikow was quoted as saying. "Merchandise costing $2,000 in Miami sells for $4,000 in Argentina. So people fill their suitcases. When they get home they sell some things, keep some and get a free vacation out of the deal."

Be that as it may, for some Anglos it might be a little vertigo-inducing, imagining the scene in Costa Rica as the recently returned vacation family unpacks its downtown-Miami-obtained, brand-new water skis, roller-skating helmets, microscopes, autographed steel tennis racquets, Nikon cameras, Gucci shoes, Givenchy shirts, electric popcorn machines, Sony televisions, Healthtex children's wear, Sortilege perfume, Levi's jeans, and riding saddle picked up at a branch of Hermès, the ultimate status-symbol leathercraft emporium of France, located in downtown Miami's Omni.

The ironies are considerable. Sixty percent of the luxury condominiums on Bickell Avenue in Key Biscayne are being bought by Latins. "It works this way," one observer was quoted as saying. "First you buy a condo and come here for Easter. Then you decide to come up for a couple of weeks in August. There's not a lot to do here in August, so one of the kids says, 'Why don't we buy a boat?' That's another $45,000. When you've spent $45,000 for a damn boat you start spending long weekends here. The next thing you know someone says, 'You ought to buy a warehouse.' "

The bottom line is that the Anglo dream of Miami Beach, which, in the fifties, was proclaimed "the sun and fun capital of the world" by Jackie Gleason, who broadcast his shows from there when television was young, is now withering. Its glitz is peeling; its hotels are lined with autographed photos of the dead or might-as-well-be — Eddie Fisher, Joan Crawford, Spiro Agnew. Its attractions, such as the Fontainebleau Hotel, with its determination never to use a little rococo where a lot would do, used to elicit the inaccurate effusion "Now, *that's* class." Today, it's changed hands and been remodeled, in an attempt to eliminate its reputation as a monument to bad taste. The legalization of casino gambling in Miami Beach has been urged — unsuccessfully — by those who unconsciously demonstrate just how low the Beach has sunk by pointing to Atlantic City, New Jersey, as a model.

Meanwhile, otherwise sophisticated Miami Anglos unself-consciously remark, "Oh, *nobody* goes downtown," despite abundant evidence that the Latin American vision of Miami is thriving. It's made a hitherto typical dying downtown one of the most bustling spots in the Islands. What they mean is that nobody who doesn't speak *Spanish* goes downtown.

Bona fide Latin American trade and commerce has exploded through the South Florida gateway.

• Between 1974 and 1978, trade to and from the rest of the Islands more than doubled, to about $6.5 million.

• As of early 1980, fifteen international offices of U.S. banks, chartered in Miami under terms of the federal Edge Act, were active. Fifteen more foreign banks, hailing from South America, the Islands, Great Britain, Spain, Israel, Canada, and Japan were setting up shop. They joined thirty international banks and a dozen international departments of local banks already there. This made Miami North America's third-largest international banking center, and its growth was not tapering off.

• Free-trade zones, in which goods remain free of customs duties while they are being assembled or transshipped, have boomed. The one in Miami alone is expected to handle $2 billion worth of goods a year, three quarters of which are expected to move by air.

• Since 1972, the number of firms engaged in the export-import business has tripled. The Miami Yellow Pages have eighty pages of ex-im listings. They show more than 300 freight forwarders.

• The seaport of Miami, which was supposed to fulfill the area's needs through the year 2000, is way overcrowded, and expansion plans are proceeding.

• The director of the Miami airport expects to see international passenger traffic at his facility jump from 40 percent of the action to 70 percent in the decade of the eighties.

And this has all happened since the arrival of the Cubans in the sixties. As one observer wrote, they "would pick up a suit at Burdines for $5 down, buy a ticket to South America, and start selling nuts and bolts to Latin countries out of a factory catalog. The trade is still dominated by Cubans, but exporters aren't pushing nuts and bolts. They sell whole factories."

While the Islands' export-import may have started as a mere mom-and-pop, pennies-a-day business run by a handful of immigrants, Anglo-dominated multinational corporations recognized a good thing when they saw it. Over a hundred have moved the headquarters of their Latin American operations to Coral Gables, a sanitized suburb of Miami. Most made the move in the late seventies.

Du Pont, North America's largest chemical company and sixteenth among *Fortune*'s 500, with sales in '79 of over $12 billion, has a Central and South American operation that includes forty-seven plants with twelve thousand employees in fourteen countries, generating $700 million in sales on an investment of $600 million. It moved its Latin American headquarters to Coral Gables from its corporate headquarters in Wilmington, Delaware, after considering eight other cities: Mexico City; San José, Costa Rica; Bogotá, Colombia; Caracas, Venezuela; São Paulo and Rio de Janeiro, Brazil; Buenos Aires, Argentina; and San Juan, Puerto Rico.

It ran an eighteen-point analysis of which city would best serve as the capital of its Latin American operations, and, according to Du Pont's Kenneth Trelenberg, this is how the hemisphere looked to a major multinational:

Buenos Aires and Bogotá were disqualified because of concern for the personal safety of employees transferred to those cities. There was quite a bit of terrorism going in those countries in nineteen seventy-eight, when this study was conducted.

Caracas was disqualified because of operational problems. That is, visa difficulties, acute shortage of hotel rooms, tax clearances needed for departure, and so forth. At that time, the Venezuelan government had its hands full trying to spend the oil money it was generating. They just had such a glut . . . Ships were sitting in the port for four to six months, trying to get unloaded. They just had too much business. And the way to slow things down is to make it difficult to get a visa.

San José and San Juan are somewhat isolated and lacking in direct air service to other locations in the area, so they were wiped out.

The remaining four cities — Mexico City, Coral Gables, São Paulo, and Rio — were surveyed and rated using the following criteria:

Number one, political stability and good business climate;

Number two, centrality of location;

Number three, regional air-transportation service;

Number four, telecommunications and mail service;

Number five, ability to maintain area perspective. Let me explain that a little bit. We have major subsidiaries in Mexico City and São Paulo and in Buenos Aires. There was a fear that there would be trouble with the local management maintaining its local perspective and the division management maintaining a regional perspective. The fear was that the regional management would always be telling them what to do, see.

The sixth category was ease of expatriate adjustment and living. In other words, living conditions. You know, [North Americans] think that they've got to go somewhere and they've got to have good clear running water and they've got to have sewerage, got to have lettuce they can eat, and vegetables, without fear of dysentery. And you've got to have a telephone in every bedroom and blah, blah, blah.

The seventh was operating costs.

The eleven other considerations included everything from how easy it would be to find a parking space near the office to availability of club facilities. But the first seven were considered important enough that they were assigned double weight. Out of a possible score of 100, Coral Gables came in at 87; Rio was second with 70; São Paulo, 60; and Mexico City, 55.

And the reasons those others bombed out [said Trelenberg], primarily were poor communications from that city to other cities in Latin America — not to the United States, but to other cities in Latin America — and poor air connections.

What it comes down to is that South Florida was regarded as the only place in the hemisphere with a truly advantageous mixing of cultures. Thanks to the Cubans, Latin Americans feel as if they're in Latin America. Thanks to the 782 overseas hemispheric flights a week out of Miami International and the efficiency of Ma Bell, Anglos still feel as if they're in the old U.S.

•   •   •

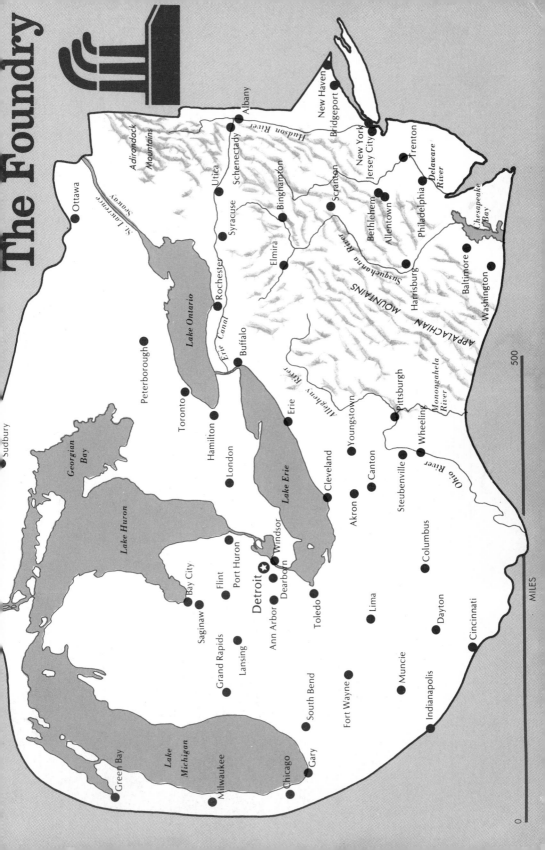

The Foundry

Sudbury ·

Ottawa ●

St. Lawrence Seaway

Adirondack Mountains

Albany ●
Hudson River

New Haven ●
Bridgeport ●

Utica ●

Schenectady ●

Binghamton
Scranton ●

New York ●
Jersey City
Trenton ●
Delaware River

Syracuse ●

Elmira ●

Erie Canal

Rochester ●

Lake Ontario

Peterborough ●

Bethlehem ●
Allentown ●
Philadelphia ●

Susquehanna River

Harrisburg ●

Chesapeake Bay

Buffalo ●

Baltimore ●

Washington ●

APPALACHIAN MOUNTAINS

Toronto ●

Allegheny River

Pittsburgh ●
Wheeling ●
Monongahela River

Erie ●

Lake Erie

Hamilton ●

Youngstown ●

Ohio River

London ●

Cleveland ●

Akron ●
Canton ●

Steubenville ●

Georgian Bay

Lake Huron

Windsor
Dearborn

Columbus ●

Port Huron ●

Bay City ●
Flint ●

★ **Detroit**
Ann Arbor

Toledo ●

Lima ●

Dayton ●

Saginaw ●

Grand Rapids ●
Lansing ●

South Bend ●

Fort Wayne ●

Muncie ●

Cincinnati ●

Indianapolis ●

Green Bay ●

Lake Michigan

Milwaukee ●

Chicago ●
Gary ●

0

500

MILES

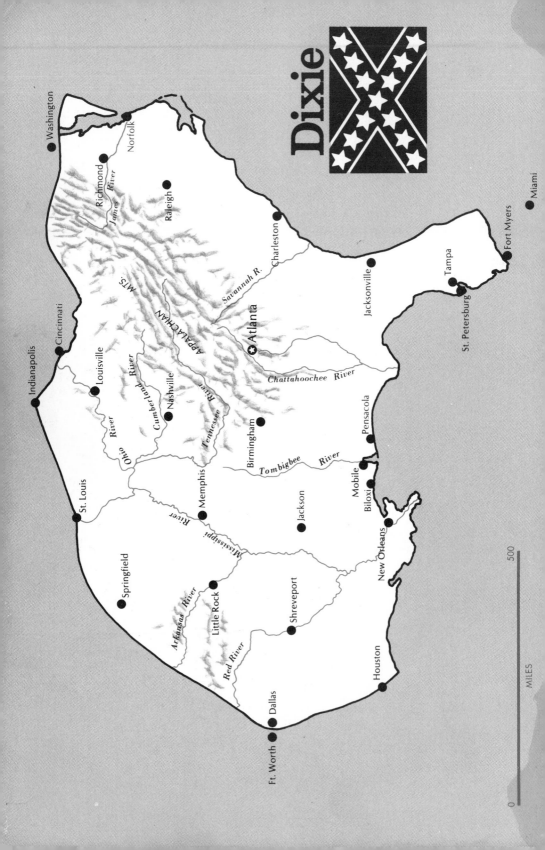

Dixie

Washington

Norfolk

Richmond
James River

Raleigh

Charleston

Savannah R.

Jacksonville

APPALACHIAN MTS.

Atlanta

Cincinnati

Louisville

Chattahoochee River

Nashville

Pensacola

Cumberland River

Ohio River

Tennessee River

Birmingham

Tombigbee River

Mobile

Indianapolis

Memphis

Biloxi

St. Louis

Mississippi River

Jackson

New Orleans

Springfield

Arkansas River

Little Rock

Shreveport

Red River

Houston

Dallas

Ft. Worth

Miami

Fort Myers

Tampa

St. Petersburg

0   500   MILES

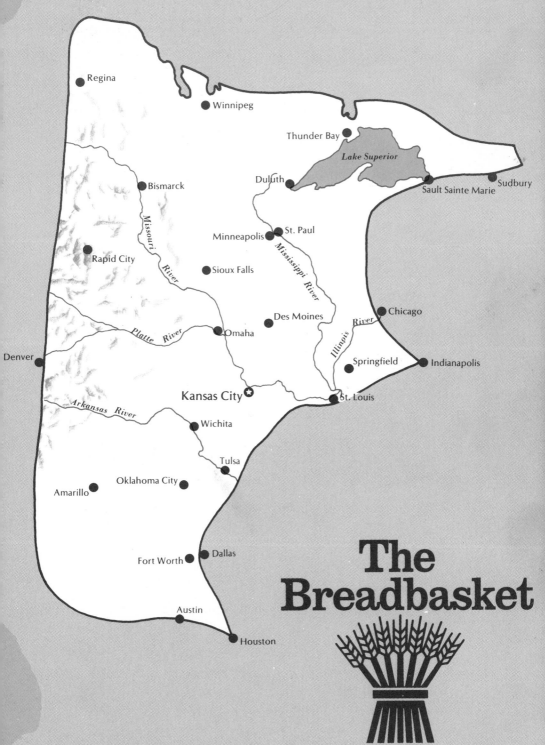

The Breadbasket

Québec

Lac
Minto

Fort Chimo

Poste de la Baleine

*Grande rivière
de la Baleine*

*Lac
Bienville*

LG2

Rivière La Grande

Rivière Opinaca

Rivière   Eastmain

Fort Rupert

*Reservoir
Manicouagan*

Lac Mistassini

Sept Iles

Île d'Antiosti

Lac St. Jean

*Peninsule
de Gaspé*

Chicoutimi

Rimouski

Îles de la Madeleine

Québec

Shawinigan
Trois Rivières   *Rivière Saint Laurent*

Hull

Montréal

Ottawa

Sherbrooke

0   500

MILES

ing for $598 were not machine guns. That was a mistake. The wrong picture was submitted with the advertising copy. Actually, his guns were factory-modified carbines. The barrels were a tenth of an inch longer than the sixteen-inch legal minimum, not snub-nose. And they were only semiautomatic. You had to pull the trigger for each shot. They just *weren't* machine guns. Machine guns were illegal. You could, of course, fire the carbine's twenty-five-round clip manually in well under ten seconds.

Could a clever gunsmith revert them to full automatic? "Not to my knowledge." He grinned sheepishly. Oh, c'mon. "Well, what the hell do you want me to say: 'No comment'?"

Senatore was most upset and confused, he said, about Dade County Public Safety Department homicide detective Gus Ewell's assertions that the guns would go to arm the Cocaine Cowboys.

The Cocaine Cowboys, as they have been locally dubbed, are a sore subject. Also known as "those crazy Colombians," they've started blowing each other away with machine guns on the city streets. For obscure, but drug-related reasons, one of their number, known as "El Loco," is thought to have been connected with the running machine-gun battle conducted by two speeding cars on the Florida Turnpike, the shots whizzing over the heads of passing teen-agers. Citizens quietly asleep in their bedroom have waked to the sound of machine-gun slugs coming through their wall from the next apartment, where an execution was in progress. The most brazen incident was the one in which a heavily armored van, which police called a "war wagon," pulled up to a liquor store in a toney suburban mall as unsuspecting shoppers went about their business in their Bermuda shorts, carrying their children. When the machine-gun fire ended, two Latinos were dead, two bystanders wounded, and the Cowboys had made a clean getaway. "This is like Dodge City," commented one detective.

Senatore said that he read only gun books, not newspapers, and he'd never even heard of Cocaine Cowboys until all the fuss started. Besides, he said, he'd made a few phone calls after the dust settled, and he'd found out that that stuff about his Uzis being a status symbol among the drug crowd was just a load of crap. The druggies, he'd been told, do not use Uzis. They use MAC-10 machine guns.

Still honestly professing his injured innocence, Senatore went to serve a customer. If there was any doubt that the patron was a member of the starched-whites yacht crowd, he dispelled it when he asked to be educated about the various powder loads available in .38 caliber pistol ammunition. What he wanted, he said, was something that would go right through a fiber-glass hull. He was rather mysterious about under what circumstances he envisioned putting a small hole into a big boat and it doing anybody any good. But he made no bones about his alarm. He feared that, with the drug trade and all, it was not at all unlikely that someone might approach him on the high seas, kill him, and take his yacht for a run to Colombia. Careful, polite questioning on the part of Senatore and a fat, bald friend of his, who'd just entered the store, revealed that the yachtsman, who was making noises about armor-piercing shells for a handgun, probably had never fired a weapon in his life. But his concern was completely justified.

"What you need," said the fat man, "is a .30-.30 for those armor-piercing shells. Fire it from half a mile away, and you can make the hull ring like a bell. Let 'em know you mean business. Hell, you don't want a pistol. A pistol's only good at close range, and by the time you can see 'em, what you need is a shotgun, not a .38."

The yachtsman, having invested in what *he* believed in, finally left the shop.

Senatore returned to me. "You know," he said, "a lot of this gun stuff is blown out of proportion. What's a big deal about an Uzi? That's not even the most dangerous gun I've got in the shop. Lookit over here. This is an antique buffalo gun, still works good as new, accurate at a distance of two miles. And here, see this? Look at it. What does it look like? A German Luger? Made right here in the States for the U.S. Army in World War One. I mean, it's so emotional.

"See that gun over there in the corner? It's marked down. Used to sell for ninety-eight dollars. I'll give it to you for forty-nine-fifty, and hell, that's a Carcano."

That's the kind of gun that killed John F. Kennedy.

MEXAMERICA

RICHARD MILHOUS NIXON always liked Coronado Island, and no wonder. It would take an incomprehensible hardening of the soul not to feel a surge of gratitude toward the Pacific Ocean for creating the beaches, waves, and breezes that give the island what is possibly the finest year-round climate in North America.

But perhaps more important to him, the island, just an hour south of San Clemente, is full of the former president's kind of people. Many of San Diego's financial heavies live on Coronado Island. Half-million-dollar condominiums are taken for granted along this beach. The houses there are the kind, like Nixon's old Casa Pacifica, that, when put up for sale, are offered through special agencies that would never think of advertising in a mere newspaper.

And Coronado Island's political views are consistent with the cash value of its ocean views. Not far from here, a successful candidate for office once proclaimed, less than half-jokingly, that he'd joined the Orange County John Birch Society in order to capture the middle-of-the-road vote.

Contributing to the sense of righteousness on the island is the plethora of retired admirals who live there. Coronado Island is the sunsetward-most piece of bread in a sandwich, the meat being San Diego Harbor, and the eastern layer being the mainland and the city of San Diego. The marvelous harbor that Coronado Island protects from the western waves is the home of the

Seventh Fleet. There's more retired Navy brass in the San Diego area than anywhere else on earth.

For them, one of the nice things about living on Coronado Island, if they can afford it, is the great view of the ships you can get from the San Diego–Coronado Bridge. Row upon row of mammoth hulls are tied up to the mainland: destroyers, frigates, tankers, freighters, troopships, aircraft carriers. Lost in a thicket of radar, the ships fade into their field of gray paint, incongruous in the land of fierce sun and bright colors.

The reason the view of the fleet is so good is that the San Diego–Coronado Bridge is so high. Because the bridge was engineered to ensure that all future floating war behemoths, no matter how conceivably large, could glide under the span on their way to make Asia safe for democracy, the approaches have to start lifting off almost a mile inland. If they did not get a running jump on the harbor, which is not all that wide, the roadways could not achieve the proper altitude while maintaining the sweeping French curves of the classic California freeway — curves that resemble a flight path more than a roadway.

There's little way to overemphasize the importance of preserving the geometry of these boring, banked curves. The pace of the Southern California autobahn is exact. On these fast, crowded roads, one changes lanes with precision, courage, and nonchalance, or one spends an inordinate amount of time in fear. Surprises are not welcome or expected. The freeway is especially not a good place for a rich, conservative Anglo to confront, on his way home, a twenty-foot-tall brown man with a book in one hand and one very big hammer in the other.

Victor Orozco Ochoa knows that well. As the mural coordinator of Chicano Park for ten years, he smiles as he thinks of the unsuspecting Republican whose car, climbing the bridge to Coronado under cruise control, is about to bring its driver face to face with the stunning giant, only one of dozens of huge, vibrant images painted on the concrete pylons supporting the on-ramps. Orozco Ochoa gets a kick out of the way Barrio Logan, the community that lives under the approaches to the San Diego–Coronado Bridge, and that created the murals of Chicano Park, startles Anglos from time to time.

It's not as if the Anglos don't have it coming.

They started the whole thing back in the sixties. That's when the city fathers of San Diego decided that a bridge to speed the affluent to their Coronado homes from downtown was a good idea, and that ripping out a long swath of a down-at-the-heels part of the city in the process was an even better one.

The hitch was that what the Anglos saw as a blighted area given over to junkyards, sandblasting, and arc-welding shops, Mexican-Americans who lived there saw as their homes and their jobs. More than that, it was their "barrio," and a barrio is not the same thing as a ghetto. It means neighborhood, but often is translated as community, and a community is not something you flee, much less casually tear down.

But the voice of the Mexican-American community was not loud then, and even if it had been, the Anglos at that time were not disposed to listen, so the bridge to Coronado began to take shape. All the people of the barrio had to show for it was what they thought was the following understanding: after the construction was finished, the neighborhood kids would be allowed to play in the shadow of the bridge, on the land that had been cleared for the tall support towers.

It's never been made completely clear what led the city to try to build on that land a parking lot for the much-hated police, rather than a playground. But there's no doubt it was a spectacularly inept move, with a predictable outcome. There was an uprising. The fragmented, acquiescent community of Logan Heights suddenly found an issue around which it could coalesce. In defiance of the city, hundreds of Mexican-Americans attacked the construction-scarred land with shovels, picks, wheelbarrows, and hand labor, making the land a park hospitable for people, not cop cars, and vowing violence if anybody tried to stop them.

And so was born Chicano Park, which today, almost a decade later, is a quiet, grassy, pleasant spot, with basketball hoops, a small open stage shaped like an Aztec temple, and a forest of these strange urban "trees," the size of sequoias, made out of T-shaped concrete, supporting five "vines" of multilevel, twisting, curling freeways high above your head leading from Interstate 5.

It's weird, standing in this park on a sunny Sunday afternoon surrounded by these Stonehenge-like monuments, gazing up at tiny cars whizzing past with tiny passengers in them. It's clear there are physically two worlds in operation here. One, in the park, is on foot, relaxed, girl-watching, having quiet conversation. The other is fifty feet straight up — directly over the heads of playing children — screaming past, encased in Detroit iron, with its thoughts definitely elsewhere, probably not even aware the road has left the ground.

It's surreal even without the mammoth murals, which from ground to highway completely obliterate the grayness of the concrete in eye-socking acrylics the color of sun-brightened stained glass.

And these murals are dizzying. On one side of a column, there is a thirty-foot-tall Virgin of Guadelupe, the brown-skinned Madonna who, 450 years ago, only a few years after the Spanish started their New World conquest, appeared to an illiterate Mexican Indian with the revolutionary message that the poor were her people, whom she would protect. Her image is inextricably, and purposefully, bound to the flip side of the pillar, on which is a stylized rendition of the pagan earth goddess Tonantzín, whose veneration the Virgin superseded.

Serpents rear their heads on these murals and scream in a style reminiscent of the horse in Picasso's *Guernica*. The snake was venerated by the Central American Indians, to the horror of the first padres, who saw it as a symbol of evil. But to the Indians, the earth was holy, and the snake was the being always closest to it, and as a result, he was a symbol of wisdom.

A thoughtful mural dedicated to a gunned-down farm laborer depicts, in Dali-like fashion, stoop-laborers chained to the cornucopias of vegetable crates they fill.

On another column Cuauhtémoc, the last emperor of the Aztec, and an eagle both fall. The artist has played complicated tricks with perspective and light to make his point about the ancestor of today's Chicanos.

And all the while, the cars roar overhead, on the way to Coronado Island.

The murals of Chicano Park are in a strange space, existing, as they do, in two such different worlds. On the one hand, though fastidious art magazines rave about them, Anglos, flashing by on the interstates, usually experience them unexpectedly, and in the blink of an eye.

On the other hand, they are statements made by hundreds of ordinary people, immigrants or children of immigrants, many of whom have not yet learned to speak English, but who, painting in groups, express themselves vividly, and with complexity of image, variety of style, and great technical ability, on the concrete of a civil works project even the Toltec would have considered to be of grand scale.

In a way, this strange space exists all over the North American Southwest, for the Southwest is now what all of Anglo North

America will soon be — a place where the largest minority will be Spanish-speaking. It's a place being inexorably redefined — in terms of language, custom, economics, television, music, food, politics, advertising, employment, architecture, fashions, and even the pace of life — by the ever-growing numbers of Hispanics in its midst. It is becoming MexAmerica.

"A binational, bicultural, bilingual regional complex or entity is emerging in the borderlands," wrote the late Carey McWilliams, historian and editor of *The Nation*. "Nothing quite like this zone of interlocking economic, social and cultural interests can be found along any other border of comparable length in the world."

MexAmerica is most evident along the 1933-mile border that the United States shares with Mexico, but it is highly visible as well in such diverse nonborder cities as Los Angeles, Phoenix, Albuquerque, Santa Fe, Pueblo, San Antonio, Austin, and Houston.

Los Angeles is not only the second-largest metropolitan area in the United States; it's the second-largest Mexican city in the world, after Mexico City, with at least 1.5 million American citizens of Mexican heritage, and an estimated half-million more illegal immigrants. In San Antonio, the tenth-largest city in the United States, there are already fewer Anglos than there are Tejanos, as some Texans of Mexican descent like to call themselves.

Within the borders of MexAmerica, the approximately eight million Mexican-American United States citizens — not counting illegals — vastly outnumber blacks, Asians, and all other minorities, reaching statewide levels as high as 36 percent. Some estimates have been published saying that as early as 1985, the Spanish-surnamed population of the United States — including people from the Caribbean, and Central and South America, but predominantly Mexicans and Mexican-Americans — is expected to outnumber the thirty million blacks in the United States.

Over one hundred million federal dollars are spent in the United States each year on bilingual education. Much of the money is spread throughout the Southwest, teaching Spanish to Anglos, and English to Mexican-Americans, with the goal of making students fluent in both. The face of the future can be seen in the kindergartens of Los Angeles, where the majority of the kids claim Spanish as their first language. Busing to enforce racial integration is hampered in portions of L.A. because there simply are not enough Anglos to go around.

In Houston, a Parisian restaurant advertised its crêpes as

"French enchiladas." In San Antonio, cigarette billboards urge you to *Saberro* [*savor*] *Salem*. In a suburb of Phoenix, street signs read Avenida del Yaqui and Calle Sahuan. In Los Angeles, Coors is advertised as *cervesa* as often as it's advertised as beer.

Western Union is diligent in supplying services in Spanish, if for no other reason than that billions of dollars in money orders are sent to relatives in Mexico by workers in the United States every year. Even Datsun advertises in Spanish, following the lead of the Bank of America.

The growing Mexican influence is evident in food, fashion, and music. Dos Equis and Carta Blanca are offered as premium imported beers in California clone bars. The standard alternative to a roadside steakhouse in the Southwest is a Mexican restaurant, exactly the role Italian restaurants play in the Foundry. Tacos and burritos are as common as lasagna and ravioli elsewhere, although Mexicans view the spreading of hot sauce over everything as an American — and especially Texan — habit as barbarous as the suggestion that pizza was invented in Rome.

White, cotton Mexican dresses with meticulous, colorful embroidery are gaining favor among Anglo women during the long, hot southwestern summers. Anglo men becoming bored with oversized Texas cowboy hats are discovering that there are dozens of styles of Mexican broadbrimmed hats — each of them specific to a Mexican state — which are at least as rakish as anything Dallas can produce.

Austin as a country-and-western-music center that produced the likes of Willie Nelson and Waylon Jennings is also becoming a cultural crossroads in which not only do U.S. and Mexican tunes influence each other, but an even greater musical gap is bridged — that between Hispanics from northern Mexico and Hispanics from the Islands.

"Norteno" music is as characteristic of northeastern Mexico and south Texas as Dixieland is of New Orleans. This Norteno music, which is sung in Spanish, is itself a cultural fusion over a century old, borrowing the beat and instruments of Germans who settled in Texas after their country was wrung by revolution in 1848. The lead instrument is a diatonic accordion (played by the musician's manipulating rows of buttons, a far more difficult task than dealing with an instrument that comes with a pianolike keyboard). Its rhythm is a catchy, but boxy, Germanic "oompha." This Norteno music is so foreign to syncopated Latino beats that Texan-Mexican kids, at a disco in Austin, when confronted by reggae or a cha-cha-like tune, sit it out, saying, "You can't dance to it." But that may be changing, because many of the Mexican polka bands of south Texas are listening to the new waves of Hispanic beats coming out of New York, Los Angeles, and the Caribbean, and are trying to adapt it to their style.

In the same spirit, Anglos like Ry Cooder are now cutting albums with Norteno sidemen, and Mexican-Americans like Freddy Fender and Johnny Rodriguez are making it big on Anglo hit charts.

In MexAmerica, languages are converging, so that an Anglo may be asked to *presta mi su credit card*. But also, a Mexican-American is confronted by a used-car-dealer whose sign says: COMPRO Y VENDO CARROS. Buy and sell cars is what it means, but "carros" is not a Spanish word. Like the commonly heard "truckos" and "hamburgesa," it's an adaptation of English. The question "Where do you work?" can even come out *"Donde puncheas?"* That lifts not only an English word, but a labor concept that certainly did not originate in rural Mexico. The question, in effect, is "Where do you punch (your time clock)?"

Increasingly, Spanish can be seen in U.S. print. Emergency warning cards on Texas International Airlines, legal advertisements in Houston, and dialing instructions on telephone booths throughout Southern California are printed in both languages. So are popular magazines, such as *Nuestro — the magazine for Latinos.*

It's come to the point where a weary official of the Mexican American Cultural Center in San Antonio told me he'd just come from an organizational meeting for a new weekly at which a ferocious argument had been waged over which of *three* languages the paper should be printed in.

One possibility was English. The second was traditional Mexican Spanish, which holds in high esteem a richly colored, quasi-poetic, Cervantesque style of writing. But the most controversial choice was, for lack of a better word, MexAmerican. This language, built on Spanish, not only relies on adaptations of English words for much of its vocabulary, but, most important, has a fast-paced, direct, United States style that says what it has to in a hurry. "Those Mexicans!" said the Hispanic official with a sigh. "They want to make a minor point, and they build up to it, and build up to it, and build up to it, and it can bore your ass off."

Jerry Warren is the editor of the *San Diego Union*, a once undistinguished if not terrible paper that is recruiting a lot of fresh talent and is beginning to make a name for itself. The *Union* has begun to do pioneering work in the coverage of politics and corruption in northern Mexico and how it affects the United States side of the border. But the reporters were frustrated by the lack of effect their English-language articles were having until Warren decided to have one particularly controversial report translated, reprinted, and trucked twenty miles south to Tijuana, where a free and feisty press is less than a sacred tradition. The appearance of biculturalism and binationalism in the form of American-style muckraking in Spanish had an explosive effect.

Ironically, Warren the border-blurrer is the same man who, in 1969, as deputy press secretary to Nixon, had to stand up and explain to doubtful reporters why Operation Intercept was a good idea. Operation Intercept was an attempt to seal hermetically the United States–Mexican border against drug smuggling. It succeeded most markedly in displaying a complete lack of understanding of the geography of MexAmerica on the part of the authorities who thought it up. Operation Intercept coincided with a dramatic rise in the sale of four-wheel-drive vehicles along the border. Local teen-agers, who knew the desert areas of the borderlands as well as they knew their own backyards, soon realized that one quick smuggling run through the vast desert, by-passing the newly toughened road checkpoints, could pay for a brand-new truck outright. Thus, what had once been a tight-knit, controllable drug-distribution network was transformed overnight into a wild, every-man-for-himself collection of individualistic and hitherto law-abiding entrepreneurs. The new arrangement exists to this day.

Spanish is also becoming the language of the U.S. airwaves. The Southwest used to have only a handful of Spanish-language radio stations. Now there are thirty-seven in Texas, twenty-three in California, six in Arizona, and four in New Mexico. There is virtually no major city in the entire United States without at least one Spanish station. Even television is changing. Broadcast and cable television bring full-time Spanish programming as far north as San Francisco, just as it brings English television as far south as Mexico City. MexAmericans who don't want to watch Walter Cronkite can catch Jacobo Zabludovsky, who's known as the Uncle Walter of Mexico.

Sometimes the cultural cross-fertilization can get very confusing, such as when an American is watching Mexican television and a show that looks naggingly familiar reveals itself to be a knock-off of the popular U.S. movie series *Benji*, named after the star, which is a dog. The plot on Spanish television is exactly the same. Only the language, the scenery, and the dog (an Airedale, not a lovable mutt) are different.

Politics are changing: Democrats in control of the 1979 California legislature put $800,000 in the state budget to encourage participation by illegal aliens in the 1980 U.S. census. The census totals determine how many congressional seats a state gets, how many presidential electors it gets, and how $50 billion worth of federal programs, ranging from school and housing aid to community-improvement projects and affirmative-action goals, are divided up. And nowhere does the law say that census totals should distinguish between residents with passports and residents without.

Organized labor is changing. The International Ladies' Garment Workers Union, which once was violently against illegal immigration as an unlimited source of cheap labor, has shifted its stance in California and is now actively and successfully recruiting undocumented workers. It realized that it would have to represent illegal aliens if it was going to continue representing garment workers. Other unions, such as farmers', retail clerks', and the textile workers', have followed suit.

Even religion is changing. Among those in the Southwest who do go to church, the majority are Catholic, and two thirds of these are Mexican-American. This, too, is altering balances. After long being ignored by the U.S. hierarchy, Mexican-Americans in the decade of the 1970s saw an average of one new Hispanic bishop named per year, an amazing statistic for such a historically glacial institution.

Father Virgil Elizondo of San Antonio, who has studied the role of Catholicism in the Mexican-American culture, suggests that there are some devotional practices that non-Hispanic Catholics take as dogma that may have more to do with the juridical minds of Irish priests than they do with the faith. Compulsory Mass on Sunday is one example he uses. In English, he points out, the Third Commandment is "Remember, thou keep holy the Lord's day." In Spanish, the commandment is much different. It's "Sanctify your feast days." There are thousands of Mexican-American Catholics who feel they are complying with God's will, thus stated, without necessarily checking in with the parish priest every seven days.

Similarly, researchers had some of their assumptions rearranged for them when they started investigating the success Protestant denominations have had in recruiting Mexican-Americans. (It shouldn't have surprised me, but it did, the first time I saw the sign in Los Angeles that read SOLON DE LOS TESTIGOS DE JEHOVA — Jehovah's Witnesses.) On asking a brand-new Baptist why she left the Catholic Church, the researcher was told, "Oh, I haven't left the Catholic Church. I go to it, too. I'm a Baptist-Catholic." Father Elizondo, taking note of people who describe themselves as Methodist-Catholic and Presbyterian-Catholic, remarked, "They'd heard of biculturalism and bilingualism, but they didn't know what to put on their computer cards when they hit bi-religionism."

The Anglo influence south of the border, meanwhile, is as casual and pervasive as the pay telephone in Rosarito, Baja California Norte, south of Tijuana, which will not accept pesos. Only dimes. Or the stop signs that have the 7-Up symbol on them. Or LA RECETA DE CORONEL SANDERS. Visit the "Coronel"?

Anglos with a stereotype of persons of Mexican ancestry as pickers of fruit and drawers of water like to forget history. Americans who mutter darkly about "alien hordes" ignore the fact that, like the French of Québec, the Spanish-speaking people of the Southwest were here first. MexAmerica bulges hundreds of miles north of the border into New Mexico, Colorado, and California, because, for example, a flourishing Spanish civilization existed at Santa Fe before the Pilgrims landed at Plymouth Rock. The Santa Fe Trail was important to Missouri frontiersmen in the early 1800s, because it opened up trade to a city then already two hundred years old. Place names, from San Antonio to Los Angeles, bespeak the ancient Spanish presence. The northern borders of California, Nevada, and Utah are at the 42nd parallel, because that's where the Spanish empire of Alta (Upper) California (as opposed to Baja [Lower] California) ended.

The conquistadors and the padres saw this region whole, without imaginary lines creating divisions between the state of Sonora and the state of Arizona. The desert was the same, the cactuses were the same, the climate was the same, and the people were the same. And the descendants of the conquistadors are still here. Hispanics in New Mexico still refer to themselves as Spanish, rather than Mexican-Americans, partially out of snobbery, but also out of a sense of historical accuracy. In Santa Fe, because of intermarriage, the lineage is thoroughly European. Mexican-Americans, by contrast, claim a far more indigenous North American ancestry. Their forefathers may have been European, but their maternal ancestors were Aztec and members of the other highly developed nations of Central America that flourished before the white man came.

The Anglo world is the latest invader of these parts, not the Indian, Mexican, and Spanish. It's the borders that have moved, not the founding cultures. There are great numbers of Hispanics in the Southwest who can't be told by ignorant Anglos to go back where they came from. They *are* where they came from.

There's a legend that has acquired popularity among some of today's young Chicanos. The origins of the great Indian civilizations like the Toltec and the Mayan have always been shrouded in mystery. But the first Aztec said they came from Aztlan, and their descriptions of it tally with what today is the United States Southwest. *Aztlan* literally means white earth, and when a bulldozer flattens the top of a hill for a San Diego subdivision, white earth is what it's pushing. The legend continues that Aztlan will someday be regained by the sons of the Aztec, and a new civilization will flourish. The land will once again be regarded as holy, and oppression be brought to an end.

Already, there are Mexican-Americans who refer to the five-state region of California, New Mexico, Arizona, Colorado, and Texas as Aztlan.

This is significant for two major reasons.

The first is a little drama that will be played out in the nation of the Islands in the early 1980s and that will actually have its most important impact in MexAmerica.

The situation is this: Puerto Rico is scheduled to vote on whether it wishes to become the fifty-first state. If it does, it's difficult to imagine, in terms of racial politics, how the Congress will either be able to turn it down or force that 98 percent Spanish-speaking island to abandon its native language.

If Puerto Rico's 3.5 million residents are then allowed to be full citizens while remaining monolingually Spanish in official proceedings, the way Québecois are allowed to be monolingually French in Canada, how is it going to be legally possible not to offer the same rights to the far more numerous Hispanic citizens of MexAmerica?

Miami is a very different place from the towns of MexAmerica, but listen to the words of its mayor, Maurice Ferré, in the context of San Antonio, El Paso, San Diego . . .

"American public opinion will have to deal with it: Do you accept American citizens that are not like you and me? They speak a different language; they have a different culture."

With heavy irony in his voice, Ferré continued:

Look, okay, I understand. It was just us Americans before. We had to accept those damn Jews and then we had to accept those damn Catholics, and even the blacks got in. And the Indians made their pitch with Wounded Knee, then came the youth movement, and now we got all these crazy kids and they've got rights. And now you got gray power to counteract black power, and Claude Pepper is passing bills left and right that say you can't discriminate against an American just because he happens to be old.

Now here come those Puerto Ricans. And they're saying, "Wait a minute. Not only can you not discriminate against me because I'm Catholic. Because I happen to have some black blood in me. And because I happen to be a youngster or a female. You can't discriminate against me because I happen to speak a different language." *That's* the line. *Permanently* speaking a different language. And that's when America really becomes America. Because [many Hispanics] are permanently going to speak Spanish. I mean, we're all Americans as long as we're all human beings and born here. And there is no distinction in the Constitution that deals with [language].

Let's get the definition. Not transitional Spanish. We're talking about Spanish as a main form of communication. As an official language. Not on the way to English. What I'm saying is that what color is to blacks, language is to Hispanics. And that's something that has to be very clearly understood.

The second extraordinarily important thing to keep in mind about MexAmerica is the many ways in which this area is viewed as the promised land by Anglos.

Both in wealth and population, it's showing the most spectacular growth on the continent. It's not hard to envision a near future in which the MexAmerican Southwest becomes the continent's dominant region — replacing the Foundry. Already, California and Texas, the first and third most populous states in the United States, have passed in wealth number two New York and all of New England combined. Four of the seven major candidates in 1980 presidential primaries, including the two successful Republicans, came from these two states — Ronald Reagan, Jerry Brown, George Bush, and John Connally. And the bulk of the population of these two states is in MexAmerica.

Houston, the border town that anchors MexAmerica on the east, is the world capital of petroleum. If you want to drill for oil in Kuwait, the Soviet Union, Mexico, or the South China Sea, "you can buy your rig in Houston, or you can dig with a silver spoon," as people in the "awl bidness" like to boast.

This is already changing world perceptions. When a European

banker thinks of his North American counterpart, he may still think of a New Yorker. But like the German industrialist who, when he thinks of North Americans, thinks of Southerners, a Saudi who conjures up an image of a North American, like as not, thinks of a Texan.

And Houston is not just a world energy capital. It's giving Boston and Minneapolis a run for their money as a medical capital, and is continuing to come on strong in electronics, space, finance, construction, and law.

At the other end of MexAmerica is Los Angeles. An argument can be made that it will soon be North America's première city, replacing New York.

The Security Pacific National Bank estimates that if the sixty-mile circle with Los Angeles at its center were to become an independent country, it would be the fourteenth wealthiest in the world. Its gross national product in 1976 would have been $91 billion, which was almost half that of all of California and a staggering one-twentieth of that of the entire United States. It is a world leader in aerospace, manufactured goods, electronics, fashions, construction, and finance, and, while other parts of the continent suffer from lay-offs and recessions, this MexAmerican capital, not weighted down with nineteenth-century industry, continues to boom. It is the air and sea hub of the West. And if the Saudi thinks of a Texan when he thinks of a North American, a Japanese banker or auto-maker undoubtedly thinks of an Angelino.

But Los Angeles' foremost importance may be its impact on the continental culture. If it is true that trends move from west to east, then Los Angeles is at ground zero of the future. It has influenced continental thinking on the worth of everything from casual sex to fresh foods.

The majority of the images of who we are — and why — come out of this world television-and-film capital. Shows theoretically set in Minneapolis, Chicago, Cincinnati, and Brooklyn are actually written and shot on stages right here. Los Angeles' major export is image-creating ideas. This is especially significant as the speculation increases that Los Angeles' visual culture is challenging, if not displacing, the print culture associated with old capitals like New York.

It is eerie how the two book ends of MexAmerica, Los Angeles and Houston, imitate each other. "With their freeways, their dispersed development patterns, their open spaces, their outdoor styles of living, their gleaming buildings, their atmosphere of gung-ho vitality and their very newness," the *New York Times* commented, "they are urban brothers. Probably no two major cities in the country look and feel more alike."

And now their urban patterns are being slavishly imitated by even newer booming urban centers in MexAmerica, like Phoenix and Tucson.

Meanwhile, the irrigated desert valleys of California, Arizona, and Texas have changed the diet of the continent, with fresh pink grapefruit available in Hartford in February, and Chicago secretaries casually ordering crisp lunch-hour chef salads as snow squalls scream in off Lake Michigan. Few stop to wonder how the produce got there, but it came from MexAmerica. Almond-growers in the San Joaquin Valley are so nonchalant about the miracles of their desert gardens that one casually talked to me about changing the eating habits of Greece. In pursuit of markets, he and his associates are convincing Greeks to use almond oil from California in their cooking, rather than olive oil from the eastern Mediterranean.

Desert sun and visions of individual freedom that continue to draw people to Southern California now lure people south to Ensenada and east to Tucson, Taos, and the metropolises of Texas. These are what demographers are talking about when they refer to the Sunbelt surge.

MexAmerica is also the land of the future because its civilization's claim to existence is as threatened as that of any place in North America. Unlike Dixie, the Foundry, New England, and other eastern nations that developed in the eighteenth and nineteenth centuries, MexAmerica simply couldn't exist in its present form until the advent of advanced aqueducts, air-conditioning, and the automobile. There is only enough water in the Los Angeles Basin under natural circumstances for two hundred thousand people. There are seven million there now, and their water comes from hundreds of miles away. When temperatures soar over 100 degrees day after day in El Paso, the old and the sick who are too poor to afford air-conditioning die, just as surely as the old and the sick who can't afford heat die in the Buffalo winter. One Houstonian, looking out over his city, remarked, "Who would have thought that, given the opportunity to do different, anybody would have built a second Los Angeles?" Phoenix is a third. These low, sprawling, centerless, brand-new cities that worship the detached single-family bungalow and the shopping center are utterly dependent on the internal combustion engine.

The entire region is obsessed with two questions: Where will the water come from to allow industry to expand, food to be grown, and subdivisions to be built? And where will the power come from to keep the climate and the immense distances at bay?

Nature, in the meantime, through earthquakes, brush fires, flash floods, mudslides, and drought, from time to time raises questions in the minds of even the most confident about whether God wanted this many people to live in the paradise of the Southwest. And what He intends to do about it.

Because MexAmerica is a watershed of the future, its boundaries can be controversial. By definition, this is a land where two cultures are coming together, so there will be two distinct views of where the process is achieving critical mass. An Anglo might try to insist that the border be drawn only where English-speakers are actually and right now in the minority. But he would have to argue with a Hispanic observer who can see abundant and growing evidence of his culture as far north as Kansas, a portion of which was once part of Mexico. He'd have to talk, for that matter, to the successful operator of the Mexican movie house in Moline, Illinois, and the politicians who woo the huge barrios of Chicago and Gary, Indiana.

Be that as it may, there is a fault line between Texas, the most colorful portion of the Breadbasket, and MexAmerican Tejas, which, you must remember, did in fact win at the Alamo. And that line leaves Dixie behind somewhere south of Beaumont, where the twenty different greens of the piney woods yield to the reds and browns of the drylands, and the gumbo begins to give way to refried beans. It encompasses the border town of Houston, and then heads out across the flatlands toward the state capital of Austin.

In Austin sit many Anglo institutions torn by the knowledge that the future lies to the south. The inadequately named Texas Railroad Commission has the awesome power to oversee energy production and distribution in this state which is the home of big oil. Temperamentally, it has been compared to King Fisher, the nineteenth-century Texan who, when asked how many notches he had on his gun, allegedly replied, "Thirty-seven, not counting Mexicans." When poor Mexican-American border towns like Crystal City can't pay their natural gas bill, it's the Texas Railroad Commission that, with enthusiasm, allows the faucet to be shut off.

On the other hand, governors of Texas, like their counterparts in California, have come to conduct their own foreign policy.

Tours of Mexico have become as important to them as trips to the Panhandle because of Mexico's supplies of natural gas, crops, and labor, on which Texas' economy is counting. As California governor Jerry Brown told an interviewer, "We're inextricably linked with those people, and the sooner we realize it the better. Mexico's not an island. If something goes wrong in Mexico City, it will be felt in Los Angeles and El Paso." In fact, Ronald Reagan's first diplomatic move as president-elect was to visit Mexico.

Austin is also a good border town because to the north and south of it exist islands of one culture unassimilated by the other. In the eastern barrio of the city, it's easy to find some of the best roast *cabrito* (young goat) in Texas. North of Austin, in Waco and Dallas, substantial Hispanic enclaves thrive. Yet south of it lies New Braunfels, the headquarters of the Texas German influence mentioned earlier.

From Austin, the border cuts across the bulk of the chaparral-covered hill country of Texas west of the Balcones Fault. It cuts under Johnson City, the Pedernales River town just downstream from the LBJ ranch. Continuing under Fredericksburg, another pocket of German-Americanism, where LBJ frequently went to church, the border cuts across the Edwards Plateau in one of its closest approaches to the Mexico–United States line.

At this point, the boundary is crossing all sorts of geographical demarcations between east and west. The 100th meridian, the two-thousand-foot elevation line, and the twenty-inch rainfall line all are important indicators that the Breadbasket civilization based on corn, wheat, cattle, and hogs cannot continue much farther west. Every north-south dividing line starting at the Appalachians takes a perverse pride in referring to itself as "where the West begins," but here it's inescapable. It's so high and dry and remote in these parts that it's a tribute to Yankee agricultural determination on the edge of madness — and to the maturing oil fields of West Texas around Midland-Odessa — that there's anybody living here at all.

Thus, no longer experiencing the southern push of the Breadbasket, when the MexAmerica boundary hits the Pecos River, it begins to head sharply north, toward the energy futures of the Empty Quarter.

Southwest of the Pecos River is the Chihuahua desert, which sprawls on both sides of the border and leads to El Paso. On the opposite side of the frequently dry Rio Grande is its bigger sister,

Juarez. Right on the Pecos is Loving County, Texas, which, with far more square miles than it has population, is one of the most abandoned places in North America.

Judge Roy Bean had a reputation. among Anglos in the Old West for being the law west of the Pecos. But all he was, was one of the first eastern Anglo interlopers, Spanish Santa Fe having been in existence for so long.

Today it can be argued that the thin eastern edge of New Mexico is a land more influenced by the Anglo culture of the Texas Panhandle than by its historic ties, but the bulk of New Mexico, like southern Colorado, is MexAmerica.

Following the eastern face of the Rockies northward, it's somewhere near Pueblo, Colorado, that MexAmerica encounters the mineral riches being raided in a fashion so characteristic of the Empty Quarter. North of here, in Colorado, gold was discovered in 1858 — the stuff the conquistadors knew had to be out here somewhere, but which the Yankees exploited. North of here is the Empty Quarter.

MexAmerica includes all of the southern quarter of Colorado as it dips and churns across the rugged and spectacular mountains that divide the continent. But at the enormous, poor, but uranium-laden Empty Quarter Navajo and Hopi reservations of western New Mexico and northeastern Arizona, it cuts back down well to the south, toward Gallup. It heads west along the line cut by romantic and fabled U.S. Route 66, through Winslow and Flagstaff, north of the Zuñi and Apache reservations, but under the Navajo, and well north of Phoenix.

Continuing under the Grand Canyon, the boundary enters California at Needles, right where the Colorado River does, although at right angles to the water, for if MexAmerica is anything, it's dry.

Southern California is perhaps MexAmerica's purest statement. *Esquire* once offered up Los Angeles to its readers as "the city of the future (and it's coming to get you)." And the magazine was right.

Thus, the boundary of MexAmerica heads north and west out of Needles, skirting under Death Valley, but well east of L.A., heading for the Tehachapi Mountains.

The Tehachapi, a mountain range rare in North America for its east-west orientation, has often been touted as the division between Northern and Southern California. That may once have been true, but it isn't now. Point Conception, on the Pacific

Ocean, where the continent takes a 45 degree right turn, is still a good dividing point between north and south. And it is at the place where the Tehachapis meet the ocean. But it's wrong to conclude then that the whole mountain range is meaningful.

The line between the Empty Quarter and MexAmerica heads north from the Mojave Desert up the ridge of the Sierra Nevada range. There's a long way to go before this boundary reaches the sea, because MexAmerica includes the southern San Joaquin Valley. This desert valley, thanks to irrigation, is the most fecund garden in the world. It is also the headquarters of one of the Southwest's more hated men, César Chavez, the organizer of the Mexican-American stoop-laborers who harvest the produce. This valley is so thoroughly MexAmerican that, although Hispanics have been United States citizens here for generations, "good" jobs, like running agricultural machines twenty feet tall and fifty feet wide, go to blacks, a development that is viewed in some circles as a calculated political statement by Anglo growers flattering to neither the Hispanics nor the blacks. The valley is not a nice place. The Oakies who migrated here during Dust Bowl days hate the Basques, who came here to herd sheep. The Basques hate the blacks. The blacks hate the Mexicans. And everybody hates Los Angeles.

The interior valley itself continues well north of Sacramento, before being consumed in the folds of endless mountains, but the MexAmerica line encounters Ecotopia somewhere around the state capital, in the drainage area of the Sacramento River, which flows into San Francisco Bay.

It seems to me that Davis, as the home of the University of California at Davis and its agricultural school, the most sophisticated in the world, is the place where Ecotopia and MexAmerica are most significantly at odds. This is the place where a philosophy of limits meets a philosophy of no limits. On the one hand, U. Cal. Davis is the home of square plastic tomatoes. It views uppity minorities who had once been reliable cogs in the agricultural machine, and who are now insisting on $3.00 or $4.00 an hour, as problems to be solved. It designs harvesting machines that can rattle and shake the vines and the trees until their fruit is loosened. It designs other machines to suck up the produce thus left lying on the ground. And then it designs strains of plants that yield produce that can stand up to the brutality of the machines.

Like everything else in nature, these remarkable accomplishments are a trade-off. Some taste and texture may be lost in the process. But that is not necessarily irreplaceable. Other machines can be designed to inject desired qualities directly into the products. You want a nice red color? You want more juice? Such a deal we have for you.

Interestingly, in the fashion of a true border town between nations, Davis is also spawning a startlingly Ecotopian community. Not only is the ag school attracting youngsters with a "back to nature" orientation that may or may not be realistic but that is giving nonchemical farming a big boost; it is becoming a town where subdivisions are going up that are designed to exclude automobiles, encourage cooperative development of backyard gardens, and explore renewable resources.

From the Sacramento Delta, MexAmerica's boundary with Ecotopia skirts well to the east of the San Francisco–Marin County–Berkeley–Oakland Bay Area, and picks up the Coast Range, the mountains that are the San Joaquin Valley's western edge. West of these mountains, even tacky San Jose, a town once thoroughly and blindly prodevelopment, is now deciding that enough growth is enough, making it borderline Ecotopian.

Down along the coast are Monterey, Carmel, William Randolph Hearst's San Simeon, San Luis Obispo. Well-off, hip, thinly populated, and beautiful, this shore is like Marin, Sonoma, and Mendocino counties north of San Francisco, and is Ecotopian.

But inland, over the rain-trapping mountains in the San Joaquin Valley, corporations with familiar names like Tenneco, Chevron USA, Superior Oil, Southern Pacific Railroad, and Standard Oil of California rule multithousand-acre agricultural baronies. Subsidized by federal water systems originally meant to encourage the "family farmer," these huge tracts of MexAmerica are where the idea of "agribusiness" was born, and where political steamrollers are applied to unacceptable ideas as readily as eight-row John Deere cultivators are used on weeds.

MexAmerica stays inside these mountains until it hits the western edge of the earlier-mentioned Tehachapi. Just north of Santa Barbara, the northernmost penetration of the Los Angeles megalopolis, is where MexAmerica returns to the sea.

From there, it has the Pacific all to itself, past San Diego and its bigger sister, Tijuana, and well into Baja California Norte.

Mexico has land laws that prohibit foreigners from owning property within thirty-two miles (fifty kilometers) of the sea, or sixty-four miles from any border. This inhibits Anglo settlement south of the border, despite attractive tax, fuel, and living costs.

But there are enough ways around the law, especially through long-term leases, that the Baja is becoming known as the "new Southern California," where life again can be sunny, bucolic, casual, unpolluted, and cheap.

The road to Ensenada, two hours south of Tijuana, has far more signs in English than in Spanish, attempting to lure gringos with promises of "ice cubes," "cold beer," "blown glass," "leather works," "western wear," "steaks," "seafood," "horseback riding," "color TV," "tennis," "heated spa and pool," "auto parts," and a 19.52 percent return on your savings account. The most prominent billboard in Spanish was the one cautioning the locals, should they get upset at this cultural invasion, to remember how important tourism is to the local economy and *smile*.

(Conversely, as one heads north from Mexico into California, one sees that the majority of the signs are in Spanish. In Mex-America, as elsewhere, entrepreneurship goes for the main chance.)

As far south as San José del Cabo, at the most southern tip of Baja California Sur, seven hundred miles from San Diego, Anglos are finding striking homes with inexpensive Pacific views.

Across the Gulf of California, in the state of Sinaloa, American agribusiness is flourishing. "If you dropped me down blindfolded in the middle of the Culiacán Valley, then removed the blindfold," one California grower with investments there was quoted as saying, "I'd be hard pressed to say if I was in Sinaloa or California's Imperial Valley." The irrigation systems, the farm equipment, the crop dusters, the packing sheds in Sinaloa — all are the latest in U.S. agribusiness technology. The fact that the workers in the fields are migrant Mexicans, too, completes the similarity to California. (Internal migration in Mexico is even greater than international migration to the United States.) Next time you marvel at the fabulous produce in the open-air markets in New Orleans near the French Quarter, turn around and look for the Mexican national freight cars on the siding. The vegetables they were hauling almost undoubtedly came from Sinaloa. Florida tomato-growers are so apoplectic about how much cheaper Sinaloa winter tomatoes are than the U.S. varieties in, say, Denver, that the Florida farmers are trying to block their sale.

This is causing serious international friction, made worse by the fact that the Mexicans know, even if most Americans don't, that Americans are flouting the spirit of the Mexican laws prohibiting foreign ownership of Mexican land, and are actually in control of much of the Culiacán Valley. One common way is for U.S.

vegetable distributors, mostly headquartered in Nogales, Arizona (half of a metropolitan complex, along with Nogales, state of Sonora), to be the controlling source of credit for the growers of the Culiacán Valley. Another way is to use a *prestanombre*, "name lender." In that scam, the land is registered in the name of a Mexican national, all right, but the Mexican national has signed a note saying he owes the value of the land to a U.S. company. Either way, the result is that American companies can grow tomatoes, without pesky interference from U.S. unions and wage and environmental laws, cheaper than they can be grown in Florida. "The new Southern California," indeed!

Yet farther south, in the dry mountains around Guadalajara and Mexico City that have been carved up into tiny, unproductive subsistence farms, lie the five states from which comes the bulk of the illegal Mexican immigrants to the American Southwest. In the states of Michoacán, Guanajuato, San Luis Potosi, Zacatecas, and Jalisco, there are few families who do not have relatives in the north. Working in the States for a period is a part of life. It's either that or starve.

East of this harshness, seven hundred miles due south of Louisiana and just west of the Yucatán Peninsula, in the Bahía de Campeche, lies what is thought to be the partial solution to two great North American problems. That's where the Mexican oil fields, thought to be of Middle Eastern vastness, are. Planners hope that they will ease not only Mexican poverty, but the world energy crisis as well.

But the southern border of MexAmerica cannot be determined by Anglo interests alone. By that standard, the resort of Acapulco, well south of Mexico City, should be part of MexAmerica, and that's silly.

No, if the standard in the United States is the significant boundary of Hispanicized North America, then the opposite standard should apply in Mexico, and the Mexican government itself obliges by offering one possible line: it doesn't ask for, or check, tourist cards or visas at the official border. The checkpoints are seventy-five miles south. One hundred and fifty thousand square miles of northern Mexico is a free-travel zone for quick trips by American citizens. U.S. Drug Enforcement Administration agents in El Paso regularly go to lunch in Juarez, just across the line in Mexico, because they think the food's better. They don't pay any more attention to the "real" border than anyone else does.

But the line could be drawn farther south than that. The line could be drawn by the broadcast cones of U.S. radio and television stations. That way, you'd know you were really south of MexAmerica when your car radio stopped producing Spanish-language music that, as it turns out, is being transmitted from Arizona.

•   •   •

MexAmerica may be the most misunderstood of the Nine Nations. Wayne Cornelius, a political scientist from the University of California at San Diego, who has interviewed hundreds of Hispanics in his work as one of the foremost experts on Mexican immigrants, has written: "The average [United States] citizen sees all the benefits of migratory movement accruing to Mexico, and all the costs being borne by the United States. He believes that Mexico as a country is profiting unfairly from the migration, by being allowed to dump its problems of overpopulation, poverty and unemployment upon the United States."

Analysis of a January 1979 national New York Times / CBS News Poll, he says, shows that the farther away from Mex-America a North American lives, the more fervently anti-Mexican-immigrant he or she tends to be.

The first problem in understanding MexAmerica is determining how many Hispanics there are in it. Even the Bureau of Census regards its 1970 count of United States *citizens* of Mexican-American heritage as inadequate, and it's not clear if 1980 was much better. Census admits that language problems, lack of community involvement, and distrust of the government data-collectors reduced the 1970 census figures to estimates. Numbers like eight million total within MexAmerica, 1.5 million in Los Angeles, 53 percent of the population of San Antonio, and 36 percent of the population of New Mexico are educated guesses.

The question of how many illegal immigrants there are is even more open to debate. Leonard Chapman, director of the federal Immigration and Naturalization Service during the Ford administration, felt compelled to announce that he was facing a "vast army that's carrying out a silent invasion of the United States," and estimated that there were twelve million illegals, which would be one and a half times the population of New York City. No one knows where he got that number.

The previous high figure had been eight million, in one of many such reports that display serious ignorance of reality. For example, one study noted that among European immigrants, only 2 percent returned to the home country, and assumed that must be true among Mexicans, too, which is crazy. The Europeans were separated from "home" by an ocean. Cornelius' interviews indicate that the majority of the Mexican immigrants don't particularly *like* living in the United States, where they are often subjected to urban or rural miseries. They are there only because even a wage of $2.00 an hour is four to six times as much as they could earn in Mexico. They return to Mexico when their seasonal jobs are over, or separation from their families becomes intolerable. Perhaps most have never seriously considered settling down in the States permanently, and as many as three-quarters say they would prefer to commute from Mexico even if they could stay in this country *legally*. By not allowing for these realities, studies that show the high illegal alien figures are, in effect, counting the same commuter over and over again as he heads north, but not subtracting him when he returns south.

Latest estimates go as low as 1.5 million illegals in the country at any one time, which, of course, is about a tenth of Chapman's. Even the Border Patrol notes that it nabs about three quarters of a million illegals a year, and figures, from the number of times its electronic sensors, buried along the border, go off, that it's getting about one in three or one in four of such immigrants. That would put the figure at three million or less.

The second problem in understanding this nation is the tendency many Anglos have of grouping all Hispanics together as one undifferentiated mass of greasers and wetbacks. Armando Morales, of the UCLA School of Medicine's Neuro Psychiatric Institute, becomes livid when he talks about the Arrid deodorant commercial that showed a Mexican spraying his armpit as the voice-over said, "If it works for *him*, it will work for *you*."

But the distinctions to be made among the Spanish-speaking are so great that they present serious problems in organizing the people politically. There's not even a consensus on how to refer to them — Hispanic, Latino, Mexican, Mexican-American, Chicano, Spanish, Tejanos, Californios, Manitos.

One segment of the society, the undocumented workers, as both Mexicans and Mexican-Americans prefer to call illegal aliens, occupies a shadow world of fieldhands, bus boys, domestics, and day laborers. Fear of deportation prevents protest of even the most unfair treatment or unsafe working conditions.

These workers are sometimes paid an illegally low wage, forced into fields that have been freshly doused with poisonous chemi-

cals, denied simple requests like an extra fan in a garment factory — which, in the L.A. sun, brings new meaning to the phrase
"sweat shop"— beaten, shot, and, in one recent case in Louisiana,
actually held in what legally constituted peonage — slavery.

Typically, the *undocumentado* embodies the classic case of culture shock, because nowhere else in the world does an advanced,
technological society like the United States abut a developing,
but nonetheless struggling nation with a birthrate higher than
that of Bangladesh, an unemployment or underemployment rate
of 40 percent, and an average age that may be as low as fourteen.

(The culture shock can cut two ways. I visited MexAmerica
right after I'd been to Dixie. In the godawful-poor Mississippi
Delta, I ended up casually talking to a newspaperman who recently had seen an old black farmer plowing a field with mules.
The reporter was still kicking himself for not instantly stopping
the car and getting out to walk a few miles with the man, talking
to him about his life and times and his animals. He was sure that
was the last working mule team in Mississippi, not counting
those kept by some white ecofreak weirdo hippies. By contrast,
I'm here to tell you there are horses and donkeys left in the southern edge of MexAmerica that are not only the proverbial primary
mode of transportation, but represent a major capital investment — even a display of relative wealth. As with the Testigos de
Jehova, I guess I shouldn't have been surprised by them, but I
was.)

Not only does the undocumentado speak a different language
from his employer literally; he speaks a different language culturally, both from his employer and the village he left behind.

"The illegals have a somewhat higher propensity to take risks
[compared with people who stay behind in Mexico]," suggests
one study. "They are more sensitive to inequalities in the distribution of wealth within their home community; they have weaker
attachments to the Catholic Church and Catholic religious symbols."

Yet typically, and at least initially, they do not speak English,
are uneducated (frequently illiterate in Spanish), are technologically unskilled, and share a decidedly non-Anglo culture
system.

For example, a publication of San Antonio's Mexican American
Culture Center includes a chart entitled "Comparative Overview
of Anglo-Saxon and Mexican Historical Cultural Patterns." Under

"system of social organization; response to stress," it characterizes the Anglo mode as: "Immediate and constant action . . .
modify the environment to fit our needs." The Mexican mode, it
says, is "passive endurance & resistance . . . modify ourselves to
fit the environment."

Under "fundamental values," it lists for the Anglo: "Control. Of
oneself, of others, of nature." For the Mexican it cites: "Harmony.
Within oneself, among others, within nature."

Under "fundamental institutions," subcategory "state," for Anglos it says, "The people are the government." For Mexicans, it
says, "The government versus the people."

Under "popular wisdom," Anglos think "Might makes right."
Mexicans, "Life is a valley of tears."

United States citizens of Mexican extraction, by contrast,
though frequently endorsing such sentiments, do not seem to let
it get in the way of their embracing acculturation. Mexican-Americans serve in the U.S. military out of all proportion to their numbers in the population. And to prove that this is not necessarily
motivated by the pay, Mexican-American leaders point to the fact
that their people are also decorated for gallantry and heroism out
of all proportion to their numbers.

While Mexican-American homes can still be found frequently
with portraits of John and / or Robert Kennedy on the wall (usually right next to the picture of the kid serving in the Marines),
Democrats cannot take for granted the liberalism of Mexican-
Americans. Not only is pacifism not a congenial issue; abortion
isn't either. Although Mexican-American poverty results in many
broken homes, family ties — in the sense of extended family — remain strong. It is not at all unusual for the woman who may be
left as head of a household to be strongly supported by cousins,
aunts, and parents. Against this tradition, and the influence of the
Roman Catholic Church, "pro-choicers" have rough sledding. Opposition to nuclear power is also not a big deal in the barrio.
Energy development is linked to jobs. For that matter, Benjamin
Fernandez, a Mexican-American fringe candidate for the presidency in 1980, ran not as a Democrat but as a Republican.

Demographers have noted a dramatic difference in birthrates
between Mexicans and Mexican-Americans. While the typical
Mexican family can have eight kids, the Hispanic United States
citizen is much more likely to have two or three. There's a growing Mexican-American middle class, which is making inroads in
small business, teaching, and government. (This helps explain the

sudden interest on the part of U.S. corporations in Spanish-language product advertising. Budweiser's ubiquitous slogan is *"Es para usted"* — It's for you.)

The United States citizen of Mexican ancestry feels a kinship to the undocumentado, at least in the geography of his mind. Many of the oldest citizens were immigrants. Some of the newest still have relatives in Mexico. They know that, as in the case of the millionaire Mexican-American Los Angeles restaurant owner who had been deported thirty-seven times before he finally became financially successful and was allowed to stay in this country, much is forgiven in the United States of those who manage to rise out of poverty.

But at the same time, some Californios — California Mexican-Americans — scornfully refer to undocumentados as "tee-jays," after the Tia Juana River they crossed to get into the United States. A "tee-jay" is equivalent to somebody who "just got off the boat."

American citizens with brown skin resent the police suspicion of them that illegal immigration brings. They resent the necessity to demonstrate constantly at random checkpoints that they actually are citizens. They resent sitting in an airport next to a couple chattering away in Vietnamese and having the authorities come up and ask *them*, not the Orientals, to show their papers.

And one of the ways such citizens display their integration into the larger North American culture is the kind of crap up with which they won't put.

In the 1960s, the Chicano movement began, fueled by young Mexican-Americans sick of second-class citizenship. The litany of oppression of Mexican-Americans — not aliens, not naturalized immigrants, but third- and fourth-generation Americans who had deep roots in the United States, but also brown skin — is a long one.

A few of the highlights include the occasional massacre at the hands of Texas Rangers. (It's amazing how different the history of the Southwest sounds when recited by the people on the wrong end of the gun. One man's band of brave knights is another man's despised Gestapo.)

Then there was the massive roundup and deportation of California Mexicans during hard times in the thirties. Like the shameful internment of the Japanese during World War II, it didn't make much difference whether you were a United States citizen or not. Brown skin? Into the train.

There were the schools where the teachers punished you if you spoke Spanish in the schoolyard.

There were the classes for the retarded where they put the children who didn't speak English too well. George Pla, a University of Southern California graduate who has become a leader of the Mexican-American community of East Los Angeles, remembers being classified as a "retard."

But then, California used to count only white children, not Mexican-Americans, when it distributed school funds.

There are the interestingly drawn voting districts. As of 1980, Los Angeles, with its estimated two million Hispanics, did not have one single Mexican-American city councilman.

Then there's Larry Ortéga Lozano, who died in the Odessa, Texas, county jail, shortly after being joined by more than a half-dozen lawmen. A pathologist said it was homicide, after finding ninety-two injuries to the body, some "in places where he would have had to be contorted" to inflict the wounds himself. The sheriff said Ortéga Lozano had committed suicide by banging his head against the cell door. The sheriff's view prevailed.

Andrés Ramirez died on the way to the hospital in Albuquerque after being beaten repeatedly on the head with a five-cell flashlight by a policeman trying to restrain him. The cop was acquitted by an all-Anglo jury.

Roberto Fernandez died in the home of his estranged wife in Pueblo, Colorado, at the wrong end of two cops' nightsticks. The cops were acquitted.

Greaser. Beaner. Wetback. Spic. Chilibelly. Frito-bandito. Hey, Pancho; hey, Cisco. What's your hurry, the tamales getting cold? Never trust a Mexican. Lazy as a Mexican. You're late; what are you, Mexican? You want my seeester? She is a virgin . . .

Ka-boom!

The riots, the Brown Berets, the Chicano movement were directed at all that. The word Chicano (feminine: Chicana) is still not used by older Mexican-Americans to describe themselves. They knew it when it's stressing of the *mestizo* (mixed-blood) aspects of the heritage, the Indian component, the ties to the hard-scrabble land, was a slur. But they will say, "My son is a Chicano," for the young have taken the name as a badge of pride. It's a political designation more than an ethnic one. Not all Mexican-Americans are Chicanos; by the same token, there are many highly successful, highly educated, non-Spanish-speaking — even blond-haired — Americans with Mexican blood who wrap themselves in the name as a form of liberation. As a mark of political awakening.

Some of the political awakening, like the reference to Mex-America as Aztlan, can take on local overtones. In Austin, for example, you can buy a T-shirt that says PUT THE J BACK IN TEJAS. Yet many Tejanos make cultural distinctions between themselves and other Mexican-Americans. Hispanics in Arizona and New Mexico, for example, are often referred to as Manitos, or "little brothers," in a mild condescension that the New Mexicans who want to be referred to as "Spanish" sometimes find irritating. One of the distinctions that Tejanos and Californios make between themselves I found amusing. Tejanos say Californios are a little flaky. Californios say Tejanos are hick. Who says brown and white MexAmericans have nothing in common?

Down California's Interstate 5, past the Chamber of Commerce's billboard that says HANG YOUR HAT IN CHULA VISTA — the hat being a sombrero — rise the mesquite-covered hills near the Mexican border that look exactly the same as their cousins farther south, save for the maze of footpaths. The well-worn trails in the dust almost seem tended — firmly packed and weedless — and in a way, they are. They're the trails padded every night by the feet of the illegal immigrants, heading north.

On such a hill, in San Ysidro, parked in formation, is a row of distinctive, pale green trucks and buses, their color a little lighter than that of the U.S. Park Service. The vans, identified in chrome by their maker as the Sportsman model, have grilles and bars over their windows, and their drivers are wearing guns, for this is the sector headquarters of the U.S. Border Patrol.

The headquarters building is a grim affair, its concrete-block walls painted an institutional beige, its floor, cheerless blocks of linoleum, its furniture, scarred metal, and its signs saying NO ADMITTANCE, AUTHORIZED PERSONNEL ONLY.

The receptionist has a Spanish accent. One employee wears over his pants a traditional, open-necked, embroidered Mexican dress shirt. Outside, in the sun so bright it makes you squint, men with dark brown skin wash the ever-present desert dust off the buses that dump apprehended illegal aliens back south of the border. Snippets of conversation between agents tantalize. "Have you seen Ricardo in the last four or five days? He just fell off the face of the earth. I hope nobody got him." Whatever *that's* a reference to.

This sector is the smallest, geographically, of any of the Border

Patrol's, but it has the most men assigned to it — 236 — for along its sixty-six miles, 337,930 illegal aliens were caught in fiscal 1979, which was nearly half the number caught in the entire United States. That works out to one every two minutes or so, round the clock, all year long. It also works out to more than 1400 illegals per agent.

This sector is so active that Don Cameron, the sector chief, a jovial old bear a year away from retirement, has become a teeny bit famous. "I just finished making a movie with Charles Bronson." He grinned. "It was about the Border Patrol. The name of it is *Borderline*. It has to do with a Border Patrol agent who's murdered in the line of duty and his friend, the senior agent, who's Charles Bronson, who sets about solving the murder. It ends up with the conviction and all that stuff of the murderer and the smuggling ring that's involved. My part was very small. I played myself. Somebody said, 'How long did you have to study to do that?' The wags around here."

The sector is so hot that since a law was enacted which allows the Border Patrol to seize vehicles used in alien smuggling, Cameron says he's accumulated so many, the men don't have a place to park their own cars. He's got four hundred down at a local military base. "I've got more used cars than Cal Worthington," Cameron only half-jokes, making a reference to one of the biggest car-dealers in California.

In fact, this sector is so hot that it has the highest attrition rate in the Border Patrol. Cameron lost a hundred officers in one year. Some transferred to other parts of the Mexican border or, better yet, to the Canadian border. Some transferred to other duties, such as investigative work inland. Some transferred to other parts of Immigration and Naturalization, like the Deportation branch. Some went to other agencies, such as Customs, or Alcohol, Tobacco and Firearms, or the FBI. Some just plain quit. And, as in the Bronson movie, a few stopped bullets. Cameron calculated that journeymen Border Patrol agents in his sector last exactly nineteen months, on average. And it's no secret why. Cameron himself estimates that no matter how hard it tries, and no matter how much danger it exposes itself to, the Border Patrol in his sector, with the existing level of manpower and resources, is at best 30 to 50 percent effective, "and nobody beyond me gives a damn.

"It's frustrating."

He worked hard with the local congressmen to get more agents in place, more money. Congress had even gone along with hiring 495 more bodies, costing $14.5 million, and he would have gotten 239 of them in this sector alone, and, God, with enough men and material, he could get enforcement of the law up to 90, 95 percent effective, he thinks. But the Office of Management and Budget pulled the plug on the increase. Too expensive. How could they do that? he asked.

"We can't keep them all out," said Cameron. "We can't seal the border. But what's going to happen to our economy if we allow Mexico to move up here *unrestricted?*"

Unrestricted. Unconsciously, Cameron hit on the key word to his dilemma and the frustrations of his men. Unrestricted. What drives the Border Patrol agents crazy is that they think they're a federal law enforcement agency and that their mission is to *stop* the breaking of the immigration laws. But their sector chief, in the depths of his soul, grasps the true mission. They're supposed to *restrict* illegal immigration. Mold it. Shape it. Channel it. Establish the rules under which it will be conducted and see that as few people as possible get killed in the process. *Stop* illegal immigration completely? Who's in favor of that? Too many people on both sides of the border benefit from the situation just as it is. The Border Patrol isn't a federal law enforcement arm. It's a *regulatory* agency. Just like the one that watches over the stock market.

"I've got to be a little careful in what I say here," said Michael Walsh, the U.S. Attorney for the Southern District of California, whose job it's supposed to be to prosecute the people that Don Cameron's boys catch, and whose manner is reminiscent of Robert Redford in *The Candidate*.

"But the thing is, from a political point of view, this is pretty much a no-win proposition. It's all discombobulated in terms of traditional Democratic and Republican positions.

"The Democrats are by and large quality-of-life people. They also, traditionally, are for the underdog. Well, here, quality of life and being for the underdog conflict. If you look at the long-term implications of relatively unchecked migration . . ."

Good-by, zero population growth.

"Now the Republicans are typically law-and-order types. And the policy that I've adopted in this jurisdiction of simply not prosecuting illegal aliens, just returning them to Mexico [in lieu of hopelessly clogging the courts, which would lead to hopelessly clogging the jails], could be the subject of a lot of attack from traditional conservative quarters.

"On the other hand, the agricultural interests and a lot of the commercial interests that profit by relatively lower prices and relatively un-unionized labor tend to be Republican. So you have the flip side of the Democratic dilemma, and the Republicans tend not to be too enthusiastic about too aggressive an enforcement posture.

"This creates a very, very difficult problem."

The situation, of course, as Wayne Cornelius points out, is usually viewed in terms of what Mexico gets out of immigration. With its high birthrate, low average age, and its cities growing at the rate of up to 10 percent per year or more as rural poor migrate to the cities in the classic pattern, Mexico has growth problems that nobody's got the money to deal with. Mexico has a developing oil industry, but it's just that, *developing*, and besides, the number of jobs an oil well creates is finite. You drill for oil with expensive Houston-made machinery, not your hands. So almost half the people are unemployed or underemployed.

No wonder it's no crime to leave Mexico for the United States, passport or no passport.

Of course, there are those on this side of the border who see this situation as a flock of *locusts* and we've got to *do* something about it, and, as the polls show, the less people know about the situation, the more likely they are to have that view. That's why it's important to remember how well the United States benefits from this deal.

Immigration as a social safety valve is not a bad governmental policy for the United States. The alternative is to have a social pressure cooker along your two-thousand-mile-long southern border, with the heat on full blast, ready to blow at any time. Nothing like a good bloody Nicaraguan-style revolution along your flank to liven up your foreign policy problems. Or, more entertaining yet, it could be a Cuban-style revolution.

Apart from the political unpleasantness that a communist Mexico a few blocks away from San Diego, El Paso, and Brownsville would entail, it would make the American businessmen who have made major investments in Mexican agriculture, industry, and tourism very unhappy. For that matter, a trading partner like Mexico, which buys $3 billion worth of stuff from the United States every year, is not insignificant. Especially just when all that oil is about to start flowing.

It's also been pointed out that the wages that the undocumentado send home are the cheapest, most efficient form of foreign aid the United States has ever stumbled on. It requires little bureaucracy. There's not a lot of corruption to it. And it actually gets to the people at the lowest levels of the society, who rarely get anything from the traditional foreign aid programs.

It's also transferring skills and technology, which certainly can't hurt Mexico's development. Granted, a great many undocumentados don't get the opportunity to learn much more than how to drive a wheelbarrow or tuck a bedsheet in hospital corners. But others are arc-welding, running machinery, and performing calculations behind store counters. These are skills your average illiterate *campesino* didn't have when he started.

Sealing the border, were that possible, would also cripple the way Mexico subsidizes the United States. For example, a San Diego State University study showed that Mexican citizens spent over $400 million in retail outlets in San Diego County in 1978. The U.S. taxes the Mexican citizens paid on these purchases amounted to almost $25 million. The downtown San Diego shopping district would lose 23.5 percent of its business if Mexican citizens stopped shopping there tomorrow. The manager of one Houston *supermarcado* figured that two thirds of his business came from the paychecks of undocumentados.

One way high-priced American jobs are saved from export to Taiwan or Japan is through the use of *maquiladoras,* "twin plants." In these factories, expensive United States–produced components are imported without duty to Mexico, where, for $1.40 an hour for a forty-eight-hour week, a hundred thousand Mexicans assemble them and ship them back with a "Made in U.S.A." stamp, duty paid on only the cost of assembly. United States makers of semiconductors and automobiles claim that without such cost savings, they would really get swamped by Asian competition.

The United States benefits even in the underground economy. The smuggling works two ways. People and drugs may come north, but almost every other store in the commercial district of Brownsville, Texas, is an appliance–electronic goods shop. They are not there for the citizens of Brownsville. At least one of the stores has clerks who speak no English. Consumer luxuries, such as color televisions, fashionable clothes, and electronic games and toys, are, along with guns, a major factor in the southbound smuggling trade.

The chronically deficit-ridden Social Security system is being subsidized by illegal immigration. A researcher who interviewed 793 undocumentados apprehended by the Immigration and Nat-

uralization Service discovered that more than 77 percent had had
F.I.C.A. deducted from their paycheck, just like everyone else. But
because the Social Security cards were forged, they can never
claim the benefits. The researcher calculated that if there are four
million illegal aliens in this country, the Social Security system
gets a $2.3 billion windfall each year.

The fact is that illegals do pay both payroll and sales taxes,
and, despite the stereotypes, make relatively few demands on services. Because of their fear of deportation, they shun all contact
with government agencies. They most especially do not trot down
to the welfare office. They often are afraid to go to the *hospital*.

The children born in America of illegal immigrants are, of
course, American citizens, and their presence does burden school
systems, especially those closest to the border. But this is one of
the ways the Border Patrol works as a regulatory agency. By definition, only the more resourceful and agile are the ones who get
through its net. This discourages the immigration of whole families. The wife and kids tend to stay in Mexico and rely on Mexican
social services, such as they are. It's the breadwinner who faces
the dangers of *La Migra*, as the Immigration Service is known. It
serves as a filter to allow through only those most likely to be
productive members of society. That's one reason there are so
many kids in Tijuana.

The undocumentados are displacing American workers, some
cry, but there's little evidence that that's true. As Cornelius points
out:

Most of the jobs in question are the least desirable in the U.S. labor
market: they involve dirty, physically punishing tasks, low wages, long
hours, generally poor working conditions, low job security (often due to
the temporary or seasonal character of the work), and little chance for
advancement . . . Among recent illegal migrants, the most frequently
held jobs were (in order of importance) agricultural field laborer, dish-
washer or waiter in a restaurant, and unskilled construction worker
. . . Where they worked alongside blacks and Chicanos, illegals usually
. . . worked in basically different jobs. For example, in a typical small
construction firm, the Mexican illegal aliens worked as laborers while
the Mexican-Americans and blacks had jobs as craftsmen. In a manufacturing industry such as meatpacking, the illegals worked in occupations
that Mexican-Americans and blacks shunned because of the working conditions.

In order for American workers to be displaced, they have to be
there in the first place, and there is no record to indicate that

American eighteen-year-olds, no matter how high their unemployment rate, are clamoring for the opportunity to spend the day bent over in the hot sun, picking carrots for peanuts. The Mexicans, by contrast, are *motivated*.

And, as U.S. Attorney Walsh indicates, there are too many conservative business interests, ranging from agribusiness to the garment industry to the construction industry, whose margin of profit is based on the flow of undocumentados for it to stop. For that matter, these businessmen know damn well that if you went into the kitchens of one of their posh restaurants and yelled "La Migra," within thirty seconds there'd be nobody there to cook or serve them lunch.

San Antonio's Mexican-American leaders are already viewing the ease with which Spanish is used in their city as an asset in forging ties to Latin America. They see an opportunity for pivotal trade relationships the way New York is important to Europe, Miami is important to the Caribbean, and San Francisco is important to the Orient. Already, Guatemalan city clerks and Panamanian junior college instructors come to San Antonio for training — in Spanish. The city leaders note with interest that Québec has discovered it profitable to be in a position to export North American technology, but to do so in *French*. In some parts of the world, notably Africa, where it's politically unpopular to be exploited by Yankee devils, doing business with the Québecois is far more comfortable for everyone involved. So it may be someday for MexAmerica.

Finally, the Border Patrol's efforts as a regulatory agency not only ensure that none but the most dedicated gets through; it keeps the peace for the undocumentado-importation industry. It fights the *banditos* who try to rob the incoming aliens. Although a frustrated agent occasionally shoots an illegal, and a frustrated illegal occasionally shoots back, by and large the violence between the patrol and its quarry is kept to a minimum. Neither side is particularly interested in, or sees the necessity of, getting into a war over all this.

The rivalry has even taken on a certain tone of clubbiness. The Border Patrol has developed a "black box" electronic detector that, when put close to a car or a truck, filters out all the engine and electrical noises and homes in on heartbeats. It is meant to detect illegals being smuggled under false floors or in car trunks. The agents call it the "garlic detector."

The Mexicans respond in kind. Some take a certain pride in

finding the electronic body-heat detectors that dot the border. And urinating on them.

• • •

It's Saturday night at the Hotel Rosarita in Baja California Norte, Mexico, and the self-described *supergroupo* Chaparral, *y su cantante*, Ruth, are getting *down*. As the strobes etch motion, and a revolving, multifaceted crystal ball flickers colored light over the jam of dancers, loudspeakers serious enough to cause aural damage if aimed 10 degrees lower, paint the room with the band's flawless imitation of Donna Summers' disco. Flawless except when Ruth rolls her *r*'s.

Disco queens with deep-slit togas and long flowing hair glide under the Spanish arches painted on the inside with stylized Central American floral patterns. Against the stucco walls stand both lithe bronzed godlets and the pale-chested, gold-chained gut-suckers. The crowd's about 45 percent Mexican; 55 percent Anglo.

The red-tuxedo-jacketed waiters serve margaritas to eighteen-year-old Americans who have migrated into Mexico for the illegal-in-California-at-their-age purpose of drinking same.

Behind the flashing, leaping guitar, bass, organ, and drums, a mural depicts a peaceful world of cactus, prickly pear, green rolling hills, blue sky, and violet clouds.

The floor and the walls of the men's room are covered with fine, ancient, hand-painted Mexican tiles. On the wall of the corridor that leads to it is a six-by-twelve-foot painting, depicting a campesino in sandals, a chicken crate on his back, walking head down, doggedly, through empty desert, blue jagged mountains in the background.

In the lobby, a sign proudly announces that the hotel is a MEMBER: SAN DIEGO CONVENTION AND VISITORS BUREAU. Another sign announces DINNER FROM $4.50 TRY OUR MEXICAN PLATE.

The phone, definitely not part of Pacific Bell, announces bilingually that it is not in service.

The prices in the gift shop are in dollars, not pesos.

A rack of brochures extols "unspoiled Baja Malibu," with its "magnificent" beach, "sparkling" air, and "affordable" luxury.

That there's a Tijuana cop with a Magnum on his hip, and that he is using a nightstick to point out the lady taking the cover charge, is mildly unnerving, but he speaks English and appears friendly.

The newsstand has a solid display of U.S. fan magazines, along with its Goody Hair Fashion Center, its Brach's Kentucky Mints, its Bayer Aspirin in "exclusive child-guard slide pack," and its *Mad* magazine paperbacks, next to its paperbacks of Robert Kennedy's biography.

On the wall behind it, yet another mural shows a mustachioed, sombreroed young man hauling in fishing nets out of a blue-green sea that contrasts nicely with the red tile of the roofs depicted nearby. In the painting, a man in a serape, holding a cold drink, leans against the massive, arched porticos of the buildings as he's yapped at by a small dog.

Back in the steamy disco, a trio of Anglo men has become rather entranced by a young Mexican lady who appears to be in her late teens and has the most fabulous hip action when she dances. Her arms, encased in what seems to be an expensive angora sweater that matches her tasteful white skirt, wave gracefully over her head as her pelvis almost clicks to the beat.

Yet discretion is apparently advised, since the young lady not only is dancing with what is obviously her boyfriend, but when they get back to their table, there, waiting for them, is a forty-ish, long-black-skirted, could it be? No. A *chaperone!*

My God! the trio notes among itself. A cultural artifact! A wealthy Mexican girl out on the town with her *señora de compañía.*

I wonder, says the most serious-looking member of the trio, his seriousness deepened by his margarita intake, I wonder, if the chaperone . . . boogies?

And with that, as the first notes of the next set start, he leaps up, strides purposefully to the other table, bows slightly, and inquires of the chaperone if she would care to dance.

She would, and they do, and as the band thunders, she gets it on. A little woodenly, it's true, but, like the dog walking on its hind legs, the trick is that it happens at *all.*

The Anglos are deeply impressed.

• • •

In San Antonio, the dozen people in the back office of the print shop, cracking open some beer at the end of a long week, debate the question the stranger has brought up. Why is it that Mexican-Americans don't vote worth a damn?

Earlier in the day, the stranger had been given the grand tour of western San Antonio — the barrios — by Carmen Badillo, the head of COPS (Communities Organized for Public Service). Like UNO (United Neighborhood Organization) in East Los Angeles,

COPS is a Mexican-American community-action coalition that hates to be called a pressure group. But in San Antonio, at least, if you don't call it a pressure group, what do you call it, a shadow government?

COPS members join together to analyze the needs of each neighborhood — more schools, better schools, better roads, storm sewers for the flash floods, low-cost housing. They assign priorities — okay, there's only so much money in the whole world: what's a "gotta" and what's a "nice-to-have." They research the availability of federal funds for specific projects. And then they go down to the mayor and the city councilmen, frequently en masse, and jump up and down until they get what they want, neighborhood by neighborhood.

By no means do they win every battle, but an eloquent testimonial to the effectiveness of COPS is that there are now white neighborhoods asking if they can join.

Badillo drove me around, showing me the victory of Barrio La Tripa COPS. Named after the tripe — animal guts — rendered at nearby plants, the neighborhood had organized to do something about the stench. COPS made the air pollution an issue in 1975, and got it cleaned up.

There was Colonia Santa Cruz, a neighborhood of modest, bright, good-looking, two-bedroom homes surrounded by well-kept lawns and suburban fences, built and bought through low-interest federal loans.

The Mayberry Project was COPS's first great accomplishment. It's a concrete gully being built through town to drain off the periodic torrential rains that regularly caused floods, which led to citizens regularly being evacuated from rooftops.

She showed me the rotted foundations and high-water lines that had been caused by the repeated flooding until COPS had made it an issue.

Christ the King COPS was responsible for the $7 million park that was under construction. Christ the King was the local Catholic church, around which the neighborhood had organized. The park would have three pavilions, she said gleefully, and a swimming pool, and . . .

Not everything was rosy, by any means. Well inside Route 410, San Antonio's encircling highway, in Holy Family parish, we found dirt streets, some steers, a goat, and chickens that looked suspiciously pugnacious.

Portions of the barrio could just as easily have been a thousand miles south. Dirt yards, fences made of sticks lashed together, unpainted wooden shacks, crooked doors, hostile faces. A tiny shop to patch flat tires. Blouses offered for sale, displayed on a chain-link fence. Produce sold from carts.

But Badillo was very proud of what COPS had accomplished, and she was certain it would do more. It was making sure, she observed, that the San Antonio power structure was producing a government of the people, by the people, and for the people, whether they liked it or not.

So back in the print shop, to which I had been taken by Henry Cisneros, a very smart, mediagenic Mexican-American San Antonio city councilman who is being touted as the next Texas senator, Texas governor, president of the United States, you name it, the argument raged. (Cisneros had invited me to talk to some "ordinary" Mexican-Americans.) Why the hell *don't* Mexican-Americans vote? they debated. If we can organize into COPS, certainly you'd think we could elect a majority to the city council, and we haven't. And in most southwestern cities, we're far less represented than we are in San Antonio, despite our numbers.

The politicians are selfish, said one man sitting on a couple of boxes of *Enciclopedia de Mexico. 12 Tomos.* They're only for themselves. They don't build up an organization, so when they get elected to higher office, they haven't groomed a young Chicano to take their place.

All politicians are selfish, said another. It's up to us to encourage these young candidates. We've got to develop them, put them in position, said another man, sitting under a display of bumper stickers the shop had produced, political bumper stickers with names like Garza, Delgado, and Gamez.

That still doesn't explain why Mexican-Americans don't vote, interjected a fourth.

Well what difference would it make? somebody chimed in. All politicians are alike anyway.

(When I had asked Badillo what COPS thought of Cisneros, the rising young Mexican-American political star, she shrugged and said, "He's a politician, like any other.")

Yeah — the crowd seemed to be coming to a consensus — the thing is, what difference does it make? The roads will get paved, and the flood waters tamed, and the parks built, and the housing put together, whether there's a Mexican-American majority on the city council or not.

I mean, what's the big deal about voting?

There are so many of us, *we're going to run things anyway.*

ECOTOPIA

PARADISE, as it turns out, smells like bee glue.

Near the crest of the Cascade Mountains of Oregon, Paradise is guarded by Three Sisters. North, Middle, and South — 10,085 feet, 10,047 feet, and 10,358 feet, respectively — the Three Sisters are snowcapped behemoths that tower over the Douglas fir near the top of the valley of the McKenzie River. In late spring, when the dogwoods bloom in the forest, the Sisters feed just barely melted light blue mountain water past Paradise, over well-rounded boulders, past the jagged snarls of uprooted giant cedars felled by winter storms.

Paradise smells like bee glue because it is surrounded by black cottonwoods. The buds of black cottonwood contain a yellowish, tangy, pungent, clean, and resinous-smelling stickum called propolis. Bees collect propolis to attach their honeycomb to their hive, hence the popular name. But the other thing propolis does is permeate the air of the forest, its aroma quickening the senses and focusing urban-jaded attention on the broken water flowing swiftly past.

Presumably it's the propolis that is sharpening the attention. The other possibility is simple fear. For Paradise is just above the rapids euphemistically called the "most interesting" on the McKenzie, and the river guide in red baseball cap, black neoprene booties, and orange life vest is giving what is cheerfully referred to as the "death speech."

"Okay," says the guide, "I'm going to go through the whole

spiel, just in case. We're going to hit heavy water almost immediately, so we're not going to have much time to practice. We're going to do a little dry run right here, okay? We'll start with the basics, and then we'll move on to what you do or don't do if you hit the rocks."

As the guide drones on, explaining the dynamics of the six-person, $2000 gray rubber raft on which we are going to ride down the mountain due west toward the city of Eugene, the speech is occasionally interrupted by gusts of slightly overshrill wisecracks and nervous laughter. No one seems entirely comfortable with the fix they've gotten themselves in, rafting the McKenzie so soon after winter.

Certainly, the ride is hardly one you'd compare to going over Niagara in a barrel. There are far more dangerous rivers in the Pacific Northwest. But on the other hand, though the air is warm, there has been considerable discussion on the trip up to Paradise about exactly how long a person would last in water this cold before suffering from hypothermia — the body's inability to maintain a constant temperature of 98.6 degrees. Hypothermia leads to unconsciousness, shock, and death. Nobody disagrees that the duration of the process would be measured in minutes.

"The hardest thing to do is shake your fear of leaning on the water. Put the paddle into the water as vertically as you can, then push it through the water, really putting your weight on it. The lower arm doesn't bend at all. It's the fulcrum point. If you hear me yell 'Fulcrum! Fulcrum!' that means straighten your arm."

The five people listening attentively to the guide look like an advertisement for sheep-raisers. They are clad from head to toe in multiple layers of wool, one of the very few fibers that will conserve warmth even when soaking wet. The raft trip had been almost scuttled because the crowd could not rustle up the requisite number of wetsuits — the rubber underwear that protects scuba divers from the ravages of ocean cold for hours. Finally, a judgment call had been made that enough wool would probably keep the crew members from doing serious damage to themselves. So, feet covered with three layers of socks had been laced into sneakers, and arms rather stiffly encased in layers of wool shirts were now being further encumbered by rigid life vests, each equipped with a collar designed to keep even an unconscious head afloat.

This is a very rocky river, and the worst is at the beginning, so if there's a chance of an accident, it's highest at the start [says the guide]. The boat is amazingly forgiving, but nonetheless, the river has a tendency to remind you that it's there. If we hit a rock head-on, the boat will come around, and we'll end up floating downstream, with time to recover. But if we hit it sideways, it's a little more risky. The boat doesn't handle it quite so well. What happens is that the boat rides up on the rock, and then gets pinned down by the force of the water. It happens with canoes, kayaks, rafts . . . It's a very uncomfortable position to be in. So we try to avoid that. But if we do hit sideways, jump on the tube closest to the rock. It's called highsiding. You almost do it instinctively, because the other side is going under. So leap for the far tube; everybody in the boat put their weight on it. It holds the boat down, and slowly it will come around. It does work. I will shout the command if it's necessary. It will all happen very quickly.

Ha, ha, ha. Oh yes. "Highside! Highside!" everybody suddenly takes to commanding each other in slightly constricted voices. It's very early on a Sunday morning. There's a great deal of interest voiced in whether there's maybe not something good to read in the Sunday paper and maybe we could try this some other time.

Now. If you should fall out of the boat, which is possible in this section, we'll try to get you back in right away. But whatever you do, don't get caught between the boat and a rock. If it looks like that's what's going to happen, just swim on down the river, and when we get to a quiet place, we'll get you back on the boat. Of course, there aren't any quiet places for the next six miles, so . . . I'm sorry. I shouldn't laugh. Really. We don't have many people fall out in this stretch. Just stay in the boat. If the boat itself should turn over, just stay with it. You'll all be together in the water. If you should come up under the boat, don't worry about it; there'll be an air pocket there that you can breathe. But it's very unlikely that the boat will turn over. I've only flipped a boat once or twice.

In an eddy near shore, a kayaker does wrist exercises with a double-bladed paddle. This kayaker will escort us down the river like a fighter pilot accompanying a lumbering bomber. The kayaker is securely bound into the craft by a neoprene skirt attached in a theoretically watertight fashion to the boat by hooks, and to the person by a sturdy belt at the waist. Getting out of a kayak in an emergency is not the world's easiest task, because a person's automatic reflex is to assume a crouched position when confronted by danger, and you can't bend your knees in a kayak; if you try, you may wedge yourself in there permanently. But as a help, the rubber shield comes equipped with a white plastic "Jesus ball." If you're in trouble, you grab the white ball, yell "Jesus!" and pull as hard as you can. The idea is that the bindings that hold you to the flimsy shell will promptly give way, leaving you to the water and the rocks unimpeded. We innocently ask the kayaker to show us a barrel roll, a basic stunt that involves turning the craft completely over and then righting it again, spending a few seconds head down underwater in the process. The kayaker drops a hand into the blue water for a moment, letting the chill slip between loose fingers. After a brief period of thought came the smiling but serious reply: "Only if you pay me."

In relatively calm water some hours later, the guide will hand over command of the raft to one of the novice river-runners, who will discover that coordinating the efforts of six oarsmen with sharply barked commands is more of an intellectual achievement than he had thought. Running a river is a lot like running a pool table. A working knowledge of physics is mandatory. The main difference is that on a raft you are the cueball, and the surface on which you're rolling is itself moving.

But just downstream from Paradise, no one except the guide was doing any thinking. "Left turn! Backpaddle! Forward! Forward! Lean into it! Stop!" came the commands, and we obeyed with surprising alacrity and coordination, focusing completely on the small pieces of water against which we were pitting our backs. Miraculously, we found ourselves whizzing between boulders and over standing waves, the nose of the keelless craft pointed unerringly forward as the drill sergeant in the stern eyed the conditions far down the river and authoritatively positioned us for new surprises even as we huddled masses were greeting the cold shocks of the old ones.

At lunchtime, on a gravelly clearing, came the first opportunity to get a really good look at the river guide and kayaker, who were so at home with the harsh forces of the river that they seemed a part of it, like the mountains and the Douglas fir and the ravens, like ancient Indians.

Both of them were women. In some parts of the continent, it's not the most common thing for a man to stare at a woman's thigh with no more prurient a thought than marvel at the articulation of her muscles.

But then again, in some parts, it's not altogether common to find a pair like this. Neither of them could have weighed more than 130 pounds, but they wore on their bones the mark of a vigorous life, shaped not by hours behind a desk under fluorescent lights that denied noon and dusk, summer and fall. These women blended into the Oregon landscape. They were healthy animals.

It seemed a bit stupid to spend time pondering how it came to be that the difficult art of slipping into unquestionable command came so naturally to Jean Carroon, the guide. After all, this is the late twentieth century, right? Isn't this what the social revolution that flowed from the 1960s was all about? Why shouldn't she be unself-conscious about her prowess at close-order drill?

No reason. Any more than an outsider should find it remarkable that in Northern California's Marin County, in the state whose southern half is dominated by the gasoline-consuming, nature-denying sprawl of Los Angeles, serious plans are advancing to transform a surplus Air Force base into a solar-powered city. After all, we've always said that human habitats that work with the planet, rather than against it, would have to be built sooner or later.

Why should it be remarkable that in Everett, Washington, under the world's largest building — the assembly plant for the Boeing 747 jumbo jet — lunchtime can find two hundred people in the sixteen-hundred-foot-long bomb shelter. Not grimly preparing themselves for Armageddon. But jogging.

Or that in the urban parks of Berkeley, California, large signs have been erected, warning residents not to drink from the creek water because it may be polluted. After all, it's not Berkeley's fault that almost everywhere else in North America it would never occur to city dwellers that pollution control may be so far advanced that the water in their parks could be *clean*.

Or that in Homer, Alaska, at the dedication of the first broadcast radio station whose signal could reach the town, five hundred people — a large percentage of the entire population of the lower Kenai Peninsula — showed up at a high school gym for the festivities. And I, a child of the sixties, now in a white shirt and tie, could slowly look around and have it dawn on me that virtually everybody else but me was on the "right" side of the age-of-thirty barrier. And that I was by far the straightest-looking person there, the others being dressed in strange ways — fringe, fur, beads — that I hadn't seen en masse for a long time. Not since those corny days when the word "counterculture" was new, to be precise. Even the elected officials were of that age and dress.

Yet there's no reason why this should be considered odd. For a long time, now, there have been many visionaries saying that the future would be formed by alternative ways of life. The only thing that's remarkable is to find a chunk of North America where such ideas are not only *not* viewed as particularly flaky, but where such a future actually is considered logical, even inevitable, and seems to be taking hold.

There are some paths into the twenty-first century that are very different from the bigger-is-better, growth-is-inevitably-good, sons-of-the-pioneers philosophies that are especially well represented in the MexAmerican and Empty Quarter nations of the West.

What's special about the Pacific Northwest is the number of otherwise ordinary middle-class suburban homeowners, major party politicians, and even captains of industry there who seem to be prepared to walk these paths. And not consider it remarkable.

The name Ecotopia for the nation of the Pacific Northwest comes from the title of a melodramatic, but nonetheless brilliant, 1975 novel by Ernest Callenbach, who edits *Film Quarterly* magazine in Berkeley. In Callenbach's book, the year is 1999, nineteen years after Northern California, Oregon, and Washington have seceded from the United States. The inhabitants of these states had taken their final look at the nuclear-and-foreign-oil-addicted, materialistic, wasteful, polluting, military-industrial-oriented, racist, sexist, soul-mangling direction in which North America was galloping headlong, and decided they wanted out. Through implausible nuclear blackmail, they had forced the rest of the country to allow them to secede and had set up their own independent nation, which they named Ecotopia. Taken back to its Greek roots, Ecotopia means home place, but the more obvious meaning lies in the contraction of Ecological Utopia, which, in the novel, is precisely what the Northwesterners proceed to build, after sealing off their borders to the insidious influences of the rest of the continent.

In the novel, the internal combustion engine is outlawed, and the capital city, San Francisco, is broken up into a chain of minicities wherein creeks flow where the traffic used to choke, and potholes are planted with flowers. The shrewd female president has guided the nation into a "stable state" economy, in which wastes are recycled, small-scale technology is the only kind there is, solar power is ubiquitous, and the work week is down to twenty hours. The country is pollution- and noise-free, and an educational-social-sexual work-play ethic stresses the equal functions of men and women as tool-bearing animals capable of improving the quality of life. Violent urges are channeled into war games, and sexual promiscuity is allowed at the four annual holidays of the solstices and equinoxes. And, oh yes, from time to time people have a meaningful relationship with a tree.

Utopianism is as North American as the Mormons, the socialists of Saskatchewan, and the textile mills of Lowell, Massachusetts. There is hardly a white person in the whole continent whose ancestors did not arrive with the firm, if starry-eyed, idea that they were going to build a better world than the one they left. Yet it would be difficult to analyze seriously an entire segment of the continent from the perspective of a melodramatized tract except for two things:

• Callenbach's vision is selling. After being turned down by twenty-five East Coast publishers who asserted that "the ecology fad is *over*," Callenbach formed a collective of friends who brought out the book themselves. Without any advertising, completely by word of mouth, the private edition sold thirty-nine thousand copies, which is extremely good by the standards of the book business. And that was before Bantam, the incongruously named publishing giant, woke up to the commercial realities and bought the rights to produce a standard paperback version. That edition had sold ninety-five thousand more copies by the end of 1979, and the sales were perking along at the unflagging rate of a thousand per month. Callenbach estimates that at least half of these sales are in the Pacific Northwest, where "ecotopianism" is a readily understood newspaper word. His success has been so marked that he is finishing a second Ecotopian volume, in which he fictionally reports the politics that led up to the founding of the new "nation." The appeal of Callenbach's idea, the scope of which has been compared to the work of H. G. Wells, Jules Verne, Aldous Huxley, and George Orwell, has been analyzed in several ways. Even the author admits that the attraction is not in the quality of the prose. One suggestion has been that Callenbach's futurism has the audacity to have a happy ending, in which the problems of the twentieth century come under human control. This is a powerful thing today.

• Second, it's working. The Pacific Northwest, politically, economically, and socially, is right now operating on some fundamentally different assumptions from its neighbors'. Most of these assumptions revolve around the more conventional concept of enhancing the quality of life. In 1979, *New Scientist*, the respected British magazine, published an article by Peter James, a member of the Institute of Planning Studies of the University of Nottingham, that asked, "Why does Callenbach sit Ecotopia in the

Pacific North-West? Is there any correspondence between his
ideal society, and the present state of things in that part of the
U.S.? The answer is a qualified yes." *New Scientist* focused on the
politics of Oregon. "Oregonians," it noted, "are an outdoor people, and are willing to follow their love of nature to its political
conclusions, in support for environmental policies at the ballot
box. The result is bipartisan attitudes within the political parties.
As former Governor Tom McCall has put it, 'No one in his right
mind wants to be caught voting against a big reason why most
people live here in the first place.' " The article pointed to the
clean-up of the Willamette River, the valley of which is the most
densely populated portion of the state. Once heavily polluted by
untreated sewage and sulfite wastes from lumber and paper
mills, it now is congenial swimming for both people and salmon,
"a success story," according to the federal EPA, "yet without parallel in the United States." And it points to the state's "more complex awareness of the results of human activities" on nature as
producing political initiatives that are taken for granted in Oregon, but are remarkable by the standards of the rest of the continent: the first Department of Energy, the first bill banning pop-
top cans and throwaway bottles, the most stringent standards in
the world for the siting of thermal power stations, tax credits for
alternative energy installations, laws that force utilities to aid
customers to conserve, a total ban on the storage of nuclear waste
in the state . . . The list is long.

But the focus could just as easily have been extended to Northern California, including the state capital, Sacramento, where
such institutions as the state Office of Appropriate Technology
(OAT) matter-of-factly pursue the mechanics of windmills and
harnessing the steam from the mantle of the earth. Meanwhile,
the state Arts Council has reorganized itself administratively into
"bioregions," arguing that whether you work with nature or
against it, the planet is going to influence your operations, so you
may as well work with it, and not draw your political lines as if
mountains and river barriers do not exist. Such ideas are so distinctly Ecotopian that Governor Jerry Brown was dismissed as
"Governor Moonbeam" during his 1980 race for the presidency of
the United States. In New England, he said things like "You don't
hear much about holistic medicine in presidential primaries,"
and seasoned eastern political reporters turned to each other and
said, "You know? He's right. You *don't* hear much about holistic
medicine in presidential primaries."

Yet the point that Brown was making might not have been regarded as particularly strange in the Northwest, where, once
some unconventional assumptions are made, hundreds of new
conclusions can be arrived at. In Ecotopia, holistic medicine can
be seen as having considerable internal logic. If you've got a Social Security or Medicare system that is financially on its last
legs, the argument goes, perhaps it's time to take a look at what
we're spending our money on. Perhaps it's wrong to gear our
medical system to the heroic treatment of biological catastro-
phes. Perhaps it would be better, and ultimately cheaper, to view
patients as whole (hence "holistic") organisms, with complicated
interrelated systems. Perhaps the thrust should be at keeping
these systems well, rather than responding to them only when
they're screwed up beyond belief. It's the same logic that a careful automobile owner applies when he's scrupulous about what
he puts in the gas tank, how he applies a rust preventive, or when
he changes the oil — that it's a lot less expensive than replacing
a blown engine or a rotted quarter panel.

The hitch with a holistic medical system is that it requires people to pay far more attention to what they eat than they generally
do now — perhaps forcing changes in the chemical-dependent
agribusiness system. It requires changes in "life style" — like
banning tobacco. And it makes your head hurt to think how you
would administer a holistic medical system through existing
massive bureaucracies. You'd have practically no choice but to
decentralize.

But, then, in Ecotopia, none of those propositions is always
viewed as crazy, either.

The Ecotopian vision extends to southeastern coastal Alaska,
the economy of which, unlike the oil regions of the far north, is
based on renewable resources, like salmon- and king-crab-fishing
and timber. And to western British Columbia, which is the warm-
est place in Canada — the only point that is normally above freezing in January. "We are a temperate island," I was told, "surrounded by a sea of envy." And even to western Washington state,
although it's the home of Boeing's cruise missile and the base for
the Trident submarine — two of the most devastating weapons
systems ever devised. Christopher M. Little, the publisher of the
Everett (Washington) *Herald,* tells of the culture shock he encountered when he moved to Everett from the East Coast. "They're
not into recreational deviousness around here," he said. The point
he was making was that office intrigue for its own sake was a

foreign concept in his new Puget Sound home — a very different situation from the Washington, D.C., law practice he had been accustomed to. In fact, he could only numbly answer no to the very first question he was asked at a staff meeting, which was "Are you into mellow?" Similarly, he tells the story of his chief production man. Newspaper production types are rarely described as the greatest triumph of human evolution. Newspaper production devices — notably the presses — are big, dirty, loud, and dangerous, and the men who run them tend to respond in kind. The system is also fast, complicated, and unforgiving, so when a newspaper production manager has a bad morning, it tends to define the top end of the scale of bad mornings.

This is why Little was so intrigued by how this Washington state production manager dealt with stress. Most of his kind release it volcanically. In Everett, the man, who is in his fifties, walks out the door of the building on his lunch break, picks up an apple or a hamburger at a nearby shoreside greasy spoon, and buys a round-trip ticket on that part of the highway system that is the Puget Sound ferry. He gets on the boat, absorbs the rhythm of the water, gazes at the snowcapped Olympic Mountains to the west, marvels at the clean, attractive city skyline to the east, and, at the end of the hour, he comes back to the office. Feeling like a new man.

I guarantee you that this is not the way it works at the *Washington Post*.

Ecotopia, for the purposes of this book, has boundaries somewhat different from Callenbach's, in that they are not hindered by arbitrary political boundaries, either of states or countries. The real Ecotopia, appropriately enough, follows biophysical borders more faithfully than any other nation. Mountains that snare the Pacific clouds and force them to drop their rain define this nation exactly. Ecotopia is the only place in the West that is blessed by bountiful water. The entire Chile-like thin coastal strip is lifted out of aridity by twenty inches of rain a year or more — sometimes much more: one hundred inches. In the West, where thirst is a preoccupation for over a thousand miles in any direction, Ecotopia is special, and the mountains that collect the moisture make it distinctive.

As mentioned in the MexAmerica chapter, Ecotopia starts where the Tehachapi Mountains meet the Pacific at Point Conception, effectively shutting off the Los Angeles urban ooze, which some Northern Californians refer to as "slurbs." Ecotopia then hugs the ocean along the central coast of California, with its back to the Coast Range, separating it from the dry, hot, heavily irrigated, agribusiness-oriented MexAmerican San Joaquin Valley.

Past the beauty of Monterey Bay, Ecotopia crosses the peninsula that encloses southern San Francisco Bay to include "Silicon Valley," the home of the semiconductor industry, which has been referred to as the basic manufacturing component of the future — the "steel of the twenty-first century." It includes the city of Oakland, which is rare in the West in being heavily black, but which has a bright future because of the supermodern containerized port facilities that have drawn most of the ocean freight business away from the capital of Ecotopia, San Francisco. (San Francisco's first industry is tourism, but it is also a major financial center and corporate headquarters town.) It then curves around the East Bay to include Berkeley, the crown jewel of the University of California system and the ideological birthplace, in the sixties, of the counterculture. It follows the Sacramento River Delta, which empties its northern waters into the bay, past Davis and Sacramento itself, across the San Joaquin Valley to the Sierra Nevada, effectively splitting California in half.

On the other side of the Sierra Nevada — Spanish for "snow mountains" — whose winter snowpack feeds the valleys to its west well into the summer, is the Empty Quarter desert of Nevada. Heading north, Ecotopia follows the mountains as they open at the Donner Pass, the crossing from the east named after the immigrant party that got trapped there in the winter of 1846–1847, ultimately surviving only by resorting to cannibalism.

After passing by the bulk of the played-out gold rush fields of the famous Forty-niners, the Ecotopian border then picks up the Cascade Mountains, as the Ponderosa pine yields to Douglas fir, passing towering Mount Shasta, which looms over the California-Oregon border. Douglas fir is a stronger building material, for its weight, than is pine, and is the basis of Oregon's most important industry — timbering.

One of the things that is hard to get used to about this area, for those accustomed to the rest of the West, is how often the vistas are framed and blocked by forests and mists. It can be claustrophobic. As in an eastern city dense with skyscrapers, sometimes the only view of the blue can be obtained by a person's looking straight up. This is the exact opposite of the "big sky" country across the mountains. Its endless lush variations on the color green also contrast markedly with the reds, browns, and grays of the rest of the West, and contribute to its being perceived as "God's country" — the perception that has led to a sharp rise in immigration, and, in turn, to antidevelopment politics objecting to the "Californication" of this wilderness.

At the Columbia River, invariably described as "mighty," and correctly so — it's second only to the Mississippi in quantity of water carried — Ecotopia crosses the Oregon Trail, the ancient immigration route to the West, made a great deal more comfortable by the existence of Interstate 80 North. (Interstate 80 South cuts the mountains in an equally historic spot, the aforementioned Donner Pass. Of all the places to cross the mountains made available by the technology of modern road-building, the interstate planners, interestingly, liked best the spots identified by half-wild, hulking mountainmen over 150 years ago.)

In Washington, while the Cascades continue north, what's on either side of them changes. The east benefits from the dams and lakes, including the quite Grand Coulee, to the extent that the region is called the Inland Empire, despite relatively thin population. Here you can find wheat like Montana's, rather than unrelieved desert. But you can also find unreconstructed, Empty Quarter–like devotion to the Hanford nuclear works, where the fuel for the second atomic bomb, the one dropped on Nagasaki, was produced. It is now the largest complex of experimental and production reactors in the hemisphere, if not the world. So beloved by the populace are these elsewhere-controversial hummers that the politics of the place are Empty Quarter — more akin to Utah or Nevada than they are to Ecotopia.

To the west, the politics and economics have been shaped by renewable resources — particularly the bargain-priced hydroelectric power from the Columbia Basin complex. There are thirty hydroelectric dams there now, and the Grand Coulee is still the largest single source of electricity in the hemisphere. Such a massive undertaking were those dams in the thirties that Woody Guthrie wrote twenty-six songs about them.

> Uncle Sam needs wool, Uncle Sam needs wheat,
> Uncle Sam needs houses 'n stuff to eat,
> Uncle Sam needs water 'n power dams,
> Uncle Sam needs people 'n the people need land.
>> Don't like dictators none much myself,
>> What I think is the whole world oughta be
>> Run by ee-lectricity . . .
> (From "Talking Columbia," by Woody Guthrie)

Now, however, their legacy is the basic industry here — strong, light aluminum, the manufacturing of which requires inexpensive energy as its most important raw material. It takes twelve times as much power to create a pound of aluminum as it does to make a pound of iron. A good-sized aluminum plant uses as much power as a city of 175,000 people, and there are only seven cities bigger than that in all of Ecotopia. A third of the continent's aluminum comes from here.

The higher, related industry is Boeing, the world's largest airplane manufacturer. It is, of course, a natural complement, being a major consumer of aluminum, but that is not *the* reason it is located here. William E. Boeing, the founder of the company, was from Seattle originally, and that obviously contributed. But more to the point, in pre–World War II days, Boeing benefited from being strategically located near a different strong, light aircraft-building material — spruce.

A flight from San Francisco to Seattle aboard one of Boeing's products is the best way to take in the most breathtaking part of the border — the volcanoes. The most scenic at two and a half miles high is the dormant Mount Rainier. But the most awesome is Mount St. Helens, which, on May 18, 1980, vaporized undreamable millions of tons of earth and rock and a medium-sized lake, and threw the result sixty thousand feet into the atmosphere of the rest of the continent in the largest explosion of any kind in North America in recorded history. These volcanoes are the eastern edge of the Pacific "Rim of Fire," which extends to South Asia.

The bulk of British Columbia is so vacant as to be clearly Empty Quarter, but Vancouver, the third-largest city in Canada and the West Coast exit for its grain, is on the shores of what amounts to an inland sea. The Strait of Georgia is the northern end, and Seattle's Puget Sound, the southern. That, plus its highly civilized traditions and handsome scenery, marks it as a part of Ecotopia. So the border, crossing the Fraser Valley, which the Hudson's Bay Company in the 1800s admired for its furs and gold, cuts east of the city and north toward the Coast Mountains for Alaska.

The fjords of this coast are as deep, cold, clear, and gorgeous as anything Scandinavia can boast, which is one of the reasons Ecotopia has attracted so many northern Europeans — Swedes, Germans, and British. The tall trees, the constant mist, and the temperate climate look a lot like the west coast of a different continent — Europe. To such people, it feels a lot like "home." At least the Russians thought so. They were among the first non-Spanish Europeans there, trading as far south as California's appropriately named Russian River, even building a fort above San Francisco in 1812. They found an advanced coastal native population, now most commonly remembered as producers of totem poles, conducting a home-grown form of conspicuous-consumption capitalism that fitted right in with the trading patterns of the Europeans. Some of the coastal Indians were also distinguished by being fat, one of the few Native American strains of whom that could be said. Of course, they lived in an area so thoroughly blessed with natural resources that it was feasible for them routinely to feast on salmon, crab, and clam, and still be burdened with so much leisure that they developed advanced crafts. Ecotopia extends north past the Alaskan state capital, Juneau, which is isolated by being two time zones east of the vast bulk of its state. Juneau is so ensconced in its damp mountain terrain that it is impossible to get to the city by road, although the approach by ferry is a stunning ocean cruise.

Climatologically, Ecotopia could extend almost to Siberia along the rain-drenched Aleutian Islands. The enormous harvests of salmon and king crab from the Bering Sea around them mark their Ecotopian natural wealth. But at a certain point, transportation problems become overwhelming. And that point is the port of Homer, which is literally the end of the road in North America. You simply can't get any farther west by car. Beyond the road's end, the natural challenges are so harsh that the rest of Alaska is a logical part of the Empty Quarter.

An examination of the topography of Ecotopia, especially from a pre–World War II perspective, yields many explanations for its current countercyclical development. From Point Conception to the Kenai Peninsula there are, for example, very few geographic reasons for cities to exist on the northern Pacific coast.

Unlike the North Atlantic, which is littered with natural harbors, there are only two major natural shelters from the winds in Ecotopia — San Francisco Bay, and the great Tacoma-to-Vancouver Puget Sound–Strait of Georgia complex inside the Strait of Juan de Fuca.

The mouth of the Columbia River is guarded by treacherous shoals and vicious wave action. (The mouth's northern edge is called Cape Disappointment.) It wasn't until World War I that engineering work on the Columbia River Bar made Portland, one

hundred miles up the river, even semireasonable as a connection
to the Pacific. To this day, the shallows and the riptides limit the
growth of Portland as an ocean connection. The largest grain
haulers still don't dare to try to make it out that river fully
loaded. Oil supertankers are out of the question. Inland from
Portland, however, barges can make it on the Columbia and the
Snake rivers all the way to Idaho.

Arcata Bay, two hundred miles north of San Francisco, in the
redwood country of Eureka, California, offers a nice shelter, but
the overland connections are terrible because of the mountains.

The rest of the shoreline is marked by narrow beaches, more
frequently pebble and rock than sand, snuggled up against highland ranging from deceptively steep hills to rugged cliffs disappearing into mountains.

There is little coastal lowland, no barrier islands, and no inter-
coastal waterway. It is not a particularly hospitable shore for approach by sea.

On the landward side of Ecotopia, the mountains offer a formidable barrier. The few choices available to the interstate highway builders demonstrate that. In fact, in satellite photos, almost
all of Ecotopia looks like crinkled tinfoil. That's why advertisements used to include the tag line "Prices slightly higher west of
the Rockies." Transportation was a problem. If the continent had
been settled from west to east, rather than the other way around,
Ecotopia might be a different place. The Cascades might have
filled the role of Appalachia, acting as a snare to trap the dirt
poor who couldn't find it in themselves to move on. But instead,
the Northwest was separated from encroaching civilization by a
thousand miles of even more forbidding mountains and desert.
So today the twelve million or so total population of Ecotopia
isn't much bigger than that of the Los Angeles Basin.

Even apart from the transportation problems, the Northwest
didn't offer the inducements to settlers that some other parts of
the continent did. Up until the World War II aluminum boom,
there simply wasn't an abundance of ways for large numbers of
people to prosper, compared to the Breadbasket or even latter-
day MexAmerica. The land is fertile enough, but most of it is at a
45 degree angle to the horizontal, which did not make it easy to
farm. Even where farming was successful, such as in the Willamette River Valley of Oregon, there were natural limits to marketing. The forces that made it difficult for people to get in, made
it difficult for grain and product to get out.

Unlike the Breadbasket, timber was abundant, which was a great comfort to European settlers conditioned to consider lumber a prerequisite to civilization. But an industry that basic does not offer a great deal in the way of an economic multiplier effect. The operators of the forests and the mills — the rapacious "timber beasts," as they were called — could become fabulously wealthy, but there was a long income drop from those few to the men who actually held the saws. Nobody ever got rich holding a hand tool, and the number of men who moved from the woods to the board room are so few as to be legends. Allied industries, such as furniture-making, are also low margin. Furthermore, in such a stratified economy, it's not even easy to be a merchant. It's just as hard to make it selling groceries to a gyppo logger as it is being a logger.

There wasn't much in the way of mineral riches to plunder after the gold rush ran its course. The short duration of even that boom is attested to by the ghost towns all over Northern California and southern British Columbia, which were left behind when it became clear how much greater the opportunities were in the Empty Quarter environs of Nevada and Colorado. There is very little oil, coal, or gas in Ecotopia. Even the bauxite to feed today's aluminum mills must be imported from Indonesia and the Caribbean.

There wasn't even much sun. Seattle likes to say that the total annual rainfall in that fair city is less than in New York, but that doesn't explain the town's suicide rate, which is the highest in North America, and is often attributed to the way the water comes down. All over Ecotopia the weather loves to hang in a difficult-to-dress-for balance of wetness that is moister than mist but drier than drizzle. The standard joke is that in summers in the Pacific Northwest, residents don't tan, they rust.

Ecotopia does have a very long Anglo history by the standards of the West. Because of a variety of explorations, 1844 has frequently been cited as the year in which the "sea to shining sea" concept sank into the popular mind in the United States, and expansionist fever took hold. The very next year, Portland was founded by Yankee traders who had come all the way around South America's Cape Horn. (The town was almost christened Boston.) Immigrants had started pouring into the Willamette Valley in the early 1840s. San Francisco became a formally Anglo city in 1846, when California was wrested from Mexico. Washington state has a shorter history as part of the United States, but it had been run by the British Hudson's Bay Company, in effect as part of British Columbia, since 1824. The 1840s were a time when Wisconsin — two thirds of a continent to the east — was only just being admitted to the United States. It would be another twenty years before Canada would be confederated. The greater part of the western American lands hadn't even been organized into territories.

So what you ended up with, as you entered the decade of rethinking that was the 1960s, was a physically isolated region that, like most of the West, was not heavily populated. (The valley of the McKenzie, where Paradise lies, did not get electricity until 1942, didn't get telephone service until 1952, and the main valley road linking Eugene with the Empty Quarter's environs to the east didn't get pushed over the Cascades until 1962.) It didn't have the diverse industry of the Foundry, didn't have the resources of the Empty Quarter, didn't have the sun-drunk boosterism of MexAmerica, and didn't have the agribusiness of the Breadbasket.

All it had was breathtaking beauty; untrammeled nature near population centers; the mildest, most temperate climate in North America, where the air never burned or froze; an economy almost totally based on renewable resources such as fish, timber, and hydro; a certain amount of social homogeneity; a long enough history that a basic agreement had evolved about the right way to comport oneself (to wit, mind your own business); and, at its southern border, a stunningly bleak and foreign example of what unlimited growth gets you: Los Angeles.

It was in the sixties that a thundering market suddenly appeared for all this, in the form of the quality-of-life revolution. The phrase "quality of life" became important in that decade because that's exactly what was disappearing all over North America. Advancing industrialization propelled by a desire for more money to spend on raising a standard of living instead brought smog, noise, and congestion to one part of North America after another. "Screwed up" is the term you hear again and again in Ecotopia, in reference to the rest of the continent. Ironically, because of its then relative industrial backwardness, Ecotopia was able to catch the wave when environmental thinking became popular.

Because of its long history of open-mindedness and education, Ecotopia was willing to pursue the new ideas. It had a mild climate. (Palm trees grow in Berkeley even though it is at the same latitude as Richmond, Virginia; if it snowed in the Bay Area, San Francisco would not exist. Can you imagine trying to get up those hills with *ice* on them?) This encouraged experimentation. (If your geodesic dome in Bolinas, California, collapses in the middle of winter, you merely get cold; in North Dakota, you would die.) In this fashion, not being screwed up became precisely Ecotopia's most valuable and marketable asset.

We're ahead of the rest of the country [said Andrew Safir, the chief economist of the state of California], in that we value our environment. And we do so, I think, for very rational economic reasons. We do lead the nation in trends, and one trend, I think, is to take your income in a nonpecuniary fashion. Salaries in the Bay Area reflect the quality-of-life differential. In New York, you work in a filthy environment so you can buy a house in the Hamptons or Vermont to get out of the crap you're living and working in. The easier thing to do is to benefit from an attractive environment directly, as we do here. In fact, nonpecuniary income in the form of nice surroundings is a better bet than pecuniary income, because it can't be taxed and isn't subject to inflation.

Walking to the windows of his corner office atop a high-rise in the financial district of San Francisco, below which the city and the bay sparkled, Safir said:

It's tough for the government to tax my view. If you live in New York, and live without a window or up inside some alley somewhere, you may earn twenty thousand dollars more a year, but the government takes ten thousand of that. Well, is my view worth ten thousand dollars? I would say the view's worth twenty, which is why it's a rational judgment to be here. From an economic standpoint, it's a simple trade-off. It's not to say that we're any more weird than anybody else.

It may not make Ecotopia weird, but it certainly makes it different. This is the first place in North American in which even the middle class has moved on the idea that a person may have to lower his monetarily described standard of living in order to raise his overall quality of life.

Think about that for a minute. In order to be better off, you may have to see *less* money? *Less* production? *Fewer* cars? *Fewer* factories? *Smaller* farms? Become *less* dependent on supermarkets, canned entertainment, and other expensive luxuries?

It's impossible to overestimate quite how fundamentally different an idea that is from the gung-ho approach that has fueled this

continent's development since the very first days the Europeans
landed.

While the other eight nations speculate about how, in times of
scarcity, they will further their current ways of life, Ecotopia asks
a profound question: Were we heading in the right direction in
the first place?

It is sometimes unnerving, the different views of what the future should look like that spring logically from this controversial
question.

Safir himself unconsciously demonstrated this when, in the
middle of a discussion about capital formation, Pacific Rim trade
patterns, gross national products, and growth curves, he mentioned, "I mean look, there are a lot of great uses for solar energy." Reaching over to his desk for a cube of transparent plastic,
he said, "These things sell like wildfire. It's a solar music box."
Walking over to a window, he said, "I'm on the governor's solar
council. Tom Hayden's the chairman of it. Now this little baby,"
he said, planking it down in the sun, "plays, of course, as one
would suspect, 'You Are My Sunshine.'" And sure enough, on
cue, the three wedge-shaped photovoltaic cells on the top of the
gadget started feeding direct current to the device, which tinkled
merrily away. As the music continued behind him, the well-paid
chief and self-described hardheaded economist of the state of California turned and said, "Now that's a real marketing piece. They
wholesale for about ten dollars, retail at forty dollars. I thought
about splitting for Aspen, and doing nothing but selling these
things."

Almost the moment you get north of the Tehachapis, you run
headlong into the kind of monumental clash of values that
springs from this kind of development-questioning attitude, and
that typifies relations between Ecotopia and its neighbors.

Because of its growth, Southern California has essentially run
out of convenient places to put the heavy industrial facilities
needed to support its megalopolises. For reasons of land cost, if
nothing else, operations that require proximity to the sea are particularly difficult to site. So it is looking north to place things like
nuclear reactors and liquefied natural gas terminals.

MexAmerican Southern California has almost two thirds of the
votes in the state, and the most compelling need for such devices,
because its existence is based, philosophically, on such conventional ideas as the one that holds that individuals will not gain a
bigger share of the economic pie unless the pie itself gets larger,

and that pie will not grow without more LNG terminals and nuclear reactors.

So plans are afoot to put such facilities, for example, between Point Conception and San Luis Obispo, to the north. The magnitude of the unpopularity of that idea among the locals, however, is awesome.

Liquefied natural gas is the most volatile chemical explosive in common use today. Very little compares to it in terms of BTUs of energy released per unit volume when it comes in contact with a spark. An LNG plant went up in Cleveland during World War II, and the enormousness of the explosion was not commonly comprehended at the time, because people had nothing to compare it to. We do now: if there's ever a serious screw-up at an LNG plant, it will blow with the force of a moderate-sized atomic bomb.

There are a lot of folk in Northern California who think the idea of putting such a plant anywhere, much less near the almost-completed Diablo Canyon nuclear reactor, is a bad idea. There are more who think that putting them near each other on an earthquake-prone coast is a *very* bad idea. Then there are those who object to the idea of putting them together on an earthquake-prone coast on which they happen to live — and not for the benefit of the residents, but for the loathed city of Los Angeles.

Finally, there are those who look out over the unspoiled, drop-dead scenic vistas of this coast, still described as "the way California used to be." When they think of the idea of an LNG facility and a nuclear reactor and the earthquakes and the unhappy locals and it all happening right here, on these beaches, with these beguiling, bosomlike manicured rolling hills, they get semi-inarticulate in their rage.

It becomes difficult to reason with these people. The differences in perceptions and premises go so far back into time and history that there's almost no talking to them. If Ecotopia were to have a motto, in fact, it would be "Leave. Me. Alone."

The rock-ribbed state of Washington offers the classic dichotomy between the Empty Quarter values of its eastern half, and the Ecotopian values of its western half. Its controversial former governor, Dixie Lee Ray, had a startling and rare capacity personally to embrace portions of both. On the one hand, she was a woman chief executive who liked to retreat into the woods of Fox Island on Puget Sound and live there with her Afghan hound, raising piglets that she proceeded to name after members of the capital press corps. On the other hand, as the last chairman of the old Atomic Energy Commission, she was one of the continent's foremost proponents of nuclear power. At one point she got so cross-cultural that she was arguing that feminists ought to favor nukes because they were liberating. No, I don't completely understand, either.

The clash in values is most acute over energy futures. Washington's development has been entirely based on cheap energy. In 1975, $24 worth of electricity from Seattle City Light, the city-owned public utility, would have cost $196 if the bill had come from New York City's Consolidated Edison. But all good things have limits, and all of the good places to put large-scale hydro facilities in the Columbia Basin have been used. Meanwhile, engineers came up with charts that predicted demands continuing to go up. So the region's utilities decided to build twenty-six coal and nuclear plants, which would produce power at ten times the cost of hydro plants. Well, from the rage of the ensuing controversy, you'd have thought that the power companies were trying to ban motherhood. This continent has not seen such opposition to an idea since Curtis LeMay suggested we bomb North Vietnam back to the Stone Age. Newspapers in the Northwest have spoken of an incipient civil war. That may be less hyperbolic than it seems because some people in the region grimly remark that whoever tries to complete those plants will have to contend with terrorist bombings and sniper fire.

This raises the amazing specter of a power company having to establish air superiority before it can start pouring concrete.

But more important, this controversy has produced a document called "Choosing an Electrical Energy Future for the Pacific Northwest: An Alternative Scenario," by the Natural Resources Defense Council. Based heavily on a study performed by Skidmore, Owings and Merrill, one of the nation's largest architectural firms, and reviewed for the federal Department of Energy by TRW, the hi-tech corporation, it argues that Ecotopia can make a massive turn-about via simple conservation techniques. It calls for the installation of twelve inches of ceiling insulation in buildings, the greater use of storm windows, and the employment of waste heat from industrial processes to do useful work (cogeneration). It claims such measures would clean the air, save the salmon industry, avoid Three Mile Island mishaps, and create jobs. All this would cost $20.5 billion, but the result would be a total saving, by 1995, of $6 billion over the cost of the thermal plants.

Such analyses have become so influential that Seattle and Portland have become continental leaders in the retrofitting of homes, offices, and factories to conserve energy. Seattle City Light even embarked on its conservation plan, which has received wide-scale public and industrial support, with the explicit intent of avoiding investment in a nuclear plant. Congressman Jim Weaver of Oregon has introduced legislation to create the Columbia Basin Energy Corporation, which would require, through power sales contracts, that within ten years "every structure regularly accessible to the public and every residence within the service area of the purchaser to be insulated, weatherized, and provided with conservation devices for the purpose of reducing the demand for electric energy to the extent deemed economically feasible."

As William Boley observed in *Oregon Times* magazine:

There's an energy war going on out there, all right, only peripherally having to do with "cheap hydro" and who gets it . . . For the real war is over two competing visions of our society. One was presented in a utility tract of the mid-'70s, entitled "Why Oregon Needs More Power": It reads, "The economic well-being of an industrialized, civilized and healthy nation is directly proportional to the amount of electric energy it uses."

The other, by essayist Edward Abbey, came after surveying [an Empty Quarter strip-mine]. He wrote, "Growth for the sake of growth is the ideology of the cancer cell."

The advanced debate in Ecotopia about which path the society should take brings up questions of fairness. An expansion of the Redwood National Park, near Eureka, California, brought bitter opposition from the loggers who would lose their high-paying jobs as a result. Preserving the wilds for tourists and backpackers were not anywhere near as important to them as a paycheck.

In Eugene, Oregon, meanwhile, there are communes of young people who replant trees in areas that have been forested. When I was there, one of the thorniest problems they faced was squaring their Ecotopian politics with the fact that illegal Mexican aliens, willing to work for practically nothing, were beginning to take their jobs away from them.

One of the most hotly contested arguments that growth advocates produce is that a "stable state" society is one that will tend to freeze those members on the bottom economic rungs, like blacks, exactly where they are.

Situations like this demonstrate that any "small is beautiful" ethic raises questions that go to the very core of how we should live. They ultimately are technological questions, and North America is a technological civilization.

Ideological Ecotopians believe history to be running in their favor. In an era of diminishing resources, more thoughtful relationships to what's left is the only reasonable pattern, they would claim.

Yet a one-year project of the San Francisco–based Foundation for National Progress that attempted to explore this societal split included a report entitled "Technology: Over the Invisible Line?" It implies that Ecotopianism is doomed.

Many thinkers of our time have had a sense that we are, or may be passing into a new culture-phase. It has been variously dubbed: Post-Industrial, Technological (Jacques Ellul), Nuclear, Supranational, Space, Megalopolitan, Behavior-Controlled, "Epoch B" (Jonas Salk), Bio-Engineering, Sensate (Herman Kahn), Post-Humanist (Lionel Trilling), and so forth.

The mere proliferation of such terminology suggests that the changes taking place are of an order qualitatively different from that, let us say, of the shift from the Renaissance to the Industrial Age. Each term in itself connotes a radical alteration of the human condition.

The report then lays down thirty propositions, with a "these opinions are not necessarily those of management" disclaimer. They start:

1. "A real culture" which is "all of a piece" is now emerging.

2. Prefigured by Nazi Germany and, less clearly and effectively, by Soviet Russia, its outlines are most perceptible in [North America].

3. It is dominated and pervaded by technology.

4. By technology is meant an integrated system of thought and action enabling us to produce any desired effect by the most efficient means. These means are only in part dependent on machines. More important, in the techno-system, are its propulsive general ideas, such as that which assumes *the prime property of the environment to be its alterability*. [Emphasis added.]

5. Technology is autonomous, universal in trend, and, unless arrested by global catastrophe, irreversible. Because, as at its optimum, it is all-controlling, it is not controllable. This is implied in technology's familiar categorical imperative: *If it can be done, it will be done. If possible, then necessary*. Phrasing it differently, the technician is the master of technology only as the fish is master of the water.

Here's the punchline:

30. If . . . all civilizations are organic . . . are born, grow and die —
then techno-society will, at some undetermined future point, change into
a new and different form. However . . . a truly universal imperium — a
world techno-society — may be different in essence from all preceding
societies and may therefore . . . be immortal — at least for the duration
of humankind. However . . . nothing prevents those who prefer a humanistic rather than a technical culture from preserving the humanistic
tradition somewhat as the monks during the Dark Ages preserved the
artifacts of classical Greco-Roman culture. At some future time, as
techno-society is replaced by another culture, it may be possible to ex-
hume our traditional culture and try to fit it into the new culture. While
this may prove impossible, there is no harm in taking a chance . . . It is
our thesis that this function of preservation — a kind of cultural deep-
freeze — is the most feasible activity open to adherents of the dying society. Active, organized opposition to the emergent techno-culture is a
sentimental exercise in futility.

Well, if Clifton Fadiman, the author of this tract, was looking
for an argument, he gets it in Ecotopia. *"Monks!* Sentimental
monks, are we?"* comes the reply.

Fadiman dismisses the ecology movement as just another technology, but in the down-at-the-heels industrial section of the flatlands of Berkeley, there's a house that is designed as the proto-
type of a brand new urban world. It is indeed a work of
technology, designed to help people "gain control of their lives,"
but it is tough not to see it as potentially revolutionary, for that.

This structure is called the Integral Urban House. It is a product of the Farallones Institute, named after the Farallon Islands,
which lie outside San Francisco Bay and are the leading fringe of
Ecotopia. The Farallones Institute is also, organizationally, a
close cousin of the Foundation for National Progress, to which
Fadiman was connected; this suggests the extent to which nobody
out here actually buys the Orwellian belief that the forces of darkness must necessarily triumph.

The Integral Urban House was bought, in run-down condition,
for $5000. A good-sized semi-Victorian in which four people ac-
tually live, it still doesn't look very prepossessing from the street.
But because of the improvements that have been made in it — in
effect, recycling it — the house could easily now be assessed at
over $100,000.

It is built on an eighth of an acre in an area seemingly designed
to display what's wrong with the conventional approaches to the
way we live in cities. Its back fence is chain link, topped with

three strands of barbed wire, put up to guard an adjacent, pot-holed, bleak, paved parking lot. You can see railroad freight cars as they thunder by only a block and a half away. A few blocks in the other direction are houses with plywood over their front windows. A feature of the neighborhood is an ugly concrete tower that is periodically torched in order to train firefighters.

The house, however, is an oasis. In the southwest corner, there is a windmill made out of recycled fifty-five-gallon oil drums, cut up and rewelded into S's to capture the wind from any direction. It drives a pump, made from an old inner tube, that raises water and aerates it. This water than flows into a large fish tank, the inhabitants of which help free the people who live in the house from frequent trips to the supermarket meat counter.

On the other side of the house are the compost bins, which, without odor, absorb all biodegradable wastes. These would otherwise require an expensive sewer system to dispose of them. Next to the bins are the chickens, a dozen of which produce more eggs than the average family can eat. They also love to eat flies.

Out back, surrounding the fish tank, is the garden. It is on raised platforms, mulched, intensively planted in the French manner, and picturesque, being interspersed with flowers and herbs, and virtually the last word on petrochemical-free organics. It is simply loaded with careful juxtapositions of, for example, marigolds and vegetables, the characteristic odor of the first supposedly discouraging garden pests attracted to the second. But the gardeners here are so far into this kind of topic that they now say they don't think marigolds work all that well as a natural pest repellent, and go on at great length singing the praises of parasitic wasps.

Inside is a Clivus Multrum composting toilet, an ingenious Swedish device that does not use precious water or any power source, and that, again, doesn't flush wastes into an expensive sewer system. Instead, it produces garden fertilizer, odorlessly and cleanly transforming excrement and food wastes into a substance with the texture and smell of peat moss.

The roof bristles with solar arrays and another, conventionally bladed, windmill. Every place where heat transfer could occur, be it the hot water tank or the walls, is insulated to a fare-thee-well.

In short, the Integral Urban House is a living, working example of nearly every "soft technology" idea ever devised for completely changing the way North Americans live in cities.

In fact, it has so many interlocking systems that Sierra Club (who else?) Books has published a five-hundred-page, coffee-table $12.95 paperback that is essentially the house's operating manual. When the book describes vegetable-growing, it starts all the way back with the classification of igneous rocks, and when it talks about the house itself, it includes a discussion of how to read a water meter.

When Page Nelson, the codirector of the house, discovered that I was calling the Pacific Northwest Ecotopia, he smiled and said, "Not yet." The unspoken implication: "But we're working on it."

The Integral Urban House and the hundreds of home-grown prototypes like it are, in effect, the research and development arm of this alternative view of the future. They demonstrate once and for all the technical and economic feasibility of the path that must be trod if we are to avoid a nuclear-and-oil-powered future.

Syn Van der Ryn, who founded the California Office of Appropriate Technology for Jerry Brown, writes in the introduction to the Integral Urban House book that when, in the late sixties, he first heard of a couple who were trying to build an urban, but ecologically oriented life, "I nodded, thinking to myself, 'Yes, Berkeley is full of eccentrics.' " But then, after the first oil shock of 1973, it occurred to him, "It comes down to this: more and more energy — material and human — is used to maintain present wasteful habits and pay for their effects. More government to administer and regulate the complex effects of centralized technologies. More dollars to treat the social and environmental diseases that result from the way we live . . . The challenge is to make cities ecologically stable and healthy places to live."

It's at least open to question whether urban North Americans are ready to get on a first-name basis with chickens in their backyards any time in the near future. The same goes for jerry-rigged windmills.

Yet in Davis, California, work is proceeding apace on what you might call the Integral Suburb. In some ways, this development is infinitely more important than anything the Farallones Institute does, because the Davis project is motivated by greed. Greed is a far more reliable and universal agent of change than is the urge to do good for your fellow man. Thus, it should be very encouraging to Ecotopians that a lot of their ideas are being used by a general contractor not simply because they're holy but because they make money. The future of any great idea is always made more bright when it's found to be profitable.

Village Homes, in Davis, is sited on a sixty-nine-acre former tomato field in this college town. Its developer, Michael Corbett, has built 70 percent of the $38,000-to-$130,000 homes there, and other contractors who build in Village Homes must adhere to extensive covenants and restrictions that Corbett has established.

The solar-conscious subdivision's innovations include extra-narrow and tree-shaded streets that absorb (and therefore radiate) less than the usual amount of heat, at times cutting air temperature by as much as 10 degrees.

The drainage system is simple and highly unusual, in that it is essentially a series of manmade streambeds and pools. It's calculated to return more than 85 percent of the rainfall to the local water table, compared with the 40 to 50 percent return rate of standard and more expensive underground systems.

Energy conservation is encouraged by the simple expedient of building carports that are too small for a gas guzzler. "Wasted" front lawns are all but eliminated by building the houses only fifteen feet from the street. Backyards, on the other hand, are large and contiguous with commonly held land so that neighbors must garden together or hire a gardener, and most people prefer to get to know each other. Some of these areas have flowered in row crops, vineyards, white clover, and small orchards. A corporation controlled by a homeowners' association is developing a small commercial center and building some apartment units, and a community center featuring a pool and a clubhouse is also run by homeowners.

"I knew there was a homeowners' association, and that's all I knew," Joyce Vermeersch, a nutritionist, told the *Los Angeles Times*. "Then I began to sense I wasn't just buying a house, I was buying a way of life," and she started to get very nervous about all this enforced neighborliness, cooperation, and self-reliance. She complained to the developer, who offered to return her deposit, but while she considered the offer, Vermeersch looked at "every house for sale in Davis in my price range," and the result was that she stayed in Village Homes.

"As the economic situation gets worse," said one UCLA analyst, "I suspect this kind of living will become more and more attractive to people in the so-called mainstream. Village Homes strikes me as the kind of place that might be more difficult to accept were it not for the economic squeeze."

In a doctoral thesis, Janice Graham Hamrin determined that Village homeowners tend to be "young professionals, well educated (often with graduate degrees), earning a moderate income, white, single or newly married, and active in a variety of leisure time activities, especially sports activities of some type," and that they tend "to consider themselves to be politically liberal, independent thinkers, artistic, to value self-sufficiency, and to believe they [can] influence what happens in the world around them." That is, they're dreaming upper-middle-class Anglo dreams.

Of course, one shouldn't sneeze at upper-middle-class Anglo dreams, because they are the ones that are in cultural control in a lot of the continent. And Ecotopia is a decidedly Anglo place. Outside the cosmopolitan Bay Area, blacks and Mexicans average 1 or 2 percent of the population, and, as in the Breadbasket, there are relatively few people of southern European ancestry, compared with the number of residents of Scandinavian and German stock. And they don't call it "British" Columbia for nothing. This does raise the question of how exportable some of these northwestern ideas are. In North Carolina, for example, there are simply tons of beautiful old log cabins in scenic settings, each heated by wood and graced by a yard full of chickens, the inhabitants of which participate in a cooperative life style. But the people who live in them do not consider themselves Ecotopians. What they consider themselves to be is poor and black. If pressed, they might describe as Utopian a situation in which they never again split another log or messed with another stupid chicken. The idea of a young, educated white couple voluntarily living the way they do — even seeking out the experience — would be, to them, almost beyond belief.

In fact, all this Ecotopian marching off into a golden future can become just a tad irritating. Ecotopia was originally settled, after all, by descendants of New England Puritans, and to this day, even its search for new futures is burdened with some moralistic self-righteousness. It's not hard to find people in the Northwest who get as rigid with distress over the idea of a person eating an additive- and sugar-laden Twinkie as a devout Empty Quarter Mormon does about someone imbibing strong drink.

Enough smugness accompanies some aspects of Ecotopia that I took a perverse pleasure in noting that the Integral Urban Chickens had a bad mite infestation that made their rear ends look as if they had been forced into a window fan.

This gets at some of the perhaps unfortunate directions all this alternative and sometimes elitist thinking can take.

Marin County is the unspeakably hip / chic suburban community north of the Golden Gate that thrives on tall redwoods, octagonal barns, alfalfa sprouts, walls made of planks nailed on the diagonal, hanging plants, and the highest achievement of the modern economic version of people taking in each other's laundry: crafts. In places like Marin — and this includes enclaves from Santa Cruz to Mendocino to Eugene to the Seattle waterfront — there is no end to the cozy shops featuring locally made pottery, woodworking, and leather-tooling. Much of it is marvelously innovative and of great technical quality, but that sometimes gets lost in the overpowering grooviness of it all. Like too much health food, it can make you sick.

Richard Ofshe, a sociologist at the University of California at Berkeley, shared in the 1979 Pulitzer Gold Medal for Meritorious Public Service. In the tiny Marin County weekly, the *Point Reyes Light*, he helped to expose the Synanon cult. He swears by Cyra McFadden's book *The Serial: A Year in the Life of Marin County*.

"Every damn word of it is true," he fulminates, as he tells of hearing conversations in which stock dividend checks arriving late held up the purchasing of food stamps. "It doesn't even go far enough." A sample:

When he flashed on Sam Stein, sitting in the gloom at the bar of the Velvet Turtle, Harvey hardly recognized him. Here he'd been looking for a freak in acid glasses all these weeks, and Sam, with a haircut so short he had skin showing over his ears and wearing a polyester leisure suit, looked more like Bob Haldeman than Hunter Thompson. Sam was going through changes *for sure* . . .

"Peace, Harv," Sam said serenely. He signaled for another gin and tonic. "Don't let it get to you."

"Sam," Harvey said . . . "What's coming down with you, anyway? I mean, why did you get your hair cut like that, with your ears sticking out? And the leisure suit. Leisure suits are *out;* they weren't ever in. Look, what are you trying to prove?"

"Leisure suits are *in* in Hammond, Indiana," Sam said. He paid for his g & t and offered Harvey the maraschino cherry. "I'm getting back to my roots, Harv, you know? I'm cutting out on Marin. They need urban planners in Hammond."

"Sam," Harvey said, "have you completely freaked out? Okay, so you're leaving Angela. That's cool; I mean, I know where you're at. But *Marin?* I mean, Jesus, you're leaving Marin for *Hammond, Indiana?*"

"Harvey," Sam said, "trust me. I know what I'm doing." He set down his drink with a shaky hand. "I can't take the whole Marin head-set anymore. Angela. Marlene. Natural foods. Cocaine. Woodacre. Flea markets. Pool parties."

"They don't have flea markets in Hammond?" Harvey asked. "They don't have pool parties? What's so goddam oppressive about pool parties?"

Sam ate his maraschino cherry himself. "The last time we went to a pool party," he said slowly, looking straight ahead, "I went into the gazebo and I *screamed*, Harvey. I flipped out. We were at the Gallaghers', you know, and Frank Gallagher fired up those outdoor speakers of his: Vivaldi, full throttle. So the Woodwards on the other side, they figured massive retaliation. They fired up *their* outdoor speakers: the overture from *Tristan und Isolde*."

Harvey noticed that Sam had a tic going in his right eyelid. "Big deal," he said. "Listen, you ever been to Winterland? I mean, noise is part of contemporary culture, you know? It's part of *life*."

Sam ignored him. He'd signaled for another g & t. "Then this guy on the next lot over — I guess he wasn't heavily into classical — he turned up these incredible Klips of his and he started playing Stan Kenton." Harvey noticed to his horror that Sam had tears in his eyes. " 'Artistry in Rhythm,' Harv," he said. "And that Japanese landscape artist with the Spanish-style across the street — he started playing 'Hawaii Calls.' He's got Klips, too. And Ginger Gallagher kept passing around organic prunes from the Torn Ranch, and Angela kept telling me how hurt she was because I didn't use the blow-dryer she bought me for Christmas, and everybody else was reciting bumper stickers and really getting off on 'We Brake for Garage Sales' and 'Another Glass-Blower for Udall' and 'Save the Wombats.' "

"Sam," Harvey said urgently, "get ahold of yourself, man." Sam's voice was rising alarmingly. "You wanna go to Hammond, go to Hammond. Whatever's right . . ."

"Plant stores," Sam went on compulsively. "Kleen-raw in the hummingbird feeder. Weekends at Tahoe. *Vasectomies*. The Fungus Faire, redwood bathtubs, mandalas, compost piles, needlepoint, burglar alarms . . ." Harvey had already begun to back toward the door when Sam's voice rose to a cracked tenor. "*Acupuncture, saunas, sourdough, macramé . . .*"

Out in the parking lot, safely back in his Volvo with the doors locked, Harvey sat shaken. He hated to give her the satisfaction, but Kate was right. Sam Stein was really sick.

You can laugh at this kind of culture clash, but it can take some terrible, tragic, bizarre turns.

In 1979, Dan White, a San Francisco supervisor elected from the outnumbered white "hard-hat" constituency of the city, shot and killed George Moscone, the mayor of San Francisco, and Harvy Milk, the councilman who was the de facto representative of the large homosexual population. When White came to trial, his defense, essentially, was temporary insanity brought on by an overdose of junk food (!). And he was let off with a wrist-slap sentence (!!). The result was a large gay riot, in which police cars were overturned and set on fire. The point of this recitation is that in San Francisco, at that time, White's actions were often interpreted as being provoked by frustration at how little power and sway working-class "straights" had in the city. They were, in effect, an oppressed minority, in a land in which it is possible to hear otherwise intelligent, educated people seriously discuss "astrological birth control" and think nothing of it.

· · ·

Considering how often, in Ecotopia, issues turn on questions of life style, and the most emotional debates are reserved for the questions of how one's life is affected by a nuclear power plant, the use of pesticides and herbicides, or a plan to clear-cut hundreds of acres of wilderness, this nation's economics have a certain through-the-looking-glass quality to them.

At the same time that Ecotopia is made a very attractive place by the ease with which a person can live simply, and relatively close to nature, Ecotopia's manufacturing base is heavily dependent on high-technology industries.

The same nation that, in its every architectural manifestation, demonstrates its affection for natural wood and its loathing of plastics is one of the world centers of superadvanced computers and the latest designs for blowing the whole planet away with nuclear missiles.

Take the semiconductor manufacturers of Northern California's Santa Clara ("Silicon") Valley, the world capital of advanced computer circuitry.

The manufacturer of a semiconductor, through a photography-like process, makes several patterns on a wafer of silicon, a component of sand (hence the nickname of the valley). The last pattern is made up of metal spun far finer than human hair. All of the patterns — etched, diffused, metallic — make up the circuit that performs the computer function. The resultant package is very small, very mass-producible, and therefore cheap.

Each of these little gadgets, as of this writing, is smaller and thinner than your smallest fingernail, and the technological revolution you keep hearing about in this field is in the advances that are being made all the time in how much "stuff" — how much circuitry — you can print on this silicon without the whole thing either shorting out or the patterns becoming so fine as to be nonexistent.

Ironically, it's at least partially an accident of this technology that these things end up being so small. When they were being developed, there simply were not that many markets which actually required semiconductors to be so tiny. How many satellites were there in the universe in which weight was so crucial? A semiconductor chip could be much bigger than it is and still fit comfortably in a hand-held calculator. While small chips are faster than big ones, a major reason for their size was a manufacturing consideration. These chips are not made one by one. They are printed in a batch on a silicon wafer, say, four inches in diameter. Each time a layer of stuff is printed on this silicon wafer, it must be, in photographic parlance, "fixed." That is, the wafer must be treated so that the stuff you've laid on will stay there. As it happens, this fixing process is achieved through the application of monumental quantities of energy. In effect, as each layer of the circuit is laid on, the whole wafer is "baked" at temperatures sometimes high enough to reach the outer limits of technology.

Each time you fire up a furnace to bake these four-inch wafers, you make an investment in energy, whether there is one complete circuit on a wafer or a hundred. Obviously, the economics of scale dictate that you want to put as many of these circuits on each four-inch wafer, and as many wafers in the furnace, as you can, thus cutting your energy costs. Then, when you've finished the entire circuit-laying process, you can cut apart the individual but identical bits of each wafer and proceed to use these computer chips however you wish. It's the same economics of scale that make the cost of small photographs less than the cost of large photographs. You can print four 4-by-5-inch photographs on the same piece of paper that one 8-by-10 would require. If the 4-by-5 will do the job for you, obviously, you go with it.

The semiconductor industry's concern with energy costs helped lead to this microminiaturization. That it will change all our lives is a side effect.

"Who knows what you can do with these things on the low end of the scale — at the consumer end?" asked Kirk Lindsay, the headquarters sales manager of Advanced Micro Devices in Sunnyvale. Advanced Micro Devices is considered an average-sized "quality" house in the semiconductor business. Everything it produces comes up to strict military specifications. "We're mainly just serving the top end of the market — satellites and military applications and the communications industry and things like that. And we're expanding as quickly as we can to do that."

Writing about semiconductors is invariably embarrassing because no matter what your projection, it ends up being outstripped by reality in no time at all. Say you accept the standard explanation of what these can do, which is to replace many mechanical controls that have slow, breakdown-prone and bulky moving parts. That's as if Marconi described what he did with radio by saying, "I've transformed sound waves into electromagnetic waves." It bears no hint of the future. There would be no way of anticipating, from that, that television would end up being used as a narcotic that effectively neutralizes the hyperactivity of jangled urban nerves.

Walking around the manufacturing operation at Advanced Micro-Devices is a similarly frustrating experience. Men and women wear the most perfect science-fiction surgical white robes and slippers designed to prevent dust from settling on the silicon wafers containing the tiny devices. They operate in rooms that are in "positive pressure." That is to say, the air pressure inside is slightly higher than it is outside so that when a door is opened, air gusts out, not in, again to control dust. That air in the photo room is bathed in a warm, orange-yellow light, because light at the other end of the spectrum — ultraviolet — is what's used to create the image on the wafer. Electron microscopes project enormous magnifications of the tiny elements of the chips onto television screens, where they are examined for flaws. But this doesn't tell you how these chips will change the world.

Lindsay attempts to offer a couple of examples of semiconductor uses that may someday seem routine:

Take the technology of watering your lawn, he says. Okay, the first level is the guy standing with his thumb over a garden hose. At some point, he decides to replace his thumb with a lawn-sprinkler attachment to the end of the hose. All he has to do then is turn the faucet on and off. But then he gets tired of coiling and uncoiling the hose. So he puts pipes underground. Then he gets tired of turning the faucet on and off. So he installs a mechanical timer with little pegs on it that turns the sprinkler on and off automatically. But that results in ludicrous situations in which you see sprinkler systems running in the pouring rain. The really efficient way of watering your lawn would be to put tiny probes in the root system of the lawn that would tell whether the roots

were thirsty or not, and then hook those probes into a micropro-
cessor, which would decide when to turn a water pump on and
off. This would be cost-effective only where water is more expensive than semiconductors — but in some parts of the continent,
someday soon, that's going to be true.

Or take energy conservation, he says. People right now use window shades or louvers either to let heat from the sun come in
through a window or to keep it out. But louvers break, and the
system doesn't work at all if you're not around during the day to
play with it, and anyway, it doesn't do anything about glare. So
maybe what you want to do is take your double-glazed window
and coat each layer with some chemical that would change colors
as an electric current was passed through it. One layer would ad-
just for heat, the other for glare, so that you'd have one combination on a cold day when light was bouncing off a layer of snow
and a different one on an overcast but muggy day. You then hook
the windows up to one end of a chip, the other end of which
would be attached to some simple sensor on the roof. And it
would run your solar heating system with maximum efficiency.

Of course, microprocessors are already controlling fuel flow in
some cars to increase mileage, and others are being worked into
your phone system to make the automobile partially obsolete by,
for instance, eliminating your trips to the bank. There's no reason
you shouldn't be able to pay your bills and conduct your financial
affairs by phone. The pushbutton keyboard, after all, is no different from a calculator.

Just remember that, as these visions of an alternative future
change your life, it is no accident that Silicon Valley is in Ecotopia.

First, it is there because it is near Stanford University, in Palo
Alto. In a successful attempt to lure high-technology scientists
from the East at the dawn of the computer age, post–World War
II, Stanford, which is called the Harvard of the West, offered its
staff an important concession. It allowed scientists to profit personally from discoveries they made in the course of university-
related research. That is, a Stanford professor who came up with
a technological breakthrough could patent his device and go into
business manufacturing it. Once there was a community of thinkers at Stanford doing just that, it was natural for them to put
their operations in the nearest town hungry for clean, smokeless,
high-paying industry, which happened to be the San Jose area,
next door. In this fashion, they could keep their eye on their con-

stantly changing operations while maintaining face-to-face communication with others who spoke their extremely exotic high-tech language.

Second, the Silicon Valley ·is in Ecotopia for the same reason the aluminum industry is. Although finished semiconductors can be assembled into final products anywhere there is a population with manual dexterity — from Massachusetts to Malaysia — the actual manufacturing sucks a lot of electricity, so it is important that the electricity be cheap, which often means renewable hydro.

Third, the engineers and other key people at the cutting edge of this industry are scarce, the competition for their services is fierce, and the salaries they command are handsome. When such a person is considering three similar job offers in, say, Massachusetts, Texas, and Northern California — all semiconductor centers of one sort or another — it is hardly unusual for the decision to be made finally on the basis of:

Quality of life.

Which, of course, links up with the environmental concerns of Ecotopians exploiting simple technologies like solar hot-water heaters.

Many semiconductor firms are now seeking to locate new facilities outside the Santa Clara Valley, simply because there is little flat ground left there on which to build plants and housing. And because of that quality-of-life concern, many companies are examining locations in northern Ecotopia: Oregon and Washington.

There is another aspect of Ecotopia's economy that is, you'll pardon the expression, disorienting: its trade with Asia appears to be more significant than its trade with the rest of North America. It's tough to nail this down because, of course, Ecotopia does not literally have customs inspectors measuring its trade with the rest of North America. But:

"We don't want to rely anymore on the establishment of the eastern states. They're Europe-oriented, and our future is with Japan and the Pacific Rim," said Richard King, director of the California Office of International Trade. "The Japanese see California as part of their Pacific co-prosperity sphere, and we better be responsive to that," he added. Presumably, when he said that, he was not recalling that "Co-prosperity Sphere" was the precise term used by World War II Japanese militarists to justify their far-flung Pacific empire. "But, of course we do see it that way," said one smiling Japanese banker in San Francisco. "We see California already as part of Japan. Oh, yes. California Prefecture."

When China began to open up its economy to the West, Seattle and Vancouver saw dollar signs. Before Mao, they had been the ports from which North America's trade with China had flourished, simply because they're the closest. And, of course, Vancouver had been shipping Canadian Breadbasket wheat to China throughout the seventies.

One of the first things the People's Republic bought when it started looking through the North American industrial candy store was a Boeing jet, which ended up going nonstop from Peking to Paris on its maiden flight. In fact, when I was at the Boeing 747 assembly plant, a plane destined for the PRC sat gleaming in its Vaseline-green protective coating, peacefully coexisting next to a plane with Taiwanese markings.

It's politically unthinkable to export U.S. oil, and oil is Ecotopian only in the sense that the Alaska pipeline ends in Valdez, but to illustrate geographic economics, Alaskan oilmen nonetheless keep pushing the idea of a new triangle trade. The idea would be to ship North Slope crude to Japan, which would reduce Japan's imports from Mexico, and the Mexican oil thus freed up would in turn be pipelined to Houston. That would be cheaper than shipping the Alaskan oil directly to the Texas refineries, as is done now. (Actually, Ecotopian attitudes do play a large role in this calculation, in that goo-laden supertankers are out of the question for Puget Sound and San Francisco Bay residents. As a result, the crude ends up being lightered through the Panama Canal to Gulf Coast refineries. The all–Empty Quarter, trans-Canada, Northern Tier pipeline is alive as a proposal largely because it's one of the few direct ways to get Alaskan crude to the Breadbasket without facing kamikaze Ecotopian environmental opposition.)

On any city street in Ecotopia you can see the extent to which it is a Pacific Rim nation. There are twice as many Japanese automobiles as there are in the East. It's been suggested that one of the reasons North American auto-makers were slow in meeting the Japanese challenge is that they didn't live on the West Coast, and weren't physically confronted day after day by the magnitude of the Asian success. You look out your Detroit window, and you still see people driving Chevys. Here, you don't.

In fact, there is some concern that Ecotopia is being reduced economically to nothing but a resource colony of the Asian industrial powers — surrendering its vital natural resources in exchange for much more costly manufactured products. Again, trade figures are slippery, because they are not usually gathered along the boundaries this chapter describes. But Pacific Rim U.S. states ran up a $3.6 billion deficit with Japan in 1978, twice the 1976 trade imbalance. Oregon pulp is fueling the Asian bureaucratic paper-shuffling explosion. British Columbia logs are used to build Kyoto homes, and Vancouver doesn't even get to keep the sawmill jobs that would result. The Japanese just want the logs. Their lumber specifications are different from North America's, and far more customized. A two-by-four is not a meaningful concept in Japan. Huge self-sufficient Japanese trawlers ply the Bering Sea, catching bottom fish North Americans are not used to eating, and not even landing in Alaska to pick up provisions, much less to generate cannery jobs. Japanese interests are buying up western farmland, thus reducing the importance even of agricultural exports. And now, of course, Japan is going after the semiconductor market. "The question is whether we want to become a banana republic," said E. Floyd Kwamme of the Silicon Valley's National Semiconductor. "The problem is that manufacturing creates more jobs than agriculture. If we think we are going to balance our trade with the Japanese by selling them beef and grapefruit, we'll end up killing our industrial base."

"The exporting of the raw materials from which our jobs spring," says George Cassidy, president of the Portland-based Lumber Production Industrial Workers Union, "is the exporting of our jobs."

"We are getting in the position of selling all our logs and fish for TVs," Ed Furia, co-chairman of the North Pacific Ocean Protein Coalition (a lobbying group), says.

And now China has started producing an airplane with startling similarities to those first Boeing 707s it bought, along with a suspiciously large supply of spare parts. At Boeing, the Chinese knock-off is matter-of-factly called the 706, and the pirating seems to be shrugged off. "What the hell," I was told. "It's twenty-five-year-old technology."

But a consideration of the 707s and China and the through-the-looking-glass aspects of the Pacific Northwest's industries raises another topic.

There is a very, very real Looking Glass.

It's flying somewhere over North America right now, refueling in midair, coming down only when its engines run low on oil, and then only after an identical sister ship takes its place. It is definitely nothing but state-of-the-art technology. It has been referred to as the "Flying Fuehrer Bunker," and it is piloted by a man with perfect vision who has a black patch over one eye. If a Soviet nuclear missile explodes within his field of vision, searing his exposed cornea, the pilot will switch the patch from his protected eye onto his now useless orb, and fly on. For the Looking Glass plane is designed to run the world's last war after all the generals on the ground are gone. It's the command post that will further the strategy of MAD — Mutually Assured Destruction — so it's designation as the Looking Glass is apt. And, of course, it's Ecotopian. It's an EC-135, which is the military configuration of a Boeing 707.

That's not Ecotopia's only contribution to MADness. Boeing builds cruise missiles on Puget Sound — twenty-foot-long, ground-hugging, pilotless little jets, with megatonage cargoes, thousands of which will be unleashed from the bellies of the B-52s if it ever comes to that. They have little semiconductor brains that read the terrain they fly over, telling them to take a left turn at the Volga River. Those semiconductors were probably built in Ecotopia.

And that's not all, either. In Bremerton, Washington, less than an hour's soothing ride from Seattle aboard one of the Puget Sound ferries, is a naval shipyard. When I took the ride out, it was harboring something I didn't ever recognize at first, nestled in among the Douglas fir and the steep hills and the pebbled beaches and the vacation homes and the sailboats tacking in the wind and the clouds washing in off the Pacific across the Olympic Peninsula. All I saw was some sort of strangely architected squarish building isolated on top of a low but very sheer gray cliff, and I looked harder and harder because, even in this land of surprises, I'd never seen geology like that, much less the building style. "That's the *Enterprise*," said a friendly local who noted my concentration. "Just back from the Middle East." The *Enterprise*. The world's largest nuclear aircraft carrier. The "building" was the operations tower. The "cliff" was the hull supporting the flight deck.

For that matter, about fourteen miles up the Hood Canal from the *Enterprise*, Kitsap County property values are soaring. Not long after this book comes out, a vessel longer than the Washington Monument is high, probably escorted by the killer whales, which like these waters, and which it resembles, in a certain way, will round Cape Flattery into the Strait of Juan de Fuca, shortcut Puget Sound by using the Hood Canal, pass the bridge that sank during a winter storm the other year, pass South Point and Lofall, and then dock in Bangor.

It will be a Trident submarine, the *Ohio*, the largest submarine ever built. At a length of two football fields, it will be, without a great deal of competition (save from the likes of the *Enterprise*), one of the world's larger naval vessels.

It's the ultimate weapon.

That's what its designers meant it to be.

It warehouses twenty-four four-story-tall Trident I missiles. Each of these missiles carries ten independently targetable warheads, each of which is aimed at a city. Not a military target; a civilian city. Each warhead is designed to produce an airburst that would cause flash blindness, hurricane winds, spontaneous combustion, thermal radiation, and radioactive fallout. And that's at the edge of its effectiveness. Closer to ground zero, it's supposed to vaporize its targets the way Mount St. Helens vaporized. Two hundred and forty Soviet cities. Flick.

That's one Trident submarine.

Kitsap County will be the home for ten.

When the *Ohio* and its nine sisters are not home in Kitsap, they are supposed to be on the deep ocean floor, waiting for Armageddon.

Nuclear war will not occur the way most people think. It will not be a question of the president hitting some button as the blips appear on the radar screen, to throw everything we've got past the incoming everything-they've-got.

Most strategists feel that it will occur in waves, in which one side throws a certain amount at a certain number of military targets. Those targets will probably throw what they've got before they are ionized. And then everybody will stand around surveying the result. But by no means will that be the end. The whole military strategy of both sides ensures that there is no way that that will be the end. The object of the game is to make sure that no matter how massive the first strike, there will be lots left to throw back.

After everybody compares the result of the first wave against the computer model of where the first wave was supposed to leave us (which will occur after the analysis of which of the thousands of possible first waves actually got thrown), there will be a rational, managerial decision made, very possibly aboard the EC-135, about how and where to target and launch the second wave. And the third, and so forth. And after each wave, the men will talk to the computers, and the computers will talk to each other, and in effect the question will be asked: "Had enough, Leonid? Had enough, Ronnie?"

While all this is happening, Kitsap County's finest will be sitting on the bottom of some ocean somewhere. Presumably, it will be the Pacific, near Siberia. But then, though these Trident I missiles can fly forty-five hundred miles, it doesn't pay to use their total range. The very planet has a nasty habit of introducing "bias." It throws up magnetic interference and such, which introduces error into the trajectory. On a testing range, this error can be compensated for, if you're familiar with it. But presumably this will be the first and last time anybody ever tries to throw several million tons of death from the depths of the Pacific at the left rear, fourth-story window of the Kremlin. So actually, it pays not to use the full range.

The point of the Tridents, the Ecotopia-based Tridents, is to sit on the bottom of that ocean until everybody has thrown everything they ever dreamed of at each other. And then the ten of them, with their 240 missiles, and 2400 warheads, are supposed to surface silently and wipe out the 2400 largest remaining population centers that are considered worth wiping out. That's why they're aimed at civilian targets. It goes without saying that the military targets will already be worthless. The cruise missiles alone . . .

Remember Nevil Shute's 1957 end-of-the-world story, *On the Beach*? It winds up with a submarine surveying North America for any signs of life. But I'll let Bill Prochnau tell it. Bill wrote a series of stories called "Life at Ground Zero" for the *Seattle Post-Intelligencer*. In a photo that accompanied it, he sits at the controls of a Trident submarine training simulator. The picture caption reads: "The firing key which in real life would send 24 life-destroying missiles into the heart of Russia is just behind Prochnau, slightly out of arm's reach."

The series, which ran just before the Salt II process was finally aborted by the invasion of Afghanistan, is a humbling example of the truths you can buy from an honor box for fifteen cents. Some of my preceding scenario is drawn from it.

In *On the Beach* [Prochnau wrote], the nuclear submarine, gray and ominous like the killer whales that swam nearby, cruised silently at periscope depth past Whidbey Island and Edmonds and into Elliott Bay, heaving to off the shoreline of Seattle.

The radar officer, Swain, took the first look, Seattle being his hometown. He saw Ken Puglia's drugstore and Mrs. Sullivan's house, with one window broken. He couldn't see his own home because that was "up Rainier Avenue, past the Safeway."

Everything looked so normal, except the people were gone.

In a moment, Swain was gone, too, out the escape hatch and into the radiation, swimming home. Just before the U.S. submarine *Scorpion* headed back to Australia, all hope for the Northern Hemisphere discarded, the skipper got one last glimpse of Swain. He was fishing in Puget Sound and waiting for the first deadly signs of radiation poisoning.

It wouldn't happen exactly Nevil Shute's way now — a 37-day nuclear exchange between the northern superpowers, many cities left undamaged, the radioactive fallout killing everyone north of the Equator, then slowly moving south to eclipse the last humans in Australia, on the beach. At least, most strategists and scientists don't think it would happen that way. In the fourth decade of the nuclear age, they don't see 37-day wars, and fallout is becoming "tolerable."

But some parts of Shute's book still seem hauntingly possible and prophetic — mankind's last lonely voyage under the sea whence he came, a sailor's return to Puget Sound whence he came.

If it ever came to the very worst, the American and Russian submarines would be the last to say goodbye — the last to threaten and probably rain death on the trigger-happy offenders in all countries. And for the American crews, Puget Sound probably would be the home to which human nature might draw them as the food ran out, finally . . .

Again and again in my travels through the Pacific Northwest, I said to people: Now look. I know you've got powerful senators like Scoop Jackson who effort mightily to bring military dollars home. But doesn't anybody at least see the ironies of building the cruise missiles here? Of basing the Trident missiles here? Doesn't anybody find it the slightest bit mad to be working on the ultimate vehicles of death in the midst of a land that reveres quality of life?

Well, I was told, you know. We've got a lot of aluminum . . .

And apart from that — it's clean industry.

•   •   •

In the Olympia Hotel, the Rotary Club of Seattle is having its Wednesday Lunch. The hotel ballroom is full of large gray men in large gray suits. The only black man I can see is on the podium, invited to discuss some meaningful social topic. There may be a couple of women, but they are no more numerous than the men with beards. There are perhaps four hundred people under the big crystal chandeliers. The master of ceremonies hits a bronze bell. Everybody stands and faces the Pacific. A spotlight hits the American flag. The spotlight apparently is on the same circuit as the fan that makes the flag billow. You can see the fan behind the flag there, making the banner ripple. Time is very important to this group. They make a big production out of starting precisely at 12:30, and ending at 1:30. People bail out of this lunch precisely at 1:30. Sometimes they cheat. 1:28. Who knows why. Maybe it's important to them. Maybe looking as if it's important to them is important to them.

Anyway, precisely at the stroke of half-past twelve, the master of ceremonies stands up and gongs this bell, and all these large gray men stand up and start singing as if their hearts would break, about this 1814 battle that occurred three thousand miles east. The piano plays, the conductor waves his arms, the fan spins, and the flag waves.

Everybody sits down.

The Episcopalian minister stands up to recite the blessing.

"Lord," he says, "it's been an exciting week."

And he goes on about Mount St. Helens, which, having just blown up, in fact has made it an exciting week.

He runs through the revised standard invocation, and he gets to the point where he is supposed to swing into the number in which he stresses how great God is, and how small is man.

But. Unself-consciously. *Instead*, he turns to these Rotarians and he says: "Let us consider the limitations on our technologies."

And they bowed their heads and prayed.

THE EMPTY QUARTER

Down at the Blyth & Fargo Co. mercantile, where he takes payments on the credit sales of groceries to ranchers and puts the cash into an Antonio y Cleopatra cigar box, Harry Bodine talks about the Wyoming frontier as if it were yesterday. He really does.

"We had two barns in town to house these horses to do our delivering with. We'd go from town to town, sometimes, with these horses. You had to have just as stylish a horse, just as nice and useful as you would an automobile or truck today.

"Being a nucleus here in Evanston with the sheep-raising, maybe in the fall of the year some man would come in and he'd trade in his horses and wagon, and we'd keep them over the winter and sell them to a different man next spring. Because they'd go fifty or sixty miles from Evanston, that's where their sheep would be. We don't have as many Basques as we used to, but they were good men. The Basques were by far the best sheep men that they could ever get.

"We'd stock two railroad cars full of sugar and maybe one of flour, but the rest of the space in our warehouses would be for oats. All the road projects were done with horse power, so oats was the gasoline of that time."

We?

"Blyth and Fargo, the store here. It was originally Blyth and Pixley, but that didn't last long; it's been Blyth and Fargo almost from the beginning. It's a general merchandise store. The country demanded a store of this kind about every hundred miles along the railroad when it was coming east, and you'll find them dotted all over Wyoming. James Cash Penney takes credit for the first chain store. But before J.C. even began to get his first store started, fifty miles over here in Kemmerer, Wyoming, we were going.

"We had ten or twelve stores operating out of this place. Now, this was before automobiles and trucks. The only access you had was the railroad. So things came in by railroad and we had little stores we'd job to around here."

When are we talking about?

"Oh, this would be, I imagine, eighteen ninety, eighteen ninety-five. The railroad came through in 'sixty-eight, and the store started in 'seventy-two."

How long have you been working here, anyway?

"I've been in this store fifty years."

Bodine is a gaunt man with an initially gruff manner that hides his real sense of wryness in front of strangers. He wears a red and green plaid shirt-jacket and a string tie fixed by a giant, honey-colored stone. He has his desk and his cigar box at the mezzanine landing. From that little cubbyhole perch behind a wrought-iron railing, he can keep an eye on most of the store, from the quarts of 7-Up to the Stetson hats and Levi's overalls.

His town, the town of Evanston, is one of the biggest in western Wyoming. Population 4462, elevation 6748, it says on the sign at the top of the bright, dusty road. Bodine continues:

I was born in Evanston. My grandfather came here when the railroad came, eighteen sixty-eight. I started here in nineteen twenty-nine, no relation to anybody, and just stayed here ever since. I was a senior in high school. The very day school began that year there was a sign down there that said, "Boy Wanted." It was almost like a Horatio Alger book. The man said come down after school. And I did and here I am yet.

I've done everything that I think I wanted to do. I got to be the general manager fifteen or twenty years ago. You know, I started out as a kid, and they always thought I was a kid. I'm afraid I'm the culprit who's made all the changes. In those days, you had counters and clerks to wait on you. You didn't have a chance to have free access to merchandise like you have now. We had a horseshoe-shaped counter. We had maybe twelve or thirteen people working, excluding the grocery department. We had seven or eight over there.

All we can do is do what we're doing and get a little bit farther behind every day, seems like. Help is scarce, and like I say, we can't compete with oil-field wages. They're siphoning off a lot of women in the oil fields.

There are jobs out there they can do, on insulation and stuff like that. And the bankers down here. One day I went in there and they had five tellers! Terrible!

You want to go upstairs and see all that stuff, you go ahead, but I can't show it to you. I'm too busy. I got two boys who are down here struggling. They can't hire any help. Bookkeepers last maybe a month, two months, five months, then they get lured away by the competition. I can't let these books pile up; they've got to be done every day.

It's toward closing time, and people are bustling along on the sidewalk outside, but there is not a single customer in the store.

Up the stairs, on the echoing floorboards, back behind the stack of mattresses, the Old West still lives.

One of the first things to catch the eye is the Wheeler and Wilson sewing machine, in a hand-carved wooden case, foot-pedal operated. It used to be the centerpiece of the Blyth & Fargo millinery department. Next to it is a Conformateur — proudly labeled "Paris, France" — a black metal torture device with hundreds of parts that shaped and fitted bonnets. It gathers dust, along with hundreds of other items stacked haphazardly in this back room. Someone, back a ways, recorded, on now-yellowed file cards, the uses of some of these devices to preserve that knowledge before everybody who remembers them has passed on.

An advertising display for Munsingwear Union Suits has a picture of two children, fittingly attired, on the lap of a young mother whose beauty fits an image decades, perhaps a century, old. A white camisole hangs near a case of button hooks — for your high-button shoes. Free-standing, not far away, is the foot-shaped platform and the big lever of the "Scholl Manufacturing Company, Chicago, Arch Fitter."

Quill pens, a curling iron with a green handle, a two-handled scythe, a horse collar, horseshoes, a horizontal butter churn with wooden paddles that roll back and forth along a shallow tray when cranked. A tin case, handsomely lettered "National Bisquit Company," still displays its glass front before which an earlier generation drooled at the sight of cookies. Another tin box stands about five feet high and contains six bins. Its gilt legend reads, "Howard W. Spurr Co., Coffee Importers and Roasters. Boston, Mass." Next to it is a two-bin Simpson hand-crank coffee-grinder of about the same height.

In the middle of the room stands an "Estey Organ Co., Brattleboro, Vt., USA" pedal organ. It has five octaves. Many of its wooden knobs are broken, but there are remaining ones, with such labels as Harp Aeolienne, Diapason, and Flute. I wonder what a Harp Aeolienne sounded like.

On top of Mr. Blyth's original desk is a stack of ledgers. Inside the one with "1888" imprinted on its spine, the beautiful but almost unreadable ornate script shows that Mike Dacey was one of the mercantile's big customers: $109.70 in purchases that year. August was his big month: $11.45. The ledger tells us that he paid off his bills, month by month. James Davis ran up a total bill of $19.55, making charges about once a season.

An Evanston town map, 1898, shows a Chinatown. The Chinese, who came to build the railroad, stayed on to mine coal for the locomotives. It was the biggest Chinatown east of San Francisco, they say. Some photos show the store clerks lined up for a formal sitting, wearing three-piece suits, with their hair parted in the middle and slicked back. A perpetual calendar from Becker Brewing & Malting Co., Evanston, counts the years.

There is an enormous, elaborately scrolled, silvery cash register on a wooden base that holds four drawers. It stands atop one of the fifteen-foot oaken counters that Mr. Bodine removed from the lower floor. An old steel tub sports a stained and peeling sticker that reads, "Old Maytags Never Die."

We don't think of any value tied up in that stuff [Bodine says]. Some people tell us it should be incorporated in some of our displays. They say it would make good conversation pieces. We did bring down a few, but the local people don't pay much attention to them, because they've grown up with them. The new people might appreciate them, but we don't get many new customers, because they're attracted to the chain stores. They know Safeway, because there's been one wherever they've been, and the stores are more or less standard. I think, in this town, those grocery stores are cutting a fat hog — that tape machine of yours don't pick up no swear words, does it? Look, here's a store without a customer in it. That isn't natural, this time of day. As the old-timers pass on, when you see a funeral pass by, you know that's one of our good customers going on down the line.

From the street, the store looks almost like a museum or a carefully designed movie set. On the green street-floor façade and the brick upper stories, there are black-on-white signs in nineteenth-century lettering:

THE BLYTH & FARGO CO.
Drygoods — Clothing — Boots & Shoes
Furniture Hardware Stoves, Groceries &c.

It is not the only place of its vintage in Evanston. Mel Baldwin, the monosyllabic editor of the *Uinta County Herald*, located on the other side of Main Street, sits at his old desk in the front of his office. It is a hand-carved rolltop, furnished with dozens of tiny pigeonholes, the very desk that the founder of the paper lugged here from the East in the last century. California antique dealer offered him $6000 for it the other day. Didn't take it, though. Sat at it for a long time now. Doesn't see any reason to change.

But change is Evanston's tomorrow — change so torrential that in the next few years Evanston will be swept from the nineteenth century into the twenty-first, with only the briefest pause for some oil workers' chair-swinging bar fights in the Whirl Inn disco in between. For Evanston is becoming the Intermountain West's newest energy boom town.

"This is the most exciting place in North America!" says Milt Hoesel, expressing a sentiment that would undoubtedly leave Harry Bodine utterly baffled.

Hoesel is sitting on the couch over by the plate-glass window in the office of Alan Graban, just up Main Street. Graban is the president of the First Wyoming Bank, Evanston. He has been here two years. Hoesel is the senior drilling foreman for Amoco in these parts.

"Where else," continues Hoesel, "would I have had the opportunity to serve on the board of directors of a bank? Was the furthest thing from my mind. All I ever knew was oil. I was born in Mandan, North Dakota. I have the same feeling Al does."

"Yeah," says Graban, "the opportunities to be made here are, well, they're just *fantastic*.

"I thought all this big equipment would be coming through town and they'd see it and it would finally sink in to the people in this town. Look out there. Halliburton. Oil-field pump truck. Oh, now this should be interesting. Wonder if he can make it past that gravel hauler. Look, you're seeing millions and multi-multi-multimillions of dollars out there.

"We've got five percent of the total oil and gas reserves of the entire United States sitting right underneath us. We're saying it's Prudhoe Bay size. They just hit a well yesterday, that — what was it, Milt?"

"It flows twelve hundred and ninety barrels of oil a day. And five million cubic feet of gas. And that's just one well. We've got seventeen fields, and they're all giants."

"Ten trillion cubic feet of gas. Write that down on a piece of

paper some time. Ten thousand billion. You see, it's beyond . . .
It's hard for people to even comprehend . . ."

Added Hoesel: "If you can stand the challenge, boy, it's all *right
here.*"

All *right here.* In Evanston, Wyoming, about a hundred miles
east of Promontory, Utah, where the golden spike was driven to
connect the continent's first coast-to-coast railroad, just a tad
over a hundred years ago. Exactly one hundred miles due west of
Rock Springs, Wyoming. Exactly one hundred miles because
that's how often the Union Pacific needed a town. The train east
needed more fuel, more water to make steam, and a fresh crew.
And, of course, a mercantile. A hundred miles to Evanston, then
Rock Springs, then a hundred miles to Rawlins, a hundred miles
to Laramie, then through Cheyenne, and on into Nebraska.

Precious little sign of humanity in between, even today.

Evanston is still a mind-scarring distance from anything except
Salt Lake City, which is across the Wasatch Range. It's a steep
climb of an hour and a half by the interstate, during which you
can still see, in the breakdown lane, a cowboy on a horse, followed by a pack mule on a short lead. Above the lobby desk at
the Dunmar Motel there are five clocks, each one with a label —
Los Angeles, Chicago, New York, London, and Evanston — and
each one an identical ten minutes slow. A list there shows that
even within Wyoming, the distances are menacing:

Gillette, 456 miles.

Cheyenne, 372 miles.

Sundance, 515 miles.

Then comes what is repeatedly referred to by the roughnecks,
the oil workers, as "the real world":

Albuquerque, 770 miles.

Amarillo, 855 miles.

Bismarck, 874 miles.

Chicago, 1313 miles.

Denver, 438 miles.

Dodge City, 788 miles.

Great Falls, 596 miles.

Las Vegas, 513 miles.

San Francisco, 832 miles.

Seattle, 877 miles.

Sioux Falls, 912 miles.

Vancouver, 1006 miles.

Evanston is not even near a commercial airport.

The only thing Evanston is near is the Overthrust Belt. And that's three miles. Straight down. Through the rock of tectonic plates that intertwined and rode over each other as the continent was formed 150 million years ago. Land 140 miles wide was compressed into 70 miles wide, leaving behind some of the most baffling but productive geology oilmen have ever had to face. The Overthrust Belt reaches from British Columbia, Canada, to Guatemala, up and down the Rocky Mountains. But it is here, where Colorado, Utah, and Wyoming meet, with Evanston its de facto capital, that the Overthrust Belt is first being conquered.

Evanston was, until recently, Mormon by an overwhelming majority. The straitlaced Latter-Day Saints greased their wagon wheels with the oil that bubbled through to the surface in 1847, when Brigham Young brought his disciplined and suffering bands west. He even left a colony behind here before he pushed through to the valley of the Salt Lake and declared, "This is the place."

But now, Evanston is becoming a boom town of a kind southwestern Wyoming has never seen before, not even in the earliest days of the frontier. An energy boom town.

"This is not the worst energy boom town *I've* ever seen," Hoesel muses. "Now, Gillette!"

Gillette, in northeast Wyoming, was the town around which preparations were made to extract vast quantities of highly valuable low-sulfur, strip-mined coal in the late seventies. Absolutely no provisions were made for the problems of the boom. Alcoholism, violence, crime, child-abuse, wife-beating . . . a bouquet of modern urban pathologies bloomed overnight in the high country. Today, you can't reach for your keys in Gillette without elbowing an amazed sociologist, come to witness this phenomenon. In fact, there is now a neurosis recognized as the "Gillette syndrome." It's found among women stuck, day in and day out, in mobile homes literally forty miles from nowhere, with zero to do except watch men poke holes in the ground. They go crazy.

"Gillette was the worst," says Hoesel, "but the horrible example around here is Rock Springs. We don't ever want to have as many prostitutes as they have, or the killings, or the drugs. Rock Springs is the emotional word in Evanston."

A short time after CBS's "60 Minutes" televised a take-no-prisoners exposé of the lawlessness in Rock Springs, a police officer who had been brought in from Brooklyn to do antinarcotics undercover work was shot right between the eyes. In a patrol car. At pointblank range. In front of two witnesses. By his boss. The sheriff. One Ed Cantrell. Testimony indicated that the victim never touched his own firearm. Yet Cantrell's case was self-defense. He saw in the deputy's eyes, he said, that he was going to draw, so he plugged him, claiming that it was perfectly possible to get the jump on a man twenty years his junior in the flicker of an eye. Expert testimony was introduced that Cantrell was one of the fastest guns in the West. He was acquitted. This was in 1979.

Either justice was done in this case, or it wasn't. You pick which thesis you find more staggering.

"Yeah, you know, Evanston isn't really that bad, yet," Hoesel and Graban agree.

"But wait till next year."

Graban, who is from Seattle, and Hoesel are traveled, educated, sophisticated men by the standards of Evanston. Although both cultivate what a New Yorker might consider country ways — come by more or less honestly — they are from a completely different world from that of the "old-timers." "Why, you talk to some of these people," says Graban, "and find they've never been on an *airplane*. One old guy has never been out of Evanston. Not even to go to Salt Lake City!"

So these two don't see things the way many locals do. The locals, thoroughly a part of the pickup-truck-and-television generation, nonetheless still eat dust in the fall, rounding up cattle from horseback. ("Well, how would you propose to do it?" I was asked.) They still heat heavy branding irons in their campfires.

"They were told about it," says Graban. "They heard it. But they didn't quite believe it. And there's thirty percent of the people in this town who *still* don't believe it. They think that now it's going to get cold, and it's been a busy summer, but it's going to quiet down next year and all those people are going to go away."

Of these erroneous fantasies, Hoesel says, "If you've lived in a little community of four thousand people all your life — well, I can see how they think this is so unreal."

But as long as energy controls destiny in North America, "this" is not going to go away in Evanston. After an isolated and sleepy century, the town and its region will never again be the same.

Graban is an amiable, dynamic, six-foot-tall, kind-of-overweight, straight-faced-joking, hell-of-a-man-if-you-take-him-on-his-own-terms kind of character. He is also a serious banker. He begins to tell a story by starting in the middle:

"I got a note on my desk here to call the mayor and the chief of police. We've got to sit down and resolve the problem of our

driveway. It's not my problem. We're doing everything according
to the law. But, last Saturday —"

Hoesel begins to chuckle, and Graban goes on:

We brought the entire downtown area of Evanston to its *knees* and traffic
didn't move for an hour and a half. Lining up at our drive-in windows.

You see, they're building a plant for Milt out there. Will separate the
hydrogen sulfide from the natural gas. Got to before you can ship it.
Three hundred million dollars. Two hundred and fifty construction workers.

Well, it just happens that we're very fortunate because there's an out-
standing, intelligent, handsome, honest bank president in this town who
has gone out and called on all these companies in Houston. So we have
all their bank accounts.

And, all right, where do those two hundred and fifty guys come at six
o'clock on Friday night to cash their paychecks? You wouldn't believe it.
Look at these pictures. This is what upsets the locals. Three lanes into
the bank. You can't even drive through town.

And then, Saturday. The policemen came out. Two of them walked out
of the police station there, stood and looked at the mess. One guy took
off his hat, scratched his head, turned round and walked back in, and
never came out again.

The point I'm making is that this is happening with two hundred and
fifty people. And Milt's drilling so much, they're probably going to start
the second phase of construction before the first is finished. So now
you're talking four or five years of construction, at least, and adding another three hundred million dollars. And Chevron is saying the same
thing. So you've got by spring six hundred construction workers in *one*
camp. Add in Chevron, that's nine hundred to twelve hundred. A billion
dollars worth of construction. So on Friday night at six-thirty, you're
going to see fifteen hundred people trying to cash their paychecks . . .

I mean, look. That's the total assets of the bank, here, those figures.
We've got ninety percent of the construction loans in town. Just ap-
proved a huge loan for a five-hundred-pad mobile-home park just outside
of town.

All the girls downstairs love doughnuts. Eighty percent of them are
Mormons, and they all weigh nine thousand pounds more than they
should, like myself, but they have great doughnuts down at the bakery
here. So when we hit thirty million dollars in assets, I said, okay, doughnuts on the bank. Guess we can afford it.

When we hit thirty-one, Janet comes in here, and says it's doughnut
time. Well, I said, you just had doughnuts the day before yesterday. Basically, last Tuesday they came in and said we just passed thirty-seven
million dollars, can we have doughnuts? That's two days ago. And they
came in today and said we had seven hundred thousand dollars more

than two days ago, and they asked if they could have doughnuts today again. I said no way. Not until you hit thirty-eight million. You heard me. No doughnuts.

And this is in a town where the first cut the nineteen-eighty census took at us said we still had only four thousand people. Well, hell, we've had twice that many *gas* hookups. Turns out they completely missed a subdivision and a trailer park. So new they didn't even know they were out there! We've got to be at least seven thousand, eight thousand.

"Our internal figures at Amoco show that we expect things to not level out until eighteen or twenty thousand," says Hoesel.

That would bring Evanston from not-even-on-the-charts to the fourth-largest city in Wyoming in well under a decade. Probably five years.

The signs of the boom are everywhere. Out in the sagebrush, a weathered old barn leans picturesquely into the never-ending wind in a fashion usually reserved for calendars or checkbooks called something like the "Scenic America Series." Right next to it, grading equipment operating at full bore planes the empty land for the cement mixers and earth movers, creating a vast and dusty trailer court, the other end of which is already being occupied. And those aluminum boxes, their silver roofs reflecting rows of glare, in turn, are right next to a thumping diesel generator, there because the utility company simply hasn't had time yet to run power lines out. It is impossible to get a motel room without reservations weeks in advance. Fifteen-thousand-dollar bungalows in town are fetching $75,000 apiece, if you can get one. People live in cars, campers, tents, old school buses. Even the shrubbery is slept under. "I got me a nice big bush," one Jerry Williams was quoted as saying. "If I could just get a little satisfaction on the love scene . . ." The week I was there, the *Uinta County Herald* had raised a stir by writing about the town's brand-new whorehouse. But for some reason, they'd protected all the identities, so the biggest game in Evanston was trying to figure out, from the cryptic clues in the story, where in hell the thing was.

One of the proudest possessions in town was a baseball cap with the legend "Caught in the Evanston Underpass." It seems that the historic main line of the Union Pacific cuts right through town, and the only way across the tracks is a two-lane cut under them in the middle of town. (You wouldn't want to try running your four-wheel-drive over the tracks, what with the coal trains ripping through with great but unpredictable frequency.) The traffic jams at the underpass are becoming legendary. "There's coming the day when the only way you're going to be able to get to the other side of town is to be born there," said one old-timer. The pleas for widening the underpass have been ignored or snarled in red tape for so long that the police are now being urged to get the Union Pacific's attention by posting a ten-mile-per-hour speed limit for these trains as they come through town. Ticket them if they don't obey. Although that begs the question of how you pull a mile-long train doing eighty miles an hour over to the side.

The Whirl Inn ("and stagger out," say the locals) called for police help seventy-nine times in the first ninety days of 1980. At the back of the bar, there's a corkboard with names written large with Magic Marker on construction paper, like the honor roll in some third-grade classroom. But this is the list of people who are permanently banned from the premises. I couldn't get a straight answer about what on earth it takes to be banned from the Whirl Inn, but I did notice an unusually large number of women's names. And there are decidedly not that many women in Evanston.

Workers from all over the world are streaming in to get the hard, dirty oil-field jobs, many of which are worth $2500 a month.

Well out into the rutted hills, where good-looking Herefords graze on the meager growth, past the A & G Oilfield Maintenance workers putting up fences to keep said cows from getting into the waste-recovery water pits next to the Lufkin pumping jacks, along a solid gravel road built up four feet above the surface so that the winter snow will drift off, beyond the stacks that flare off bright orange plumes of natural gas against the azure, cloudless sky, stands Urroz No. 1. That well is being worked by a blue number labeled "Star Drilling Co., Inc., Rig No. 11." It's so big that even the thought of moving it from location to location is exhausting.

Trailers are parked around the rig. In one of them, where computer display screens set into thin wooden paneling monitor geological events thousands of feet underground, half a dozen people are having a bull session. The senior geologist, Ted Solarz, has recently been based in London and has just come here from the North Sea.

Jim Crow is from Ogden, Utah. He's the twenty-four-year-old Oilind Safety Engineering supervisor who handles the equipment that guards against accidents associated with the highly poisonous hydrogen sulfide gas that is mixed in with the natural gas. Before the bottom dropped out of the housing market, he had been a plumbing apprentice and never dreamed of working in the "oil patch." But when he was laid off, he visited his brother, working the Overthrust Belt, for three days. Then he wandered into an office to see if they were hiring, got a job, drove back to Ogden, packed his stuff, and moved. "Just like that," he says. Now his father, who is in construction, is thinking of joining him to build 125 houses.

Eugene (Butch) Connor is driving a rig, hauling water to the site for the Big K Company. A bull-shaped man, with a dusty cowboy hat of astounding size, and a mouthful of very big white teeth, Connor is from Eastern Montana up by Canada. What he really wanted to do, he said, is ranch, but there are just no jobs for a cowboy, so he's in Wyoming with his wife and two small children.

Bill Perreault grew up in Santa Monica, California, but now considers Flagstaff, Arizona, home. In fact, he works a two-week-on, two-week-off schedule as a geologist, monitoring the computer screens, and when his two weeks off comes up, he drives the sixteen hours one way to Flagstaff, where he's got a girlfriend.

"Yeah, there's virtually nothing to do here except drink," says Crow. "There ain't even any women to dance with. A gal this wide who's been beaten with an ugly-stick can come up here from Ogden and be a queen."

"In fact, they're fought over," says Perreault.

"You can see a guy pass out on a table with the change to a hundred-dollar bill underneath him," adds Crow. "I've seen it a number of times."

There are few opportunities for peaceful recreation in southwestern Wyoming. There were two separate reward notices on the wall of the Whirl Inn. One was for information leading to the arrest and conviction of anybody breaking up the furniture. The other was for information leading to the arrest and conviction of anybody shooting livestock. "That last one is the one they're real serious about," said one pool player, observantly.

Crime of all sorts has taken quantum leaps. "Five years ago nobody locked their houses," I was told. "Now you damn well better. There was this one gal, did you hear this one? She came in to the hospital for tests and went into Dr. Morris' office just absolutely doubled up, broken up, laughing so hard. It seems that she was expecting, and one of the tests, she needed a urine sample, and the only thing she found around the house was a little half-pint whiskey bottle. And so she filled the whiskey bottle about two-thirds full and it was sitting in the front seat of the car, and she came into the hospital, laughing till she cried. The nurse asked her what in blazes had happened, and when she finally got control of herself enough to explain, it turned out that somebody had stolen the bottle."

The growth is occurring so fast that Evanston needs half a dozen more of everything. Schools, police cars, office buildings, garbage trucks, sewer lines, restaurants, shopping centers, doctors, planners, clerks . . .

Evanston is unusual at this point, however, in that, after a little prodding, Amoco and Chevron started acting like the model corporate citizens they always claimed to be and coughed up a million bucks up front, which was instantly spent on modular school classrooms, police cars, police officers, the hospital, the sheriff's office, a new ambulance, and a mental health clinic. In virtually every other energy boom town, the companies have acted as if they had nothing to do with the problems of growth, and merely pointed out that once production started, the locals would be drowning in tax revenue. Of course, that resulted in every single problem showing up two to four years ahead of the tax money to combat it. But in Evanston's case, the companies even went one step further. Amoco, Chevron, and Champlin Petroleum (a subsidiary of Union Pacific) set up the Overthrust Industrial Association, designed to sort out and struggle with the effects of the boom.

"We are unique," said Amoco's Bob Bizal, in announcing the group's formation, "because we want . . . not to hide the symptoms of growth-related problems, but to solve the underlying causes."

And what gives you pause is that he's right. This is unique. And look where it's got Evanston.

For this is hardly the isolated concern of a small town in Wyoming. Evanston's name could be Craig, Rifle, Crested Butte, Lynndyl, Denver, Calgary, or Fairbanks. They are all in the nation of the Empty Quarter, the nation that, in the coming decades, is facing the most spectacular and profound assault on its ways and means of any of the nine.

In 1980, Exxon issued a study of energy futures. It repeatedly stressed that the study was not meant to be seen as Exxon's *plan* for what is the Empty Quarter. It was merely Exxon's view of the inevitable,

led to [by] a growing conviction that rapid development of a synthetic fuels industry in [North America] is a critical . . . need.

Known recoverable reserves of coal and oil shale — even after deducting coal to be used conventionally and the energy to be consumed in the process — are capable of providing synthetic fuels equivalent to one trillion barrels of oil.

That's three times as much energy as the U.S. Geological Survey estimates can be provided by the country's remaining proved and undiscovered reserves of oil and gas. And it's enough to sustain a synthetic fuels industry producing 15 million barrels of oil a day for 175 years.

Saudi Arabia today produces about nine million barrels of oil a day. Its technical capacity to sustain such production is expected to start declining soon after the year 2000, if political considerations do not force the issue earlier.

Exxon allows that producing fifteen million barrels in the United States "will be complicated by the fact that much of the industry will have to be concentrated in arid, sparsely populated parts of the West."

In fact, Exxon figures that of that projected fifteen million barrels, almost 80 percent would have to come out of the nation of the Empty Quarter. Over half would come out of the Piceance and Uinta basins alone — the area in the vicinity of Evanston.

Exxon figures the project would cost $800 billion in 1980 dollars. It would involve piping water hundreds, perhaps thousands, of miles to the Empty Quarter.

By the year 2010, according to Exxon, the effort would employ 480,000 people in mining, 390,000 in processing plants, 250,000 in construction during peak years, and 8400 in design engineering.

Of course, servicing this kind of industry would multiply the number of jobs by three to five times. Multiply that figure by the number of families supported by those jobs, and you're talking about eight million people in the lower fifth of the Empty Quarter alone.

That's twenty-five times the current population of Wyoming.

There is a portion of Saudi Arabia, dry and unpopulated, whose energy resources are dwarfed by those of North America's Intermountain West. In Arabic, it is called Rub 'al Khali: the Empty Quarter.

It is after that region of the Middle East that this part of North America is named.

The North American Empty Quarter is easily the largest of the Nine Nations. It contains perhaps a quarter of all its land. It doesn't contain even one twenty-fifth of the continent's population, today.

The vast majority of the U.S. portion of that land is controlled by the federal government, a condition that has triggered the "Sagebrush Rebellion," as the drive to gain more local control over this region's future is called. The portion of the Canadian Empty Quarter that is conducting its own version of the Sagebrush Rebellion in Ottawa is called "the sheikdom of Alberta" because of its energy riches and its demonstrated interest in going its own way, which may be even more serious than Québec's. All over the West, the developers of the Empty Quarter are called "blue-eyed Arabs," and that appellation is apt.

No one knows exactly how much in the way of energy resources the Empty Quarter contains. Just when geologists thought that they could safely say that there were no more major conventional oil fields left onshore in this continent, advanced technology cracked the Overthrust Belt, and the rest is the history of Evanston.

Trapped in the Athabasca tar sands of Alberta alone, there is more oil than in the entire Persian Gulf.

Empty Quarter Indians alone — Acoma, Colville, Hopi, Navajo, Ute, and Wind River, among others — control an estimated 50 percent of the continent's potential private uranium resources. Other tribes, including the Blackfoot, Sioux, Crow, Spokane, and Northern Cheyenne, control a full third of all western low-sulfur, strippable coal — at least a hundred years' supply. They have all formed an organization called the Council of Energy Resource Tribes, and have sought advice from OPEC about the development of their riches.

The amount of oil locked up in shale rock, and the so-called heavy oil, which comes in the consistency of fudge, is thought to rival the stuff locked up in the tar sands.

And, says Tom Reagan, head of the United Bank of Denver's energy and mineral division, which has grown by 60 percent a year for almost a decade and now has the largest energy loan portfolio in the Empty Quarter, "It's tough to look into the future. But I think more than half of our portfolio for the next ten years will be in conventional oil and gas."

And that doesn't count the gold. Or silver. Or molybdenum. Or copper. Or lead, beryllium, iron, zinc, potash, sodium, magnesium, vanadium, selenium, cadmium, or the hundreds of other metals and minerals without which the twentieth century would screech to a halt.

As a result, this land, which is at present the most unpopulated, weakest-voiced, least-developed, who-cares? (Idaho's license plate boast is FAMOUS POTATOES) region of North America, faces a future in which it will be chewed up and spit out to light the lights from Los Angeles to Boston.

Of course, this plan is not without flaws. First, this is among the driest places in North America, and every single development scheme demands vast quantities of water.

This land scars easily. The wagon-wheel ruts of the Oregon Trail are still visible in Wyoming and Idaho, after almost a century and a half.

And the Empty Quarter is the repository of most of the continent's spirit-lifting physical endowment. It has the only sizable quantities of Quality One air left in North America, air through which you can see a hundred miles. From Mount McKinley to the Grand Tetons to the Grand Canyon, it is the site of some of the continent's most spectacular and precious vistas. It has the only major stretches of wilderness left. It's literally where the deer and the antelope, and the wolf, grizzly, black bear, elk, caribou, lynx, Dahl sheep, cougar, snowshoe rabbit, and American bald eagle, play.

This is the land the energy-minded cynics are calling the National Sacrifice Area.

In sketching the Empty Quarter, geographically, one starts with the fact that it is definitively the West. The classic definition of the West was everything on the map to the left of the 100th meridian. If you took the vertical border between the Texas Panhandle and Oklahoma, and extended it north and south through the continent, you'd have that old dividing line which has been magic to geographers for over a century. It's important for several reasons, the most crucial of which is that in the vicinity of that arbitrary mark is a boundary of nature's. West of it, the average rainfall is below twenty inches. That is so arid that the question "Where will the water come from?" affects every human activity in such a fundamental way that Easterners, who are used to having water just fall down from the sky, never get used to it. You can't locate a factory, build a house, plant a radish, or dedicate a national park in the West without first sorting out what the water situation is. Thus, the 100th meridian helps define a watershed of thinking as well as of moisture.

Also near the 100th meridian is another of nature's boundaries, west of which the land is above two thousand feet in elevation. The Empty Quarter is not just dry; it's high and dry. Where it's not mountains, it's "big sky" country, where the stars really do seem clearer and closer, and that patch of pale white that you think is a cloud turns out to be the best view you'll ever have of the galaxy of the Milky Way.

The line also has great poetry to it. John Wesley Powell, the great explorer and student of the West, was immortalized in a work by Wallace Stegner called *Beyond the Hundredth Meridian*. By contrast, *One Hundred and Four Degrees, Twenty Seconds West of Greenwich* would scarcely have had the same ring.

But even in the most conventional terms, as North America matures, it's difficult to lop off half a continent at this surveyor's line and say it's of a piece.

What it boils down to is that when people talk about the "West" these days, they aren't really talking about the West. They're talking about the Empty Quarter.

Ecotopia, where rain falls in Amazonian quantities, does not share the most fundamental similarity with the rest of the West. It's not dry. Similarly, politicians discussing the problems of the West invariably end every generalization with the phrase "except [heavily populated] California." And the hot Southwest has such a different climate (palm trees), different culture (Spanish), different history (the earliest development in North America, rather than the latest) that it, too, demands to be trimmed off.

What you have left is the Empty Quarter, that repository of values, ideas, memories, and vistas that date back to the frontier. That's what is really meant by the "West."

If you carve the border with a little more precision, you can see some of what makes this nation what it is. The Empty Quarter starts at the Beaufort Sea, beyond the "other" continental divide, the Brooks Range, which decides what water will flow into the Pacific and what will flow into the Arctic Ocean. That's the location of Alaska's oil-rich Prudhoe Bay. This is as good a spot as any to dwell on the "Emptiness" of the Empty Quarter. Arco and Sohio–BP have increased the population density of the North Slope by 40 percent by importing two thousand men and women to drill the tundra. But even adding their numbers to the five thousand or so Eskimos who live north of the mountains, the eighty-seven thousand square miles of the North Slope is not what you'd call crowded. Nor is the rest of Alaska, which is solidly Empty Quarter except for the strip of its relatively temperate Pacific coast discussed in the Ecotopia chapter. And even at that, Alaska is coming close to having more people than Wyoming.

Alaska is so special in the raucousness attendant on every single discussion of its future — and, for that matter, the wisdom of joining the Union in its recent past — that it was discussed in the Aberrations chapter. But in many ways, the bulk of Alaska is distilled Empty Quarter. Its mineral wealth, for example, has always engendered great greed. From the Klondike gold rush of 1897 to the oil rush of the 1970s, wave after wave of fortune-hunters have fueled boom-and-bust cycles.

The Yukon Territory, Northwest Territories, and British Columbia, also Empty Quarter, except for the western seacoast, demonstrate another truth about this nation: you can't get there from here in your Buick. In the northern Empty Quarter, going by rail or truck is, in many cases, a novel way to travel. The airplane was the most important invention this world had ever seen. Before that, the biggest breakthrough had been the steamboat. Such land lines as exist in the lower Empty Quarter were not, in fact, designed to facilitate the needs of this nation. The politically important rail line uniting the coasts of Canada in 1885, for example, was meant to link the Pacific coast with the Breadbasket and the Foundry, not the Empty Quarter. At the time of Confederation, in 1867, there weren't three thousand people in all of Alberta. In fact, Alberta and Saskatchewan weren't admitted as provinces until 1905. If the roads had been built with the Empty Quarter in mind, there'd be more interstates running north-south, rather than east-west. To this day, you can't get over the Coast Mountains to Juneau, the capital of Alaska, from British Columbia or anywhere else by car. No roads.

South of the 49th parallel, the arbitrary United States–Canadian line, the Empty Quarter–Ecotopia boundary curves down around the Cascade Mountains, which block moisture-laden clouds from the sea, causing the aridity so characteristic of the Empty Quarter. The Cascades turn into the Sierra Nevada of California, but the blocking of the vital rain continues, because of that geology, all the way down the eastern edge of California, past Las Vegas, until the Hispanic influence becomes so strong that the MexAmerica boundary looms.

The huge Navajo reservation, with some of the shrewdest, if, to Anglo tastes, somewhat unsavory, Native leadership of any Indians, is definitely part of the Empty Quarter. Peter MacDonald, the leader of the Navajo, is also the chairman of the OPEC–minded Council of Energy Resource Tribes.

Thus, the line cuts across central Arizona to New Mexico, where the Spanish were thriving before John Alden introduced himself to Priscilla Mullens. The line continues up to Colorado, and stops at the wheat fields of the southeastern Colorado Breadbasket, at the plains east of the Rocky Mountains' Front Range.

The distinction between the Empty Quarter and the Breadbasket is most clear in Colorado. The mountains slice the state in two, temperamentally, politically, and economically, with as much precision as the Cascades split Washington and Oregon.

Eastern Colorado is like Kansas, Oklahoma, the Texas Panhandle, and the eastern strip of New Mexico — wheat-and-sorghum country, flat, and, being west of the twenty-inch-rainfall line, so dry that irrigation is almost imperative.

The cities at the feet of the Rockies, like Colorado Springs, Denver, and Boulder (which are clotting into a Front Range megalopolis), Cheyenne, Billings, and Calgary, all belong to the Empty Quarter. They were originally important as cowtowns. Calgary — skyscrapered, sprawling, culinarily sophisticated (every nation should have a French minority) — is still famous for its Stampede, arguably the hottest rodeo in the West. All these towns are now important as staging areas for the assault on energy and mineral wealth.

The farms of eastern Colorado look eastward to Kansas City and other markets where prices are set. From the brand-new Amoco building in the Empty Quarter's capital city of Denver, the view down 17th Street is westward, toward the mountains. (Except when that view is obliterated by the forest of construction cranes building new energy-company office buildings and banks. Or when the smog of this rapidly growing city — sometimes the worst in North America, beating even Los Angeles — isn't so bad as to swallow the snowcapped peaks.)

Heading out of Cheyenne, Wyoming, a regional boundary a decade ago might well have followed the Rockies sharply toward the northwest. To the east of these mountains, eastern Wyoming and Montana were then more Breadbasket-like, although often designated as the last outpost of the Old West. To this day, white-faced cattle and black-faced woolly sheep graze on ranges so immense that they are not fenced. Viewed from the air, dryland wheat and barley fields checkerboard this remote, sparsely settled land.

But these high, flat vistas have of late seen their politics and people jerked around hard. Now the Empty Quarter line must proceed so far east that it is at least due north out of Denver, to include the infamous coal boom town of Gillette, which is so far east that it is almost in South Dakota. Sleepy little legislatures like Wyoming's for decades had met infrequently and were content to do the bidding of the stockmen and the Union Pacific Railroad.

Once the most controversial and long-range issue discussed by these citizen-lawmakers — whose horizons may perhaps be characterized as limited — were grazing rights. Now they are trying to figure out how much to tax Exxon, a question that is not only of enormous complexity, but whose answer will determine the future of generations. Unlike Ecotopia, development is a religion in the Empty Quarter, which has done with so little for so long. Being in favor of only moderate, planned growth makes you a right-winger in Ecotopia, just a few notches west of the John Birch Society. In the Empty Quarter, an identical stand puts you over on the opposite end of the political spectrum, marking you as a suspected liberal. So no one wants to vote for confiscatory taxes on development. But if the taxes on Exxon's schemes are too low, the Empty Quarter will have nothing to show for all the minerals that will have been gouged out of the ground except the attendant problems left behind.

And on top of that, these legislators, who, for example, in Wyoming, get paid $30 a day when the legislature is in session (plus $36 for lodging, meals, and other expenses), are making their decisions while confronted by the most expensive lobbyists and lawyers the oil companies can afford.

Even assuming everything is honest and aboveboard (and it would be unkind to speculate on the odds of that being likely), clearly, the world has changed here. There are new gambles, with payoffs undreamed of by the most imaginative cattle baron. Thus, despite their agricultural background, Wyoming and Montana have rapidly become Empty Quarter.

In fact, there is a temptation to draw the Empty Quarter line even farther east — even farther into the Plains — into the Dakotas. Not only do the Dakotas, for example, share problems of aridity, unthinkable empty distances, and major coal deposits, but, interestingly enough, North and South Dakota have become quite active in the Western Governors' Policy Office — WESTPO. This group of U.S. governors, which is attempting to augment the meager political influence of their individual states by pooling efforts, is classically Empty Quarter in makeup. WESTPO does not include Washington, Oregon, or California, states whose most heavily populated areas lie in others of the Nine Nations. But it does include Alaska, whose scant population, consequent lack of political clout, and various problems with the federal government are the right credentials. Now, even the Dakotas, which for generations have been considered satellites of Minneapolis, are looking west.

East has always hitherto been the direction from which the newspapers came, the direction students took to college or university, and the direction in which crops were shipped — and if the Dakota governors buck this old tradition, it is testimony to the powerful dilemmas they share with their Empty Quarter neighbors.

But there's one basic reason to stick with this boundary heading north from Denver and not including the Dakotas. It describes where private ownership of land becomes less than common; where federal control over the land becomes dominant.

East of this line, the feds control 2 percent, 5 percent, 0.3 percent of the total acreage. West of this line it's 40, 50, 60, 90, 96 percent. West of this line, it's national parks, national monuments, national forests, national wildlife refuges, public lands, and Indian reservations until the heavens cry for mercy. And the decisions of the bureaucrats of the Department of the Interior, the Bureau of Land Management, or the Bureau of Indian Affairs have far more weight than the opinions of any elected officials. In the federal district — the District of Columbia — the government controls far less land, in percentage terms, than it does west of the Empty Quarter line.

This is not all bad, despite what Empty Quarter politicians would have you believe. West of the line, the federal government spends vast amounts of money on water projects, agricultural benefits, and defense contracts and military bases. West of this line, the feds are sometimes the only ones standing in the way of avaricious private interests. In other words, what nonresidents who claim a stake in the continental patrimony view as the rape and ruin of some of the world's most spectacular scenery.

Be that as it may, west of this line is also where the classic Empty Quarter controversies start. This is the yelling and screaming and jumping-up-and-down boundary. West of here, everything is literally a federal case.

West of here, I've run into real unpleasantness when I've told people I work in Washington. West of here, when asked where I was from, I started mentioning that I live in Virginia. It is this sort of anti-eastern sentiment — far more significant, politically, than any North-South distinctions such as Frost Belt–Sun Belt — that Ronald Reagan rode so skillfully into the White House.

As the line heads north into Saskatchewan, drawing the boundary between the Empty Quarter and the Breadbasket in Canada involves the same weighing of agricultural versus energy interests as it does in Montana. Not too surprisingly, the Creator has arranged things such that the balance of western oil versus eastern grain, western dryness versus eastern rain, works much the same way north of the 49th parallel as it does south.

"The concept of a North American common market is thoroughly accepted in western Canada," says Stanley Roberts, the president of the Calgary-based Canada West Foundation. Canada West is a respected and feared regional think tank which holds that the resource-rich western provinces are being shamelessly exploited by the populous industrial eastern Canadian Foundry. The most serious battle lines are being drawn over the Canadian government's insistence that the Canadian Empty Quarter in effect subsidize the East, by shipping its oil there at prices way under that of the world market — as much as 50 percent. This is viewed as especially egregious because development of synthetic fuel resources are not economically feasible except at high world prices.

The complaints of the Canadian West are exacerbated by the fact that the upper house of Canada's parliament, its Senate, is an appointed and virtually powerless chamber. Thus, the western provinces don't even have the minimal guarantees provided by two strong senators, unlike each western U.S. state, no matter how thinly populated. In 1980, the Liberal Party formed a government in which not one member came from west of central Breadbasket Winnipeg, Manitoba. North American regional distinctions are always most stark north of the 49th parallel.

There isn't much sympathy for a common market east of that lakehead — Lake Superior. But west of here, ninety-nine percent of the people and all of the governments are in favor of a free common market with the United States [says Roberts]. There's no question about it. None. It's where we are governed, over here in the East, that there's opposition. They have their Autopact, which is for all practical purposes a common market, but we have nothing. This is the big split in the country, you see. All Canadian public policy is made in Ottawa by people who live in this eastern region. And so no matter how much we might want free trade up here, we ain't gonna get it, because we're not even invited to the negotiating table, like GATT [General Agreement on Tariffs and Trade, a UN agency].

But if the Americans are willing to pay for the petrochemicals what they're paying their own people, then there's just no problem. The classic example of the eastern fix being in, for us, is that we must pay huge tariffs when we want to import steel from the U.S. or Japan, because Stelco [the Steel Company of Canada] has enormous political clout in the East. You've just got nothing but free-traders out here in the West.

The provinces have more control over their own provincial domestic affairs than any state in the United States. It's at the national level, in the central government in Ottawa, where western provinces in particular have no muscle at all.

Alberta has it in her power to pull the plug on this shaky Confederation, but that's a strange kind of political clout, a blackmail kind of clout. [Alberta premier Peter] Lougheed has the power to turn the [oil] taps off. But then the federal government has the power to turn them back on again. That's clear-cut. Our prime minister does have those emergency declaratory powers. The last time the prime minister used it was in nineteen seventy, during the so-called Québec incident. [In 1970, Pierre Trudeau in effect put Québec under martial law during a series of Québec separatist terrorist attacks.] He might use it again. But that's not politically·thinkable. Because he'd lose the West. It would be the end of Confederation. The Québec model is now the established precedent. The [unsuccessful 1980] Québec referendum [on sovereignty-association] has just established for all provinces their right to hold a referendum to determine whether or not they should stay in Canada. It didn't make any difference that the referendum was lost. The fact that they had the referendum at all was the big thing for the provinces.

Yes, we've got a strange sort of alliance with Québec out here. We're empathetic with them. They're allies in the sense that they have the same kind of concerns about Ottawa making decisions that affect them without including them. We make shoulder-to-shoulder stands on many issues. Québec and the West vote in bloc. And one of the things they vote in bloc on, surprisingly enough, is their opposition to bilingualism. They want to be monolingual French. We want to be monolingual English.

And I think you'll find that there is a higher level of separatist sentiment in British Columbia than there is in Alberta. It's just been there longer, because of the mountains and things. It's been there for generations, so people aren't paying much attention to it. It's a new thing in Alberta or Saskatchewan, so people are relatively excited about it.

The Saskatchewan coal, uranium, heavy oil, and tar sands are west of this line running north from Denver. The major difference between the Canadian Empty Quarter and that of the United

States — and it is a difference that will be disappearing in the next decade — is that the Canadian portion in many ways is developing its potential faster. Because the provinces have more internal control over their resources than do the states, Canada has gone through far less noisy national disagreements that slow down the process.

But both in Canada and the United States, this is obvious: if our short-term futures will be shaped by new limits, then the Empty Quarter is on the potter's wheel of history.

The twenty-first century is coming to get the high country.

Ironically, two dreams that start from a similar premise are at war in the Empty Quarter.

The first is that of the overwhelming number of North Americans who have never been surrounded by limitless crystal air, absolute desert silence, real Stone Age wilderness, today still like the world the Indians knew.

It represents to a lot of people a freedom that is meaningful only when compared to the confines of the city. There's a tension that is not even recognized until the absence of it makes you realize that the telephones and the sidewalks have gone away.

This dream has become a very popular one, and has resulted in sleepy towns like Boise and Boulder growing at a startling clip because of factors the locals are only beginning to get used to, much less understand: calculations, for example, that a Chicagoan or an Angelino might make, that a dynamite trout stream within ten minutes of work and skiing thirty minutes distant are worth a $10,000 cut in pay to many young executives recruited by Boise Cascade.

Moreover, for every Foundry executive who actually ups and leaves to try to make it on thirteen acres of cherry orchard near Flathead Lake, Montana, or who adopts a lonely life as a forest ranger in Colorado or as a desert rat in Nevada, there are a hundred thousand who envy him — and there is a political content to that.

Knowing that the option to escape the rat race exists, if you have the guts, is a prerogative of which many city-dwellers are envious, even if they actually do nothing more rural than tend a spider plant. The knowledge that the wilds exist is becoming as important as the knowledge that the theater exists. There are an amazing number of people who may never take advantage of either, but who would be plenty upset if the options were taken away.

And thus the irony that the opposite dream about the Empty Quarter works off the same premise: if you don't like the way Los Angeles is headed, the answer may be in Utah. Only this other dream assumes that the cure for Los Angeles is there for the taking: more coal, more shale oil, more of any resource you'll ever need for development and growth, all conveniently located where few people live — the Empty Quarter.

All you have to do, so this dream has it, is go in there and dig it up. Crush it. Refine it. Burn it. What are the alternatives? Hand over the continent to the Arabs? Watch the Los Angeles Basin return to the desert from which it came?

And thus the argument between empire and environment is drawn in this land, which, as I've said, scars easily, deeply, and for a long time.

Notice, too, that the argument is drawn by dreams of different species of outsider. Very few people who actually live in Utah or Alberta want to see their land either locked up or chewed up. But they probably are not going to have overly much to say about the matter. That's what it's like, living in a colony.

And make no mistake about it. Between the U.S. federal control of such huge quantities of the land and resources of the Empty Quarter, and the Canadian West's political impotence, this high, arid, resource-rich, beautiful, often still pristine Empty Quarter is the last colony of the rest of North America.

In understanding the Empty Quarter, before all considerations of Arabs and oil prices, one must realize that it is shaped by water. "Water," said one planner, "is the testicles of the universe out here."

Twenty inches of precipitation a year or less. Sometimes a lot less — four, five, eight inches — a fifth or a tenth of what Atlanta gets. Much of it is in snow clinging to the mountains, which, when it melts, runs off in a rush in a few spring weeks. There it is. If you don't grab it, you lose it. None of the water projects in this land create a drop. They all do only one thing: store the precious commodity and then allocate it to someplace else at an extraordinary price in concrete, manpower, and energy, and in a highly politicized fashion.

But there are no futures without water. With water, you can irrigate high plains and mountain valleys and even desert to grow food. With water you can create mighty industries; processing the oil shale of the Empty Quarter into synfuel, for example, requires from two to seven barrels of water for every barrel of oil produced, depending on whom you believe. With water, you can create cities of charm and grace in the middle of alkali, the green grass along the sidewalks of Salt Lake City, fed by built-in sprinklers being a prime example. With water, you can have wild rivers that charge the spirit, like the Snake, the river Jimmy Carter rafted on in 1978.

As a backward, overlooked part of North America, the Empty Quarter never had the opportunity to face the tough choices it's having to now. Taming the land was the imperative. Making the desert bloom. Pitting your brains and your back against a harsh nature, and being proud when your brains and back won.

It's something of a shock, socially and psychologically, for the residents of this land, who in many ways retain the values of pioneers, to be asked to think in terms of limits. If they had been thinking in terms of limits for the last century or so, they wouldn't be here today. This land doesn't make anything easy.

But the signs are all there that choices must be made. *Fortune* magazine noted that water was an "emotional" issue in the Colorado River Basin, and all of it was assigned to uses other than oil shale. Yet it quoted an Energy Department official as asserting that "enough water can be begged, borrowed, bought, or won in court to support a one-million-barrel-a-day industry."

The coal-fired Intermountain Power Project in Lynndyl, Utah, is offering $1750 for an acre-foot of water that the valley's farmers can pay only $10 a year for. Suburbanites will pay a great deal to keep their swimming pools full and their lawns green. Yet the influx of new residents — and new voters — to the Empty Quarter is very much tied to the quality of life.

And quality of life around here means nature, which it is politically unacceptable to denude.

Decisions must be made.

Another limit is air. Clean air. One fabled battle occurred in Utah over the Kaparowitz power project. To be located in the southern part of the state, it offered some compelling logic. It would be located right on top of some of the richest coal land in Utah, so transportation costs would be low, and it also was a site that offered not only enough water to cool the monstrous plant, but water so salty that it wasn't good for much else.

The only hitch was that the Kaparowitz site was surrounded by North America's most fabled national parks, including the Grand Canyon, and some sentimentalists allowed as how generating electricity for export to L.A. was not as important as being able to see these wonders without having to peer through the smog from coal burning, and they won.

So now there's another plan, the aforementioned Intermountain Power Project, also known as Son of Kaparowitz, to the north of the old site. It's farther away from the coal than its proponents would like it to be, but, then again, it's far enough into the desert and away from the national parks that fewer screams are heard over air quality. So the project will be built. But this gets us back to water.

There is so little water near Lynndyl, that people get to pick only one future. For generations, that choice has been agricultural, and in Mormon Utah, the very symbol of which is a beehive, that's more than just a livelihood; that's a statement. It's a family-oriented way of life. It speaks to the idea of stewardship, taken from scriptural references to man being given dominion over the land, from which he is to bring forth plenty.

Seventeen thousand irrigated acres are going out of production near Lynndyl. The farmers have sold their waters to the Intermountain Power Project. They've traded futures.

Northwestern Millard County is the valley of the Sevier River, a valley of jagged mountains to the left, right, front, and back. Dawn and dusk are the prettiest times, when the phrase "purple mountains' majesty" becomes quite real, and in the foreground the golden stalks of barley offer a striking palette.

At other times, when the sun hangs huge, this is gray, brown, unforgiving desert, startling to an Easterner who is used to seeing his planet in its natural state, covered by vegetation. Fat cattle find nourishment in the blue-gray greasewood, sheep grass, buffalo grass, four-wing salt bush, and particularly the Indian rice grass, but the Lord knows how. In the sand hills and the sheer mountain rock, trees can't find a home. The most unnatural color in the Empty Quarter is deep, rich alfalfa green. It's as eye-catching a shock as browns and violets in a polluted industrial river. It's the absolute sign of man. The only evidence of wildlife in this valley is the plastered tufts of fluff on the asphalt road every few hundred feet, testimony that there are an awful lot of slow jackrabbits in the 150 miles between Salt Lake and Delta.

In Lynndyl, Phill Nielson runs eight hundred head of cattle on fourteen hundred acres, six hundred of them irrigated. His granddad came here from Denmark in 1870, one of the very first settlers.

Phill Nielson, a bishop of the Mormon Church, is the man who has been instrumental in organizing local farmers to sell out their water rights to the four mammoth power belchers of IPP, 750-megawatts each.

"The water is directly related to the land," he says. "If you take out a fifth of the water, you take out a fifth of the land. The Sevier River is the most used river in the United States and maybe the world. We start at the top of the Sevier River and water the ground and the water comes down, through, and comes back out. You go down to another dam and you catch the water and rewater. We're not exactly sure how the IPP sale will affect this farm yet, but I sold forty percent of my water, and I'll probably cut forty percent of my operation. Maybe fifty. Six hundred acres to three hundred, three hundred and fifty. It would cut my cattle [herd] in proportion."

Some parts of the Empty Quarter are luckier than others in their water supply. When it comes to the choices of agriculture, industrialization, urbanization, and wilderness, places like the Front Range of Colorado get to pick three out of four. In some parts of Montana, the choice is two out of four. But in Lynndyl, it's one out of four. The sad little trickle called the Sevier "River" can serve either a power plant or agriculture, but not both.

Nielson sees his water sale as a way of getting out of the farmer's chronic problem — debt. But he also sees it as a way to regain his children. "We export about ninety percent of our young people out of this area. Only about ten percent stay. With IPP, we hope to reduce that until we're down only to about forty or fifty percent.

"Six hundred and fifty full-time jobs when it's operating. But we figure with the multiplier effect, that will create three times that. Eighteen hundred jobs. Supermarkets and barber shops and movie-show houses and everything else." Although he can't say what makes him think local kids, rather than boom-town immigrants, will get all those jobs.

He says he has one son-in-law, trained to operate the control board of a power plant, who's living far away. He wants to return to Lynndyl, and this IPP project is the chance. Nielson just doesn't know about the future of another son-in-law, who wanted to farm.

He also doesn't know where California and Japan are going to obtain the alfalfa that came out of this valley at the hefty price of $100 a ton. They're just going to have to get it somewhere else.

This last drives Nielson's neighbor, Bernard Jackson, wild.

Jackson has been one of the most vociferous, if lonely, opponents of the sale of water rights to IPP. He almost drags a visitor out to his fields, digging his hand into the crops, talking about the six tons, eight tons of food per acre his desert garden will produce. "What's a higher use than food?" he sputters. "You've got to eat!" But he's sued the bastards and sued the bastards, and he's not willing to admit it to anybody but an outsider, but he's pretty sure he'll lose. Agriculture will lose. The future is going off in a different direction.

"They're making a lot of money!" protests a Utah planner. "It's not as stark as that! Some of the lands they're giving up are marginal. With the money the family makes from the water sales, the kids can do anything they want. They can raise thoroughbred racehorses if they want. There are going to be a lot of millionaires coming off that thing!"

All true. And if, in exchange, they give up a way of life, that's just the way it is. Life can be tough in the Empty Quarter. Lord knows, the riches are tempting.

The Empty Quarter has at least half of North America's coal, with Montana alone having three times the proven reserves of West Virginia, and Wyoming, twice that of Kentucky.

Much of the stuff is near the surface. The Rawhide Mine, near Gillette, has been called "the coal-miner's dream," with seams running 110 feet thick, thinly covered by sand. Coal companies consider that fortunate for several reasons, not the least of which is that fewer people get killed stripping dirt off coal than they do when they're thousands of feet underground, as is common in the Appalachians. Also, the towering draglines that actually do the work are a great deal less expensive than an army of United Mine Workers, who tend to get their lungs clotted with coal dust and then demand pensions.

In fact, the coal companies are very pleased with the union situation, or lack of it, in the western coal fields. Many of the strip-miners aren't organized at all, and others have signed up with such diverse organizations as the Operating Engineers and the Brotherhood of Electrical Workers. The United Mine Workers' position was so weak in the West that during the crippling hundred-day national coal strike of 1977, UMW locals in the western states agreed to a separate contract when the strike began, and missed only one day's work.

The best news is that this coal is relatively low in sulfur, the most notorious pollutant associated with coal burning. Sulfur in the air causes rain itself to turn acidic, killing the rivers, lakes, and cropland on which it falls. If United States law, which fails to recognize the distinction between high- and low-sulfur coal, is finally altered, this western coal will have a significant economic advantage over its eastern competition. Eastern coal is impossible to burn cleanly without the use of expensive and temperamental anti-air-pollution devices called scrubbers.

In fact, the main thing wrong with Empty Quarter coal is that it isn't even remotely near anybody who can use it.

But the coal companies are working on this problem. One idea is the unit coal train. A unit coal train has five locomotives and a hundred or more coal cars, each car with a hundred tons of coal in it. A mile or so long, the coal train clips along at maybe fifty miles an hour through every little Empty Quarter town between the mine and wherever it is going, since many U.S. Empty Quarter towns were railroad-oriented.

When these trains are ripping through town, or across your backyard, should you have decided that you liked the looks of the Big Horn Mountains in your front yard, they represent a substantial hazard to your livestock and your children. If the trains slow down, they can be even more troublesome, because a train a mile long does not quickly clear a highway crossing. A house can catch on fire, or a person can get a heart attack, and if the responding fire truck or ambulance finds a unit train between where it is and where it's got to go, there's nothing to do but wait.

Outfits like the Burlington Northern or the Chicago and North Western railroads currently plan to push one of these trains through little two-thousand-population burgs like Lusk, Wyoming, once every half-hour or so, around the clock for the rest of time or until the coal runs out. The local smart money is betting that the coal will last longer.

But that doesn't mean there is no other choice. There are slurry pipelines. Slurry pipelines take millions of gallons of the water that is so scarce in this part of the world, load it up with as much crushed coal as it will take and still stay liquid, stuff this mixture into a long tube, and pump it where it's going. If that should be Arkansas, for example, you may not have brought coals to Newcastle, but you have introduced a great deal of dirty water to a place that, inasmuch as it borders on the Mississippi River, does not consider the commodity a novelty.

Incidentally, railroad companies view slurry companies as competition. Therefore, they tend to frown on slurry companies who want right of way over or under their tracks, which is why you shouldn't hold your breath for the arrival of pipelines.

Okay, there's got to be a better way, right? What about all this synfuel stuff. The Germans in World War II made gasoline from coal. What's wrong with that? Isn't the country's stated goal the production of over a million barrels a day of oil equivalents from coal by 1990?

Yes, well, that's true. The only hitch is that synfuels from coal cost about twice what Saudi sweet does, and there's a question about that gap closing in the near future, since coal conversion is a high-technology-dependent process, and technology is inflation-ridden. Thus, as long as the price of oil goes up, the price of making a replacement for oil goes up. It will be a while before coal-dependent synfuels can compete, unaided by Moral Equivalent of War (MEOW) grants.

Furthermore, there are enormous medical questions that surround coal gasification. Tar and ash are inevitable by-products of all coal conversion. Coal tar is one of the most potent cancer-causing substances known to man. It's so virulent that in the early days of cancer research, coal tar was exactly what they spread all over the white mice, knowing that if this didn't kill off the little buggers, nothing would. No one has even begun to grapple with the question of how the waste from a million-barrel-a-day coal-conversion industry could be kept out of the environment in perpetuity.

And, of course, there's the ever-present problem of water. A synthetic fuel plant requires as much as ten billion gallons of water a year, and current plans are for a dozen or more plants in the valleys of the Yellowstone, Big Horn, Tongue, and Powder rivers in the coal-rich eastern plains of Montana and Wyoming.

If all the water goes to synfuels, ranching may disappear. Ranching has been the bedrock of this land for a century. It's the very symbol of the West. But, then, no one is completely sure that this fragile, arid land can be reclaimed well enough to support cattle economically after it has felt the bite of the strip-miner. So the question of whether there will be enough water to sustain this way of life may be moot.

All right, forget about exporting the coal or the coal products. Why not burn the coal right where it is, and export the electricity? Well, this gets you back to the Lynndyl situation and the questions it raises about water and air. But the future of this region is not completely tied to coal. The Empty Quarter is also richer in oil shale than the Middle East is in crude. In the seventeen-thousand-square-mile area at the intersection of Colorado, Utah, and Wyoming, for example, lie the world's largest known deposits of shale, containing about six hundred billion barrels of oil. If you take this area — more than twice the size of Massachusetts, with deposits as much as fifteen hundred feet thick — and every day mine the equivalent of the dirt moved to dig the Panama Canal, crush it in a large still, and then refine it, you'd have enough gasoline to last you almost a century.

What's more, this promises to be the cheapest alternative to Arab oil, only a few dollars a barrel more expensive than the highest priced stuff from Iraq.

Of course, oil-shale processing requires so much water that it may have to be piped in from Canada or the East at a dollar or two a barrel.

But more interesting are the questions raised about what to do with the trillion tons of tailings that would be left behind after the oil was separated from the shale. That's literally mountains of waste. Apart from what it would do to the scenery, when it is hit by rain, it would leach off minerals, from boron to molybdenum, into the Colorado River, which is already so saline that by the time it hits Arizona, it can poison farmland. Also released into this river, which provides the drinking water for millions, would be as-yet undetermined quantities of petroleum-related carcinogens like benzo(a)pyrene (BAP).

Furthermore, the process gives off lots of sulfur, the substance that produces the acid rain. One of the more thought-provoking decisions that will have to be considered concerning oil shale is how high the smokestacks associated with the process should be. The higher they are, the farther up into the atmosphere pollutants are released. The farther up they start, the farther downwind they come down. Downwind from the Empty Quarter is the Breadbasket.

"If the synfuels program becomes operative," notes historian K. Ross Toole, "the effect on the lush farmlands to the east is very frightening to contemplate." But, then again, there's the question of what happens when the wind hits the tailings, much less where the wind takes the pollutants. The dust from the tires of trucks working on these projects has occasionally been so bad that the Environmental Protection Agency has had to shut down operations temporarily because of the choking conditions. No one knows how much dust could come off a trillion-ton mountain of oil-shale tailings.

Many hundred miles north of Rifle, Craig, and the other Colorado towns at the center of the oil-shale concerns is Fort McMurray, Alberta. Once, Fort McMurray was the last outpost of civilization, where the road ended and trappers and traders began to make their way by boat up the Athabasca River through connecting lakes and waterways all the way to the Great Slave Lake. Now, Fort McMurray is the center of yet another source of Empty Quarter riches: tar sands. Again, there's more oil up here than there is in the Persian Gulf. In Alberta, it has actually been turned into synthetic fuel since 1978. But, again, a few factors give one pause. Up here, the good news is that you don't have to worry about screwing up farmers and ranchers, because you're north of where agriculture and stock-raising are even a marginal way of life. The bad news is working with an asphaltlike substance mixed with grit at temperatures that hover around 40 below for weeks. At Fort McMurray, the stuff is strip-mined, and reclaiming the land in a climate with a growing season of twelve weeks or less is a neat trick. Syncrude, the company running the operation, has set aside three cents per barrel for the job.

Meanwhile, this town of seven hundred people living close to the land, with only occasional contact with the outside world, has overnight become a city of twenty-seven thousand, with hotels, a municipal pool, three indoor skating rinks, a golf course, a Sears, a Safeway, movies, bowling alleys, regularly scheduled commercial airline service, banks, inflation, pollution, crime, juvenile delinquency, drugs, and a Kentucky Fried Chicken stand. The Good Fish Indians have gone into the cleaning business. Everybody's making a lot of money.

What else? Well, there's heavy oil. One famed energy writer likes to characterize it as the chocolate mousse of petroleum. It's about as easy to pump.

There's uranium. The Empty Quarter has very nearly all of North America's uranium. Coincidentally, it has more than its share of radiation-related problems. The Rocky Flats nuclear weapons plant, which builds "triggers" for hydrogen bombs, is located right on the edge of the most heavily populated area in the region — Denver. There are those who think this unwise, and they periodically gather together in groups of several thousand, storm the gates, mix it up with the local constabulary, and get themselves arrested. They then try to politicize their trials, and the judge tries to stop them, and this goes round and round.

There's St. George, Utah, which is just downwind from the Nevada nuclear bomb test site. Everyone's appalled at the number of cancer deaths there, and equally upset by the way the federal government repeatedly denied that there was a connection between the bombs and the deaths, although they knew damn well that it was so.

In the desert of central Washington state, there is the Hanford nuclear reactor and disposal site. The facilities are central to the area's economy, but even the locals get upset when sloppy procedures, occasionally associated with the way nuclear waste is handled as it is trucked long distances across the Empty Quarter, are discovered.

If you prefer your radiation to come directly from the sun, the Empty Quarter has significant solar potential — and geothermal, too. In fact, the federal government likes Empty Quarter exotic energy so much that it wants to use solar and geothermal exclusively to run one of the most deadly weapons systems the world has ever seen — the MX missile system. No, they don't want solar and geothermal to fire the missiles. They want solar and geothermal to run the railroad on which the missiles will ride all up and down Nevada and Utah.

Why, you may ask, does the Pentagon want missiles on railroads? Well, it seems that the MX is the Pentagon's idea of the old shell game. They want each missile to have several widely separated launch sites, and a railroad to drag it from one site to another. The theory is that with such a system, the Soviets will never know which launch site contains a missile and which is empty, and thus won't know which one to attack.

This is an ambitious concept. In fact, it's the largest public works project in the history of man, dwarfing the Pyramids. Whenever a North American planner thinks in terms like these, it's almost inevitable that this thinking will sooner or later center on the Empty Quarter. There is no chance, for example, that such a project would ever be considered for New Jersey. It seems impossible enough to get Interstate 95 completed through New Jersey, let alone an MX missile program. So there you are, five hundred empty miles of Utah and Nevada — Salt Lake to Reno (covering a distance equal to that from Buffalo to Chicago). But Nevada and Utah won't mind. If they do, who cares? It's not that they have many votes in the House of Representatives.

But suppose they were to make a stink? Suppose that the Empty Quarter were to point out that this large a construction project would demand unheard-of amounts of water that should be used some other way? Suppose it were to point to the dust and the pollution? Suppose it were to observe that the construction jobs would be short-lived, going largely to outsiders, like those which were created by the Alaska pipeline? Suppose it were to object to the idea that when these military installations were finished, they would be manned by Alabama crackers with a hitch in the Army, rather than locals? Suppose, for that matter, that it questioned the wisdom of causing every pointy-nosed missile on the Soviet side to be turned toward the vicinity of Salt Lake City?

Well, the Pentagon figures, you'd just have to sweeten the pot. That's where geothermal and solar come in. Not only are they secure energy sources; they're attractive ones. Utah and Nevada are being told that they will be the hotbeds of development of these razzle-dazzle industries. It is being put as if they will be the new Silicon Valley.

Interestingly, there is some local opposition to the MX. It comes from people who are afraid that if the missile system is constructed, the land for hundreds of miles around it will be locked up in a military reservation. If that were to happen, they point out, it will never be possible to exploit the alumina reserves.

The alumina reserves could be chewed up and spit out to produce aluminum. In fact, they could close the circle for Utah, catapulting it into the advanced, industrial world. Remember the coal-fired electrical plant in Lynndyl? Well, if you figure things right, you could take the power from that plant, and, instead of feeding it to L.A., you could use it to process the alumina reserves of Utah into aluminum. And if you did that, you could take this light, versatile metal, which has such great potential in the twenty-first century, and make it the cornerstone of a bright, job-rich, industrialized land, producing airplanes and automobiles. You could avoid the mistakes that the people who managed the gold rush in Colorado of the mid-1800s made. You could avoid the mistakes that the people who ran the copper rush in Butte, Montana, in the early part of this century made. You could avoid the mistakes the people who ran the molybdenum mines quite recently made. Theoretically.

Westerners [said one very thoughtful and sincere observer], don't go along with a lot of this living in harmony with the elements. That was a notion that the Indians had. The earth lived. It was a being. Gouging it hurt. Beautiful Indian poetry.

There's a notion here that the resources were made to be developed, are to be developed. That's part of our optimism. One thing that disturbs me about the East is the notion that they've lost their nerve. They've lost their confidence. You don't have that out here. People are aggressive about the land. I don't believe they want to spoil it; that wouldn't be palatable public policy. But by the same token, they're not offended if a power plant goes up. What they can be outraged by are some incredibly silly regulations about visibility requirements — environmentalists' pipe dreams about vistas.

I see us having a pretty shiny region. There's just an optimism out here, that you can change things, that you can fashion and shape the way things are going. We're not pushed around by forces. We recognize that they are there, but you can screw it up, or you can catch the wave.

•   •   •

In the course of writing this volume, I've tried to stay fair. I've tried to let the voices of the North American people come through. But the fact is that I've spent my adult years in the Foundry, and I must, in all candor, admit that that affected my perceptions of the Empty Quarter. I couldn't help myself. I found myself asking folk, again and again: Have you ever been to Cleveland, South Bend, Trenton? Have you ever seen what an industrialized nation can look like? Are you sure you know what you're doing? I couldn't get over the enthusiasm I met in this, the land of the proverbial wide-open spaces, for coal mines and steel mills and boom towns. Is it that this land is so big that its inhabitants just flat can't believe that it can be seriously altered by the works of man? Could it be they're right?

Even Alan Graban, the Wyoming banker whose professed motivations are "avarice and greed," sensed what I was saying.

I guess the toughest thing is the rancher, comes in to buy his groceries. Got a nice car, a zillion acres, the mineral rights under it. Along comes Milt [the drilling foreman] and a bunch of his guys and says gee whiz, we'll give you a hundred bucks an acre if you let us drill and it takes him about a month to think about it because goddamn, this is ranching country and you're not going to come in and mess it up.

But they come in and drill a few wells, maybe three miles out of town, one on each side of the house, and one flows seven million cubic feet of gas a day, and the other flows five hundred barrels, and he's a millionaire overnight.

And then he comes in with momma and he sits down with his banker and hands you a check for a hundred and fifty-eight thousand dollars for the first month's royalties. And he hasn't the foggiest notion what to do.

We're set up where we take them down to Arthur Anderson, who has

an expert in oil depletion and oil accounting; we take them bodily down
there and they are most happy and this guy is a tremendous person and
he introduces them to the tax ramifications and what have you and turns
them over from that point to the First Security Bank and Trust so that
they can set up living trusts and that sort of thing and maybe protect
. . . Well hell, they've got more money now than they'll ever need, but
then he comes in with the next month's check and he sits down and
smiles and says, "This is the first time in my life that I can afford to be
a rancher."

The nice thing is that the people who are getting the royalties are the
old-timers who struggled and lived here all their lives. But the thing that
scares me is that they don't have the knowledge. You see, they got the
ranch from their father, and their father from their grandfather, and now
the father gives it to the son. The only difference is that there's a thousand acres, and when they transferred it from grandpa to their father at
a buck an acre, it was nothing.

There's no way you're going to tell Internal Revenue that with two
producing oil wells on both sides of your house that that's worth a dollar
an acre. Or there's a housing development on three sides, or a mobile-
home court. With the land selling for five thousand dollars an acre.

All of a sudden, the guy's land is worth five million dollars. And the
guy dies and Uncle Sam says, okay, in the next six months now we need
a check for three quarters of a million dollars, and you tell them that
and they don't believe you.

The kids say, but Dad! God! Make your will! Get your trust set up!
Protect Mom! What if you pass away? She's got to sell half the ranch just
to settle your estate tax! Well, I'll think about it, he says. You know, kids
don't know anything. They're dumb. Every one of them, as far as the old
man is concerned. Dumbest things that ever walked on legs. Useless as
tits on a boar. It's just a whole other world for them.

I hope we're not making these people look like idiots. Some of them
are very smart. Very, very clever. They're great at ranching. It's Evans-
tonitis, somebody called it. It's a feeling that they have been here,
there's no need to go anywhere else, they've raised their family, they've
retired here, they've enjoyed it, and why has all this happened?

I mentioned my concerns to Jerry Mallett, of the American Wilderness Alliance in Denver. You're obviously optimistic about the
future of the wilderness, I said. Why? Where's the constituency
for saving the land?

Well, he explained, there are ranchers out here who are eager
to keep the federal lands surrounding their spreads from roads
and development. It will keep the price of land down and save
their way of life. One shouldn't underestimate the number of elk
hunters either, he said. There are far more applications for hunt-

ing licenses than there are "harvestable" animals, and no politician in his right mind wants to cross them, and they are numerous. But, he candidly admitted, the bottom line is the Easterners, and the people hugging the West Coast. They're the ones who have seen what can be done and has been done to the land around them. The Wilderness Alliance is in fat city, he suggested. As long as the majority of the continent's votes are in the places that have been most screwed up, the wilds have a fighting chance.

But the other thing I wondered about were the Latter-Day Saints. The Saints are the fastest-growing church in North America. Their organizational abilities are formidable. When floods hit Idaho, semi-tractor-trailers loaded with relief supplies were rolling out of Temple Square in Salt Lake before the Red Cross had received the first phone call from national headquarters. It's a wealthy church. Tithing 10 percent of income is still a highly respected tradition. It actively proselytizes, and it takes care of its own.

And if one were to map the stiffest concentration of Saints in North America, from Nevada to Utah, Colorado, Idaho, Wyoming, Montana, and Alberta, and set it next to a map of the most intensively assaulted energy portions of the West, those two maps would be identical.

Karl Snow is a Utah state senator and a professor at Brigham Young University. Named after the man who brought the Mormons west, BYU, in Provo, is right at the base of the towering Wasatch Range, with sheer cliffs pushing straight out of the backyards of some dorms. Speaking of straight, whatever you've heard about BYU is probably true. Coca-Cola is not sold on campus, because of its caffeine content, which makes it strong drink. I watched a colleague reach for a cigarette behind closed doors in the office of a political science professor. The professor, who is Mormon but not overly devout, blanched. He didn't himself mind the reporter smoking, he said, but somebody might smell it, and "eyebrows would be raised," as he put it.

(Jeans are not acceptable dress for women going to class. So dresses are the order of the day. Thank the Lord that fashion, as I write this, favors longer hemlines. When I finished my set of interviews at BYU, I went out of my way to find the nearest place to get a beer. I wasn't all that thirsty. I just felt an overpowering need to sin. There may be another campus in North America where the nearest bar is three miles away, and is very lonely, at that; but if there is, I don't know where. But I digress.)

Karl Snow is a thoughtful, liberal Republican, not the most common breed in the Empty Quarter.

We've worked for a long time to shift from dependency on agriculture. People think of us as a rural state, which we are not. We are highly urbanized. But you're right. There's a real shift going on. At the outset, Brigham got here and he wanted the people to be farmers. He didn't want too much preoccupation with mining. He wanted to keep the people in cohesively knit groups. Miners were the outsiders, the Gentiles, the explorers. We can't say he kept them from mining entirely, because he sent a mission to southern Utah to mine iron. The Iron County Mission. But that was in the direction of self-sufficiency.

I'd like to think it's not naïve, but I'm not so sure we know exactly what we're doing, either. Although I do believe that the development of our resources, particularly coal, and maybe oil shale and those kinds of things, are deliberate. Those are clear-cut statements of public policy, not only in speeches, but in legislation that would facilitate and back up that kind of move. We've fought to bring industry in here for at least twenty-five years.

Yes, we've been concerned with what kind of industry. But that goes more to the concern over outsiders coming in. We have a project over on the mountain called Four Seasons. There's been more litigation over that project in the forest over there than anything else that's gone on in the state of Utah. It's a ski resort. And Provoans are concerned about the change in life style that it will bring. Because you get a ski resort out here and it's a lot different from a Brigham Young University. I mean, there are a few environmentalists around. But basically, it's the drinking and the smoking and the sex. I mean, that's been the biggest battle in this community for the last two years.

Yet I think if you took a vote in this community, it would be ten to one in favor of Four Seasons, because we see it as an economic survival issue. We are so dependent on Geneva Steel out here that when the Environmental Protection Agency comes out and says we're going to impose some restrictions that cost one hundred to two hundred million dollars in corrections, and U.S. Steel says we can't do it, this community gets upset.

And yet I can remember when I was a kid, when this community was very concerned about Geneva Steel coming, concerned about the kinds of values it might bring in. "Well, you're going to bring in the foreigners who aren't going to like the kind of life that we like." It's not the Gentiles as such. Gentiles are well accepted in this community if their values . . . It's not being a Mormon; it's whether your values would coincide. You can't even buy beer over at the grocery store over there. He could sell it, legally, but he just won't.

The only reason we originally embraced Geneva Steel was that it was part of the war effort. And today we'll defend it with our lives. We'll exchange it for pollution. We have told EPA in a downtown rally . . . seven thousand people turned out at that rally! There's never been a political campaign that has ever drawn over a thousand people. Seven thousand people came to that rally downtown to tell EPA to go to hell. Because it's economic survival! It's jobs!

If we tie this to the culture, the thing I can see is that we're committed to self-sufficiency and opportunity for our children. We want them to stay home. We educate them; we spend half our tax dollars on education. Highest in the nation. We want them to stay home.

We want to broaden our base. Develop our resources. Provide jobs. And every time we try, either the Department of the Interior or the EPA gives us a hard time. In Utah, the Sagebrush Rebellion is over the fact that the federal government owns so much of the land that is our economic base.

And you know what the growth situation is here. This state has the highest birthrate in the nation. And that's Mormon policy. So we need jobs for our children!

• • •

Minding my own business, in a roadhouse a long way from Provo. A very long way. Comes the call from the next table.

"What you looking at that map there for, boy? Where you from, anyway?"

Virginia.

"You from anywhere near that Williamsburg restoration place?"

Kind of.

"Saw a television special on that the other night; they done a hell of a job, ain't that right?"

Yes, they've done quite a job.

"Quite a job! They done better than that! They done a hell of a job! Ain't I right? Tell me I'm right. Don't ever tell me that I'm wrong. You looking for the Wild West?"

(Pause.)

Yes, I guess you could say that.

"Well, you found it. You know why we wear these big hats?"

No, why do you wear those big hats?

"To keep the pigeons from s****ing on our lips!"

• • •

"I've got a particular bias," said Kent Briggs, the young executive assistant to Scott Matheson, the governor of Utah, sipping a very expensive beer in the stylish confines of the Vail, Colorado, ski resort *boîte*.

"I was raised up on a farm in Idaho, and so I don't really get off on a lot of this stuff about the joys of the ethereal experience in the great outdoors."

An articulate dreamer of big dreams, Briggs had been discoursing about the future of his land, noting that it had no tradition of being screwed over, as did, for example, West Virginia.

"To me," he said, "I'll take the TransAmerica Building over the Great White Throne any day."

The TransAmerica Building is a pyramidical San Francisco skyscraper that some critics contend is the ugliest building in North America. The Great White Throne is a sheer, three-thousand-foot monolith that is the symbol of Zion National Park.

It's a different mind set [he continued]. People in the *East* . . . I understand that they've fouled their nest there. But we don't believe we have to do that. We'll have to make some compromises. You can expect that there's going to be some winning and losing.

But I believe in the city. The city is what puts the finishing touch on a human being. Civilization was not possible until the Neolithic revolution, until we ceased becoming nomads and became stable in one spot and started developing a culture.

Culture cannot take place on a farm in Idaho. Hell, going to school was a profound experience for me. I went to Idaho State University in Pocatello. I remember sitting on the steps, the first day that classes started, and the dean of the college of liberal arts was telling us what to do.

He was a great dean. He said, "You'll have to have a two point [grade average] at the end of one year. However, the first semester, a one-six will *suffice*. We will allow you to *hover* there for one semester. And that is sheer *magnanimity* on our part."

Playing with his glass, his voice was hushed as he returned to being nothing but a husky farm boy.

I said, "My God!" No one had ever talked like that before! I remember sitting there and shaking my head and saying, "Wow! I've found a home!" Because, God! that was an incredible experience to be exposed to that kind of stuff. It changed me. Changed me profoundly.

So I value institutions like colleges. I've got this thing about colleges; I've got this thing about *cities*. I'm not going to be offended to see an oil derrick on the Great Salt Lake. Amoco. Punched two wells, hit oil. High sulfur content, but the oil is there.

You got to bring that stuff *up!*

To me, it's a symbol of man's *progress!*

THE BREADBASKET

In the hush of the high-ceilinged expanse of teak and cork, near the soaring walls of glass, below the enormous chandeliers, oblivious of the hundreds of people who filed, blinking, into the bright, lofty space through a low portal, the three men talked of cathedrals.

"One is pretty similar to the other," said one thoughtful acolyte. "Basically, they're worshiping the same monolithic higher power. You know, the rules are different, just as the ritual is different. But essentially, these things tell us how to live. Very often where to live. How we dress.

"They make a lot of demands on us. You can kid about the rituals, but I think the guidance that they give to a large number of people is exactly what they want. In many cases, it is exactly what they need."

"The hat thing is very old," chimed in another disciple. "Nobody here wears a hat. But they used to. If you were going to sell for Hallmark, you wore a hat. But then Mr. Hall's blood vessels on his forehead began to enlarge, and it gave him headaches. So he took his hat off, and all the hats came off."

The man munched on his English muffin; stirred his coffee. To his left, on an open balcony, where the choir might sing if this were really a church, were the stacks of a law library. The chandeliers high above his head were enormous coronets, for the cathedrals of which he spoke had been a metaphor for corporations, and the vast room was the employee cafeteria of Hallmark Cards, whose totem is a crown and whose incantation is "When you care enough to send the very best." The Missouri morning sun streamed in, sparkling off the Christmas decorations.

A large chunk of Kansas City is beginning to look a lot like Hallmark these days. Five hundred million dollars of one family's money is being plunked down on what had once been the eyesore of Signboard Hill, at the southern edge of downtown, to build a city within a city of hotels, office buildings, condominiums, and specialty-store shopping complexes in what has come to be known as Crown Center. This theme park to what might be called high-quality capitalism owes a large debt to Walt Disney, a Kansas City boy who was disappointed to see his Disneyland ringed by taco stands. He told his friend Joyce C. Hall, the founder of Hallmark, to make sure not to make the same mistake — to make sure he bought enough land so that his monument, the Hallmark headquarters, wouldn't get overrun by blight, and Mr. Hall took the advice to heart.

In an urban setting in which space is usually measured by the square foot, privately held Hallmark has eighty-five acres. Because Hall, like Disney, believed that his products could help civilize the raw, gangly, unsophisticated population that was at the core of his market, Hallmark's headquarters are surrounded by artifacts of a taste that time has honored as good. The lobby of Hallmark tells the story. The paintings of Salvador Dali abut those of Norman Rockwell, who is hard up against Winston Churchill, who's next to Saul Steinberg, who is the neighbor of Grandma Moses. The juxtapositions are breathtaking. The comments on the plaques, like the one with the Grandma Moses collection, are straightforward enough. It points out that "no other single artist's work has ever achieved such popularity at Christmas as hers." Like that of all the other artists, her stuff sells.

Not only is the design at Hallmark clean and modern; it is, on one occasion, bold. In what has been termed the ultimate act of architectural preservation, the Crown Center Hotel has exposed the hill on which it is built to the indoor inspection of its guests. For four stories or so, the hill, lavishly planted, discreetly lit, and crossed by catwalks, marches up the inside of the hotel, leading to the swimming pool. At its base is a Trader Vic's.

At this time of year, for eighty-five acres of Kansas City to look like Hallmark, it has to look a lot like Christmas, and it does in a fashion that is stereotypically perfect: The Mayor's Christmas Tree. Fairy lights in the leafless trees. On the corporate skating rink, an old man struggles to master the art of gliding backward as a bright-cheeked blonde twirls around her tottering child. Lighted silhouettes of peace doves ten feet across. Bright ribbons and bows. It begins to dawn on you that Christmas would look and be different in North America if there had never been a Joyce C. Hall.

But at Hallmark they've known that all along. "Santa Claus," points out one high executive in the design end of the business, "has changed quite a bit over the years." In the early fifties, she points out, on our cards we wanted the old boy to be a ruddy, cottony-bearded cartoon of himself. But in the early sixties, as we became more sophisticated, we looked for a more stylized old elf. We went most overboard, she says as she sketches, over this Santa Claus more or less in the shape of a Christmas tree–like cone. We thought that was just clever as the dickens. In the late sixties, Santa took a back seat to pleas for "Peace." In the middle seventies, he made a strong come-back, but this time in the old-fashioned Thomas Nast–like etchings of another century, reflecting our contemplation of where we'd been. Now, for some reason, we're losing our affection for St. Nick again. We're getting into bells and birds.

This interest in birds, the executive feels, does not bode well for those interests inclined to pay less than strict attention to environmental concerns.

Now, you can believe that or not, as you see fit, but as Don Hall, the son of the founder and the president of the corporation, said:

We promote communications between people. I guess the reason greeting cards became popular is because people hate to express things themselves. They've become reluctant to say something meaningful to someone else either in person or in a letter. They feel awkward in their ability to do that. So this has been a method of people finding something that's very meaningful to someone else and sending it through the mail. People are no less sentimental. They just need more help in the expression of it.

Our computer would tell you that quote squareness unquote is a universal thing. We don't go after the gay market, for example, but you name a situation, assuming you know a liberated gay who wants to communicate with another one, and I'll find you a card that would be suitable. They buy our cards.

The implication is that, no matter what our status, Hallmark knows who we are and where we're coming from, and has for a long, long time. It's not too surprising that, in all its works, Hall-mark stresses that it is "of Kansas City."

From the early part of the last century, when trade was opened with the Spanish over the Santa Fe Trail, to the opening of Oregon, California, and Colorado, Kansas City was a pivotal place. Not far from the exact geographic center of the United States, it was where Easterners became Westerners. To this day, it is a great marketing-research location, because of its utter typicality. Even urban employers will tell you that its friendly, open, hard-working people are still a product of the prairie.

As Paul Gruchow, the editor of the tiny *Worthington* (Minnesota) *Daily Globe*, wrote:

The prairie is like a daydream. It is one of the few plainly visible things which you can't photograph. No camera lens can take in a big enough piece of it. The prairie landscape embraces the whole of the sky. The sensation of its image is globular, but without the distortion that you get in a wide-angle lens. Any undistorted image is too flat to represent the impression of immersion, which is central to the experience of being on the prairie . . .

The essential feature of the prairie is its horizon, which you can neither walk to nor touch . . . We are helpless as babies about this: whatever we can see and do not understand and must acknowledge, we make over in our own image. The moon, the sea, the prairie all present insurmountable barriers of distance. We cross them on the craft of egocentricity. The moon becomes the marker of time and the dwelling place of desire. The sea becomes the mirror, the bosom. The prairie becomes the breadbasket.

The Breadbasket, of which Kansas City is indisputably the capital, is that North American nation most at peace with itself. It is the nation that works best.

Based on the most prodigiously successful agriculture the world has ever known, the Breadbasket has built an enviable, prosperous, renewable economy.

The Breadbasket produces three quarters of the continent's wheat and corn, and much of its cattle and pigs. The continent's need for wheat can be met by Kansas, North Dakota, Oklahoma, Manitoba, and the Breadbasket portion of Saskatchewan all by themselves. In 1978, Kansas, Nebraska, and Minnesota, in combination, produced a pound of wheat, corn, beef, or pork for each of 261,808,230 people to eat every day for a year. That's a meal a day for a year for the entire population of the United States and Canada, with some left over for Mexico. The Breadbasket accounts for 18 percent of the world's exports of wheat. By contrast, Saudi Arabia accounts for 14 percent of the world's production of oil.

Even though the majority of its people are not farmers, the Breadbasket can afford to be choosy about the manufacturing it accepts. Unlike other nations, it does not feel obligated to leap at an increase in low-paying jobs. Nor does it have to embrace the boom-town syndrome. "With rapid growth," one corporate chief pointed out, "all kinds of things go wrong. You lose your ability to stay within your plan."

And staying within the plan is high on the Breadbasket's list of priorities. If you like roller-coaster rides, don't come to the Plains. Stability, here, is a virtue.

The Breadbasket, appropriately enough, starts in the wheat country of Saskatchewan north of Denver near Alberta. Well to the dry side of the 100th meridian, the line represents the place where carbohydrates become more important than hydrocarbons. There is grain in the oil country of Alberta, and minerals in the farm country of Saskatchewan, but this line describes a shift in primary interests.

The same is true as the border skirts the eastern edge of Wyoming and Montana, cleaving most of those places from the Dakotas, heading for the Front Range of the Colorado Rockies. The mountains that dramatically meet the plains at Denver offer the most distinct food-mineral line, and they continue down the eastern edge of New Mexico. From there, the Breadbasket line passes through West Texas, where herculean efforts are being expended in keeping the oil fields of Midland and Odessa productive. Without them, the influence that could be characterized as Empty Quarter would diminish. But it's hard to claim this part of the world as MexAmerica yet. The harsh, masculine culture predominant here may be beholden to the Spanish, who named, if not invented, everything here from the lariat to macho. But it surely is Anglo. The Panhandle is still informed by straightforward, colorful, do-or-die ambitions that Dakota ranchers easily recognize. It's Breadbasket.

From there, the line walks across central Texas, following the impact of the Hispanics to the state capital, Austin, where it enters the cultural battleground described by the triangle connecting three of the United States' ten largest cities — Houston (fifth), Dallas (eighth) and San Antonio (tenth). It is the triangle in which MexAmerica, the Breadbasket, and Dixie clash.

Heading north, the boundary splits Dallas and Fort Worth at

Runway 17 Left, the main north-south piece of concrete of the most heartless airport in the world — immense DFW International. Fort Worth, which hates to hear itself called a cowtown, is Breadbasket. The border then concedes Oklahoma's southeast corner, known as Little Dixie, to its appropriate nation, skirts the Ozarks, and splits Missouri in half, cutting well south of Kansas City. This is an interesting border. Even the weather respects it. The Arctic winds that make Breadbasket winters so insufferable battle the high fronts off the Gulf of Mexico around these parts. Local meteorologists have been known to split their forecasts into two completely different sections to accommodate different conditions separated by only a few dozen miles. Not too surprisingly, the U.S. National Severe Storm Forecast Center is in Kansas City.

The swift Missouri River leaves the Breadbasket after its extraordinarily long trip from northern Montana as it joins the Mississippi at St. Louis, just below the junction with that important eastern Breadbasket river, the Illinois.

The Breadbasket border marches across south-central Illinois corn and hog land into west-central Indiana before being met by the pincers of two eastern nations: the gritty industrial Foundry, with more of a past than a future, in northern Indiana, and rolling Dixie, in southern Indiana.

The Plains continue across Ohio all the way to the Alleghenies, but the Breadbasket nation does not. The Breadbasket's most typical agriculture is heavily equipped, heavily capitalized, and with substantial acreage. The farm's proprietor is an owner or a manager too busy trying to outwit the gods of the harvest to have a full-time city job. By contrast, in the Foundry, there are a fair number of "sundowners" — steelworkers, for example, who keep a farm going for the extra income or the quality of life, but who couldn't financially swing a complete dedication to crops.

Thus, the Breadbasket ends at the point where farms with five hundred acres or more, representing a value of over a million 1980 dollars in land alone, become unusual. The Breadbasket ends at a point where the *average* farmer pushes out less than $30,000 worth of food per year from his spread.

The Breadbasket ends at a point where less than 80 percent of all land is dedicated to farming. (There are sizable farms within the Kansas City limits.) For all practical purposes, then, the eastern edge of the Breadbasket is in western Indiana, and Indianapolis, as we saw in the Foundry and Dixie, is a crossroads town for those two nations, as well as for the Breadbasket.

From Indiana, the Breadbasket curves back around, giving Chicago a wide berth. Chicago has nothing to say to the farmlands of downstate Illinois, as any political observer can tell you. It's part of the Foundry, as are the other industrial centers hugging the western edge of Lake Michigan, like Milwaukee and Green Bay. The Breadbasket starts thirty or so miles inland from the lake, in Wisconsin's impeccable dairy country. With the Lake Superior wheat ports of Duluth in the States and Thunder Bay in Canada to its back, the boundary then heads into the corn country of rural Ontario before ending at La Belle Province — Québec. Across Ontario, Manitoba, and Saskatchewan, of course, the northern border of the Breadbasket is the point at which even barley, the grain with the shortest growing season, can't make it.

In preparing this chapter, it occurred to me that I started off with the least detailed image of what set the Breadbasket nation apart from any of the nine. On examining why that would be, I realized that my images were based on news events, and there just isn't that much big news out of the Breadbasket. Could it be, I wondered, that the news exists, but is just not being reported? No; the Breadbasket is littered with good newspapers from Kansas City to Minneapolis to Winnipeg. The *Des Moines Register*, for example, keeps winning Pulitzer Prizes for its national reporting. Of course, its topics are frequently agricultural, and those are of limited interest to folk on the coasts. But that's a fault of the people who think that food is grown wrapped in plastic, not that of the *Register*. What news there was, was being reported.

I finally came up with the theory that perhaps news occurred most typically when and where the social fabric was being torn; an absence of news of continental concern constituted the presence of social calm — and that this was the most identifiable characteristic of the Breadbasket. I found my theory popular even among Breadbasket journalists.

In Sioux Falls, South Dakota, for example, in the spring of 1979, an avowedly gay high school senior decided he wanted to take a male date to the prom.

Sioux Falls is a nice town. I should say "city." In the seventy-seven thousand square miles of South Dakota, there are fourteen places with a population over five thousand, and Sioux Falls is far and away the biggest, with about seventy-five thousand people.

The falls after which the town is named modestly tumble the Big Sioux River over hard red rock. The rock, which in its natural state looks as if it had been laid down by a giant stone mason, was quarried by men for some of the handsome older buildings, like what is now the Sioux Land Heritage Museum. The hydro power was important for milling grain back in the 1870s. The granary is gone now, lost to some misguided soul who used the old building to store paint, right up until the explosion. The flume that carried water to an also-abandoned hydroelectric plant is now a picnic site, with a roof, four picnic grills, and a pleasant view. (The falls share a small park with the sewer-maintenance division trucks, but you can't see them from the flume.) Separated from the falls by the all-important railroad tracks, which lead to faraway markets, is the downtown. It's got a modern, if not terribly large, convention center. (The city is still served by commercial propeller-driven aircraft small enough so that they do not have fold-down snack trays on the back of their seats.) It's got a Comprehensive Employment Training Act (CETA) program. The Arkota Ballroom, the Frontier Club Saloon. An honest-to-god Orpheum movie house. A Hallmark store. An automobile-free downtown pedestrian shopping mall. Minerva's Corner Creperie. Lots of stuff.

But by nobody's standards was it a likely location for a battle-line of the sexual revolution.

Nonetheless, according to the National Gay Task Force, Sioux Falls broke new ground that May. It was the first place in the United States to deal positively with a kid who insisted on his right as an American to bring the date of his choice to his own senior prom.

Sioux Falls rose to the occasion. When the senior showed up at the dance in earrings and a powder-blue tuxedo, on the arm of a member of the local gay coalition, camera lights ignited and reporters jumped to life, but the disruption was brief and largely ignor   The two melted into the throng, indistinguishable in their boutonnieres and brightly colored clothes. The only special treatment they got was a lot of room on the dance floor.

"What's the news in all this?" wailed the principal of Sioux Falls Lincoln High School. "What do they think we are in Sioux Falls, a bunch of people with big thick red necks letting fairies go to the prom?"

The week before, NBC's "Saturday Night Live" satire show had intimated just that, and more.

But the principal didn't think he was being liberal. He didn't think he had a choice. "The rules," he pointed out, "only say one prom-goer has to be a senior. They could take their mother if they want. Homosexuals have rights, too; you have to accept that. Getting myself in a situation as an advocate of gay liberation is humorous to my friends. But I'm not promoting it. There are some real confines to the law."

The students themselves shrugged it off with jokes and went to the prom with a good time in mind. It was a typical school dance, with the band showing up late and dancers slung around each other's shoulders. In fact, one student said, as she left early, that she thought it was boring. That was all fine to those who wanted to get the prom invited back the following year to the downtown Holiday Inn's Embassy Room. The Holiday Inn is one of the classiest locations in town.

In his office, cluttered with mail and newspaper clippings, with a "why me?" look on his face, the principal lamented, "We have this feeling the press used Lincoln to make a point. Most people in this community can separate the legal and moral issues. If people will forget it, it will all be fine."

The press most certainly did make a point. The point is that Sioux Falls has a delicate sense of what constitutes social limits. As does the rest of the Breadbasket, which is as straightforward as the landscape.

In fact, in a time of change in the way we look at the value of work, the desirability of marriage and having a family, how trustworthy our governments are, and what constitutes patriotism, the Breadbasket has come to be the ratifier of what constitutes a truly mainstream continental idea.

Opposition to the Vietnam War was at first considered the province of effete, intellectual snobs from the East and West coasts. That canard wasn't silenced until Paul Harvey, the widely listened to radio voice of Breadbasket news and views, turned against Spiro Agnew's notion of the universe. Admittedly, Harvey's conversion was less than that of the other Paul on the Damascus Road. His full attitude was that the war was stupid and wrong because we refused to let the generals have their heads and get it over with. Although he vigorously denies it, there are also those who think it no accident that his change of heart about the war came precisely at the time that his son was about to turn eighteen and become draftable.

But be that as it may, the war was over, politically, when the Breadbasket turned against it.

The tale is told of the high school teacher in a small Great Plains town who, in the late sixties, was discovered living with a man to whom she was not married. Her students still speak in awe of waiting for the explosion from the resident keepers of a morality that hadn't changed for a century. When it didn't come — when there was nothing but a few puffs of gossip and grumbling — these kids, now adults, marked the day. That war was over, and change had won. What had started in Berkeley had come to Nebraska. In North America, what had been a question of sin had been turned into a problem of etiquette.

By contrast, the most bitter strike in the history of Peoria, Illinois, occurred in 1979–1980, at the huge Caterpillar construction equipment works. One of the most significant issues was whether the company could compel its employees to work overtime. Just a few years before, it would have been unthinkable in the Breadbasket to value leisure over the honest gains from hard labor. Especially at Caterpillar, the very symbol, worldwide, of being ready and able literally to move mountains. The length of the strike demonstrated that the social importance of work has not been settled on this continent. Laid-back is still a regional idea. It doesn't necessarily play in Peoria.

Abortion is a social issue that pro-choice forces thought had been settled with their legislative victories. Again, they had not counted on the Breadbasket. If a person really believes that the termination of a fetus is murder, in this part of the world he is simply not going to compromise. In 1978, in Iowa, Dick Clark, one of the more gifted men in the U.S. Senate, a liberal on the issue of abortion, was defeated by an opponent with less than half his candlepower. Pundits suddenly discovered "single issue" politics. That fight is not over.

Some avant-garde sections of society, of course, don't see the Breadbasket as the ratifier of anything. They just see it as behind the times and, for that matter, not too smart. For generations, some of the holders of cultural mirrors, like Harold Ross at *The New Yorker* magazine, made it clear that they had little use for the "old lady from Dubuque." Not too surprisingly, Plains folk ended up defensive. To this day, a visitor to the Breadbasket who, when asked, must admit that he lives in the East, repeatedly has to put up with natives going through their "aw shucks" routine.

Before the stranger has a chance to peep the slightest opinion about his surroundings, the local goes through this song and dance, shaking his head and allowing as how it's tough to find fresh abalone in Tulsa and the Library of Congress isn't in Wichita, and he knows how that must weigh heavy on the mind.

He doesn't believe a word of it. He's just trying to find out if the outlander is ignorant enough to bite at the statement. His conviction is that the Breadbasket is the best place to live in the whole world.

The defensiveness is not based on the Breadbasket's being insular. From "The University," as Texans refer to the school in Austin (one local wit referred to his alma mater as The Harvard University, just to keep things straight) to the University of Wisconsin at Madison, an excellent and enormous system of land-grant colleges make superior educational opportunities here universal. The question is how intellectually isolated other people are. It's not uncommon to hear people remark that it seems to them that the East is less parochial than it used to be.

The Breadbasket, in fact, is the home of a highly sophisticated sense of international interdependence. Ordinary people here make everyday calculations about events on the far side of the globe.

In the Breadbasket, for example, a lot of people's income, directly or indirectly, is tied to the weather in Siberia. In Manitoba, which is sparsely populated by the standards of North Dakota, good times and bad are very much tied to whether the virgin grain lands of the Soviet Union are attacked by hail or drought.

If Mother Russia must purchase millions of tons of grain to maintain her people's standard of living, there are a limited number of places where she can get it, the North American Breadbasket being far and away number one.

Around Portage la Prairie, if the Canadian Wheat Board doesn't screw up and sell too low, or make the mistake of having all its hopper cars at the wrong end of the continent at harvest time, for farmers such purchases will mean money for vacations where the wind does not blow, nice Christmases, new buildings, bigger tractors.

In Moline, Illinois, a good year at Portage la Prairie means the president of the United Auto Workers local can breathe a little easier. Moline is the headquarters of John Deere, the leading farm equipment manufacturer in North America and the world. As long as most of the planet finds the production of cheap food as elusive a goal as the production of cheap energy, his union's jobs are secure.

In Kansas City, the agricultural research division of the Federal Reserve Bank is keeping a close eye on John Deere. Deere is attempting to revolutionize China. It has made some sales of its gigantic food factories on wheels — there's no other way to describe a turbo 7700 combine — to the peasant society of the People's Republic. Will there be more?

In Omaha, they're watching the Fed. Double-digit interest is killing the operators, to whom a line of credit in the spring is as crucial as a line of water.

In tiny Spirit Lake, the resort town on the edge of Iowa's "ocean" (if the lake for which the town is named were circular, the locals boast, it would be three miles in diameter!), this all means a great deal to Berkley Bedell.

Bedell, who parlayed $50 in profits from the paper route he had as a teen-ager into a multimillion-dollar fishing tackle industry today, doesn't spend much time in his home town of Spirit Lake any longer. But he does get back as often as he can. A chain of events that perhaps starts in Siberia can affect him a great deal in Washington, D.C., because he's the congressman from the Sixth Congressional District of Iowa, the northwestern corner of the state that snuggles up against Minnesota, South Dakota, and Nebraska.

Early one cold, crisp morning, Bedell, thin, scholarly-looking, with wire-rim glasses and carefully parted black hair, dressed in a checkered western suit and a butterfly-shaped belt buckle centered by a big swirled gemstone, was starting what he calls an "open door meeting" in the basement of the Spirit Lake City Hall.

The "community room" there in Dickinson County is a spartan affair, its buff cinder-block walls dirty from having had too many posters taped up and taken down. It is decorated with a printed sign designating it a fallout shelter. Hand-lettered signs indicate that this is where you get your driver's license and, no, you'd better not smoke. The red paint on the concrete floor has acquired a few cracks. As the light brown, metal folding chairs are dragged from the closet, the talk is of Iran.

This was a time at the beginning of the hostage-holding in the American embassy in Tehran, an affront to the dignity of the flag that folk took personally. They wanted to discuss it with their congressman.

Not that that was the only thing on their minds. One man just wanted to know if the congressman could get the Army Corps of Engineers to stop draining a lake across his corn field. His harvesting normally would be done by now, he said, but he couldn't get into his field for the mud. The congressman nodded to the young aide, in her peach-colored suit and waffle-stomper shoes, taking notes. Let's look into that, okay? he said. He turned back to the farmer, sympathetically and seriously, and said he didn't know what he could do, but he'd try to work something out.

None of the congressman's other inquisitors looked much different from the man with the water problem, who was beefy, wearing a heavy red-plaid mackintosh, jeans, and galoshes. Only one man among the constituents wore a tie. Only one woman had paid a lot of attention to her make-up.

At this point in the Iranian crisis the polls were showing an overwhelming goddamnit-let's-*do*-something attitude among the general populace, but that wasn't the tone here. It was far more studied.

The folk dismissed out of hand the suggestion of an invasion. Interestingly, it wasn't from a particular sense of pacifism or isolationism, but from a genuine doubt that the volunteer army could swing one successfully. People who signed up for the military in this day and age weren't any too bright, they observed matter-of-factly.

Massive bombing runs didn't hold much appeal. Won't we destroy our own people? they asked. Besides, the real trick is to get rid of this government without doing any more damage to the oil fields than we absolutely have to. I think we should shut off the food supply now, one woman said. That wouldn't work, a guy four seats over said. The Russians would just sell it to Iran for twice as much and, knowing us, we'd then turn around and sell the Russkies more corn.

How about getting the shah out of the United States? Bedell asked. Everybody in favor of that? Egypt had offered to take him. No, sending him to Egypt isn't the greatest idea, said one grizzled man, thoughtfully. Libya has never forgiven Egypt for signing the Camp David accords, he said, and those crazy Libyans are always spoiling for a fight. Sadat's got enough troubles. Don't hand him that one. I hadn't thought of that, said Bedell.

How bad a shape are we in, in terms of oil? one fellow asked. As long as the Saudis and the Iraqis hang in there, we're not going to face anything more than a price increase, are we? Bedell allowed as how that was the impression the State Department briefings conveyed.

The talk turned to how we get ourselves out of this mess once and for all. Bedell called for a show of hands. Six people were for coupon rationing of gasoline. Four were for a fifty-cent-a-gallon tax on gasoline. Five didn't know. The talk passed to another issue.

It was an invigorating morning, and not an atypical one for Bedell that weekend, as he went from Sioux County to Plymouth, O'Brien County to Ida.

Here he was, over a hundred miles from a city with a population in six digits — two hundred miles from Des Moines — and the ordinary voters were casually and competently discussing the inner workings of Iran, Iraq, Libya, Egypt, Israel, Saudi Arabia, and the Soviet Union. Most important, they were relating these faraway places to their own lives.

"How do you like our dumb Iowa farmers?" he asked me at one point, smugly.

This smugness is the caution about the Breadbasket. It's so quietly confident of its own innate superiority that some dangerous traits are shrugged off.

A notable lack of racial conflict, for instance, might lead one to believe that the Breadbasket was one of North America's more tolerant nations. Not so. It simply is so homogeneously Anglo that it doesn't have as many opportunities to hate as elsewhere. North and South Dakota, for example, have virtually no blacks. Minnesota, 1 percent. Iowa, 1.4 percent. But such opportunities as the Breadbasket has to discriminate, it takes. I asked one Jew in Kansas City, prominent in business and philanthropy, what it was like for him living in the Breadbasket, and he told me of the time in the late 1970s when his friends pressed him to apply for membership in a prestigious and discriminatory country club. Surely they couldn't turn *you* down, his friends said. He did and they did. He says he finds it kind of funny now. (Pause.) But, he acknowledges, his son doesn't.

The governor of Iowa got considerable recognition when he very publicly welcomed Vietnamese and Cambodian refugees to his state at a time when many other locations were shrinking from the idea. That was honorable. Within months, however, grim stories started leaking out from the small towns where these Southeast Asians had settled. The locals were running them out. They were just too different.

A United Church of Christ minister shook his head when asked about his parishioners who worked at a nearby maximum security prison. The inmate population was almost 100 percent black, and the guards were almost 100 percent white, and the careful way he put it was that some of his flock really enjoyed their work.

Nowhere in the Breadbasket is it agreeable to be a Native American. "Drunken Indian" is still one word in a lot of the

Plains states. Oklahoma, until 1890 formally Indian Territory, is one of the more schizophrenic places on the continent. A certain amount of that is tied to the disdain in which Indians are held, at the same time as many whites acknowledge having some Indian blood in them somewhere along the line.

The most ironic comment on tolerance in the Breadbasket, in fact, came from the black executive to whom I had been carefully steered by a corporate p.r. man. Yes, he said, there was one golf course that a Jewish friend of his had played, but only because he'd come as the black man's guest.

Attitudes toward tolerance go back to the way the Breadbasket was settled. A lot of North Americans forget that the Breadbasket was the last frontier.

In the mid-1800s, the Plains were considered something to get across on the way to someplace "good," like the woods of Oregon, or Utah, if you were Mormon. The Plains were referred to as the Great American Desert. There were all sorts of barriers to settlement. Since there were no trees, there was no wood for building material. Houses had to be made of sod. There was no firewood. Heat came from buffalo chips or hay. There was no wood for fencing. Fences would await the development of barbed wire, in 1874. Even governing institutions were based on woodlands culture — a town meeting assumes it's easy to get to town.

So many cowboy movies and TV shows have had dramatic mountain and desert vistas that many think that the Ponderosa was the birthplace of the western myth. But the real Dodge City, as it happens, is in Kansas, not Nevada. Virginia City was a gold-mining town, not a cowtown. Not coincidentally, Boot Hill is also in Kansas. There are no mountains in Kansas. And by our present understanding, there are no deserts, although a century ago that was debatable.

Because of the incredible success of agriculture here (an acre of central Illinois can produce twice as much corn as an acre of central Virginia, and for centuries, settlers thought that Virginia was the best of the New World in farming), people tend to think that this Breadbasket land has been pacified for a long time. Again, not so.

Breaking the prairie to the plow was difficult. The tall grasses would send down roots a foot and a half, some of them as thick as a finger. There's only so much that a man with a horse and a fire-hardened wooden sod-buster could do to land like that. But far more critical was the defeat he faced a few years after he did break the prairie. The soil, which can be as much as seven feet deep, so black and rich that it looks like two-year-old compost, turns to clinging gumbo after being turned a few times. It would stick to an iron plow like lard, forcing a farmer to stop and clean off the blade every ten feet, making productivity impossible. It wasn't until John Deere, the founder of the firm that bears his name, developed a way of bonding steel to the implements, so that the mud could slide off easily, that the revolution in the Breadbasket could begin. Until then, it was very literally cowboys and Indians. Nomads, not "nesters."

But now, families with no North American history at all, by the standards even of other parts of the West, make a big deal out of centennial celebrations of their arrival on the land. Newspapers write stories about the most notable. Private histories with photographs of every single family member back to great-grandparents are published.

One hundred years ago, unlike the case in most of the rest of North America, the technology that made settlement at all possible here was brand new. The final solution to the Sioux, Cheyenne, Pawnee, Blackfoot, and Crow problem was still being worked on. The massacre at the dot on the South Dakota map called Wounded Knee was a decade in the future. Oklahoma wasn't open to the white man. A system for getting grain to market or for importing coal and other necessities was still being patched together.

The reason it's so easy to forget that this model of stability we call the heartland is so young is those who settled it: to a bedrock of Anglo-Saxonism was added Germans, Swedes, Germans, Norwegians, Germans, Finns, Germans, Ukrainians, Germans, Poles, and Germans.

Throughout central and western Europe a century ago, "America fever" rose to epidemic proportions, fanned by the glowing advertisements of steamship, railroad, and land companies.

According to the 1880 census, 73 percent of Wisconsin's population was of foreign parentage, 71 percent of Minnesota's, 66 percent of the Dakotas', and 44 percent of Nebraska's. In these years, the amount of land under cultivation in the continent doubled, and the increase came here.

To this day, all across the Breadbasket you'll find people who'll say they can't get over how "dark" the population is in other parts of the country. And they mean *Italians*. They're still getting used to southern European stock in these parts, no less Puerto

Ricans. Winnipeg television still broadcasts Ukrainian programming. When you find anomalies like the Jewish pig farmer in Sioux City, Iowa, who says he has no idea what his product tastes like, and you ask him how he happened to get into a business that has to be unusual for a man who keeps kosher, inevitably the tale starts in Russia.

The Breadbasket is so homogeneously northern European, in contrast with other nations that are absorbing wave after wave of blacks and Hispanics, that what passes for ethnic conflict here has to be imported from a Europe of hundreds of years ago. An Illinois minister pointed out that one of his recent German Protestant predecessors had spent thirty-eight years denouncing German Catholics as creatures of the devil. The German Catholic priest who was his opposite number returned the favor religiously. This ended only in the 1960s. Martin Luther died in 1546.

In Minnesota you can still find automobiles to be a sectarian issue. One denomination drives Fords and another drives Chevrolets, because one wouldn't dream of buying a car from an infidel. The only-somewhat-kidding line in the Democratic-Farmer-Labor Party is that some elections are decided by which side of a certain mountain in Croatia the candidate's ancestors were from.

This is not to say that, for example, the Irish and French don't maintain a rivalry in New England. But the difference is that those two groups have tended to join forces in recent years in response to a perceived threat from, say, Jamaicans. You don't have much of that kind of new wave of immigration in the Breadbasket.

This self-satisfied sense is reflected in the energy issue. Gasohol is a matter of keen interest out here. Fuel that can, in part, be made from grain, leaving behind a high-protein feed supplement as a "waste" product, obviously would be.

There is considerable debate surrounding the question of whether gasohol will ever be economically sensible without high subsidies. One side says that no matter how high the price of petroleum gets, ethanol and methanol will always be more expensive to produce because they take so much energy to distill. The other side says that even if that is the case, burning coal to produce electricity to cook a chicken is enormously inefficient, compared with cooking the chicken directly over a coal fire. Yet nobody is arguing against that conversion technique, so why are they demanding miracles from alcohol?

But none of this has anything to say to farm machinery, which runs on diesel fuel, not gasoline.

Yet the research and development department of John Deere is not very interested in redesigning the tractor. When I talked to Fred Stickler, the director of the technical center in Moline, about what his people were working on, he talked to me about coatings, not about fuel. He was very interested in a paint that will stand up to both the salt spray of a long export voyage and the blistering sun of the tropics. When I asked him whether, because of energy concerns, John Deere had any plans to make their monsters smaller, or to fuel them with hydrogen or some other exotic alternative, he looked at me as if I were crazy. He allowed as how some tinkering was going to have to be done to the engines of his products in order for them to burn synthetics made from coal, but to him it was perfectly clear that the last drop of diesel fuel burned in North America was going to be burned in a John Deere tractor. It's God's plan. Do you want food or not?

This is not to say that all is sanguine on the flatlands. The rise of the American Agriculture Movement in the wheat fields of eastern Colorado and the cattle and irrigated cotton country of the Texas Panhandle made that clear. Frustrations over the price of land, fertilizer, seed, water, fuel, money, and equipment bubbled over there first. But the protests spread to every other farm region. Soon tractors were circling the Mall in Washington, D.C., and a red and black Massey-Ferguson tractor was roaring up and down the Reflecting Pool. The battle cry was "Parity," an idea that held that farmers ought to make as much profit per acre, proportionately, as they did at the turn of the century. Almost everyone recognized this as a fairly naïve concept, considering how much farming had changed. But it didn't make the farmers' anger at society any less real. The facts are that farmers are simply not rewarded, either monetarily or psychologically, in proportion to the importance of their accomplishments. Not only do North Americans eat cheap, by the standards of the rest of the world, but they get the foreign currency to buy their petroleum thanks to agricultural exports.

So what really galls the farmers is that, in exchange for this miracle, the system is so wrong-headed as to make it increasingly difficult for their kids to follow in their footsteps.

About an hour east of Peoria, off a two-lane road known locally as the Flanagan-Gridley Blacktop, after the towns it connects, is the farm of Glenn and Marge Hillman. The tallest thing on the farm is the utility pole, at the top of which is incongruously bolted an enormous quartz-iodide high-intensity highway lamp. The light is the color of the moon's on a night when that glow is so bright that it can illuminate the contrail of a transcontinental jet. It not only lights the whole farmstead; it serves as a beacon. The night is very black in farm country. There's no back-splash of light against the clouds, as there is in cities. The black ground meets the black sky at a horizon marked by scattered tiny blue-white lights, just as powerful as the Hillmans', but distant. The ground may not be table-flat out here, but folk casually point to this landmark or that grain elevator or the other town, and you can see it plain, although it's fifteen miles away. That's farther than Manhattan Island is long. The eye may take in well over one hundred thousand acres at a glance here. Folk say the beacons are a service to travelers forced to set out for help after a break-down. But the real comfort is to the people who live here; they can look out of a clear night and remind themselves that they are not, in fact, alone.

The harsh light shows a tidy farmstead, actually on the small-ish side for this region. Surrounded by corn and soybean field, limitless the way buffalo once were, is the tan-brick, white-roofed ranch house shaded by a half-dozen carefully nurtured trees. The barn houses machinery, including the combine, the corn planter, the two plows, the discer, the field cultivator, three of the four John Deere tractors, one of which has four rear wheels to float over and dig into wet ground, and another of which is equipped as a front-end loader. The round, squat, corrugated, gun-metal-gray truncated silo, where corn is dried by liquefied propane gas and stored, is surrounded by the clean, white, farrowing, wean-ing, and finishing buildings, linked by pipelines of grain, in which is produced, every year, a third of a million pounds of pig.

Marge Hillman introduces herself as "Mom." She looks it. Not much over five feet tall, she is ample of build, easy of smile, and her silver hair is cut in a style that used to be called a pixie. Which is not a bad description of her personality. Glenn Hillman, who is also not overly large in his olive-drab jumpsuit, has the ears of a yeoman. Like Lyndon Johnson's, they're fleshy and bris-tled. Initially phlegmatic, once warmed up he's an avid conver-sationalist — even something of a philosopher.

About sixty, they've got five kids, all pretty much grown, by whom they're trying to do right. Three are removed from the di-rect doings of the farm. Bob, thirty, the oldest, is making his fame and fortune as a reporter in the state capital, Springfield.

Carol, twenty-eight, the number two child, is a teacher, married to Russell, who is in a formal partnership with his farmer dad and brother, a few miles away.

Jane, twenty-two, single, is teaching Amish kids in a public school that walks a very thin line between the constitutional separation of church and state.

That leaves Scott, twenty-four, and Richard, twenty-one. Both live within a distance considered long for walking by a human but reasonable by a dog, and both want to farm real bad. Scott, who is single, has a degree in agricultural economics from the University of Illinois in Champaign-Urbana. Richard, married to Joyce, a beautician, is a crack John Deere diesel mechanic. Back in their teens, Scott and Richard figured out that their bents and skills could complement each other in a future farm partnership if they trained in these areas. That's how long they've assumed that their future was with this land. The question is whether they'll be allowed to make it.

For the fields that appear so empty are full of high-finance, personal deals, and family histories with a biblical quantity of "begats." The acres that used to go off at a couple of hundred dollars apiece can bring $4000 now. Folk say that it's only a matter of time before it hits $10,000.

Farmland costing that much makes exactly as much sense as gold going for dozens of times its intrinsic value as an industrial metal. On the one hand, it's crazy. On the other, it's a commodity that is there, tangible, and basic, should come a crash. In between, it's an enticing investment for advocates of the "bigger fool" theory — the theory that holds that no matter what you pay for Breadbasket farmland, there's a bigger fool who will pay more.

Whatever the pressure on land prices, there's a key truth in farming out here: it is absolutely and physically impossible to push enough food out of the land to pay off a mortgage at these prices.

Every economic and personal calculation flows from that fact.

Glenn and Scott Hillman, father and son, farm 440 acres in two separate but highly interconnected operations. But only 80 acres belong to either of them — the 80 that Scott lives on but Glenn owns.

Of the 240 acres that Glenn works — has worked for twenty years, on which he built a home and raised his kids — not an inch of it belongs to him. It originally belonged to the father of Marge Hillman, née Mooberry. When old man Mooberry died, he passed it on to Marge, her two sisters, and her brother.

It doesn't make much sense to divide 240 acres into four 60-acre parcels around here, since you can barely turn a combine around in plots that small, or so the locals exaggerate. So the four siblings hold the 240 acres in common for Glenn to farm.

That's working out all right now, but when one of the aunts passes on, it's going to be a hassle, figuring out how to reimburse the estate without carving up the countryside. If the Hillmans want to continue working the land, they'll have to come up with a quarter to a half a million dollars for those piddly 60 acres.

And that won't be easy.

The Hillmans senior consider a year in which they make $25,-000 a good one. The only way they got up the money to pay for the 80 acres that Scott lives on is by leveraging Marge's equity on her share of the Mooberry inheritance. In other words, Marge's share of her father's land has appreciated so much in value that the Hillmans can borrow against it to go deeper into debt to buy more land to expand their operation to, presumably, gain some advantages of scale. This makes slightly more sense when you realize that when income tax time rolls around, the more money you make, the more advantageous it is for you to be in debt, because interest payments are deductible. Thus, the bigger your farm, the more the government will pay for you to get even larger. And the more you owe the bank, the better off you are.

(If you think this is Catch-22, don't get into a conversation with Glenn Hillman about why he keeps his sows for only two breeding cycles. It has nothing to do with biology. It's because of his reading of the law on capital gains. Accelerated depreciation comes in here somewhere, too.)

So much for Glenn's 240 acres. Of Scott's 200 acres, we've accounted for the 80 that Glenn owns. Another 40 is also part of the maternal ancestral inheritance.

The other 80 he farms for the bank.

"A lady owned it and she died," Scott explains, "and the bank downtown is handling the estate and I'm their tenant. I farm it on a fifty-fifty basis. They pay half of everything except fuel. We have to pay for the fuel.

"There were literally hundreds of guys trying for the land. Everybody just goes crazy for land around here. Young guys, old guys, everybody. I'm surprised I got those eighty acres. But I guess I was from around here, and on top of that I had all that money borrowed from that bank."

"All that money" refers to the loan he got for many more thousands of dollars than Scott has years of age. It went to buy some basic equipment for him to get started as a farmer. He owns half of the combine with his dad, for example, and had to put up a collection of confinement-feeding buildings for his hogs.

(Glenn Hillman used to let his hogs roam free over about 20 acres, but at $4000 an acre, he can't afford to let land sit by and be idly rooted by contemplative porkers. The land is in corn, so now the hogs are in concrete confinement buildings. Land is so dear around here that a right of way between a highway and some railroad tracks — barely two tractor sweeps wide, and obstructed by telephone poles, at that — is leased from the railroad by 4-H-ers and planted. It's the only way for the kids to work any land. In fact, even planting fencepost to fencepost is meaningless these days. Since most animals are now locked up, the fences aren't necessary anymore, and they've been taken down to free a few more feet of land for plowing.)

Scott's doing okay, paying off his big equipment loan. "You can make hogs pay out all right," he says, while noting offhandedly that he's not paying his father any rent on the land. "You can't pay the loan on the *land*," he explains patiently. "You don't make *that* much."

He's just saying that of all the little wieners his ninety sows and three boars produce this year, about a thousand of them will survive cold, heat, porcine cannibalism, stomach upsets, scours, and fluctuating market conditions to reach 220 pounds. At 220 pounds, the pigs will each have eaten about twelve bushels, or almost 700 pounds of corn, plus about 100 pounds of soymeal protein supplement, some minerals, some antibiotics, and whatever else animal science and their own ornery intelligence have let them get at, and they will be made into bacon. If Scott gets forty cents a pound for his pigs, he'll consider himself blessed, and that will be his entire return on his education, his labor, his equipment, his fuel, and his land.

As he points out, if he and his father, who produces about fifteen hundred hogs per year, weren't in pork, they'd be dead. If they were raising corn just for the grain market, they'd need 700 or 800 acres. Each. In order to support a family.

Which gets us back to Richard, young Richard, the John Deere mechanic who's waiting for his turn at the land. He's living in a farmhouse not far from his father and Scott, but the geometric furrows that surround the house, carved by a tractor that came as close to the farmyard's trees as it dared, were not made by him. He wanted to farm this land, but when the old man who owned it retired, he rented it to an older, established neighbor whom he'd been dealing with for decades.

This older farmer needed more land, more land to pay for his machinery, the machinery that keeps on coming bigger and more expensive in order that one man can till more and more land.

Economists call that productivity, but for Richard it means he'll have to keep working at his job in town instead of working in the fields. Not only can't he afford to own any land; there isn't even any land to tenant. It's all spoken for by the established growers, and when one retires, he moves into town, rents his house to youngsters like Richard, and leases his land to his friends. His farm, in effect, disappears, gone to economic imperatives.

The only hope that Richard has to get his hand in is for his father to retire and rent the land to his son, and that's a mildly ghoulish wait. Glenn is talking retirement, but the talk doesn't seem to carry much enthusiasm with it.

And on top of all this, all the Hillmans' efforts to continue their family's heritage of working the land doesn't speak to the rights of Bob, Carol, and Jane, the three kids who have made other life arrangements. How will they get their fair share of their inheritance when their parents pass on? If they sell the land to get the money that is coming to them, the price will be so high that their siblings who want to farm won't be able to afford it.

And this is not just a private concern. All over the Breadbasket, especially in urban industrial contexts, people genuflect in the direction of values they believe are taught by the family farm. Rarely are they articulate about what they mean, but as people stumble toward an explanation of what they value in their friends and neighbors around here, the words are *always* "open," "friendly," "hardworking," "there when you need them," "down to earth." And these are virtues that are perceived as being linked to fresh memories of rural life. On the farm, you can't call in sick or go on strike or demand time and a half. By the same token, as long as you never *expect* people to look out for you when you're down on your luck, you can frequently assume that they will. The question is, how long can these values survive, estranged from their roots? One generation? Two? No one dares guess.

This "we're all in it together" ethic extends itself socially and politically. Socially, there are pervasive — some would say stifling — pressures not to flaunt wealth, or to ascribe success to "luck." Corporate officers note how few scions become playboys.

Suits come in brown, not gray or blue. Politically, there is still a constituency for bringing the other guy along economically (as long as he isn't too different from you). For example, the only significant difference between the U.S. and Canadian portions of the Breadbasket is in their brands of collectivism.

In the Breadbasket, the Depression, which was seen as the creation of eastern vested interests, led to an eruption of what was called "prairie socialism." The urge was to band together to face the banking, railroad, and industrial powers. In the States, this move was largely channeled into Populism, and its legacy today is maverick politicians like Democratic presidential candidate George McGovern of South Dakota, who lost so spectacularly to Richard Nixon in 1972. (North Dakota still has a state bank; Minnesota, a Democratic-Farmer-Labor Party.) Practically, this movement led to the New Deal farm policies of dedicating federal tax dollars to guarantees, subsidies, and credit reform. But perhaps one of the most enduring monuments to the period are the great cooperatives, such as Farmers Union. Farmers Union sells a man his seeds, fertilizer, machinery, and fuel, and then buys his crop. It is considered a great free-enterprise institution because every farmer owns a share. But the intent of a co-op is to insulate its members from rapacious private interests. It is meant to redistribute Easterners' income, not its members'. Co-ops have come to wield so much rapacious economic clout of their own that, often as not, the goal is met. Yet it is hardly rugged individualism.

In the northern Breadbasket, it is a cliché that people from Manitoba have far more in common with Americans to the south than they do with people in Ontario, their industrial sister province to the east. Minneapolis is being redeveloped with Canadian money. (The head of the American consulate in Winnipeg speaks with awe of Canadians in his parts driving three hours south to Grand Forks, North Dakota, for a *winter* vacation. They check into a motel and have a sauna. All the Canadians say they like American service. You don't have to ask for a second or third cup of coffee in the restaurant, and you don't get charged for it. It is not clear to the consular officer why this is worth a three-hour drive in winter, but, then, when I talked to him he was new to his post.)

But this is not to say that the Breadbasket is a seamless web, politically. In Canada, the Depression was met with an enduring and straightforward socialism. In Saskatchewan, for example, the government is still openly socialist. By the same token, the Canadian Wheat Board, a monopoly, which controls every aspect of the grain market from the moment a farmer's capitalist combine cuts a stalk, is socialist.

In the Canadian Breadbasket, every wheat farmer gets the same price per bushel for his grain as his neighbor, each year. There is no agricultural roulette, as there is in the States. To the south of the arbitrary surveyor's line known as the 49th parallel, every farmer tries to deliver his crop at precisely the right time to catch a fluctuation of a few cents on the commodities market. In Canada, that's considered a sucker's game, in which the little guy, playing the market without the inside dope of governments and trading giants, is doomed to lose. In the United States, the Wheat Board is considered a bureaucratic morass, unable to move fast enough to catch the trend. The "little guys" in this game, they point out, are million-dollar growers.

The argument goes round and round, but the reality is that the whole Breadbasket ultimately is a mixed public-private system, from which the multinational grain traders, like Cargill and Continental, buy and profit. Admittedly, the systems started from two different points, but socially, these institutions don't make a whole lot of difference. The repartee at the coffee shop on opposite sides of the border may differ, but it's not as if any farmer anywhere in the Breadbasket is getting wealthy on grain sales.

Which is not to say that no one in the nation of the Breadbasket is talking about anyone becoming rich as a sheik. Lined up against rank upon rank of high-priced academicians, economists, and diplomats, there is the occasional "ignorant farmer," who, with CARGILL 941 baseball cap in hand (Cargill 941 is a brand of hybrid seed), asks, stubbornly, "Explain to me again why we can't form a cartel?"

I have to admit that no matter how often it is explained to me, I, like the farmers, am too ignorant to grasp fully the reasons that are given against the Breadbasket forming a grain cartel and dramatically hiking grain prices. The most succinct answer I have received that I understand is the one that goes: "A cartel is like a gun. If you intend to draw it, be prepared to shoot it, and if you shoot it, shoot to kill."

That is, if you can't stomach the idea of a lot of innocent people in, say, Calcutta, starving to death while our elevators burst with grain, don't talk about a cartel. Although the target of a cartel may well be an OPEC, inevitably it's somebody else who'll get hurt first. And in the meantime, other people — both those who don't like to see the poor starve, and those who can control basic resources like bauxite or copper — will be retaliating.

That, I understand. We may be too charitable a continent to play hardball with food.

Similarly, it may be possible that the United States has exploited its neighbors for so long that it is impossible for a North American Breadbasket common market to come together. It could be that, no matter how much Regina has to say to Omaha, Washington and Ottawa will never get together.

Be that as it may, let me quote Warren C. Robinson, a Penn State economics professor, about grain cartels:

Objection. There are too many wheat-producing countries to make a cartel workable.

Reply. In fact, there are far fewer wheat-exporting countries of any consequence than oil-exporting ones. Over 80 percent of wheat exports in recent years were supplied by four countries: the United States, Australia, Canada and Argentina. The U.S. alone represents some 40 percent.

Objection. Wheat can be replaced by many other food grains and cereals in human consumption.

Reply. True, and so can petroleum be replaced as a source of energy. But the substitution of rice or potatoes or some other source of carbohydrates in family diets would be difficult for many nations. [The U.S. is also in a strong export position in corn, soybeans, and rice.]

Objection. High wheat prices will encourage other nations to increase supply for their own domestic use and also for export.

Reply. Certainly, almost any country can produce wheat, but the dominance of the grain trade by a handful of countries is based on historical-geographical advantage. The price must rise considerably before it is possible for Saudi Arabia, for example, to become an efficient wheat producer.

Objection. An international price-fixing agreement would cause U.S. food prices to rise, also.

Reply. Not necessarily. The government could calculate anticipated U.S. domestic needs and undertake to export only the "surplus." A two-price system requires only that the government act as the sole exporter of wheat. [The way the Canadian Wheat Board already does.]

Objection. The OPEC nations import a minor fraction of the world grain trade.

Reply. The OPEC nations as a bloc account for about half the world's wheat imports.

Objection. Such blatant self-interest in foreign economic policy will invite retaliation and open economic warfare.

Reply. Perhaps. But is it not equally possible that OPEC and other nations may come to see the United States as an adversary which has finally learned the new rules and must be taken seriously again?

That's the end of the professor's Q & A. There are a few questions that I could add:

Objection. Aren't most nations hostile to North America less dependent on imported grain than we are on petroleum?
Reply. Yes. The United States is up to 50 percent dependent on imported oil, and nations vulnerable to a grain cartel are perhaps only 15 percent dependent on imports. Yet it only takes a 3 or 4 percent disruption of petroleum imports to rock North America.
Objection. Doesn't a great deal of grain go to the feeding of meat animals? Wouldn't a decline in grain shipments lead to folk eating more bread and less steak?
Reply. Tell it to the Polish and the Egyptians. Relatively minor belt-tightening, in the literal sense of the phrase, has led to riots and strikes, even under the most austere regimes.
Objection. Couldn't importing nations, like the Soviets, simply devote more resources to the growing of grain?
Reply. The Soviet Union has spent decades and billions of rubles trying to become self-sufficient in food. It was a major humiliation for them to turn to the West for grain. It was only because they were forced to improve the quantity of meat in the diet of the average man that they are in this market at all. If U.S. grain embargoes are ineffective, it is for the same reason that the Saudis cannot pull off an oil embargo of a country single-handedly. You need a cartel to make embargoes work. This should not obscure the point that there is less slack in the Soviet demand for sausage than there is in the American demand for gasoline.

•   •   •

The road that takes you east out of Sioux City, Iowa, past the stockyards, which claim to be the final destination of more hogs than anywhere else in the world, and almost as many steers, is Gordon Drive. And Gordon Drive is one of this continent's foremost culinary triumphs.

On Gordon Drive, early one December eve, was a Bonanza Sirloin Pit with a sign on which crawled letters, like those on the electric news board in New York's Times Square. On this sign the message was: REMEMBER, IT WASN'T THE DINOSAURS THAT SURVIVED. IT WAS THE LIZARDS. MAKE YOUR CHRISTMAS RESERVATIONS NOW.

Now I know this is true, because I committed at least four misdemeanors, if not felonies, in my car until I was sure I had written the message down right. I'd done enough traveling by then to know that there were folk in certain extremities of this continent who were so limited as perhaps not to believe that the Bonanza Sirloin Pit in Sioux City was taking reservations for Christmas. But what did they know? They probably couldn't tell the difference between an iguana and a Tyrannosaurus rex.

I'd been warned by students of authentic North American eats that I was in for a treat when I came to the Breadbasket. This was the land, I'd been told, for which the 1957 Chevrolet and warm summer nights were invented. Nowhere, my tutors had assured me, could one indulge in a ten-course meal-on-the-move as on the Plains. But nothing prepared me for the gastronomic marvel that is Gordon Drive.

It wasn't just the Bonanza Sirloin Pit. Nor was it simply the proximate location of:

Hardee's char-broiled burgers.

Kentucky Fried Chicken Sunday special four course meal $1.99.

Arby's featuring Arby's roast beef sandwich Rockwell Christmas glasses coming.

Seven-Eleven try our sausage and biscuit sandwich.

Pizza Hut all you can eat $2.39 pizza, pasta, salad bar, Monday thru Friday.

Mr. Doughnut.

The Palmer House food fuel boat washing.

Taco John's.

Godfather's Pizza take one home to feed your mob! Taco pizzas now here!

Wendy's old-fashioned hamburgers give Wendy's gift certificates.

Sambo's.

Burger King home of the Whopper.

Hinky-Dinky.

Nor was it the abundant competition from bastions of local enterprise such as Bogner's prime rib, seafood, steaks, lunch, breakfast, cocktails.

I have to admit the idea of day-old Twinkies at the Wonder Bakery Thrift Shop almost brought me to my knees.

But what finally rendered me prostrate was the grain elevators, which towered over all, like the beer cans of a leviathan with a taste for fries. Painted on each of the silos was one letter, looming through the night. Put them all together, and they spelled F-E-E-D.

I found it humbling to be in the presence of an agricultural civilization that obviously cared so deeply about its supper.

This is heady business, distinguishing an "old-fashioned" hamburger from a "Whopper," and when it comes to the glories of Breadbasket food, I must admit that my observations are merely those of the dedicated amateur. However, I would like to take for my text the distinctions between Gates and Sons Bar-B-Q in Kansas City, Missouri, and Arthur Bryant's, five blocks east, down Brooklyn Street.

I recognize that far more distinguished chops than mine have been taken at this subject. It was Arthur Bryant who, after all, casually stepped outside his restaurant one day to find it surrounded by flashing police lights and Secret Service limousines. The movers and shakers of Kansas City had decided that it was important for the president of the United States to get a decent meal. "If I known you was coming," Bryant reportedly told Jimmy Carter, "I would have baked a cake."

And I know that this is not simply a regional debate. The prevailing New York view, for example, is that Arthur Bryant's is the last word in barbecue.

In that, I'm afraid, New York has it wrong. There's no question that Arthur Bryant's has the meat. But Gates's has got the sauce. "Got the sauce, got the *sauce*, got the SAUCE," in the words of my senior Kansas City barbecue adviser.

This is a difficult observation to refute.

Granted, Gates's lacks ambiance.

Gates's ceiling is a bright red, as are the seats of the chairs supported by stainless-steel tubes. The spanking clean banquettes are also red, with buttons fastening the stuffing to the back. There are live cacti in clay pots along the window.

After every order that's shouted to the chef is drawled out, long and loud, the word "pulleeze." As in, "Draw, pulleeze." A "draw" is a beer taken from a tap. Exhaust fans, sucking gases redolent of animal fat, are so efficient at Gates's that it's hard to tell the place from a McDonald's by smell. In fact, if you ask the folk at Gates's what a "beef and a half is," they'll look at you as strangely as if you'd asked about the origins of a Big Mac. A "beef" is a sandwich with fourteen machined slices of meat. A "beef and a half" has twenty-one slices. (As does the ham and a half, and the combo [beef and ham] and a half.)

On the wall near the entrance, approximately two feet wide by three feet high, is the distinguished portrait of Mr. Gates, the founder. His portrait is illuminated by a wagon-wheel chandelier.

Mr. Gates is a black man with a blue suit, at three-quarters profile. In his own way he looks a little like Colonel Sanders.

The only thing that saves Gates's — which now has six locations — from sterility, in fact, is the stainless-steel shrine to the thin, savory, crimson nectar, served piping hot over everything — shrimp, lamb, sausage, chicken, short ends, long ends, and slabs. The Sauce is so good that it can be bought separately, for people have been known to bring the humble contents of their lunch pail into Gates's, hoping for it to be raised to glory by a laying-on of The Sauce.

Outsiders find it astonishing that Arthur Bryant's, by contrast, can have as much ambiance as it does and not be a violation of the health code. Bryant's is a statement, from its Bubble-Up machine, to its Continental II Stereo-Round Jukebox, to its Gottlieb's Volley Pin-Ball machine, to the clock from Hurst's Diamond Shop.

If you cock your hand, monkey-wrench fashion, with your thumb held parallel to the last two joints of your fingers, opposing digits held wide enough apart to clamp around a size seventeen neck, you're ready to grab a four dollar, Arthur Bryant's combination sandwich. It is three pieces of white bread, separated by an indeterminate number of hand-hewn slices of ham and beef. The chef shared with me the secret of its preparation. "I stop when it look big enough," he explained. He then applies his signature. Clamping the extravagance together so that it will fit on one plate, he leaves his four distinguishing fingernail marks in the top piece of bread. Behind him, on open fires, snaps hot fat. Additional sauce is offered in wine cruets.

The juke box is in excellent voice, ranging from the Delfonics to Wilson Pickett to B. B. King. The clock on the wall showing Central Time has one of the twelve letters of Arthur Bryant's name at each point where traditionally there are numbers. There are also clocks showing Pacific, Mountain, and Eastern Standard Time. They are covered with arcs of grease, as, in fact, is everything in the place. The Pacific clock is broken. The meat is fantastic. As you sit there, belching discreetly, eyes half-lidded in pleasure, considering what miracles can be wrought from mere hickory smoke at the ministrations of a true artist, it is barely thinkable that even greater ecstacy would be attainable if you just had a little of Gates's Sauce.

•   •   •

There are few natural reasons for Minneapolis, Minnesota. Its only God-given advantage to speak of is that it is as far north on the Mississippi as navigation is practical, although that's true only during the months when the river isn't frozen solid, which are not many. If, in the last century, you were to draw a line between the two coastal commercial hubs of New York and San Francisco, attempting to figure where in the midlands to make your fortune, Minneapolis, four hundred miles northwest of Chicago, would not have been the place. In Kansas City, you could see that it would be almost impossible to fail, since Kansas City was bound to be the crossroads of everything. But it would take a miracle to make Minneapolis a center of the arts, education, philanthropy, and wealth. To this day, booster publications note that "air pollution is low because Twin Cities weather is one of frequent air mass change." Which means that the wind howls like a banshee. Never in this century have there been *two* cold snaps of below-zero temperatures for a nonstop week and a half, the locals boast.

Thus, it is with some amazement that one considers what Minneapolis, with all the physical assets and liabilities of, say, Buffalo, has become.

If the 550 U.S. corporations with sales in excess of $1 billion were distributed among states according to population, Minnesota would have one. Instead, it in fact has twenty-four. They are epitomized by such highly sought-after organizations as 3M, Honeywell, and Investors Diversified Services (IDS).

More theater and concert tickets are sold in Minneapolis–St. Paul than anywhere other than New York City. Beyond that statistic, the place is loaded with real, live, ordinary people who animatedly, and with fresh memories, discuss the last play they went to.

An astonishing 77 percent of the high school graduates go on to higher education, and this from even the most isolated rural area or ethnic neighborhood. The area is a fascinating one for demographers, since it is approximately the sociological continental divide. It is about here that kids stop being fascinated by Boston and New York City, and start becoming mesmerized by Denver and L.A.

Big business here leads the continent in giving away pretax profits to charity. The average contribution is twice the continental average. It is paced by Dayton-Hudson, which gives away five times the continental average. Dayton-Hudson used to be a local department store. It's now become a major retailing chain, spawning division after division, giving away good money as it goes.

Politics are clean. Minnesota's donation to national leadership is generous, Vice-Presidents Hubert Humphrey and Walter Mondale being examples.

Even the winter has been tamed, after a fashion. The tailgate parties in Bloomington before, during, and after the Minnesota Vikings games have become legendary. It is true that the all-time tailgate party was attended by four hundred and was held inside a tractor-trailer. It is not true that the survivors were still being dug out in March. By the same token, snowmobiling has introduced a whole new dimension to the concept of the pub crawl. Bundled up in layer upon layer of twenty-first-century fabric, crowds of twenty-five or thirty couples venture out on snow machines, spending a Sunday in the sun in outrageous temperatures, visiting one schnapps house after another, frequently stopping to tighten a fan belt or take a nip or whatever.

Twentieth-century technology generally has made a big difference in everyday life in Minnesota. Dozens of blocks of downtown Minneapolis are linked by skyways, second-story passages that allow people free movement from shop to shop without fear of the cold. (This is not unlike downtown Houston, which, through underground connections, guards its populace from an equally absurd, if opposite, climate.) Serious, man-high snow-eating machines to keep the roads clear have also dramatically changed transportation. It's actually fairly hard to get snowed in in Minnesota.

So perhaps it should have come as no surprise that when the first, landmark study quantifying quality of life entered the public dialogue, the state that ranked second in amenities, after California, was not only a Breadbasket state, but a northern Breadbasket state: Minnesota.

It may be a coincidence, but Minneapolis is also the home of the Cultural Change Surveillance System. The CCSS, as it is called, is run by General Mills, and it's certainly no accident that General Mills is headquartered in Minneapolis. Like Cargill, Pillsbury, International Multifoods, and others, the wheat tier of the Breadbasket was an obvious home base for a milling-and-marketing outfit.

The Cultural Change Surveillance System was set up by General Mills to make sure it had our number. Says G. Burton

Brown, the cautious, scholarly head of the operation: "Everything that's going to happen in the future is going to be a direct outgrowth of something that's happening in the present. Nothing just takes place absolutely without precedent. I think that's virtually a complete little piece of truth right there."

So what the CCSS has done is set up a collection of monitors with a very eclectic periodical reading list, and every time the word "change" or "new" or some synonym pops up, these folk write a short report. And these reports turn into changes in the way we eat.

What did we do when we saw the women's movement coming? [asked Brown]. Well, the most obvious examples have to do with working women and your convenience products. One of the biggest problems the working woman has is of preparing a good-tasting meal conveniently, with as little advance planning as possible, and the products we've created keep this in mind.

Hamburger Helper really started out with the observation that, working or not, one of the most pervasive problems women have is figuring out another way to serve hamburger so that the family won't get tired of it. Hamburger Helper offers a little variety. Something that is appealing, the family will like it. It's wholesome. Easy. Not much clean-up. Top-of-the-stove kind of thing. Not much time.

Stir and Frost [cake mix] literally started with the sociological development of smaller families, and people wanting less cake, and not wanting to clean up pots and pans. We actually drew a little picture of this product, and see, the pan's in there, and on the side of the box was Step One, Step Two, and Step Three.

I think we called it Little Cake and then another version, All-in-One-Cake, or something like that. And we told them what it would cost, and we put it into our little concept test system. And it came up near the top.

Cheerios are big things among young mothers for keeping kids quiet. You can just put them on the tray there and the kid can pick them up and mush them around and if they fall on the floor so what. The new, college-educated mother likes them because they're very low in sugar. People think that's important now. We've even backed some additives out of some of our foods. Especially some of the colors. We did that in the case of Cheerios. I remember a test in which we compared uncolored Cheerios with the more golden version that we had been marketing up to that time.

The energy problem is taking us toward food you don't have to cook. For example, Pillsbury has no-bake pies. I haven't tried one, but it's probably a graham-cracker crust with a pudding filling. It's a response to the energy crisis. Oh, yeah! Really! I definitely would say so!

We haven't found a way to be particularly helpful to elderly people. That's another one we've studied a number of times. We're certainly aware that they're the segment of the population that is the most rapidly growing, and will be for a long time. Some of the parameters we've examined are digestive, the minerals and things, the special dietary requirements that old people have. The problem is economics, at least partly. I don't know how you solve that problem. Another problem is that it's no fun to eat alone. You don't feel like preparing anything. Meals are no fun if you're eating by yourself. We've talked about it at meetings. Could this be the starting point for something? It's pretty hard to find a solution other than to invite somebody over.

But what about Minneapolis? I asked. Is Minneapolis a good place from which to watch North America? Would the company that invented Betty Crocker be different if it were not part of the Breadbasket?

Well [said Brown], take one of the first things we noticed when we first set up the Cultural Change Surveillance System. Organic foods. The interest in organic foods, which had been limited to only a few people for many years, was becoming broader. It wasn't strictly organic foods, but natural foods, and foods that weren't processed, and foods that weren't made by major manufacturers.

And it wasn't just this band of screwballs who had been associated with it in the past. It was an expanding group of academics, nutritionists, even students. A pretty broad base of people. So we thought that there was reason to believe that trend might expand and continue. This was the middle of 'sixty-nine.

I do think that it is probably true that if and when something begins to take hold here in Minneapolis, it proves something. Take granola, for example. Granola was that sort of thing. As far as I know, it started in Colorado. We were aware of the organic foods, natural foods, interest. And we were aware of granola as a specific manifestation of it. But when we began to see granola in some of the stores around here, around the university . . .

Yeah, I think that kind of told us something.

The way these Cultural Change Surveillance System reports have distilled forces of great passion and scope, and focused them on our bellies, may ignite the tempers of the high-minded.

But there's another way of looking at it. To those who have watched with a touch of anxiety the social upheavals of the last few decades, who have viewed with trepidation one convention after another being turned on its head, the CCSS may be reassuring.

It may be comforting to know that no matter what goes down in our society, there are always folk in the Breadbasket who are minding the store.

QUÉBEC

SIX HUNDRED MILES north of Montréal, the land is so wild and forbidding that even the moose won't put up with it. Around La Grande Rivière, where the snow begins to blow in mid-September, but stops soon after Christmas, when it becomes too cold even for that, the caribou begin their range.

The fishing is terrific in this crumpled, glacier-scoured plain. The land is so tattered with lakes and ponds that, despite the thousands of years the Indians and Eskimos — Cree and Innuit — have lived off it, there are untold numbers of waters where trout and pike have never been disturbed by man.

Before they are covered by winter, exquisitely fragile and microscopically detailed mosses hug the pink, marblelike granite and quartz. They are, in places, plush doormats, dark green and velvetlike. Nearby are cool patches of pale lichens, a green on the edge of ice-blue. Accented by the crimson of dying vines, they beckon you to a crouch, the better to study and marvel at their world, so impossibly tiny compared with the black spruce that tower sixty feet over them, taller than some office complexes, unclimbable, remote.

Across La Grande Rivière there are more majestic black spruce, in sparse stands. It's important to focus on the idea that those far trees are every bit as big as the ones that dwarf both you and the moss, because the sight of what has been done to this stretch of the northern bank of La Grande numbs the mind and blows out any sense of scale.

QUÉBEC   363

The trees on the far bank, despite their size, are mere after-thoughts of the landscape, which is thoroughly dominated by an improbable, incongruous, canyonlike staircase that has been blasted into the rock.

Try to imagine two football fields of solid granite, laid side by side, with a great deal of space to spare in the end zones. Imagine that on the right sideline, where the bleachers should be, there is a sheer rock wall the height of a three-story building, running the length of the field and more.

On the left sideline of the left-hand football field, there is a sheer drop-off as deep as the right-hand wall is high. Beyond the end zones, in either direction, are two more sheer granite walls. Each of these is three times as high as the sideline wall.

What you've got is a plain two hundred feet wide and four hundred feet long. The thirty-five-foot-high right sideline wall and the thirty-five-foot-deep left sideline drop-off exist because this plain is part of a terrace.

This terrace consists of eighteen of these plateaus, stepping smartly down from the top of the valley of La Grande Rivière to its shore — a distance of over half a mile, a sight that would be impressive enough, even if these giant's stairs were not sunk one hundred feet straight down into the rock of the slope. This hundred-foot drop is what yields the towering walls at the end zones of our metaphorical football fields.

Standing, looking at this broad, deep, manmade canyon in the wilderness, two and a half hours by prop-jet from civilization, you try to reach for some perspective. Craning your head back, you take another look at the tallest branches of your friend the spruce tree. You think of what it would take to fell this giant, cut it up into cordwood, and then haul it away, truckload after truck-load. It's a job that's within human comprehension, and the com-prehension is that the job would be hard. Hell, just getting the truck this far north would be hard. Then you look back to the canyon, which is to the tree as the tree is to the tiny lichen, and try to imagine what it took to carve those right angles and straight lines into the granite, and you can't do it. How do you move that much earth when on the *average* day of the year it's 7 degrees below freezing? How did they get the rock out of there? How much dynamite did that take? What kind of fundamental craziness did it require even to think of doing such a thing?

I relate all this by way of introducing Québec, the most improb-able, and yet most undeniable nation of the nine. Québec, a small collection of six million people, relatively few of whom speak English, surrounded by hundreds of millions of Americans and Canadians who do, built this canyon.

Yet the canyon, by the standards of Québec, is something of a yawn. It's a straightforward piece of work. All it is, is a safety device. It's a spillway to dump unwanted water out of the reservoir of a hydroelectric complex called LG 2. It's nothing compared to the dam that holds back the river. That's almost two miles long, and taller than the United Nations building is high. The tiny speck you see crawling along the top of it is a 110-ton, $400,000 Caterpillar 660 belly-dumping earth mover, the tires of which cost $7000 apiece and are taller than a man. The reservoir behind it covers more than a thousand square miles, which would drown the entire state of Rhode Island. To fill the reservoir, three rivers — the Eastmain, the Opinaca, and La Petite Opinaca, which used to quietly flow west into La Baie James — have been diverted by more dams so that they now flow north, into La Grande Rivière. If not another drop of water were added to it, it would still take Los Angeles more than forty years to drink the resultant lake dry.

If rock-moving awes you, consider the caverns and tunnels four hundred feet underground that house and serve the turbines. If ordinary dump trucks had been used to haul the rubble from the excavations, and one had been loaded every ten minutes, twenty-four hours per day, every day without letup, it would have taken over six years to clear these caves.

The main "machine room," where the dynamos are located, is something out of science fiction. It's reminiscent of the vast underground hangar in the movie *Star Wars*, from which the rebels launch their fighters in the final attack against the Empire. The most significant difference is that the real thing at LG 2 is a great deal larger than the imaginary cavern in the film. It's much longer than either the 110-story Sears Tower in Chicago or the World Trade Center in New York is tall.

It's fifteen stories high, and more than half that wide. A grid of man-sized high-intensity lamps glare down from the entire length and width of the roof, casting a strange, shadowless light. Metal screeches against metal as men hanging inside control cubes confidently and at high speed jockey machines that offer no obvious explanation of their function.

When all the generators housed in this room are spinning, they produce more energy than six nuclear reactors of the Three Mile Island type.

QUÉBEC 365

And this is just LG 2, which began to produce power in late 1979. There are also an LG 3 and LG 4 to come in phase one of La Baie James–La Grande Rivière project over the next few years. (LG 1 will come later.) And that's just phase one. Also on the drawing boards for this hydroelectric basin, which is the size of England, are installations at the unpoetically designated LA 1, LA 2, and EM 1 sites. And that's not all. La Grande Rivière de la Baleine — the Great River of the Whale — even farther north than La Grande Rivière, is scheduled to be tamed.

And this is just the new construction. Even without it, Hydro Québec, the Tennessee Valley Authority–sized outfit that is behind all this power, produced so much surplus electricity in the summer that it has a contract to help light and air-condition New York City.

And this is all done totally by the fiercely and proudly French province of Québec.

Québec's existence is utterly improbable. It's so unlikely that a French civilization should exist in North America hundreds of years after Louis XIV and Napoleon had written off the continent, that the Québécois have worked it into their nuclear-holocaust jokes. What races will survive World War III? The Chinese and the Québécois. The Chinese because there are so many of them, and the Québécois because if they've survived the last four hundred years, they'll survive anything. Québec is that part of North America that is so distinct from the rest, and against such odds, that it takes pride in serving to define what a nation is — and can be.

Québec, the largest province in Canada, is three times the size of France — even larger than Texas. Its population is larger than that of Ireland or Denmark. The cornerstone of its civilization is that, despite being surrounded by English-speakers, over 80 percent of the population speak French as their mother tongue, and the overwhelming majority speak no English at all. Québec is becoming relatively diversified, economically, with raw and semi-transformed materials, like pulp and paper, iron ore, lumber products, aluminum, asbestos, and copper, going to the States; manufactured goods and food products, ranging from textiles to yogurt, being traded within Canada; and high-technology know-how, the most prominent being hydroelectric and transportation expertise, getting exported to other continents. Québec is strategically located, controlling both sides of one of North America's greatest trading rivers, the St. Lawrence, which is the major way out of the Great Lakes to the sea.

By the standards of North America, the population is amazingly homogeneous. Most people can easily trace their roots back three hundred years or more to the arrival of their first ancestor in Québec. It's a place with a long-standing and well-founded sense of oppression at the hands both of the Anglophones (the local word for English-speakers) and the Catholic Church.

But most important, it's a place where the people feel like a nation.

In food, music, fashions, values, education, ways of thinking, politics, and other important ways, Québecois have become, or are becoming, in their famous slogan, *"maitres chez nous"* — masters in our own house.

Nationhood is such an obvious reality in the minds of the Québécois that most of the talk about the subject is by English-speakers explaining it to each other, not by Québécois themselves.

In Québec, for example, a discussion of whether the province will make it on its own economically, when it gains some sort of a divorce from Canada, is not considered a discussion about nationalism. It's regarded as a practical discussion about what one should do about this pre-existing nationalistic "French Fact." The point of this distinction is that it is logically possible to demonstrate that Québec could do badly, in economic terms, as a nation. But it would be dead wrong thus to draw the conclusion that nationalism does not, or should not, exist. For, ultimately, nationalism is a human, not an economic, reality.

Conversely, Québécois would point out, all the arguments in the world which lead to the conclusion that Canada makes sense economically cannot logically convince you that the diverse collection of entities called Canada is a nation.

It's clear as consommé to the Québécois how they are different from English Canada, not to mention the United States and, for that matter, France; and the rest of this chapter will examine these differences. What's less clear to them and, for that matter, some Americans, is in what sense English Canada is so different from the United States in the deepest, gut terms in which they describe nationalism. Some Québécois have come to refer to English Canada's collective identity as "mapism," not "nationalism." The idea is that, compared to Québec, the only thing Canadians hold in common are the same maps, with the same arbitrary surveyors' lines drawn on them. "Canada," the government of Québec has observed archly, "is obliged to use a certain ingenuity to define itself as a distinctive culture."

Thus, discussions of French-English separation in Canada start off on a fundamentally wacky basis. The minority says of the majority, as one Québec poet said, "Canada does not exist — just does not exist — other than on paper, and it *has* never existed and it *will* never exist."

When English Canada is forced by this argument into the incongruous position of attempting to explain what a poor Prince Edward Island fisherman has in common with an Alberta rancher who has oil interests, it starts skating dangerously close to the admission that they, for example, both watch reruns of "M*A*S*H," and both admire full-sized Chevrolets.

This strange situation did not arise overnight. In fact, it started almost four hundred years ago. When Champlain founded Québec in 1608, the Québec problem was born.

Today, in the Place Royale, the meticulously restored lower city of ancient mansions, pubs, docks, and warehouses at the foot of the cliffs of old Québec, there is a museum that houses a wall-sized map, entitled, in French, "Québec, Capital of an Empire."

Housed in an intimate, dramatically lit grotto reminiscent of a chapel, the map outlines a French-explored North America that is, in fact, quite awesome. From Québec it traces the western slope of the Alleghenies all the way to the Gulf Coast and then sweeps the continent to the west beyond the Rockies. It shows all the major river basins — the Ohio, the Illinois, the Mississippi, the Missouri.

It includes Toronto (originally Fort Rouillé, 1749); Pittsburgh (Fort Du Quesne, 1754); Uniontown, Pennsylvania (Fort Necessité, 1734); Detroit (Fort Ponchartrain du Détroit, 1701); Vicksburg, Mississippi (François); Natchez, Mississippi (Fort Rosalié, 1716); Montgomery, Alabama (Toulouse, 1714); Mobile (de la Mobile, 1701); New Orleans (Nouvelle Orléans, 1718); and Point Comfort, Texas (St.-Louis, 1695).

Also, Sault Sainte Marie, Green Bay (St.-Francois Xavier), Atchison, Kansas (Cavagnol); Prairie du Chien, Wisconsin (St.-Nicolas, 1690); Winnipeg (Fort Rouge, 1738); Dorothy, Alberta (La Jonquière, 1752); Memphis (Assomption, 1739), and, of course, St. Louis, Missouri.

Near the map, in a historical note pointedly not accompanied by an English translation, but carefully phrased at a level that an Anglo with a few years of high school French can struggle through, it's observed that for 150 years after Champlain established the French presence in America, explorers and merchants fanned out across the continent from Québec.

At its height, the note continues, the French Empire in "Amerique" covered almost all the continent with the exception of Florida and Mexico, which were occupied by the Spanish. As for the English, they hugged only the Atlantic coast south of the Gaspé Peninsula.

Unfortunately, France's interest in North America was short-sighted at best. Throughout the monarchies of the seventeenth and eighteenth centuries, France wanted maximum exploitation of the New World with minimum development. In the seventeenth-century France of Louis XIV, the object of government in Europe was the consolidation of central authority and the reduction of the autonomy of satellite powers. The last thing that was wanted was encouragement of a Québec that could stand on its own, if critical ties to the homeland were severed. In the eighteenth century, France was characterized by regimes that could be referred to, in their relations with the New World, only as corrupt, rapacious, stupid, and a few decades away from being on the wrong end of a guillotine.

Thus, by the mid-1700s, there were nearly fifty thousand French-speakers in the land that would become Québec, but the society in which they had organized themselves was oddly constructed so as to be better at surviving the challenges to come than it was at resisting them.

The French settlers, or *habitants*, made some major adjustments to the institutions and patterns of thought of the Old World in their first 150 years.

For one thing, the traditional French political tripod of manor lord, priest, and peasant was severely damaged, and with it the link to secular authority. In a harsh environment like Québec's, the *seigneur* — the fellow who had received the land grant from the Crown and who in turn subdivided it among the habitants — was a poor imitation of the protective nobility of feudal France. He was hardly in a position to ensure the settlers protection from the startling new range of adversities of the St. Lawrence wilderness. So, in the face of ugly winters and unhappy Iroquois, the habitants organized themselves cooperatively, rather than hierarchically, even altering the centuries-old pattern of laying out farms so that it would be easier for one neighbor to help another rather than rely on the civil authorities.

Under such an arrangement, there wasn't a great deal of need for a bureaucracy. Social and agricultural affairs were taken care of informally, within the limits of the settlement made up of equals, and without a great deal of attention paid to the peasant ways of Europe.

In fact, as the habitants developed this new culture, they began to see themselves as different from the other French-speakers — the adventurers and urban imperial administrators, military men, and merchants who were still European, still not committed to North America.

Thus, two societies developed in New France, one metropolitan, educated, literate, and dependent for markets, wages, and ideas on the ties to the old country. The other, the ancestors of the bulk of today's Québécois, was self-sufficient and, except for the maddening habit of thinking, acting, and speaking in French, utterly North American. While the habitants, for example, might not have had a clue as to how to behave amid French sophisticates, they certainly had some ideas about how to behave around, say, a North American bear, a development not unusual in pioneer societies.

As the habitants thus assigned less importance to life in a secular municipality, the ever-present parish priest moved into the power vacuum.

The priest was literate, which meant he was needed whenever a legal document like a will or a bill of sale was required. He was the guardian of recorded history — the records of births, marriages, and deaths. (In fact, he was so good at maintaining the public records that, to this day, Québec's genealogical records are among the finest in the world.) The demands made on him as a spiritual overseer were brisk, because the French settlers were notorious for letting the good times roll, a cultural trait nurtured to this day.

But the key element in this march toward the future was that the priest's first allegiance was not to France. Ultramontanism was a very hot issue at this time. It held, essentially, that there should be one Church, independent of who was in power in what country. The Jesuits, specifically, of New France were great believers in this theory, so maintaining the culture of the empire was in no way as important to them as was reporting directly to the home office in Rome.

This was the kind of rickety social structure which was smashed by the British when they conquered the French colony by force of arms.

The taking of the city of Québec in 1759, when the British general Wolfe overcame the defender, Montcalm, on the Plains of Abraham, resulted, in 1760, in the ending of a series of border wars between the two European powers. The Conquest also settled, for exactly two centuries, the fate of the Québécois: an overwhelmingly French society was to be ruled by the English.

The lack of resistance on the part of the habitants to this arrangement after the Conquest was based on the burdensome treatment they had received at the hands of the old French ruling class, coupled with the amazingly tolerant, for its era, attitude of the British.

On the one hand, to the habitants who were well into their second and third generation as North Americans by now, France was becoming increasingly irrelevant. The old country had never really embraced New France except as a get-rich-quick scheme. In fact, the habitants had come to associate the transient French with scandals, extortions, and internal bickerings associated with the lining of their own pockets even at the expense of advancing the cause of the empire.

One of the major reasons the habitants gave of their lives and resources in the fight with their French cousins against the British before the Conquest was a misguided self-interest. They believed that with the French in power, all they had to deal with was the burden of corruption. With the British in power, they firmly believed, their language, religion, and way of life would be destroyed.

But the British, after the fighting, offered a canny deal that, for all practical purposes, started to freeze the development of Québec society right where it was. All sides ended up accepting it with gratitude. The habitants got to keep what they wanted — their rural French North American society. The French elite was saved from instant ruin, although in short order they found themselves in decline, as some merchants and administrators left for greener pastures and others were crippled by the disruption of their lines of credit and sources of goods on the continent. The British got the peace and quiet that they would have loved to obtain from their thirteen Atlantic colonies to the south. And the big winner under the new English Protestant regime, ironically, was the Roman Catholic Church, which became the executor of this deal, and thus, in effect, the real wielder of secular power over the vast majority of the inhabitants of Québec.

"The political authority of a Protestant society," writes Alfred Dubuc, "thus became the defender of the values and institutions of the Catholic Church, while the religious authorities of French-Canadian society upheld, in the eyes of their flocks, British institutions."

The influential *independentist* sociologist-historian Marcel

Rioux, in drawing political observations from these develop-ments, says, "After the Conquest, Québec society, far from contin-uing to develop like other Western societies of the era, becoming industrial, urbanized, and secular, on the contrary draws inward upon its popular and rural elements and, instead of becoming more urbanized, becomes more folklike. We observe, among other phenomena, a greater predominance of agricultural occupations; a greater scattering of the population among the rural parishes; more social homogeneity; reinforcement of moral and religious norms; less important internal stratification and differentiation; and finally, a more restricted territorial, occupational, and up-ward mobility."

And that's a polite way of saying it. What you had, until the "Quiet Revolution" began in 1960, was a society that, in hind-sight, was amazingly backward and ingrown by North American standards.

In fact, many Québécois now date the dark ages of their society not from the Conquest of 1760, but from the 1830s, when the dem-ocratic liberal secular elite from within the Québécois society be-gan to try to wrest power away from the Church and the English. This resulted in armed revolution by 1837, but the *Patriotes*, as they were called, were defeated by the same old coalition: French Catholic denunciation from the pulpit, and professional English military tacticians on the ground. It was after the crushing of the Patriotes that the Québécois, while still far and away the major-ity in Québec, began to think of themselves less as one of the races destined to rule North America than as a minority. In order to convince themselves that their survival was worthwhile, they immersed themselves in their ancient traditions, and thus was launched 150 years of petrifying conservatism.

It's tough to draw a parallel between the Québécois experience of the last two centuries and anything in the rest of North Amer-ican history, although it has been tried.

Pierre Vallières, a leader of the now-defunct radical, terrorist FLQ — Front de Libération du Québec — wrote a book, while in prison in the late 1960s, called *White Niggers of America*. "To be a 'nigger' in America is to be not a man but someone's slave," it reads. "For the rich white man of Yankee America, the nigger is a sub-man. Even the poor whites consider the nigger their infe-rior. They say: 'to work as hard as a nigger,' 'to smell like a nig-ger,' 'as dangerous as a nigger,' 'as ignorant as a nigger.'"

He then goes on to expound a liberation struggle that equates the French-Canadian population with "niggers, exploited men, second-class citizens."

There surely are vivid comparisons to be drawn between American blacks and French Canadians. Every Québécois has his share of stories. The most pointed, perhaps, are the ones about Anglo bosses demanding that their underlings "speak white." Separatist Parti Québécois founder, René Lévesque, once referred to his English opponents as his "white Rhodesians." There are those who have been spat on or beaten up for speaking French in their own land. There are the jobs denied and school doors closed even to English-speakers with a French accent. There's the chic Québécoise refused service in a restaurant or boutique in the heart of her home town of Montréal for not speaking English. The workers in Anglo-owned asbestos mines brutally suppressed by thugs paid for by their own government. The "two solitudes" of English and French lived side by side for generations, never communicating with each other. Alarmingly, there was also the built-in sense of inferiority that might cause a grandmother to refuse to buy a stove built in Québec because if it was built by her own kind, "it can't be any good."

But that comparison doesn't completely satisfy. To get a sense of the Québécois, you have to throw in a little American Indian, for example.

By North American standards, the Québécois have been here since the dawn of time. Not only were they entrenched well before the Pilgrims landed (as were, for that matter, the Spanish in Sante Fe), but the whole society, from the Conquest to the present, is remarkable in the relationship it has to the land.

I found myself in a high-rent economic think tank in Montréal in 1979, in casual conversation with a quick, bright, bilingual Québécoise. She happened to ask how a plodding Anglophone like myself had come by such a French name, and, showing off the genealogical research I had done, I told her my great-great-great-great-great-great-grandfather had helped found the town of Boucherville, across the river and slightly downstream from Montréal. In fact, I said, puffing out my feathers, I was about certain that I'd found the house he'd built in 1670, which was still standing.

"Oh!" she said in all seriousness. "You mean you've been denied your patrimony?"

Patrimony is such an odd word in North American English that it wasn't until hours later that it dawned on me that she was expressing sincere sympathy for my having to put up with strangers living in my eighth-generation ancestor's house.

The point is that, though many things have changed for the Québécois in this century, the acres of Québec, its rivers and mountains and towns, are still integral to their nationalism. Even to those natives who shrug at the cold, rocky soil and deplore the ancient agrarian ways, it simply makes no sense to talk about a collective identity that does not reflexively relate to this land, their land.

In the early 1960s, when the Quiet Revolution was beginning in Québec, a poet and songwriter named Gilles Vigneault came out with "Mon Pays" ("My Country"). It blew minds the way Bob Dylan's "The Times They Are a-Changin'" electrified Anglo young people at about the same time. And it was about nationhood and the land. "My country," he sang, "is winter." It's like reading the words of original Native Americans from the last century talking about the buffalo and the Plains and themselves as inseparable concepts. One is not, without the other.

By the same token, Québec has had its own trail of broken promises.

Anglos were not the only people with an American Dream. Québec had one, too, and it also was one of being an American people, with culture, values, and language spreading from sea to shining sea. This didn't end with the Conquest of Québec, for the French continued to push on like the English and Americans to conquer the continent. In fact, at the time of Confederation, in 1867, when English-speaking Ontario and French-speaking Québec united in an uneasy union called Canada, and then convinced two eastern colonies to join them as provinces, not only were there abundant French-speaking Acadians in the Atlantic provinces, but there were major settlements of intermarried Indian Québécois, called Métis, in the prairies. In 1869, when the land they considered their own was bought by Canada from the Hudson's Bay Company, these French-speaking Métis, led by Louis Riel, rebelled against the territorial government and demanded provincial status with protection for land rights and the French language. It was granted, and Manitoba became a province in 1870. When their land rights were threatened again in Saskatchewan, they rebelled again, but this time they were crushed by Canadian troops, and Louis Riel was put to death.

The execution, which took on the proportions of a martyrdom, marks the clinching embattlement of the French people. For them it soon became clear that their future horizons would not be broad if the rest of Canada had anything to say about it. Although the British North America Act, which set up Confederation, stated that existing Catholic (that is, French) and Protestant (that is, English) school systems were to be maintained, in 1871 New Brunswick, the heart of Acadia, dropped sectarian public schools in blatant violation of that core treaty, on which the ink was hardly dry. No one stopped it.

In 1890, Manitoba, the land of the Métis, did the same thing, and, though the federal government at first tried to keep the dual schools, it soon capitulated to the provincial government. In 1905, when Alberta and Saskatchewan were created, the federal government tried to set up the mandated dual school systems, but caved in to local English opposition. In 1912, Ontario limited to the first two grades the use of French as the language of instruction; in 1914 it closed some publicly supported French-language schools, and the federal government made no attempt to stop it.

The list goes on. In both World War I and II, the Québécois had no reason whatsoever to be interested in fighting and dying for England. Thus, they voted on each occasion to allow Canada to join the fray on the condition that there would be no draft — that such sacrifices as had to be made should be made by those who wished to volunteer for it. That promise, too, was soon broken.

Thus did a once-continental people find themselves backed into a reservationlike situation, despite every promise.

But even leavening the black analogy with that of the American Indian doesn't completely relate Québec to the rest of the continent's experience. Québécois have a lot in common with Hispanics. For one thing, obviously, they speak a language that isn't English. For another, they share a religion that was despised for generations by Anglo Protestants.

In fact, Arthur R. M. Lower, writing about Québec in 1900, said, "In Québec, the first loyalty was to the race and to the church. If a choice had to be made between the two . . . the race would be put first. French Canadians were so peculiarly a band of blood brothers, they had come through so much since the Conquest, were so conscious of the hostility of the English, that there is nothing surprising in this devotion to the 'race.' It was devotion stimulated by every possible device in order to assure the French what has already seemed to them the one thing needful, '*la Survivance.*' " This passage would hardly sound strange to Mexican-Americans. They sometimes refer to themselves as "La Raza," the

Race. In Texas, the Hispanic political party is called La Raza Unida.

But beyond that, Québec's history has important parallels to Hispanic homelands.

The national inferiority complex of both Mexico and Québec, for example, was strongly shaped by military defeats inflicted by Anglos. Mexico's trauma was losing California, Nevada, Utah, Arizona, Colorado, New Mexico, and Texas during the 1840s. Québec's was its Conquest.

Both Cuba and Québec saw their economies ripped off by Anglos. In the case of Cuba, it was exploitation of its rich agriculture. For the Québécois, it was the sale of its minerals and timber at a fraction of their true worth.

Both Puerto Rico and Québec are involved in strained confederations with Anglo governments. Both have outspoken independence movements.

But perhaps most important, the proposed solutions to Québec's problems have similarities with these countries. Without even going into the question of revolution, which Québécois seem to consider unthinkable, there are parallels.

For example, as John D. Harbron, an Anglo Latin American scholar has pointed out, Parti Québécois economic pronouncements owe a debt to Mexico: "Québec [were it to achieve separation] would not be the first North American republic to establish state capitalism based on a strong nationalist ideology. Mexico has developed such an economy since the 1930s, with control of foreign ownership and state intervention in such key industries as energy, transportation and communications."

There are indeed close similarities between Pemex, the Mexican national oil corporation, and Hydro Québec. They both control vast energy resources. They are both mainstays of their respective economies. They were both created by the wresting of power from Anglos via nationalization. And the creators of each were told that such backward people as Mexicans or Québécois couldn't possibly handle such sophisticated institutions.

One of the foremost "radicals" pushing the creation of Hydro Québec in the early sixties later said, "I remember this middle-level executive [at one of the companies about to be nationalized] saying, 'Do you people really think you can run this company as well as we can?' He was so filled with contempt. Of course he was English-speaking and the company was English-owned, as they all were. I remember thinking, 'You bloody so-and-so. You're just like the British were a few years ago, saying the Egyptians could never run the Suez Canal.' It was the same paternalistic contempt — the colonial master speaking to the backward native. 'We'll show you, you bastard,' I thought.''

And they did. The name of the man telling the above story of when he was a young government minister is René Lévesque, who, in 1976, took over the very government of Québec with his Parti Québécois. His reminiscences appeared in a very long article, carried by an anxious *New York Times*, that explained to English-speaking North America where he was taking Québec.

Hydro Québec, like Pemex, is a source of great national pride not only to politicians, but to ordinary citizens. If Mexicans now take great satisfaction in sticking the high cost of their petroleum in the ear of Anglo North America, and even greater pleasure in the fact that their oil is being pumped by their people, in their language, the parallel for Québec would be Manic 5.

Manic 5 was the name of a hydroelectric project on the Manicouagan River built in the late 1960s. Although dwarfed by later achievements at La Baie James, when it was being built, Manic 5 became part of the Québec national myth. Songs were sung about it; legends told. Men went off to work on it as if on a crusade.

As the novelty of proving that Québécois are capable of performing great feats wears off, working for Hydro Québec has come to be considered merely a good job. Hardly a heroic one.

Nonetheless, Hydro Québec still holds the capacity to startle the well-meaning person who knows the twenty-first century when he sees it, but who always rather thought it would speak English. For example, in La Baie James, if you don't know that *boyaux d'incendie* are fire hoses, and a blaze breaks out, you're one crisped Anglo, because that's the only way the emergency equipment is marked.

There is one last minority with which Québécois have a great deal in common, and that is the Dixie white. While it may seem incongruous that a people like the Québécois could have something in common with blacks, Indians, Hispanics, and the heirs to the Confederacy, it's nonetheless true. A lot of the problems of the Québécois, like those of unreconstructed Mississippians, were their own goddamn fault.

Not only did Québec, before the 1960s, like Dixie, spend a lot of time being ingrown, insular, backward, backward-looking, and religion-ridden, but both blamed their condition on their conquerors while lovingly nurturing their plight through local institutions folk subscribed to almost unquestioningly. Furthermore, modern Québécois, like modern Southerners, realize this, and admit it when there are no Yankees around.

At the turn of the twentieth century, many Québécois rejoiced that their land was less than industrialized, thus less materialistic and more spiritual. The boast was a thanks to God that, rather than being the stokers of a foundry, the French were the guardians of the flame of Faith. In the twenties and thirties, according to sociologists, bishops would write to the few French-Canadian factory owners, asking them to pay low salaries to their employees. The hope was that the workers would return to the land, the heavily romanticized rural life, over which the Church — the keeper of the culture — had maximum control.

In 1936, one curé, one pastor sermonized: "You won't believe me. I went to Montréal. And around midnight there were some people walking on the sidewalk! What on earth were they doing there? Thank God you [the faithful] were asleep. You are going to heaven because you lead a normal life. You breathe fresh air. You go to bed. But Montréal! Those people will all go to hell!"

This kind of stuff now makes Québécois wince in exactly the way a Georgian does on hearing old hymns to the "southern way of life."

It's amazing how fast things have changed since the Quiet Revolution, Québec's own "Prague Spring." A people that once identified themselves as rural, Catholic, obedient, long-suffering losers have awakened to the fact that they are urban, industrialized, capable, in power in their own land — and in serious danger of having to take responsibility for their own future.

The awakening was presaged by the death of Québec's premier Maurice Duplessis in the fall of 1959. A Huey Long–like despot with a penchant for handing over Québec's national resources to Americans and English Canadians for a tiny fraction of what they were bringing in neighboring provinces, Duplessis ruled with a feudal iron hand, the last embodiment of the theory that a subdued Québec was the best of all possible worlds and the ultimate flowering of French culture. This despite the fact that even within their own land Québécois made less money per capita than just about any other ethnic group save the poor despised Indians.

In June 1960, after a brief interregnum, a liberal, Jean Lesage, was elected premier, and the water broke. "The Quiet Revolution," says Rioux, "was more a mental liberation, a development of critical attitudes towards men and affairs than it was revolutionary action per se. It was, above all, a re-evaluation of ourselves, a reappearance of a spirit of independence and of enquiry which had been smothered in the snows of a hundred year winter. Québécois grew confident that they could change many things if they really wanted to. They began to shrug off the fatalism of a conquered minority who had come to think that they were born to lose."

The first thing that happened was the take-over by the Québec provincial government of the French public schools, hitherto controlled by the Church. With that was born the attempt to shift a system geared to educating students for, at best, the nineteenth century, into one that was, in fact, going to produce kids who would take power in the twenty-first.

In 1962, under the slogan "masters in our own house," came the nationalization of the electric companies and the creation of Hydro Québec. René Lévesque, the young Liberal cabinet minister who fought so strenuously for provincial control of this, the bedrock of the economy, thus created in Hydro Québec a consumer for the French technicians, managers, and engineers who, it was hoped, the new school system would soon produce.

In 1967, the year of the hundredth anniversary of the Confederation of Canada, Charles de Gaulle, in the heart of the French province of Québec, cried *"Vive le Québec libre!"*— Long live free Québec! — thus not only straining relations between Canada and France for years to come, but, frankly, confusing the hell out of most Québécois, who hadn't quite gotten that far in their thinking yet.

In 1968, as pressure for a solution to "the Québec problem" mounted, dashing, formidable Pierre Trudeau was elected prime minister of Canada, with a mandate to keep Québec in the federation. The same year, Lévesque founded the Parti Québécois. Gathering together the shards of previous independence movements that had had narrow appeal, and more of a political-education function than anything else, Lévesque forged the Parti as a clear-cut attempt to gain power and then independence.

In 1970, the social upheaval in Québec reached a crisis. Extremists, who didn't believe change was occurring in as rapid and sweeping a fashion as desirable, had punctuated their thoughts with terrorist bombings. But in October 1970, the FLQ kidnaped a diplomat and a provincial cabinet minister. The federal government declared martial law in Québec, and the Canadian Army occupied the province. Civil liberties were suspended. Hundreds of arrests and searches were conducted without warrant. The next day the cabinet minister was found dead in the trunk of the car in which he had been abducted.

Canada is a peaceful country, and these events were more shocking even than Kent State in the United States. To this day, both sides are so traumatized that, no matter what happens in the Québec drama, there seems to be an unspoken agreement that further violence, either in the cause of revolution or its suppression, is unthinkable.

The violence did establish, however, that something uncrushable was astir in Québec. Separation was clearly going to be on the agenda. In 1976, the Parti Québécois surprised everyone, including itself, by sweeping into power in the provincial election. (Lévesque himself didn't think he'd win until 1977.) Its platform was that Québec was a nation, had always been a nation, would take into its own hands its national affairs, and anybody who said it couldn't be done could go to hell.

And, in fact, now even the Québécois are sometimes awed by the change they've made take place.

Less than a decade ago, Québec's language, for example, was scorned by Anglos who dismissed it as a patois that did not deserve to be called French, much less learned.

But since French has been legislated as the sole official language of business and government in Québec, you can find a University of Québec economist scanning the front page of *La Presse* and saying, "Here. Look at this. This is the revolution."

Indeed, the story he pointed to was amazing. It reported that the number of English-speaking parents attempting to enroll their children in total-immersion French public schools was ten times what the school system was prepared for.

As Michel Roy, a prominent Montréal editor, noted:

I know a lot of people who are learning French like mad. It's fantastic to see that. They want to integrate into this society. One reason is economic. But another reason is that they feel unhappy when they are rejected if they do not speak French. And more than ever today in any public place one is asked would you parles francais, please.

Yet another reason is that the French society in Canada in this turmoil of the last twenty years is something interesting. I know many young lawyers and doctors in the English community who just like to talk to the young French-speaking people, to go to the French theater, to read books and get involved. It's just fun. Even in Toronto, people find it interesting and will try to read French, just to see what's going on.

Another measure of how far things have come is how rapidly the Church has lost power. Since its authority as an elite was inextricably intertwined with the old secular order, it crumbled under the assault on other values. Not only did it lose communicants in droves, but it lost nuns and priests at a rate so extraordinary that Québécois now feel a little sheepish at how long the Church was considered a bastion of their nationalism. The change suggests strongly that the Church's foundations had been rotting for a long time, and the only reason it stood so long was for lack of attack. The Québécois know well the wisdom of the line from the Pogo comic strip: "We have met the enemy, and he is us." The speed with which the Church lost influence in Québec is still as much of a puzzle as the speed with which Islam gained power in Iran. As one anthropologist observed:

Religion became another cultural trait. It was never discussed. There was no opposition. It was the thing to do. It was a given.

When spring comes, the habitant discards his mittens. The Quiet Revolution came, and religion became a thing of the past.

In my village, nobody had ever met a Protestant. You didn't have to fight for your religion. When a cultural trait becomes so ingrained, so naturalized, it no longer means what it was supposed to: revolutionizing your life. It was a custom. Something you had to do.

The anthropologist could take a great Gallic delight in recounting in ribald detail the manner in which, even in the forties and fifties, and even in the small rural parishes, Church teachings on such matters as eating fish on Friday, abortion, fornication, moderation in the use of alcohol, and respect for the parish priest were routinely ignored.

You have to remember [he said], what Mass was. Sunday was a holiday, and you put your good clothes on, and you go to see your neighbors, and you arrive as late as you can. In one village [near Québec City], there were these big processions and the priest said everybody had to be there. Everybody took his place in the procession, so I took a place in the procession, and there were two files. The priest was walking down the rows, and, when he was at the far end, the people near me were laughing and telling dirty stories. It was terrible. The priest came near us, and he was telling the beads, and everybody bowed his head, and when he was gone, they'd go back to telling their dirty stories.

One of the more interesting results of Québécois becoming more secular is that an important characteristic of their old national identity has disappeared: their high birthrate.

Besides its geographical identity, one of the reasons that Québec is a nation, rather than merely a cultural subgroup, like Boston Irish or San Francisco Chinese, is that there are so many of them relative to the population of the rest of Canada.

Québec, with over six million people, has 27 percent of Canada's population, which is twice as big a share as either blacks or Hispanics have of the total U.S. population.

Not only is the group sizable, but for generations it was dramatically reinforced by the introduction of tiny new members of the society. "During the last two centuries," demographer Jacques Henripin notes, "world population has multiplied by three, European population by four, and French-Canadian population by eighty, in spite of net emigration which can be estimated roughly at eight hundred thousand."

In the thirties, the population was growing so fast that the French language was gaining ground in Canada, and it was generally expected that New Brunswick would soon become the second province to have a French-speaking majority. At the time of the 1941 census, persons claiming French as their mother tongue made up only 26 percent of the adult population of Canada, but over 36 percent of all children younger than four years. Had these conditions continued, French would have become the major language in Canada.

But today, that amazing cultural condition, tied to rural and religious values, in which to be Québécois often was synonymous with being from a family of six, ten, twelve children or more, is disappearing. The birthrate now has plummeted to zero population growth levels. There is serious political significance to that because, as one pundit put it, Québécois used to have to wait until the census results came to know if their nation continued to exist. If there were no French population growth to match the inevitable losses to emigration and cultural assimilation, Québec could disappear in the fashion of Louisiana Frenchness.

As a result, Québec has an intense interest in running its own policy on the considerable number of immigrants it receives. Already, the language laws force the children of the Italians, Poles, Vietnamese, Africans, and so many others who move to the province, to be educated in French, not English. This is meant to ensure that the proportion of French-speakers in the province does not decline.

The continued attractiveness of Québec for immigrants, despite the fact that, all things being equal, they would prefer to learn English, the language usually associated with opportunity in North America, speaks to the question of economics.

In the sixties [says the head of the biggest bank in Québec, stepping out of his chauffeured blue Mercedes diesel], people who were emotionally committed to federalism, for all kinds of good reasons, launched the argument that it was totally and absolutely impossible for an economy the size of Québec's to survive independently.

That line of argument is wrong. If you say that a country the size of Québec, with a population the size of Québec, is much too small by world standards, then it doesn't take much to extrapolate and find that Canada doesn't make much sense, either.

It's obvious that there is no economic argument that can demonstrate that you *have* to be federated, or you *have* to be sovereignty-associated, or whatever. What economics can tell you is what the costs are.

The "whatever" the banker referred to, of course, is independence. But the "sovereignty-association" is the Parti Québécois' proposal to create a new relationship with Canada in which Québec would share with that nation a common currency and a dedication to a lack of internal travel restrictions, but in everything else, Québec would be a different color on the geopolitical map. It would have complete control over a long list of its own affairs, ranging from taxation to diplomacy to military affairs.

The *Péquistes*, as Parti Québécois adherents are known, favor sovereignty-association because they realize that, though the Québécois desire for an end to inferiority is strong, it is less than suicidal. The polls repeatedly show that, while the people support a new political arrangement, they've gotten used to eating regularly and watching their color television, and they're not in favor of losing what they've got.

In May 1980, in fact, a referendum asking the Québécois whether they wanted to go their own way was soundly defeated.

The question, surely, was unique in North American politics: "The government of Québec has made public its proposal to negotiate a new agreement with the rest of Canada, *based on the equality of nations.* (Emphasis added.)

"This agreement would enable Québec to acquire exclusive power to make its own laws, levy its taxes, and establish relations abroad — and at the same time maintain with Canada an economic association including a common currency."

The *nons* beat the *ouis*, 60 percent to 40 percent. The Québec Anglo vote was 87 percent against. But even among French-speakers, it lost. An immense women's *non* vote turned the tide.

But interestingly enough, by losing this battle, the Parti Québécois may end up winning the war.

Predicting the future of Québec's relationships with the rest of the continent is an idiot's game, which I won't indulge in. But I will report one scenario that achieves a certain level of plausibility.

The following is history:

Part of the reason the vote on sovereignty-association went so overwhelmingly *non* is that Prime Minister Trudeau, himself a Québécois, eloquently promised the people of Québec, in French, that if they turned down the PQ proposal, he would personally guarantee that the Canadian constitution would be overhauled. In this overhaul, he promised, many of Québec's concerns would be affirmatively dealt with in the context of a "renewed federalism."

True to his word, in September 1980, he called a constitutional convention, at which he and the provincial premiers attempted to become the fathers of a new, stronger Canadian federation.

It was a complete bust. Trudeau wanted to create a Canada in which even more power was centralized in Ottawa. All the other provinces in this, the most loosely confederated Western democracy, beginning to see the wisdom of Québec's arguments, pushed for more autonomy to settle their own affairs internally. Québec's Lévesque, interestingly, played the role of sober statesman at the convention. He got high marks later for bargaining in good faith. It was the *other* Canadian provinces that could not arrive at any kind of agreement. Without making too much of this, their disagreements broke out along the lines predicted by the Nine Nations theory.

Here is where the scenario starts:

Trudeau, an ardent federalist, so this thinking goes, will push to write his own centralist constitution, and then go over the heads of the provincial premiers by appealing directly to Canada's voters to accept it.

If this ploy fails, then Canada, either as a matter of practical fact, or as a result of independence votes in Alberta and the rest of the West, will be put on the path of increased separatism. After all, even if the Québec vote failed, it *did* establish a precedent for a vote on independence elsewhere in Canada.

Thus, as early as 1983, Canada could start the path of dividing according to interest groups: the New England–like Maritimes going one way, Québec going another, Foundry-like Ontario going a third, the Empty Quarter environs of Alberta going a fourth, and Ecotopian British Columbia and Breadbasket-like Saskatchewan and Manitoba trying to figure out with which neighbor to align themselves, or whether to go their respective ways.

If this scenario were to hold up, the ironies would be boundless. For one thing, it would be unlikely that these newly decentralized provinces would push for U.S. statehood. Why trade one kind of federalism for another?

Another irony is that if Canada had simply let Québec go when it started agitating, the rest of English-speaking Canada might have found enough in common never to push things so far as to have that de-unifying constitutional convention.

Don't get me wrong. Trudeau's "renewed federalism" still could win out. Nationhood is a strong concept. Just because the concept "Canada" is not the most logical one in the world — because of the way its population hugs the United States border, it's been compared to a farm two hundred miles long and one mile wide — doesn't mean it does not retain great emotional power, even among the Québécois. In fact, the "Québécois" have only recently called themselves that. They used to refer to themselves as "les Canadiens." The others were "les Anglais." Canadian national symbols, from the maple leaf to the beaver to the national anthem, "O Canada," were developed by French Canadians for French Canadians. Even the federalists among French Canadians, such as Claude Ryan and Pierre Trudeau himself, strongly assert themselves as Québec nationalists, nonetheless. No, I don't completely understand, either.

This Canadian nationalist fact deeply depresses the die-hard independentists along the university-surrounded Rue St.-Denis in Montréal. But it's a reality that underscores the importance of calculating the real costs of a free Québec or any other "nation."

Calculations like these are so complicated and such fascinating pieces of futurology that one suspects some economists want to see Québec's independence just to compare it to their computer models.

The questions raised in such an analysis serve to define nationalism. For example, federalists claim that Québec now receives more in federal tax money than it pays out. Péquistes say that, though that may be so, the nature of the payments is in welfare checks, and this reflects the poverty caused by centuries of economic oppression. If Québec were to run its own affairs, they say, its money could be used to create jobs, *à la* Hydro Québec. Even if such an attempt were to fail, they add, it would be the Québécois trying and failing, rather than some Anglos whose motives Québécois have every reason to suspect.

Federalists, especially in the far West, say that Québec should be thankful for the markets they provide. After all, they claim, if Canada didn't exist, it would be a lot cheaper for British Columbia to buy its clothing from California or from Asia than from the province of Québec. Péquistes say that, first of all, in the twentieth century, a unified Canada is a British dream, not a French one. If British Columbia wants to create a customs union with Seattle, rather than with the new nation of Québec, fine. It may be economically disruptive, but not as big a blow to Québec as would be the emotional devastation that would grip English Canadians at the idea that their Atlantic provinces would become the eastern portion of another Pakistan. (Pakistan, before half the country revolted and became Bangladesh, also had an East and a West completely separated by another country, India.)

For that matter, a completely independent Québec would be free to explore American markets and tailor its customs policy to the possibilities it found there. If British Columbia wished to open its borders to cheap processed food from the western United States, it would be equally possible for Québec to nurture new import-export relationships in the eastern United States, not to mention Europe and Africa, which it can't now.

There is that tacit political alliance between Québec and the western province of Alberta on this score. When oil-rich Alberta locked horns with the rest of Canada over whether it should sell its petroleum to the other provinces at the world price or at a subsidized rate, remember that Québec, despite its having to import all its hydrocarbons, supported Alberta. Provinces must not be denied control of their resources, Québec solemnly declared, and that includes to whom it sells and at what price.

Speaking of oil, say the federalists, what about the fact that Québec doesn't have any?

That question really frosts the Péquistes. Why not, they ask, point out that we have no elephants? No coconuts? What does that have to do with nationalism? Québec does import oil at the rate of a European country like, say, Germany. But the medium-term energy outlook is brighter for Québec than for a great number of industrialized nations.

Obviously, for openers, Québec does have all that hydro power. While, admittedly, that won't run a car or a jet, it's so cheap in Québec that 80 percent of the new homes built there are electrically heated, and older homes are converting to electric heat at the rate of thirty thousand or forty thousand units a year. Industries like wood pulp are switching over to electricity to dry their products. What's just beginning to dawn on Québec, too, is the magnitude of the opportunity it could have, exporting this electricity to the Foundry and New England. Already Québec exports hundreds of millions of dollars of power, much of it to Consolidated Edison, the much-maligned New York City utility. And that's surplus power. Con Ed needs electricity most during the summer months to run air conditioners. Québec has lots to give at that time, since Hydro Québec's big season is in winter.

But there's another big export possibility. New England has systematically denied itself new nuclear plants, oil refineries, and even its own large-scale hydroelectric developments, on environmental grounds. Its power needs in the 1980s and 1990s will be so expensive that it may pay Hydro Québec to start damming rivers from which Québec itself doesn't need the power but New England does.

Hydro Québec already supplies Vermont with 7 percent of its power, and talks are under way with other parts of New England, notably Massachusetts and Rhode Island, about their needs.

Nor is that the only way energy can be exported. The most expensive raw material in the manufacture of aluminum is energy. With aluminum in demand for everything from lightweight engine blocks, which increase an automobile's fuel efficiency, to subway cars and airplanes, aluminum could easily become a key Québec energy export.

In fact, economists already point to transportation as one of the most important factors in the development of Québec's economy — the sector, along with services, that will help replace Québec's dependence on the old, slave-wages, rural-craft-like industries like shoes and textiles.

•   •   •

Québec, as a nation, as a French, North American, independent, proud nation, is such an odd quirk of history that it's possible to spend a portion of an evening sipping cognac in the grand old Hôtel Château Frontenac, pondering how this could possibly have come to be.

Below the romantic, turreted, and bespiked castle of the Château, in the ancient quarter of Québec City, the seagulls loiter, wings outstretched, oblivious of the imposing and impossibly steep heap of green-copper-roofed granite and brick hotel entrenched on the cliffs of the old city of Québec.

They circle the restored Batterie Royale, a collection of black, muzzle-loading cannon poking through imposing bulwarks of mud and twig. These hulking antiques, on their wooden carriages with wooden wheels, command a clear, 150 degree field of fire, up and down the narrow St. Lawrence, over which the mighty freighters now glide, tugs at their side.

The presence of the guns invites — demands — speculation about how easy it would be to drop a tanker in this channel, blocking Great Lakes shipping as thoroughly as a wreck in the Suez Canal disrupted oil shipments from the Middle East.

An explanatory plaque — in French only, of course — says that in the reign of Louis XIV, Frontenac, governor-general of New France, installed here a similar battery of cannon in the defense of Québec. This artillery came on hard times, through history, until 1977, when archeologists restored the site. On July 3, 1978, the 370th anniversary of La Capitale, these ten pieces of artillery which I see before me, of the model of 1733, were dedicated at this Batterie Royale, in the name of the government of France. Master of ceremonies, René Lévesque, premier of Québec.

Far above this hardware, a bar called the Saint-Laurent, at the bow of the hotel named after Governor-General Frontenac, looms over a panoramic view of the river from atop the Plains of Abraham, where this Québec nonsense started almost four hundred years ago. It's a handsome, wooden, round room with a ceiling carved like the spokes of a ship's wheel.

The foul-weather shutters on the windows are open. The sun's gone down. The yellow lights of harbor traffic reflect off the calm river, as do the arctic blue-green streetlamps of the suburbs on the far hills.

Above the tall wainscoting are the strategically placed models and oil paintings of sailing ships and expanses of plush red velvet inlaid with the national symbol of Québec, the fleur de lys.

Amid the leather upholstery, subtle lighting, and polished brass ship's instruments are placed loveseats, on one of which is a couple taking advantage of the design. They talk. She laughs. He flips up the collar of his sports jacket. She strokes his cheek, his hair. He brushes her arm. She is chic, in a three-piece suit. They kiss. This is ridiculous. There are forty people in this bar. They haven't made Grade B movies out of stuff like this since the forties. Where did she learn to do stuff like that?

This is just too outrageously romantic to fit on this continent. But this is Québec, where public displays of sensuality happen in ways that give clues to national character.

They leave. A husky gent with a mustache and a sweater embroidered with reindeer sits down in their place. I stare so hard, he waves.

Québec, when it comes right down to it, ends up being a nation, not because of industry or armies or stirring political rhetoric, but because when you're there, even if you were to ignore language, you know it's no place else.

The thought processes are different. It's bracing to hear Québec politicians talk about what they're up to in fifteen- or twenty-step tight, Jesuitical, geometric logic. In Washington, it's rare to hear a premise clearly stated, a theory methodically deduced from it, and a conclusion formally offered.

In Washington, similar conversations inevitably become so complex that the language lapses into the jargon of a specialty, be it defense or energy or journalism, in which a lack of knowledge of the meaning of shorthand words that express entire ideas leaves even a thoughtful person out in the cold.

This is not to say that one system is necessarily better or worse, or more or less honest. It's just to say that it's special to hear a Québécois say, "His reasoning is faulty." In Washington, you'd never question anybody's thought process; you'd question his *data*. (Not to mention his motives.)

The sense of time and place is different.

To love Québec, for example, is to love the Pontiac Firebird Trans Am with a 205-bhp, 301–cubic inch V8 and a flaming eagle painted on the hood. Québécois are the worst gas guzzlers left in the world, statistics show. Any street in Québec is testimony to their affection for full-sized LTDs and vroom-vroom Corvettes. Similarly, to hate Québec is to hate traveling at ten or twenty kilometers over the limit and be passed by such a behemoth, through whose dust can be discerned only the words on the license plate: *"Je me souviens"* (I remember). It's a formidable combination in the 1980s to drive like a Frenchman in high-horsepower North American iron.

Their prides are different. Québécois make a very big deal over how terrific their women look, and, indeed, compared to some of the brown thrush understatements of which English Canadian women are capable, Québécoises can be very attractive. Women here are routinely referred to as *"très chic,"* and, in fact, the most striking statements are made by women whose heels are higher, make-up and perfume more pronounced, and fashions more Europe-conscious than others. Yet, by contrast, in, say, Denver, women can and do make a positive statement by pointedly avoiding being "fashionable," and acquiring a studiedly natural look. Even the politics and culture of good looks are different in Québec from those elsewhere.

They swear differently. And not just because it's in French. In order to get nasty, they don't modify with references to excrement or sex. They modify with words like "tabernacle," "sanctuary," "chalice," and "host." If you really want to lean into a curse, you string them all together, until you get something like: *"Lui, c'est un maudit, chrisse, 'osti, calisse de tabernac'."* That'll get you a bar fight anyplace in the Gaspé.

They even think about their similarities with the rest of the continent in a different fashion. In making the point that, while Québec was French, it was also a distinctly North American culture, one observer said, "Our culture is the way we do things; the way we eat. When we have breakfast, we eat cereal, we eat eggs, we eat bacon."

It's tough to imagine another North American culture trying to bring attention to its singularity by the fact that it eats bacon and eggs.

But, of course, in Québec eating is very important to the way of life. One social scientist tells the story of an elaborate questionnaire sent to both English and French businessmen in Québec in an attempt to determine differences in the way they operated.

The first thing the observer discovered was that the English manager called a meeting in the conference room of his subordinates, where the group formulated their responses.

The French, seeing how extensive the questionnaire was, eagerly seized on the opportunity to hack away at the problem over a long lunch.

No less an authority on gastronomic bliss than Calvin Trillin of *The New Yorker*, who, when in a strange town, automatically distrusts the ethnic cooking of any group not strong enough to elect at least two aldermen, characterizes Montréal as the city in which he was rendered speechless by the fettucine Danielle he encountered in an Italian restaurant on Rue Notre-Dame Ouest.

(For that matter, I ran into an excellent steamed gingered whitefish on the Rue de Bleury in the course of talking to a Vietnamese restaurateur about immigration. Presumably, in his previous life, an air traffic controller for the evacuation of Saigon, this gent insisted on relating everything he could in metaphors of military defeat, and talked of drumming up more business for his restaurant through the study of voodoo. But I digress.)

Québec's food is so much a part of its culture that it is the final rebuke to those who insist that the interstates and the reprobates have rendered North America as homogeneous and undistinguished as powdered vanilla pudding.

Québec brought a small tear to my eye late one September evening. Forced by horrendous plane connections to break a vow, I found myself in the Montréal Airport Hilton. With town so far away, the wake-up call so early, and my stomach growling, I took myself, with resignation, to the hotel coffee shop. The ambiance was so thoroughly of Atlanta or Houston or Toronto that I was hardly surprised, merely a little depressed, when the hostess illegally failed to greet me in French.

As she led me to my table, I listened to the well-done-sixteen-ounce-T-bone-steak-with-baked-potato-and-salad-with-Roquefort meals being snarfed down all around me and realized that, for the first time in days, I was totally surrounded by English-speakers.

To find out how many different versions of cheeseburger I was faced with, I picked up the menu, only to notice. At the bottom. Handwritten. In French: *"Lapin aux pommes."* Rabbit with apple. A meal of the country. Which turned out to come with a delicate sauce, finely flavored with, I believe, Calvados.

In Québec, I thought with a sigh, picking clean the bones, you can't get a bad meal even at the Hilton.

In Québec, it dawned on me, they resist.

ACKNOWLEDGMENTS
SUGGESTED REFERENCES
INDEX

ACKNOWLEDGMENTS

The Nine Nations of North America, I frequently found myself feeling, was less a book than it was a conspiracy. Eight hundred people all over the continent contributed interviews, information, advice, and encouragement to this effort. It quite simply could not have been done without them. I regret that I cannot thank each of them here. Any errors of fact, emphasis, or interpretation in this book are entirely my fault. But:

Nancy Balz, my long-suffering and slightly clairvoyant Breadbasket–Scandinavian-rooted researcher, knew what was going on in my thinking before I did. She watched as the mosaic was going together and handed me the right-sized facts, sometimes even before I knew I needed them. (She, in turn, was aided, particularly in the statistical computations, by Michele Coleman. With all this subcontracting, I sometimes felt as if I were running a CETA program.)

Lou Cannon, former chief of the *Washington Post*'s Los Angeles bureau and now its chronicler of the Reagan White House, Joel Kotkin, formerly of that bureau, now an author, and Bill Curry, formerly of the *Post*'s Houston bureau and now with the Denver bureau of the *Los Angeles Times*, were responsible for first seeing portions of North America as new nations. Without their visions, none of this would have been started.

I am especially indebted to Curry for the prodigious number of hours he spent marking up the manuscript.

Benjamin C. Bradlee, the executive editor of the *Post*, Howard Simons, the managing editor, and Richard Harwood, the deputy managing editor, first gave me the job from which this book sprang, and then gave me the leave of absence to write it.

Bill Greider, the assistant managing editor for the national report of the *Post*, originally urged me to write the newspaper article that this volume develops.

Richard Kahlenberg of Los Angeles first convinced the editors of Houghton Mifflin that they should give me the money to write this book, and then convinced me to take it. If anyone is the godfather of this volume, it is he.

I plundered the work, files, ideas, and Rolodexes of dozens of present and former staffers of the *Washington Post*, most egregiously: Henry Allen, Stuart Auerbach, Daniel J. Balz, Fred Barbash, John F. Berry, John M. Berry, David S. Broder, Warren Brown, Bill Claiborne, Dusko Doder, Doug Feaver, Larry Fox, Martha Hamilton, Art Harris, Margot Hornblower, Haynes Johnson, Lee Lescaze, Kathy Macdonald, Dave Maraniss, Suzanna McBee, Peter Milius, Dan Morgan, Bill Peterson, T. R. Reid, Bill Richards, Pat Roberts, Ward Sinclair, J. P. Smith, and the late Laurence Stern.

Those whom I have not already mentioned who served as compasses, orienting me in my travels, included:

In New England, Stacy Jolna, WEEI News Radio 59, Boston, and John Cole, of Brunswick, Maine.

In New York, Sam Allis of the *Wall Street Journal*.

In the Foundry, Bob Joffee of the *Trenton Times*, John Boland of *Barron's*, Baltimore, and Oscar Paskal of the United Auto Workers, Detroit.

In Dixie, John Pope of the *New Orleans States-Item* and Tom Houck of WGST News Radio 92, Atlanta.

In the Islands, Joe Wright of the *Miami News*, Madeleine Blais of the *Miami Herald*, and Frank Soler, founding editor of *El Miami Herald*, then with Editorial America, an outfit that produces seventy-five million Spanish-language magazines a year out of Miami, including the Latin version of *Cosmopolitan*. (In Bogotá, I guess you could just call a reader a *chica Cosmo*.)

In MexAmerica, Chris Cook of the *San Diego Union* and his wife, Chrissy; Richard Gingras of KCET-TV, Los Angeles; Al Senia of Phoenix; and Archie Green of the University of Texas at Austin.

In Ecotopia, Paul Grabowicz of the *Oakland Tribune* and Julie Schwerzmann; Barry Lopez ("Desert Notes," "River Notes," "Of Wolves and Men," and other writings) and Sandy Lopez of Finn Rock, Oregon; Joel Connally of the *Seattle Post-Intelligencer* and Chris Little of the *Everett Herald*.

In Alaska, Howard Weaver of the *Anchorage Daily News*; Jim Rhode of the Alaska legislature, Juneau; Tom Gibboney, editor of the *Homer News*, and his wife, Kathy; and the commando biologists of Alaska Fish and Game, Fairbanks, particularly Lloyd Lowry (commercial fish), Kathy Frost (marine mammals), and Bob Stephenson (wolves). Stephenson owns one of the Norton 850 Commandos (motorcycles).

In the Empty Quarter, Molly Ivins, then with the Denver bureau of the *New York Times*; Paul Brinkley-Rogers, formerly with the *Boise Idaho-Statesman*; and Karl W. Mehlmann, president and general manager of

The Brown Palace Hotel in Denver, whom I have never met, but who apparently is responsible for maintaining the character of the hotel that became my favorite in North America.

In the Breadbasket, Steve Isaacs and Austin C. Wehrwein, of the *Minneapolis Star*, William S. Johnson of Hallmark, Kansas City, and C. Guyton Anderson III and his mama, the venerable Maurine F. Anderson, of Oklahoma City.

In Québec, Mario Polese, of the Institut National de la Recherche Scientifique and Père Robert Gareau, both of Montréal.

I often thought that, though this volume required reporting help from all over the continent, it could have been written only in Washington. Nancy Balz and I, of course, had access to information from the embassies of Canada and Mexico and the files of researchers in the Bureau of the Census, congressional offices, federal agencies, and resident trade organizations. Jack Roney of the Department of Agriculture was more than helpful in a maze of statistics. The U.S. Geological Survey, with enough maps probably to paper the globe literally, was often inspiring.

But most important was the Library of Congress. Both its resources and its staffers never ceased to amaze us. In the case of the Library of Congress, U.S. taxpayers can be proud of how their tax dollars are spent; may its budget double. Next time you come to Washington, set aside a couple of days just to begin to look around the vast rooms that house only the map collection. If you ask politely, they may even show you the ancient globe locked away in a climate-controlled vault that shows what Christopher Columbus thought the planet looked like, and where he thought he was going.

Special thanks to Dana Pratt, director of publishing, who offered early and key encouragement. The entire staff of the geography and map division, as well as Gerald F. Parsons, Jr. of the Archives of Folk Song, contributed important leads.

Robie Macauley, the senior editor of this book, who always seemed to me to be the pluperfect New Englander, despite his long-standing ties to Chicago, made his foremost contribution to this effort when he said, "As Joe Stalin said, we gotta have a *plan*," and then produced one. His assistant, Larry Kessenich, offered a number of intriguing suggestions, all of which were illegal.

The manuscript was copy-edited by the fanatically devoted Frances L. (Pixie) Apt, of Belmont, Massachusetts. It was lawyered by Paul Weaver of Boston.

The maps at the center of this tome were developed by Dave Cook and Dick Furno, both master cartographers, formerly with *The National Geographic*, now with the *Washington Post*.

The jacket photo of me was taken by Frank Johnston, also of the *Washington Post*. Frank's major qualification for this assignment was being the first photographer on the ground at the Jonestown, Guyana, massacre.

My parents, Roland and Gloria Garreau, of Pawtucket, Rhode Island, offered continuous support, enthusiasm, health suggestions, and, in concrete ways, made it a lot easier to finish this project.

Finally, my thanks go to Pegi Leonard and Jackie Geoffrion of Southern Office Supplies, Warrenton, Virginia. They stood over their Xerox machine hypnotically watching the green bar go zick-zick, zick-zick, nearly ten thousand times as this manuscript was produced.

SUGGESTED REFERENCES

The publishers of this volume have decided that they won't have anything to do with making it longer than it already is. Thus, the following is far from being a complete list of the works consulted by me and Nancy Balz in the course of our putting out the book. That list would run to thousands of items.

What we've done, then, is compile something of an eclectic reading, viewing, and listening list for the monolingual English-speaking layperson intrigued enough by this book to wish to delve further into some topics raised here.

The list is definitely not one of prime sources. *The California Water Atlas*, the novels of Faulkner, *The Almanac of American Politics*, and the songs of David Allan Coe have shaped my thinking a lot, and you will find them in the following pages. But many of the other suggestions are for the benefit of the nonprofessional wishing to learn more while being at least moderately entertained with reasonably basic material.

Professionals interested in my prime sources — some of which are exotic indeed — are invited to get in touch with me through Houghton Mifflin Company, Boston. I would be especially interested in hearing from graduate students in search of dissertations topics who have access to very fast computers, some research money, and a high boredom threshold.

ON REGIONALISM AS A WAY OF SEEING

The following are largely academic works. The geographers, especially, have fascinating stuff. The cultural geographers are eminently readable. All their works have extensive bibliographies, which can send you off in yet more directions.

Alexander, John W., and Lay James Gibson. *Economic Geography*. 2nd edition. Englewood Cliffs: Prentice-Hall, 1979.

A textbook that introduces what its title clearly states it to be. A lot of others allude to the connection between economics and geography, but Messrs. Alexander and Gibson lay it out.

American Demographics. Ithaca, New York. Monthly.

A magazine in a newly popularized field that a layperson can read. It has been of increasing academic interest since computer met census data.

Association of American Geographers. *Annals*. Washington, D.C. Quarterly.

Gastil, Raymond D. *Cultural Regions of the United States*. Seattle: University of Washington Press, 1975.

Glassie, Henry. *Pattern in the Material Folk Culture of the Eastern United States*. Philadelphia: University of Pennsylvania Press, 1968.

Gould, Peter, and Rodney White. *Mental Maps*. Harmondsworth, England: Penguin Books, 1974.

Harries, Keith D. *The Geography of Crime and Justice*. New York: McGraw-Hill, 1974.

Odum, Howard W., and Harry Estill Moore. *American Regionalism: A Cultural-Historical Approach to National Integration*. New York: Henry Holt, 1938.

The work that is the grandfather to others here.

Rooney, John F., ed. "Scratch Atlas I." Unpublished work of the Society for Survey of North American Cultures. Norman: University of Oklahoma, 1974.

Right now, these people have more words and ideas than they have maps of their own, so I've put them here, not with the atlases. Their project is in its infancy, but already they have maps locating pizza parlors in Pennsylvania, and country-and-western groups' show circuits. Enterprising commercial publishers, please take note.

Stewart, George R. *Names on the Land: A Historical Account of Place-Naming in the United States*. Boston: Houghton Mifflin, 1967.

Mr. Stewart's book is a very readable series of essays on the process of naming, suitable for a literary person's own library and containing much information on an item-by-item basis. There are also many place-name dictionaries in libraries.

Zelinsky, Wilbur. *The Cultural Geography of the United States*. Englewood Cliffs: Prentice-Hall, 1973.

Wilbur Zelinsky today is the dean of North American cultural geographers.

A CONTINENTAL APPROACH

These books, by virtue of their graceful writing about North America, by their collection of facts, or both, help give the real flavor of the whole.

American Folkways Series. New York: Duell, Sloan and Pearce.

A 1940s look at our region-by-region history, social life, and customs, written in a descriptive style. Some well-known writers who contributed to this series over the years include Hodding Carter, Oscar Lewis, and Carey McWilliams.

American Guide Series. Various publishers.

This series of more-than-travel guides was the result of the 1930s Federal Writers' Project of the U.S. Works Progress Administration. Many of the essay sections on individual states still stand as well written and historically informative. Some of the books in the series, such as the one on Pennsylvania, are being reprinted in their original form. Others, like the California guide, have been periodically revised.

Area Handbook Series. Washington, D.C.: Government Printing Office.

A wealth of factual information in a convenient travel guide–size on foreign lands brought to you by the feds who send diplomatic and military people to such spots as Mexico, Haiti, the Dominican Republic, and Cuba. Encyclopedic information on the backwaters for the spouse of an E5.

Barone, Michael, et al. *The Almanac of American Politics, 1980.* New York: E. P. Dutton, 1979.

Bedtime reading for political junkies. A monumental biennial achievement.

Broder, David S. *Changing of the Guard: Power and Leadership in America.* New York: Simon & Schuster, 1980.

Canada Yearbook. Ottawa: Statistics Canada. Annual.

de Tocqueville, Alexis. *Democracy in America.* Garden City, New York: Anchor Books, 1969.

"News analysis" written in 1835 that bears periodic reading and rereading. This is a full edition, but some may find an abridged edition more appealing for the reread.

Gunther, John. *Inside U.S.A.* New York: Harper & Brothers, 1947.

This is still the most amazing job of painting the United States, state by state, in existence. It is insightful, incisive, and entertainingly written. I still have difficulty imagining how he did it as fast as he did.

Kerouac, Jack. *On the Road.* New York: Viking Press, 1957.

Also available in a paperback edition. Penguin Books, 1979.

McNaught, Kenneth. *The Pelican History of Canada.* Harmondsworth, England: Penguin Books, 1976.

Peirce, Neal. *The Megastates of America: People, Politics and Power in the Ten Great States.* New York: W. W. Norton, 1972.

Twenty years after Gunther, Neal Peirce, a syndicated columnist who works for the *National Journal*, went back to retrace his steps. The result was this book, followed by nine regional books, the latest on the Great Lakes region. Chockfull of facts, many of them political, which, unfortunately, dates some of the older volumes.

Phillips, Kevin H. *Emerging Republican Majority*. New Rochelle, New York: Arlington House, 1969.

> I'm not sure I buy the political thesis set forth in this book, but the cultural geography, with maps, is terrific.

Rhodes, Richard. *Looking for America*. Garden City, New York: Doubleday, 1979.

The States and the Nation Series. New York: W. W. Norton and the American Association for State and Local History.

> Grants from the National Endowment for the Humanities underwrote this ambitious publishing venture timed for Bicentennial-inspired reading. Nevertheless, the small volumes, such as the Louisiana one by Joe Gray Taylor, do provide a service: an Establishment view of each state's history in fewer than 200 pages published by a commercial publisher.

Steinbeck, John. *Travels with Charley: In Search of America*. New York: Viking Press, 1962.

Thernstrom, Stephan, ed. *Harvard Encyclopedia of American Ethnic Groups*. Cambridge, Massachusetts: Harvard University Press, Belknap Press, 1980.

Thompson, Hunter S. *Fear and Loathing in Las Vegas*. New York: Random House, 1971.

———. *Fear and Loathing on the Campaign Trail, '72*. San Francisco: Straight Arrow Books, 1973.

Toffler, Alvin. *Future Shock*. New York: Random House, 1970.

Trillin, Calvin. *Alice, Let's Eat*. New York: Random House, 1978.

> Calvin Trillin is to my mind the finest writer on North America appearing in periodicals today. Look especially for his "U.S. Journal" pieces in *The New Yorker*. This book makes for some pretty funny reading and for great eating on the road.

U.S. Bureau of the Census. *Statistical Abstract of the United States*. Washington, D.C.: Government Printing Office. Annual.

> While I was writing this book, we used the 99th and 100th editions. A friend of mine has a copy on his night table for bedtime reading. I prefer *The Almanac of American Politics*, but to each his own.

Wattenberg, Ben J. *The Real America: A Surprising Examination of the State of the Union*. Garden City, New York: Doubleday, 1974.

> This one has an enlightening introduction by the author's colleague Richard M. Scammon.

Watts, May Theilgaard. *Reading the Landscape of America*. Revised and expanded edition. New York: Macmillan, 1975.

World Almanac and Book of Facts. New York: Newspaper Enterprise Association. Annual.

NEWSPAPERS

The *Los Angeles Times*. Daily and Sunday.
The *New York Times*. Daily and Sunday.

The *Wall Street Journal*. Daily.
The *Washington Post*. Daily and Sunday.
> If you have time to read only one, make it the *Wall Street Journal*. It provides the most consistently thoughtful and interesting reading on the great "out there."

ATLASES

Adams, John S., and Ronald Abler. *A Comparative Atlas of America's Great Cities: Twenty Metropolitan Regions*. Minneapolis: University of Minnesota Press, 1976.

American Heritage Pictorial Atlas of United States History. New York: McGraw-Hill, 1966.

Atlas of Mexico. Austin: Bureau of Business Research, University of Texas, 1975.

Canada. Surveys and Mapping Branch. Geography Division. *National Atlas of Canada*. 4th edition, revised. Toronto: Macmillan, 1974.

Crabbe, David, and Richard McBride, eds. *World Energy Book: An A–Z Atlas and Statistical Source Book*. New York: Nichols Publishing Co., 1978.

Dixon, Colin J. *Atlas of Economic Mineral Deposits*. Ithaca: Cornell University Press, 1979.

Geraghty, James J., et al. *Water Atlas of the United States*. Port Washington, New York: Water Information Center, 1973.

Halvorson, Peter L., and William M. Newman. *Atlas of Religious Change in America, 1952–1971*. Washington, D.C.: Glenmary Research Center, 1978.

Kahrl, William L., et al. *The California Water Atlas*. Sacramento: Governor's Office of Planning and Research and the California Department of Water Resources, 1979.
> The most beautiful book I own.

Kerr, D. G. G. *Historical Atlas of Canada*. 3rd edition, revised. Don Mills, Ontario: T. Nelson and Sons, 1975.

Paullin, Charles O., and John K. Wright. *Atlas of the Historical Geography of the United States*. Washington, D.C.: Carnegie Institution of Washington and the American Geographical Society of New York, 1932.

Quinn, Bernard, and John Feister. *Apostolic Regions of the United States, 1971*. Washington, D.C.: Glenmary Research Center, 1978.

The Rand McNally Road Atlas: United States, Canada, Mexico. Chicago: Rand McNally. Annual.
> I mauled and destroyed seven copies of the 55th edition (1979) in my travels. It was, along with my tape recorder, my most used tool.

U.S. Bureau of the Census. *1974 Census of Agriculture: Vol. IV, Special Reports, part 1, Graphic Summary*. Washington, D.C.: Bureau of the Census, 1978.

U.S. Environmental Science Service Administration. Environmental

Data Service. *Climatic Atlas of the United States*. Asheville, North Carolina: National Oceanic and Atmospheric Administration, 1977.

U.S. Geological Survey. *National Atlas of the United States of America*. Washington, D.C.: U.S. Geological Survey, 1970.

U.S. Office of the Federal Register. *Directory of Federal Regional Structure*. Washington, D.C.: Government Printing Office, 1979.

MAPS

Küchler, August Wilhelm. *Potential Natural Vegetation of the Coterminous United States*. New York: American Geographical Society. Manual, 1964. Map, 2nd edition, 1975.

Map of Population. Chicago: Rand McNally, n.d.
    Populations for U.S. counties based on final 1970 U.S. Census data.

Ranking Christian Denominations by Counties of the United States, 1971. Revised edition. Washington, D.C.: Glenmary Research Center, 1974.

Southern Regional Council. *Poor Families as Percent of All Families / Counties of Eleven Southern States: 1969*. Atlanta: Southern Regional Council, 1973.

———. *Black Population as Percent of Total Population / Counties of Eleven Southern States: 1970*. Atlanta: Southern Regional Council, 1973.

"U.S. Broadcasters Along the Canadian Border." The *New York Times*. September 25, 1979.

U.S. Bureau of the Census. *Residential Energy Uses*. Washington, D.C.: Government Printing Office, 1978.
    A beautiful map made with sophisticated techniques that showed me how out of date a map could be before it was even published. Nineteen seventy is history for most of the Nine Nations' energy situations.

U.S. Bureau of the Census: Geography Division. *Distribution of Older Americans in 1970 Related to Year of Maximum County Population*. Washington, D.C.: Government Printing Office, 1976.
    This was an early map made by the bureau with a computerized cartographic technique to promote the use of statistical maps as an analytic tool. The map uses data from the 1970 census of population. When the 1980 data start rolling from the machines, we ought to see some fascinating maps.

———. *Number of Persons of Spanish Origin by Counties of the United States: 1970*. Washington, D.C.: Government Printing Office, 1973.

———. *Percent Change in the Negro Population by Counties of the United States: 1960 to 1970*. Washington, D.C.: Government Printing Office, 1974.

———. *Standard Consolidated Statistical Areas and Standard Metropolitan Statistical Areas; Areas Defined by Office of Federal Statistical Policy and Standards, April 1979*. Washington, D.C.: Bureau of the Census, n.d.

————. *Year of Maximum Population by Counties of the United States.* Washington, D.C.: Bureau of the Census, n.d.

Data from the 1970 U.S. census of population.

U.S. Bureau of the Census: Geography Planning Staff. *Population Trends by Counties of the United States: 1940 to 1970.* Washington, D.C.: Government Printing Office, 1978.

U.S. Bureau of Indian Affairs. *Indian Land Areas, General.* Washington, D.C.: Bureau of Indian Affairs, n.d.

Indian lands and related facilities as of 1971.

U.S. Defense Mapping Agency, Topographic Center. *Major Army, Navy and Air Force Installations in the United States.* Revised. Washington, D.C.: Defense Mapping Agency, Topographic Center, 1979.

U.S. Department 'of the Interior. *Forest Types.* Washington, D.C.: U.S. Geological Survey, 1969.

————. *Territorial Growth.* Washington, D.C.: U.S. Geological Survey, 1969.

————. *United States of America Showing the Extent of Public Land Survey: Remaining Public Land, Historical Boundaries, National Forests, Indian Reservations, Wildlife Refuges, National Parks and Monuments.* Washington, D.C.: U.S. Geological Survey, 1965.

U.S. Energy Information Administration. *Federal Energy Regulatory Commission Regional Boundaries.* Washington, D.C.: Department of Energy, 1979.

U.S. Federal Aviation Administration. *International Jurisdictions of FAA Regions.* Washington, D.C.: Federal Aviation Administration, 1977.

West Indies and the Caribbean. Cosmopolitan edition. Chicago: Rand McNally, n.d.

NEW ENGLAND

New England is probably the most literate of the Nine Nations. This volume was published in Boston by the same company that first published Henry David Thoreau. It still has the original contract for *Walden* filed away someplace. The first half of any chronological North American literary litany will yield New Englanders, from Cotton Mather on. Therefore, I mention some other items.

Bryan, Robert, and Marshall Dodge. *Bert and I and Other Stories from Downeast.* Cambridge, Massachusetts: Bert and I Records, 1958.

These are recordings of "Yankee" humor, but they are not listed frivolously. North America does not express itself only in writing. It talks and sings, too.

Blair & Ketchum's Country Journal. Brattleboro, Vermont. Eleven issues a year.

New England's *Southern Living.* See Dixie references.

Estall, Robert C. *New England: A Study in Industrial Adjustment*. London: G. Bell and Sons, 1966.

Hale, Nancy, *New England Discovery: A Personal View*. New York: Coward McCann, 1963.

L. L. Bean catalogue. Freeport, Maine. Seasonal.

O'Connor, Edwin. *The Last Hurrah*. Boston: Little, Brown, 1956. Also the film, John Ford, director, with Spencer Tracy. Columbia Pictures, 1958.

The Lowell Team. *Lowell, Massachusetts: Report of the Lowell Historic Canal District Commission to the Ninety-fifth Congress of the United States of America*. Washington, D.C.: Government Printing Office, 1977.

Maine Times. Topsham, Maine. Weekly.

Miller, Perry. *The New England Mind: From Colony to Province*. Cambridge, Massachusetts: Harvard University Press, 1953.

Nearing, Helen, and Scott Nearing. *The Maple Sugar Book: Together with Remarks on Pioneering As a Way of Living in the Twentieth Century*. New York: Galahad Books, 1970.

New England Economic Review. Boston: Federal Reserve Bank. Quarterly.

Thoreau, Henry David. *Walden; or, Life in the Woods*. New York: E. P. Dutton, 1910.

Owners News. Randolph, Vermont: Vermont Castings, Inc. Quarterly.

Yankee. Dublin, New Hampshire. Monthly.

THE FOUNDRY

Alperovitz, Gar, and Jeff Faux. *An Economic Program for The Coming Decade*. Washington, D.C.: Exploratory Project for Economic Alternatives, 1975.

Mitgang, Lee. "Deteriorating Bridges, Streets, Sewers Plague U.S. Cities." *Washington Post*. December 27, 1979.

MVMA Motor Vehicle Facts and Figures, '79. Detroit: Motor Vehicle Manufacturers Association of the United States, Inc., 1979.

Peterson, George E. "Capital Spending and Capital Obsolescence: The Outlook for Cities." Conference on Federal Impacts on the Economic Outlook for Cities, April 5–6, 1978.

Policy and Management Associates, Inc. *Socioeconomic Costs and Benefits of the Community-Worker Ownership Plan to the Youngstown-Warren SMSA*. Boston: Policy and Management Associates, Inc., 1978.

Procter, Mary, and Bill Matuszeski. *Gritty Cities: A Second Look at Allentown, Bethlehem, Bridgeport, Hoboken, Lancaster, Norwich, Paterson, Reading, Trenton, Troy, Waterbury, Wilmington*. Philadelphia: Temple University Press, 1978.

"The Reindustrialization of America." *Business Week*. June 30, 1980.

The Rouge: The Image of Industry in the Art of Charles Sheeler and Diego Rivera. Detroit: Detroit Institute of Arts, 1978.

Samuelson, Robert J. "The Auto: A Prosperous Past, A Dubious Future." *National Journal.* March 15, 1980.
> Samuelson writes regularly in the *National Journal* on Foundry topics.

Sternlieb, George, and James W. Hughes, eds. *Post-Industrial America: Metropolitan Decline and Inter-Regional Job Shifts.* New Brunswick, New Jersey: Center for Urban Policy Research, Rutgers, The State University of New Jersey, 1975.

United Automobile, Aerospace, and Agricultural Implement Workers of America. *What's in a Typical UAW Contract?* Detroit: UAW Education Department, 1980.

U.S. House of Representatives of the 96th Congress, 1st Session. Committee on Interstate and Foreign Commerce. Subcommittee on Oversight and Investigations. *Waste Disposal Site Survey: Report Together with Additional and Separate Views . . .* Washington, D.C.: Government Printing Office, 1979.

United States Steel Corporation. *The One-Leaf-Book Story of Steel.* Chicago: Educations Graphics, Inc., 1970. Revised 1975.
> A marvelously clear and concise discussion of the history and manufacture of steel, printed in the size and shape of a fold-up road map.

Urban Institute, Washington, D.C. "Cleveland and Cincinnati: A Tale of Two Cities." *Policy and Research Report*, vol. 10, no. 1, Spring 1980.

"Where the Funds Flow." *National Journal.* Special Report. June 26, 1976.
> The seminal argument that federal funds are being drained from the Foundry to elsewhere.

ABERRATIONS

Hawaii life series. The *Los Angeles Times.* July 1–November 23, 1979, intermittently.

The Home Section. The *New York Times.* Every Thursday.
> How the other one tenth of 1 percent lives.

McPhee, John A. *Coming Into the Country.* New York: Farrar, Straus & Giroux, 1977.
> The modern classic on Alaska.

National Journal. Washington, D.C. Weekly.
> Only in the District of Columbia could this periodical attempt to thrive.

The Washington Monthly. Washington, D.C.
> Ditto.

DIXIE

American Institute of Architects, New Orleans Chapter. *A Guide to New Orleans Architecture.* New Orleans: New Orleans Chapter, American Institute of Architects, 1974.

Ayres, H. Brandt, and Thomas H. Naylor, eds. *You Can't Eat Magnolias.* New York: McGraw-Hill and the L. Q. C. Lamar Society, 1972.

Bass, Jack, and Walter DeVries. *The Transformation of Southern Politics: Social Change and Political Consequence since 1945.* New York: New American Library, 1977.

Brunson, E. Evan, and Thomas D. Bever. *Southern Growth Trends: 1970–1976.* Research Triangle Park, North Carolina: Southern Growth Policies Board, 1977.

Carney, George O. *The Sounds of People and Places: Readings in the Geography of Music.* Washington, D.C.: University Press of America, 1978. An academic on a fascinating popular topic.

Cash, W. J. *The Mind of the South.* New York: Random House, Vintage Books, 1941.

Dylan, Bob. *Nashville Skyline.* New York: Columbia Records KCS-9825, 1969.

Egerton, John. *The Americanization of Dixie: The Southernization of America.* New York: Harper's Magazine Press, 1974.

Faulkner, William. *Absalom, Absalom!* New York: Random House. Vintage Books, 1936.

"Is Dixie Dead? A Survey of the American South." *The Economist* (London). March 17, 1979.

Junior League of Lafayette, Inc. *Talk About Good!* Lafayette, Louisiana: Junior League of Lafayette, Inc., 1969. Gumbos, étouffées, and other fine Cajun cooking.

Liner, E. Blaine, and Lawrence K. Lynch. *The Economics of Southern Growth.* Durham, North Carolina: Southern Growth Policies Board, 1977.

Morris, Willie. *North Toward Home!* New York: Dell, 1967.

Nitty Gritty Dirt Band, et al. *Will the Circle Be Unbroken.* Los Angeles: United Artists, Inc. UAS-9801, 1972.

Powledge, Fred. *Journeys Through the South: A Rediscovery.* New York: Vanguard Press, 1979.

Ransom, John Crowe. *I'll Take My Stand.* Baton Rouge: Louisiana State University Press, 1977.

Reed, John Shelton. *The Enduring South: Subcultural Persistence in Mass Society.* Chapel Hill: The University of North Carolina Press, 1974. John Shelton Reed, who teaches sociology at the University of North Carolina at Chapel Hill, has written a variety of delightful monographs on Dixie, including the marvelously titled "Below the Smith and Wesson Line: Reflections on Southern Violence." He has pioneered in the view of Southerners as an ethnic group.

Southern Exposure. Chapel Hill: Institute for Southern Studies. Quarterly.

Southern Living. Birmingham, Alabama. Monthly. Masquerading as a very popular magazine, this is the acculturation manual to the most recent New South.

The Southern Quarterly: A Journal of the Arts in the South. Hattiesburg, Mississippi.

THE ISLANDS

Buffett, Jimmy. *Changes in Latitudes; Changes in Attitudes.* New York: ABC Records AB-990, 1977.
    Especially the title cut.
————. *Volcano.* New York: MCA Records, Inc. MCA-5102, 1979.
    "Boat Drinks," on side 2, is this nation's anthem.
Drug war series. The *Miami News.* April 25, 1979.
Hispanics in Dade County, Florida, an unpublished and untitled study. Miami: Dade County Government, 1978.
"Key West: Smuggler's Island." The *Miami Herald.* March 16, 1980.
La Charanga. *La Charanga en el 79.* New York: TR Records, Inc. TR-145, 1979.
    Especially side 1, cut 4, "Miami." This lyric Spanish love song to the city was a hit at the same time that a much-touted, very expensive, quite different, unsingable English-language song of the same name was being pushed unsuccessfully by the Chamber of Commerce.
U.S. Senate of the 96th Congress, 1st Session. Committee on Governmental Affairs. Permanent Subcommittee on Investigations. *Illegal Narcotics Profits* . . . Washington, D.C.: Government Printing Office, 1980.
Wilkins, Mira. *Foreign Enterprise in Florida: The Impact of Non-U.S. Direct Investment.* Miami: University Presses of Florida, 1979.

MEXAMERICA

Acuña, Rodolfo. *Occupied America: The Chicano's Struggle Toward Liberation.* New York: Harper and Row, 1972.
Baird, Peter, and Ed McCaughan. *Beyond the Border: Mexico and the U.S. Today.* New York: North American Congress on Latin America, 1979.
Coe, David Allan. *David Allan Coe Rides Again.* New York: CBS Records, KC 34310, 1977.
    "If That Ain't Country," side 2, is the essence of a new wave 1970s country song.
Cornelius, Wayne A. *Mexican Migration to the United States (with Comparative Reference to Caribbean-Basin Migration): The State of Current Knowledge and Recommendations for Future Research.* San Diego: Center for United States–Mexican Studies of the University of California at San Diego, 1979.
————. *America in the "Era of Limits": The "Nation of Immigrants" Turns Nativist Again.* La Jolla: Center for United States–Mexican Studies of the University of California at San Diego, 1979.

Eagles. *Desperado*. Los Angeles: Asylum Records, SD5068, 1973.

The whole album, but especially the title cut and reprise.

Ehrlichman, John. "Mexican Aliens Aren't a Problem; They're a Solution." *Esquire*. August 1979.

Jennings, Waylon. *Honky Tonk Heroes*. New York: RCA Records, APLI-0240, 1973.

An authentic statement, still.

Jimenez, Flaco. *Flaco Jimenez y su Conjunto*. El Cerrito, California: Arhoolie Records, Inc.,3007, 1977.

El Rey de Texas (the King of Texas), Norteno accordionist, Tejano folk hero, and MexAmerican cross-over artist.

McWilliams, Carey. *Southern California: An Island on the Land*. Santa Barbara: Peregrine Smith, 1973.

Merk, Frederick. *Manifest Destiny and Mission in American History: A Reinterpretation*. New York: Random House, Vintage Books, 1963.

"MexAmerica: A Five-Part Series." The *Washington Post*, March 26–30, 1978.

Nelson, Willie. *Shotgun Willie*. New York: Atlantic Recording Corp., SD7262 0598, 1973.

The dean of outlaw country and western.

Nostrand, Richard L. "The Hispanic-American Borderland: Delimination of an American Culture Region." *Annals of the Association of American Geographers*. December 1970.

Paz, Octavio. "Mexico and the United States." *The New Yorker*. September 17, 1979.

Reeves, Richard. "Boom." *The New Yorker*. December 24, 1979.

———. "Vulnerable." *The New Yorker*. November 5, 1979.

Standefer, Jon, and Alex Drehsler. The Border Country series. The *San Diego Union*. January 6–10, 1980.

Villarreal, José Antonio. *Pocho*. With an introduction by Ramón E. Ruiz. Garden City, New York: Doubleday, 1970.

The most sensitive discussion of the new breed of person who is the Hispanic MexAmerican.

ECOTOPIA

Advanced Micro Devices, Inc. *Report*. Sunnyvale, California. Annual, with charts.

Arthur D. Little, Inc. *A Regional Analysis: Economic and Fiscal Impacts of the Aluminum Industry in the Pacific Northwest*. Cambridge, Massachusetts: Arthur D. Little, Inc., 1978.

Bean, Walton. *Boss Ruef's San Francisco: The Story of the Union Labor Party, Big Business, and the Graft Prosecution*. Berkeley: University of California Press, 1972.

Berg, Peter, ed. *Reinhabiting a Separate Country: A Bioregional Anthology of Northern California*. San Francisco: Planet Drum Foundation, 1978.

Callenbach, Ernest. *Ecotopia: The Notebooks and Reports of William Weston*. Berkeley: Banyan Tree Books, 1975.
> Also available in a paperback edition. Bantam Books, 1979.

Carlson, Roy, ed. *Contemporary Northwest Writing: A Collection of Poetry and Fiction*. Corvallis: Oregon State University Press, 1979.

CoEvolution Quarterly. Sausalito, California.

East-West Journal: Common Sense for Modern Times. Brookline, Massachusetts. Monthly.
> What *Southern Living* is to Dixie, the *East-West Journal* is to Ecotopia.

Enetai. Seattle. Semimonthly.

Fadiman, Clifton. "A Technological Culture?" *Center* magazine. March / April 1977.

Farallones Institute. *The Integral Urban House*. San Francisco: Sierra Club Books, 1979.

Frye, Richard. "The Economics of *Ecotopia*." *Alternate Futures*. Winter 1980.

Martech Company. *Foreign Investment in the Pacific Northwest*. Vancouver: Pacific Northwest Regional Commission, 1975.

Prochnau, Bill. "Life at Ground Zero." A series. The *Seattle Post-Intelligencer*. November 11–18, 1979.

Semiconductor Industry Association. *Yearbook and Directory*. Cupertino, California.

Seriatim: Journal of Ecotopia. El Cerrito, California. Quarterly.

U.S. General Accounting Office. *Region at the Crossroads; The Pacific Northwest Searches for New Sources of Electric Energy. Report to the Congress of the United States*. Washington, D.C.: Government Printing Office, 1978.

Van der Ryn, Sim. "The Sustainable City." *Pacific Sun*. March 16–22, 1979.

THE EMPTY QUARTER

The works of Wallace and Page Stegner and Bernard DeVoto are premier writings from / about / of the Empty Quarter. I suggest the Stegners' *Atlantic* article about the Rocky Mountain region and DeVoto's introduction to one of Wallace Stegner's works because those particularly influenced me.

For reasons of my own, I do not find compelling the works of two other Empty Quarter writers, Edward Abbey and Tom Robbins. However, others do. They are the most commercially successful novelists singing the Empty Quarter.

Barnet, Richard J. "The World's Resources." A series. *The New Yorker*. March 17, 31, and April 7, 1980.

Billington, Ray Allen. *The Far Western Frontier: 1830–1860*. New York: Harper and Row, 1962.

Canby, Thomas Y. "Our Most Precious Resource: Water." *The National Geographic*. August 1980.

Cannon, Lou, and Joel Kotkin. "Embattled West." A series. The *Washington Post*. June 17–20, 1979.

Commoner, Barry. "Once and Future Fuel." *The New Yorker*. October 29, 1979.

Council of Energy Resource Tribes. *Indian Energy Resources*. Washington, D.C.: Council of Energy Resource Tribes, n.d.

Federation of Rocky Mountain States, Inc. *The Rocky Mountain Region: A Unity of Interests*. Denver: Federation of Rocky Mountain States, Inc., 1975.

Fielder, F. M., ed. *Canadian Mines Handbook: 1976–77*. Toronto: The Northern Miner, 1976.

Fred C. Hart Associates, Inc. *Federal and State Environmental Regulatory Requirements Impacting Synthetic Fuels Development*. Washington, D.C.: Department of Energy, Assistant Secretary for the Environment, Office of Technology Impacts, Division of Policy Analysis, 1979.

Griffiths, Franklyn. *Northern Foreign Policy*. Toronto: Canadian Institute of International Affairs, n.d.

"Harmony in Diversity: A New Federalism for Canada." Alberta Government Position Paper on Constitutional Change, 1978.

High Country News. Lander, Wyoming. Biweekly.

Lightfoot, Gordon. *Don Quixote*. Burbank: Reprise Records MS-2056, 1972.
>   Especially "Alberta Bound."

MacEwan, J. W. Grant. *A Short History of Western Canada*. Toronto: McGraw-Hill Ryerson Ltd., 1968.

Mulder, William, and A. Russell Mortensen, eds. *Among the Mormons: Historic Accounts by Contemporary Observers*. Lincoln: University of Nebraska Press, 1973.

"A Progress Report on Alternative Energy Sources." *Fortune*. September 24, 1979.

Robinson, J. Lewis, and Walter G. Hardwick. *British Columbia: One Hundred Years of Geographical Change*. Vancouver: Talonbooks, 1973.

Stegner, Wallace. *Beyond the Hundredth Meridian: John Wesley Powell and the Second Opening of the West*. With an introduction by Bernard DeVoto. Boston: Houghton Mifflin, 1954.

Stegner, Wallace, and Page Stegner. "Rocky Mountain Country." *Atlantic Monthly*. April 1978.
>   With photographs by Ansel Adams.

Tyson, Ian, and Sylvia Fricker. *Four Strong Winds*. New York: Vanguard VRS-9133, 1963.
>   Especially the title cut.

University of Georgia at Athens. School of Law. *A Multi-State Development and Trading Authority: Preliminary Analysis of Basic Issues*. Draft for the Office of the Governor. Helena: State of Montana, 1979.
>   If the Empty Quarter is a nation, this is its economic manifesto.

THE BREADBASKET

Caterpillar Tractor Company. Annual reports and product line brochures. Peoria, Illinois.

Duncan, Patricia D. *Tallgrass Prairie: The Inland Sea*. Kansas City, Missouri: Lowell Press, 1979.

Emerson, Robert L. *Fast Food: The Endless Shakeout*. New York: Lebhar-Friedman Books, 1979.

Ervin, Jean, ed. *The Minnesota Experience: An Anthology*. Minneapolis: The Adams Press, 1979.

Grain Handling and Transportation Commission. *Grain and Rail in Western Canada*. Ottawa: Government of Canada, 1977.

The Furrow. Moline, Illinois: John Deere and Company. Eight issues a year.
> Published worldwide in nine languages with thirteen North American editions. Perhaps the *Southern Living* of the Breadbasket.

Husar, John. "Illinois — Wasteland in the Making." The *Chicago Tribune*. December 9–13, 1979.

John Deere and Company. Annual reports and product line brochures. Moline, Illinois.

Leventhal, Harold, and Marjorie Guthrie, eds. *Woody Guthrie Songbook*. Grosset and Dunlap, 1976.

Meinig, D. W. *Imperial Texas: An Interpretive Essay in Cultural Geography*. Austin: University of Texas Press, 1969.

Morgan, Dan. *Merchants of Grain*. New York: Viking Press. 1979.
> The most important single source on the grain trade.

——. "Rivers of Grain." The *Washington Post*. August 12, 1979.

Sosland, Morton I. *Prospects for Agriculture in the Year 2000*. Kansas City, Missouri: Midwest Research Institute, 1976.

U.S. Department of Agriculture. *Crop Production: Annual Summary*. Washington, D.C.: Crop Reporting Board.

West, Richard. "The Last Frontier." *Texas Monthly*. Vol. 5, no. 11, November 1977.

——. "The Sons of the Pioneers." *Texas Monthly*. Vol. 6, no. 9, September 1978.
> There are a number of writers who have attempted to deal with the incorrect notion that Texas is one place. One of the most useful is Richard West, who contributes evocative reports on regions of Texas to the *Texas Monthly*.

QUÉBEC

Accent Québec. Series, consisting of short reports and basic studies. Montréal: C. D. Howe Institute.
> Contents: "On the Meaning of 'Economic Association,'" by Roger Dehem; 1st quarter, 1978. "The Québec Textile Industry in Canada," by Caroline Pestieau; 2nd quarter, 1978. "Canada's Official-Language

Minorities," by Richard J. Joy; 3rd quarter, 1978. "The Structure of Quebec's Exports," by Carmine Nappi; 4th quarter, 1978.

> In ideological terms, the C. D. Howe Institute is something of a strange duck. It is a think tank that, though sympathetic to the plight of Québec, is completely federalist. It's as if the Brookings Institute in Washington, D.C., were combined with the American Enterprise Institute.

"Canada: Time for Choices." A series. The *New York Times*. May 16–18, 1979.

Casanova, Jacques-Donat. *America's French Heritage*. Montréal: La Documentation Française and Québec Official Publisher, 1976.

"An Exercise in Failure." *Maclean's*. September 22, 1980.

> *Maclean's* is Canada's *Newsweek*. This piece discusses, with sophistication, the 1980 constitutional convention.

Feldman, Elliot J., and Neil Nevitte, eds. *The Future of North America: Canada, the United States, and Québec Nationalism*. Cambridge, Massachusetts: Center for International Affairs, Harvard University, 1979.

Harbron, John D. *Canada Without Québec*. Don Mills, Ontario: Musson Book Co., 1977.

Henault, Claude. "What Quebecers Really Are Saying" series. The *Gazette* (Montréal). September 24–27, 1978.

Kopkind, Andrew. "Québec: A Declaration of Independence But No Revolution." *Working Papers*. September / October 1978.

Lafortune, François, and Gilles Vigneault. *Où la lumière chante*. Québec: Presses de l'Université Laval, 1966.

> Photographs and text of "Québec, première ville Française en Amérique." Gilles Vigneault is the de facto poet laureate of Québec.

La Politique Québécoise de developpement culturel (*A Cultural Development Policy for Québec*). Montréal, 1978.

> Contents: Vol. 1, A General View: The Culture Under Consideration. Vol. 2, The Three Aspects of the Policy: Ways of Life-Creative Activity-Education.

> Also available as Editeur officiel. The most thought-provoking and authoritative work on Québec nationalism published in English.

MacLennan, Hugh. *Two Solitudes*. Toronto: Macmillan, 1978.

> A Québecois *Gone with the Wind*.

Morin, Claude. *Québec Versus Ottawa: The Struggle for Self-Government, 1960–1972*. English edition. Toronto: University of Toronto Press, 1976.

Notes on Canadian Federalism. Ottawa: Canadian Unity Information Office, 1978.

Rioux, Marcel. *Québec in Question*. Translated by James Boake. Toronto: James Lorimer and Co., 1978.

Stanford Research Institute. Business Intelligence Program. Long-Range Planning Service. *Québec Separatism*. Menlo Park, California: Stanford Research Institute, 1977.

Société d'Énergie de la Baie James. *Progress Report*. Montréal: Société d'Énergie de la Baie James, 1978.

La Société Généalogique Canadienne-Française. *Mémoires*. Montréal. Quarterly.

The *Southern Living* of Québec.

Vallières, Pierre. *White Niggers of America*. Translated by Joan Pinkham. Toronto: McClelland and Stewart Ltd., 1971.

INDEX

Mount Rainier, 257
Mount St. Helens, 257, 283, 286
Mount Shasta, 255
Mount Waialeale, 118
MX missile system, 320–21
Myrtle Beach, South Carolina, 132–33

Nast, Thomas, 330
Nation, The, 211
National Aeronautic and Space Administration, U.S., 26
National Center for Economic Alternatives, 10, 15–16, 82
National Gay Task Force, 335
National Institutes of Health, U.S., 102
National Journal, The, 103
National Semiconductor, 281
National Severe Storm Forecast Center, U.S., 333
Natural Resources Defense Council, 265
Nelson, Page, 270
Nelson, Willie, 137, 212
Netherlands Antilles, 181; anonymous corporations in, 191, 192, 193, 194
New Brunswick, 17–18
New Canaan, Connecticut, 66
New England, 6, 8, 12, 14; agriculture in, 18–19; boundaries of, 16, 17–18, 66–67; character of, 39–40; computers in, 40, 43–44; decline of, 38; drivers in, 41; economy in, 19; educational institutions in, 29; elitism in, 28–30; energy in, 9, 10–11, 19–22, 23–26, 36–37; industry in, 14–16, 19; nuclear power plants in, 23–26; politics in, 27; poverty in, 16, 28, 30; scenery in, 19; spatial confusion in, 41; taxes in, 27–28, 30; technology in, 39; and Thoreau, 47–48; transportation in, 37, 38; wage structure in, 38; water supply in, 38; windmills in, 26–27; wood stoves in, 15–16, 30–33, 41, 42
New England Telephone, 27
Newfoundland, 17
New Hampshire, 22–26, 28

New Haven, Connecticut, 66–67
New Jersey, 65
New London, Connecticut, 66
New Orleans, Louisiana, 141, 143–44, 156
New Orleans, University of, 164
New Orleans States-Item, 165
New Scientist, 251–52
New York City, 60, 66, 72; bankruptcy of, 123, 124; and "I Love New York" campaign, 123; parts of, belonging to Foundry, 122; transvestite disco in, 98–99; viewed as aberration, 99–100, 122–27 *passim*
New York Daily News, 125
New Yorker, The, magazine, 123, 136, 337, 389
New York state, 80, 218
New York Times, 18, 104, 198, 376; on Canadian investment in U.S., 74; on Florida drug trade, 189; on Houston and Los Angeles, 219–20
New York Times/CBS News Poll, 228
Nicaragua, 182–83
Nielson, Phill, 313–14
Nixon, Richard M., 70, 167, 175, 207, 214, 351
North Carolina, 142
North Carolina, University of, 151
North Chicago Rolling Mill, 59
North Pacific Ocean Protein Coalition, 281
Northwest-Alaska Native Association (NANA), 112
Northwest Territories, 304
Nova Scotia, 17
Nuclear power plants (reactors): Dixie's reliance on, 9; Ecotopia's opposition to, 263–64; Seabrook, New Hampshire's, 23, 24–26
Nunn, Sam, 195
Nunnery, Bob, 175
Nyad, Diana, 178

Oakland, California, 255
Occupational Safety and Health Administration (OSHA), U.S., 106, 140
Ocean City, Maryland, 132